# Tobias SMOLLETT

*a reference guide*

*A*
*Reference*
*Publication*
*in*
*Literature*

Everett Emerson
*Editor*

# Tobias SMOLLETT

## *a reference guide*

ROBERT D. SPECTOR

G.K.HALL&CO.

70 LINCOLN STREET, BOSTON, MASS.

*Library of Congress Cataloging in Publication Data*

Spector, Robert Donald.
  Tobias Smollett, a reference guide.

  (A Reference guide in literature)
  Includes index.
  1. Smollett, Tobias George, 1721-1771—Bibliography.
I. Title. II. Series: Reference guide in literature.
Z8822.5.S63    [PR3696]    016.823'6        79-28423
ISBN 0-8161-7960-3

*This publication is printed on permanent/durable acid-free paper*
MANUFACTURED IN THE UNITED STATES OF AMERICA

# Contents

# Preface

Tobias Smollett's importance in English literary history is unques-
tionable. It is no small achievement to have written two novels that
remain readable two hundred years after their first publication, and
both <u>Roderick Random</u> (1748) and <u>Humphry Clinker</u> (1771) continue to
engage audiences and stir critical interest long after the works of
most of Smollett's contemporaries have become historical curiosities.
As a shaper of the English novel, Smollett ranks in significance with
Defoe, Fielding, Richardson, and Sterne. If he has never enjoyed the
eminence of Fielding, at one time or other he has been considered
superior to the rest. Praised by Keats, Byron, and Lamb, and imitated by writers from the eighteenth through the twentieth centuries,
Smollett must be regarded as a novelist of the first order. Even
during the Victorian era, when his harsh realism and bold expression
dropped his reputation to its lowest point, tribute was paid to
his caricature, humor, and vigorous style. He found supporters in
such literary giants as Thomas Carlyle and Charles Dickens, and his
influence on the latter would in itself warrant continued interest in
his work. The author of a novel that Thackeray described as "the
most laughable story that has ever been written," Smollett must be
acknowledged as a major figure in the history of the eighteenth-
century novel.

Nor is Smollett's importance restricted to the genre of the novel.
As a typical eighteenth-century man of letters, he wrote in virtually
all the existing forms. His lyric poems, hailed by many of England's
great poets, stand among the finest examples of their kind during
his period. If his satiric poetry and dramas are less successful,
they are nevertheless significant indices to the taste and influences
of his time, reflect on the larger body of his work, and frequently
are part of the intriguing and bitter literary controversies of his
age. Smollett played a large role in the development of journalism
in its earliest stages. As co-founder and editor of the <u>Critical</u>
<u>Review</u>, he produced a periodical remarkable in its energy and forth-
rightness and an influence on the great reviewing journals of the
next century. His <u>Briton</u> engaged in polemical debate with John
Wilkes' <u>North Briton</u> and became itself a part of the history of the
peace negotiations that concluded the Seven Years' War. In the pages
of his <u>British Magazine</u>, he published <u>Sir Launcelot Greaves</u>, the

first serialization of a novel by a major author. Smollett guided the editing of large historical enterprises, translated Gil Blas and Don Quixote, and, together with Thomas Francklin, brought the massive works of Voltaire before an English public. His History of England, still a pleasure to read today, enjoyed an "unprecedented sale" in its own time. But most important of all, in his Travels through France and Italy, Smollett created a work of art that remains among the best examples in its genre.

Smollett's interest for historians, literary or otherwise, does not end there. No account of the picaresque novel is complete without reference to Smollett. His use of the Gothic requires notice in historical and critical works on that genre. His name obviously appears in assessments of the influence, reputation, and significance of Cervantes. For the naval historian, Smollett's Roderick Random provides a ready and valuable source. His treatment of mental institutions in Launcelot Greaves and his portrait of Bath in Humphry Clinker appear in treatises by sociologists, medical researchers, and social historians. Medical journals record the details of his friendships with the Hunter brothers, William Smellie, and John Armstrong, or consider his Essay on the External Use of Water, a devastating attack on the medicinal benefits of the waters of Bath and other spas. The areas in which interest in Smollett exists are seemingly endless--including certainly translation, historiography, travel literature, and linguistics.

It is no simple matter, then, to compile a comprehensive list of secondary works on Smollett's life and art, and Paul-Gabriel Boucé may be correct when he writes that "any single-handed attempt at a bibliography is doomed to fail: only an international team working in close cooperation will be able to cope with the job." To be sure, previous secondary bibliographies hardly inspire confidence. The best work has been done by Fred W. Boege in Smollett's Reputation as a Novelist (1947), a diligent study in the vicissitudes of the writer's critical fortunes, and by Boucé himself in his various works on Smollett, particularly the notes and bibliography in The Novels of Tobias Smollett (1976) and his "Eighteenth- and Nineteenth-Century Biographies of Smollett" (1971). But these are, of course, not inclusive, and Donald M. Korte's An Annotated Bibliography of Smollett Scholarship 1946-1968 (1969), while helpful, is extremely limited, even for the period it covers. The most extensive bibliographical works on Smollett, by Francesco Cordasco, are, unfortunately, more often a hindrance than a help. Although Cordasco incorporates corrections and additions made by Boucé, into his earlier lists (1947 and 1948), his recent bibliography (1978) demonstrates the same careless scholarship as his previous collections. His entries cannot be trusted, and his annotations too frequently suggest unfamiliarity with the works he is describing.

My own reference guide is not intended to be all-inclusive, but it offers more than twice the number of entries previously included in a single volume. It would, indeed, have benefited from an "international team" of scholars for its items from France, Germany, and Italy, let alone Japan and the Soviet Union. For its coverage of the last three years, particularly 1978, there are undoubtedly omissions due to the vagaries of scholarly publications--late appearances of journals and the inaccessibility of foreign material. I have attempted the broadest listing possible, but, although I have included many short references, I have deliberately omitted others. Comments on Smollett abound in works on other writers--Fielding, Dickens, and Melville, for example--and I have noted a good many, but I have tried to make the listing representative rather than complete. I have treated material in histories, literary histories, and encyclopedias in the same way. My concern has been to present as wide a variety and as complete a treatment as feasible within the limits of such a compilation.

In the course of my work, I have been helped by many individuals and institutions, and I am pleased to acknowledge my indebtedness to some of them. I am especially grateful to the Newberry Library and the National Endowment for the Humanities for a fellowship that enabled me to begin this study. My fellow Smollettians, particularly Paul-Gabriel Boucé and George S. Rousseau, have generously answered many questions and offered helpful material. In various ways I have been encouraged and aided by Professors Morris Golden, Arthur Cash, John Middendorf, and the late Professor James L. Clifford. Numerous items have been brought to my attention by Hedda S. Spector, Stephen Brett Spector, and Eric Charles Spector. Without the good services of librarians in the United States and Canada, but especially those at Long Island University, I could not have completed this work.

R.D.S.

# Chronology of Smollett's Publications

## Chronology

The Adventures of Sir Launcelot Greaves (book: 1762)

1761    Edited, with Thomas Francklin, The Works of Voltaire
        (to 1769)

1762    Edited Briton (to 1763)

1766    Travels through France and Italy

1768    Edited Present State of All Nations (to 1769)

1769    The History and Adventures of an Atom

1771    The Expedition of Humphry Clinker

1773    "Ode to Independence"

1776    Translation of Adventures of Telemachus

# Abbreviations

| | |
|---|---|
| AL | American Literature |
| ANQ | American Notes & Queries |
| BNYPL | Bulletin of the New York Public Library |
| EA | Études Anglaises |
| ECL | Eighteenth-Century Life |
| ECS | Eighteenth Century Studies |
| ELN | English Language Notes |
| HLQ | Huntington Library Quarterly |
| JEGP | Journal of English and Germanic Philology |
| JHI | Journal of the History of Ideas |
| JNT | Journal of Narrative Technique |
| MLN | Modern Language Notes |
| MLQ | Modern Language Quarterly |
| MLR | Modern Language Review |
| MP | Modern Philology |
| NCF | Nineteenth-Century Fiction |
| NLH | New Literary History |
| N&Q | Notes and Queries |
| PBSA | Publications of the Bibliographical Society of America |
| PLL | Papers on Language and Literature |
| PMLA | Publications of the Modern Language Association of America |
| PQ | Philological Quarterly |
| RES | Review of English Studies |
| SBHT | Studies in Burke and His Time |
| SEL | Studies in English Literature |

## Abbreviations

| | |
|---|---|
| SP | Studies in Philology |
| TLS | London Times Literary Supplement |
| UTQ | University of Toronto Quarterly |
| YES | Yearbook of English Studies |

# Writings about Tobias Smollett

## 1746

1   ANON.  "Monthly Catalogue," <u>London Magazine</u>, 15 (August), 428.
    Announces publication of <u>Advice</u>.

## 1747

1   ANON.  "Monthly Catalogue," <u>London Magazine</u>, 16 (January), 56.
    Announces publication of <u>Reproof</u> as sequel to <u>Advice</u>.

## 1749

1   ANON.  Extract from Sermon, <u>Gentleman's Magazine</u>, 19 (March),
    126.
        Praises liveliness of <u>Roderick Random</u> and sees it as
    warning against promiscuity.  Perhaps by Samuel Johnson
    (Paulson and Lockwood, 1969.22).

2   [CLELAND, JOHN].  Review of <u>The Regicide</u>, <u>Monthly Review</u>, 1
    (May), 72-79.
        Praises the play and the comic abilities of the author
    of <u>Roderick Random</u>.

## 1751

1   ANON.  Review of <u>Peregrine Pickle</u>, <u>Royal Magazine, or Quarter-
    ly Bee</u>, 2 (January-March), 396-97.
        Comment on <u>Peregrine Pickle</u> suggests success of <u>Roderick
    Random</u>.

2   ANON.  Advertisement for <u>Peregrine Pickle</u>, <u>Royal Magazine</u>, 2
    (January-March), 466.
        Praises Lady Vane's <u>Memoirs</u> as superior to rest of the
    novel.

1751

3  ANON.  Review of <u>The History of a Lady of Quality, or the</u>
<u>Adventures of Lady Frail</u>, <u>Monthly Review</u>, 4 (February),
308.
  Describes Smollett's advertisements warning of false
memoirs of Lady Vane and contrasts this one with Smollett's
humorous and entertaining writing.

4  ANON.  "The Heroines: or, Modern Memoirs," <u>London Magazine</u>,
20 (March), 135-36.
  Poem on Lady Vane's morality in <u>Peregrine Pickle</u>.

5  ANON.  Review of <u>A Letter to Lady Vane</u>, <u>Monthly Review</u>, 4
(March), 376.
  Lady Vane omitted her worst traits in her "Memoirs" in
<u>Peregrine Pickle</u>.

6  ANON.  Review of Pamphlet Comparing Lady Frail and Lady Vane,
<u>Monthly Review</u>, 4 (March), 376.
  Attacks Lady Vane's character in <u>Peregrine Pickle</u>.

7  ANON.  On <u>Peregrine Pickle</u>, <u>Magazine of Magazines</u>, 1 (April),
287.
  <u>Peregrine Pickle</u> among the progeny of Pope's <u>Dunciad</u>.

8  ANON.  "To Lady V--e," <u>Ladies' Magazine</u> (June).
  Attacks Lady Vane in <u>Peregrine Pickle</u>.  Printed in Buck,
1925.4.  Same poem in <u>British Magazine</u> (May) according to
Boege, 1947.1.

9  ANON.  "On the Two Celebrated Miss G--," <u>London Magazine</u>, 20
(June), 279.
  Poem attacks Lady Vane in <u>Peregrine Pickle</u>.

10  ANON.  "On Miss Gunning's First Coming from Ireland," <u>London</u>
<u>Magazine</u>, 20 (December), 568.
  Includes attack on Lady Vane in <u>Peregrine Pickle</u>.

11  ANON.  <u>A Letter to the Right Honourable the Lady V--ss V--</u>.
<u>Occasioned by the Publication of Her Memoirs in the Adven-</u>
<u>tures of Peregrine Pickle</u>.  London: W. Owen, 47 pp.
  Attacks her morality.

12  ANON.  <u>A Parallel between the Characters of Lady Frail and the</u>
<u>Lady of Quality in Peregrine Pickle</u>.  London: R. Griffiths,
47 pp.
  Lady Frail better drawn.

13  [CLELAND, JOHN]. Review of <u>Peregrine Pickle</u>, <u>Monthly Review</u>
      4 (March), 355-64.
         Approves of Smollett's didacticism and naturalness and
      rejects charges of vulgarity. Notes relationship to pica-
      resque writers and fictionalizing of real persons.

14  CLÉMENT, PIERRE. "Lettre IV" and "Lettre VII," <u>Nouvelles Lit-</u>
      <u>téraires, &c. de France & d'Angleterre</u>, (March), p. 2 and
      (May), pp. 1-4.
         Letters from Paris and London on <u>Peregrine Pickle</u>, but
      more particularly on Lady Vane and her "Memoirs."

15  [COVENTRY, FRANCIS], <u>An Essay on the New Species of Writing</u>
      <u>Founded by Mr. Fielding</u>. London: W. Owen, pp. ii, 23, 25.
         Smollett a poor imitator of Fielding. Reprinted 1962.4.

16  [GRIFFITHS, RALPH]. <u>Review of History of Miss Betty Thought-</u>
      <u>less</u>, <u>Monthly Review</u>, 5 (October), 394.
         Praises the interesting "digressive essays" in
      Smollett's works.

17  [HILL, JOHN]. <u>The History of a Woman of Quality: or, The Ad-</u>
      <u>ventures of Lady Frail</u>. London: M. Cooper and G. Woodfall,
      xii + 227 pp.
         Hill's rival to <u>Peregrine Pickle</u>.

18  Maty, Dr. Review of <u>Peregrine Pickle</u>, <u>Journal Britannique</u>, 4
      (April), 429-30.
         Reproaches Smollett's licentiousness, but praises his
      humor.


<u>1752</u>

 1  ANON. Review of <u>History of Betty Barnes</u>, <u>Monthly Review</u>, 7
      (December), 470.
         Remarks on Smollett's superior talents, along with
      Fielding and Coventry.

 2  [FIELDING, HENRY]. "The Journal of the Present War," <u>Covent-</u>
      <u>Garden Journal</u>, no. 2 (January 7).
         Mock battle of the books scoffs at <u>Roderick Random</u> and
      <u>Peregrine Pickle</u>.

 3  GOODALL, W. <u>The Adventures of Capt. Greenland</u>. London: R.
      Baldwin, I, 6.
         Includes Roderick Random among heroes receiving public
      approval.

1752

4   [KENRICK, WILLIAM]. <u>Fun: A Parodi-tragi-comical Satire</u>.
    London: F. Stamper et al., Scene 1 and passim.
        Pokes fun at <u>Roderick Random</u> and <u>Peregrine Pickle</u> and
    plays on the character of Trunnion.

5   [THORNTON, BONNELL]. <u>Have at You All: or, the Drury-Lane</u>
    <u>Journal</u>. London: Publick Register Office, pp. 14, 17, 29.
        Comic description of Smollett and Fielding's rivalry
    after the publication of <u>Peregrine Pickle</u>.


                    1753

1   ANON. "Advertissement," in <u>Histoire et Avantures de Sir</u>
    <u>Williams Pickle</u>. Amsterdam and Leipzig: Arkstee & Merkus,
    I, i-iv.
        On problems of translating the work and its general
    characteristics.

2   [COVENTRY, FRANCIS]. <u>History of Pompey the Little</u>. Dublin:
    George Faulkner, p. 8.
        Comments ironically on moral purpose of the "Memoirs of
    a Lady of Quality" in <u>Peregrine Pickle</u>. Reprinted 1974.11.

*3  FRÉRON, LOUIS S. On French Translation of <u>Peregrine Pickle</u>,
    <u>Lettres sur quelques Écrits de ce Temps</u>, 100 (1753), 226ff.
        Balanced judgment of <u>Peregrine Pickle</u>. Cited in Joliat,
    1935.5.

4   [GRIFFITHS, RALPH]. Review of <u>Ferdinand Count Fathom</u>, <u>Monthly</u>
    <u>Review</u>, 8 (March), 203-14.
        Praises Smollett's genius, but finds main character im-
    plausible and unedifying. Finds Fathom's repentance, story
    of Monimia and Melville, and that of Don Diego more satis-
    fying. Also discusses Smollett's use of the picaresque.

5   [HILL, JOHN]. <u>The Inspector</u>. London: R. Griffiths et al.,
    no. 24, I, 99-104.
        Quarrels with Smollett over Lady Vane in <u>Peregrine</u>
    <u>Pickle</u>.


                    1754

1   PILKINGTON, LAETITIA. <u>The Third and Last Volume of the Mem-</u>
    <u>oirs of Mrs. Laetitia Pilkington</u>. London: n.p., pp. 8-9.
        Verse condemns false, immoral heroes like Roderick
    Random.


                    4

## 1755

1   [GRIFFITHS, RALPH]. Review of Smollett's Translation of Don
    Quixote, Monthly Review, 13 (September), 196-202.
         Praises the translation and finds it, if less accurate,
    more in the spirit of the original than Jarvis's.

2   [KIDGELL, JOHN]. The Card. London: J. Newbery, II, 294.
         Among fictional couples attending wedding celebration
    are Roderick Random and Mrs. Booby, the former Pamela
    Andrews.

*3  [WINDHAM, WILLIAM]. Remarks on the Proposals Lately Published
    for a New Translation of Don Quixote. London: W. Reeve.
         Attacks Smollett's knowledge of Spaniards and their
    language. Cited in Boucé, 1976.9.

## 1756

1   ANON. Review of the Critical Review, Gentleman's Magazine, 26
    (March), 141-42.
         Severe judgment of Smollett's periodical.

2   ANON. Review of A Compendium of Authentic and Entertaining
    Voyages, Critical Review, 1 (May), 309.
         Praises selection, organization, and editing in
    Smollett's work.

*3  ANON. An Abstract from the Monthly Critical Review of the Ad-
    vertisement Prefixed to the History of Valencia by Don Juan
    Fernandez, Principal of the Inquisition at Estremadura.
    London.
         Attack on the Critical Review. Cited in Jones, 1942.4.

*4  ANON. An Appendix to the Critical Review of March Last.
    London.
         Attack on the Critical Review. Cited in Jones, 1942.4.

*5  [HUGGINS, WILLIAM]. "The Author of the Observer Observed,"
    The General Evening Post (June 15).
         Attack on the Critical Review. Cited in Jones, 1942.4.

6   [MURPHY, ARTHUR]. "Trials of the Authors of the Monthly Re-
    view," in The Gray's-Inn Journal. London: W. Faden, for
    P. Vaillant, II, 273.
         Erroneously suggests John Hill's connection with the
    Critical Review.

1756

*7   PARSON, JAMES.  Letter, The General Evening Post (September
        15).
            Attack on the Critical Review.  Cited in Jones, 1942.4.

*8   PATTEN, THOMAS.  St. Peter's Christian Apology as Set Forth in
        a Sermon on I Peter. III. 15, 16.  Oxford: S. Parker and
        R. Clements, 87 pp.
            Attack on the Critical Review.  Cited in Jones, 1942.4.

9   [SMART, CHRISTOPHER].  "From Edmund Curl, to the Principal
        Author of a Thing, Called the Critical Review," Universal
        Visiter [sic] and Monthly Memorialist, 1 (March), 139-40.
            Attack on Smollett's periodical.


                            1757

1   ANON.  Review of The Reprisal: or, the Tars of Old England,
        Critical Review, 3 (February), 157-60.
            Acknowledges play's lack of stagecraft, but praises its
        inventiveness, characterization, and imitation of nature.

2   ANON.  Review of The Reprisal: or, The Tars of Old England,
        Monthly Review, 16 (February), 179.
            Dismisses play in a single sentence.

3   ANON.  Review of Complete History of England, Critical Review,
        3 (May), 449-58 and (June), 481-99.
            Review of first three volumes praises their honesty,
        clarity, and authenticity.

4   ANON.  Discussion of Criticism in the Critical Review, Liter-
        ary Magazine, 2 (September 15), 426-27.
            Assumes Smollett's responsibility for reviews and mocks
        their methods.

*5   ANON.  Review of Smollett's History, Bibliothèque Impartiale,
        16 (October), 293.
            Unfavorable review, perhaps by an English correspondent.
        Cited in Joliat, 1935.5.

*6   ANON.  Review of Smollett's History, L'Etat Politique de
        l'Angleterre, 8 (1757-59), 180.
            Translation of criticism from the Monthly Review.  Cited
        in Joliat, 1935.5.

*7   ANON.  True Merit, True Happiness. Memoirs of Mr. S.  London.
            Attack on the Critical Review.  Cited in Jones, 1942.4.


                              6

*8    BOWER, ARCHIBALD.  The Second Part of Mr. Bower's Answer to a
      Scurrilous Pamphlet.  London.
           Attack on the Critical Review.  Cited in Critical Re-
      view, 3 (1757), 150, 190-92.

*9    [DOUGLAS, JOHN].  A Letter to the Author of the Critical Re-
      view.  London.
           Defends William Hunter's work from attacks by reviewers.
      Cited in Jones, 1942.4.

10    [GOLDSMITH, OLIVER].  Review of A Complete History of England
      to 1748, Monthly Review, 16 (June), 530-36.
           Despite effective style fails to provide evidence, ori-
      ginal observations, or pertinent evaluations, and character
      sketches have been overpraised.

11    [MURPHY, ARTHUR].  "Letter on Criticism," Literary Magazine,
      2 (January-February), 26-30.
           Attacks reviewing methods of the Critical.

12    [MURPHY, ARTHUR].  Review of Gray's Odes, Literary Magazine,
      2 (September-October), 422-26, (October-November), 466-68.
           Several attacks on the Critical Review for treatment of
      Gray's work and an attack on Smollett as historian.

13    [MURPHY, ARTHUR].  Review of Smollett's The Reprisal, Literary
      Magazine, 2 (January-February), 36-38.
           Attacks Smollett's reviews in the Critical and berates
      lack of comedy in the play, noting its failure in the
      theater and its derogatory treatment of Scotsmen.

14    [RUFFHEAD, OWEN].  Review of Shebbeare's The Occasional Critic,
      Monthly Review, 17 (October), 373-74.
           Deplores not only Shebbeare, but Smollett and the Criti-
      cal Review.

15    [SHEBBEARE, JOHN].  Appendix to the Occasional Critic.  London:
      n.p., 34 pp.
           Severe attack on the Critical and particular denuncia-
      tion of Smollett as a hack writer.

16    [SHEBBEARE, JOHN].  The Occasional Critic: or, the Decrees of
      the Scotch Tribunal in the Critical Review Rejudged.
      London: M. Cooper, 168 pp.
           Savage attack on Smollett and Scotsmen on the Critical
      Review.

## 1758

1    ANON. Review of <u>Complete History of England</u>, <u>Critical Review</u>,
     5 (January), 1-17.
         Notes small errors in this fourth volume, but finds it
     equal to first three and stresses lack of bias.

*2   ANON. Review of <u>Complete History of England</u>, <u>Journal Encyclo-
     pédique</u> (March).
         Attacks Smollett's partiality and anti-French senti-
     ments. Cited in Joliat, 1935.5. Also notes review in
     September, 1764.

*3   ANON. Review of Smollett's <u>Complete History of England</u>,
     <u>Mémoires de Trévoux</u> (October and December).
         Accuses Smollett of plagiarism from Rapin-Thoiras.
     Cited in Joliat, 1935.5. Also notes reviews in June, Octo-
     ber, November, and December, 1759.

4    ANON. Review of <u>The Reprisal</u>, <u>Theatrical Review: for the Year
     1757, and Beginning of 1758</u>. London: n.p., pp. 48-50.
         Savage review of Smollett's play.

5    BROWN, JOHN. <u>An Estimate of the Manners and Principles of the
     Times</u>. London: L. Davis and C. Reymers, II, 75-76.
         Attacks <u>Critical Review</u> and its methods.

6    COMBER, THOMAS. <u>A Vindication of the Great Revolution in
     England in A.D. MDCLXXXVIII</u>. London: J. Robinson, 149 pp.
         Severe attack on Smollett's <u>Complete History of England</u>
     as a Jacobite work and on the <u>Critical Review</u> for its
     approval.

7    [RUFFHEAD, OWEN]. Review of <u>Complete History of England</u>,
     <u>Monthly Review</u>, 18 (April), 289-305.
         Although an entertaining novelist, Smollett is no his-
     torian, and his work is an inaccurate, biased Scottish,
     Tory, and Jacobite account.

## 1759

1    ANON. Review of <u>Modern Part of an Universal History</u>, <u>Critical
     Review</u>, 7 (January), 1-14, (February), 158-60, (March),
     216-25; 8 (September), 189-99, (October), 261-71, (Novem-
     ber), 352-66, (December), 469-80.
         Generally favorable reviews. That of January, perhaps

by Smollett, hails the enterprise as rivaling the work of European academies.

2   ANON.  Review of Grainger's A Letter to Tobias Smollett, Critical Review, 7 (February), 141-58.
        Defends Smollett, noting he has never acknowledged connection with the Critical and denying that he wrote article on Grainger.

3   ANON.  Letter, London Chronicle, 5 (April 14-17), 361-62.
        Attack on the Critical.

*4  ANON.  Review of Smollett's History of England, Mercure de France (October).
        Cited in Joliat, 1935.5.  Also cites reviews in December, 1760 and June, 1764.

5   ANON.  The Life and Real Adventures of Hamilton Murray. Written by Himself.  London: F. and J. Noble, I, 4.
        Smollett among those authors with whom he cannot compare.

*6  ANON.  Tyburn to the Marine Society: a Poem.  London.
        Attack on the Critical Review.  Cited in Jones, 1942.4.

*7  FORTESCUE, JOHN.  Dissertations, Essays, and Discourses.  2 Vols.  London.
        Attack on Critical Review.  Cited in Jones, 1942.4.

8   FRÉRON, LOUIS S.  "Histoire d'Angleterre," L'Année Littéraire, 5 (1759), 338-54.
        Dislikes Smollett's anti-French sentiments in History of England, but moderately favorable to the work.

9   GOLDSMITH, OLIVER.  An Enquiry into the Present State of Polite Learning in Europe.  London: R. and J. Dodsley, Chapters 10 and 11, passim.
        Includes Critical Review among the inadequate periodicals that are dull and fail to encourage learning.

10  GOLDSMITH, OLIVER.  "A Reverie," in The Bee, no. 5 (November 3).  London: J. Wilkie.
        Fictive piece denies Smollett fame as an historian, but grants it as a novelist.

11  GRAINGER, JAMES.  A Letter to Tobias Smollett, M.D. Occasioned by His Criticism upon a Late Translation of Tibullus.
        London: T. Kinnersly, 25 pp.

1759

Response to review in the Critical attacks Smollett's knowledge, taste, and manners.

12   [HILL, JOHN].  Observations on the Account Given of the Catalogue of the Royal and Noble Authors of England, &c. in Article Sixth of the Critical Review, No. 35 for December, 1758.  London: H. Woodgate and S. Brook, 40 pp.
Defense of Horace Walpole and his work from an attack in the Critical Review.

13   [KENRICK, WILLIAM].  A Scrutiny; or, the Critics Criticis'd.  London: n.p., 68 pp.
Attacks the Critical Review.

14   [MARRIOTT, THOMAS].  The Twentieth Epistle of Horace to His Book, Modernized by the Author of Female Conduct and Applied to His Own Book...an Answer to the...Critical Review.  London: W. Owen, xxii +14 pp.
Attack on the Critical Review.

*15   MOLYNEUX, THOMAS MORE.  Advertisement in Newspaper.
Responds to unfavorable review in Critical of his treatise, The Target.  Cited in Critical Review, 8 (1759), 28.

*16   [N., M.].  A Letter to the Critical Review.  London.
Supports review's unfavorable treatment of Horace Walpole's Catalogue of Royal and Noble Authors of England.  Cited in Critical Review, 7 (1759), 453-57.  Yale Walpole, XIII, 32, attributes letter to William Wynne.

17   [REED, JOSEPH].  A Sop in the Pan for a Physical Critick: in a Letter to Dr. Sm*ll*t.  London: W. Reeve, 24 pp.
Vehemently attacks Critical Review and Smollett, particularly The Regicide.

18   SEAMAN, A.  On Review of The Conduct and Treatment of John Crookshanks, Esq., London Chronicle, 5 (January 13-16), 50.
Attack on the Critical Review.

*19   WESTON, W.  The Safety and Perpetuity of the British State under the Influence of Political and Religious Zeal.  London.
Attacks the Critical.  Cited in Critical Review, 7 (1759), 430.

<u>1760</u>

1    ANON.  Review of <u>Modern Part of an Universal History</u>, <u>Critical</u>
      <u>Review</u>, 9 (January), 20-32, (February), 81-92, (March),
      161-77, (April), 245-60, (May), 325-41, (June), 457-65; 10
      (July), 1-19, (August), 81-90, (September), 161-78, (Novem-
      ber), 329-37, (December), 409-21.
          Despite minor criticism, generally very favorable re-
      views of Vols. 13-24.  March, August, and September reviews
      have been attributed to Smollett.

*2   ANON.  Review of Smollett's <u>History of England</u>, <u>Journal des</u>
      <u>Journaux</u> (February).
          Based on Fréron, 1759.8.  Cited in Joliat, 1935.5.

3    ANON.  "To Dr. Smollett. An Ode," <u>Lloyd's Evening Post and</u>
      <u>British Chronicle</u>, 6 (February 20-22), 179.
          Highly laudatory poem on Smollett as historian.  Re-
      printed in full in Knapp, 1949.12.

4    ANON.  "On the Present State of Literature in England,"
      <u>Imperial Magazine</u>, 1 (December), 519.
          Some praise of Smollett as a novelist, but severely
      critical of him as an historian and writer for the <u>Critical</u>
      <u>Review</u>.

5    ANON.  <u>The Battle of the Reviews</u>.  London: R. Marriner, 159
      pp.
          Attacks Smollett and the <u>Critical</u> in a triumphant mock-
      battle with the <u>Monthly</u>.

*6   ANON.  A Letter to the <u>Critical Review</u>.  London.
          Attack on the <u>Critical</u>.  Cited in Jones, 1942.4.

*7   ANON.  <u>Louisa: or, Virtue in Distress. Being the History of a</u>
      <u>Natural Daughter of Lady ****</u>.  London.
          Attacks the <u>Critical</u>.  Cited in Jones, 1942.4.

*8   ANON.  <u>Remarks on Mr. Robert Dossie's Institutes of Experimen-</u>
      <u>tal Chemistry</u>.  London.
          Attack on <u>Critical Review</u>.  Cited in Jones, 1942.4.

*9   ANON.  <u>A Review of the Works of the Rev. Mr. W. Hawkins</u>.
      London.
          Responds to the <u>Critical</u>'s unfavorable review of his
      <u>Works</u>.  Cited in <u>Critical Review</u>, 9 (1760), 214-17.

1760

*10   ANON. <u>Two Letters to the Reviewers Occasioned by the Account</u>
      <u>of a Book Called Memoirs</u>. London.
          Attack on the <u>Critical Review</u>. Cited in Jones, 1942.4.

 11   [BOSWELL, JAMES]. <u>A View of the Edinburgh Theatre during the</u>
      <u>Summer Season, 1759</u>. London: A. Morley, pp. 49-50.
          High praise for Smollett's <u>The Reprisal</u> upon performance
      in Edinburgh. Reprinted 1976.8.

 12   COLMAN, GEORGE. "Preface," in <u>Polly Honeycombe, a Dramatick</u>
      <u>Novel of One Act</u>. London: T. Becket, p. viii.
          <u>Roderick Random</u>, <u>Peregrine Pickle</u>, and <u>Ferdinand Count</u>
      <u>Fathom</u> on list of popular circulating-library novels being
      ridiculed.

 13   [GOLDSMITH, OLIVER]. "The Description of a Wow-Wow in the
      Country," <u>Public Ledger</u> (February 16).
          Puff for <u>Sir Launcelot Greaves</u> as it appeared in <u>British</u>
      <u>Magazine</u>.

 14   K. "To Dr. Smollett: an Ode," <u>Lloyd's Evening Post, and</u>
      <u>British Chronicle</u>, 6 (February 20-22), 179.
          Praises <u>Ferdinand Count Fathom</u> and <u>History of England</u>.

 15   [LEMAN, TANFIELD]. Review of <u>Modern Part of an Universal His-</u>
      <u>tory</u>, <u>Monthly Review</u>, 23 (October), 257-70, (December),
      467-85.
          Generally critical of editing of Volumes 1-13.

*16   LOVETT, R. <u>The Reviewers Reviewed</u>. London.
          Attack on the <u>Critical Review</u>. Cited in <u>Monthly Review</u>,
      22 (1760), 340.

 17   [MURPHY, ARTHUR]. <u>A Poetical Epistle to Mr. Samuel Johnson,</u>
      <u>A.M.</u> London: P. Vaillant, passim.
          Attacks judgment of the reviewers on the <u>Critical</u>.

*18   NIHELL, ELIZABETH. <u>An Answer to the Authors of the Critical</u>
      <u>Review</u>. London.
          Attack on the <u>Critical Review</u>. Cited in Jones, 1942.4.

 19   STEVENS, SIMON. <u>A Journal of Lieut. Simon Stevens</u>. Boston:
      Edes and Gill, passim.
          Includes the adventures of Captain (later Major) Stobo,
      the original of Smollett's Lismahago in <u>Humphry Clinker</u>.

1761

*1  AMICO, AMICUS. The Critical Reviewers Criticised, I.  London.
      Attack on Critical Review.  Cited in Jones, 1942.4.

2   ANON.  Review of Modern Part of an Universal History, Critical
      Review, 11 (January), 5-18, (February), 81-91, (March),
      169-83, (April), 257-65, (June), 421-34; 12 (July), 6-15,
      (August), 81-103, (September), 161-78, (November), 321-35.
         While noting minor blemishes, praises work as a major
      contribution in the public interest.  January, February,
      August, September, and November reviews have been attribu-
      ted to Smollett.

3   ANON.  Review of Translation of Voltaire's Works, Critical
      Review, 11 (May), 377-81.
         Praises translation, editing, and annotation.

4   ANON.  Review of Sir Launcelot Greaves, Journal Encyclopé-
      dique, (June), p. 101.
         Praises novel, making comparisons with Don Quixote.

5   ANON.  Introduction to Volume, Court Magazine, 1 (September),
      6.
         Attack on Critical Review.

6   ANON.  "Essay upon the Most Remarkable Periods of English
      Literature," Court Magazine, 1 (September), 16.
         Praises Smollett as a writer of comic romances in the
      tradition of Cervantes and Le Sage.

7   ANON.  Introduction to Account of Books, Court Magazine, 1
      (September), 35.
         Accuses Critical reviewers of partiality and defective-
      ness.

8   ANON.  Review of the Continuation of the Complete History of
      England, Critical Review, 12 (October), 283-95, (November),
      335-47.
         Declares own impartiality despite Smollett's supposed
      connection and praises his great skill as an unbiased his-
      torian with extraordinary literary merit.

*9  ANON.  Review of Continuation of the History of England, Jour-
      nal Etranger, (November), pp. 63ff.
         Favorable review.  Cited in Joliat, 1935.5.  Also cites
      a review in July.

13

1761

*10  ANON. Review of Smollett's <u>Continuation of the History of</u>
     <u>England</u>, <u>Journal Encyclopédique</u>, (November), p. 106.
          Cited in Joliat, 1935.5. Also cites a December, 1765
     review.

 11  ANON. Evaluation of Contemporary Writers, <u>Court Magazine</u>, 1
     (December), 169.
          Attacks <u>Critical</u> and speculates on reviewers.

*12  ANON. <u>An Address to those Formidable Societies of Gentlemen,</u>
     the <u>Authors of the Two Reviews and Court Magazine</u>. London.
          Attacks <u>Critical</u>. Cited in <u>Critical Review</u>, 12 (1761),
     399.

*13  ANON. <u>Dr. Wilson's Remarks upon Some Passages of the Critical</u>
     <u>Review, for, October, 1761. Art. V.</u> London.
          Attacks <u>Critical</u>. Cited in <u>Critical Review</u>, 13 (1762),
     274-84.

*14  BOWER, ARCHIBALD. <u>History of the Popes</u>, Vol. V. London.
          Attacks <u>Critical</u>. Cited in <u>Critical Review</u>, 11 (1761),
     229.

 15  CHURCHILL, CHARLES. <u>The Apology. Addressed to the Critical</u>
     <u>Reviewers</u>. London: W. Flexney for the Author, 20 pp.
          Full-scale attack on Smollett and the <u>Critical</u>.

 16  [LEMAN, TANFIELD]. Review of <u>Modern Part of an Universal His-</u>
     <u>tory</u>, <u>Monthly Review</u>, 24 (January), 33-44, (February), 89-
     101, (March), 169-82 [mispaged as 109-22], (May), 285-93,
     (June), 365-73, (Appendix), 445-55.
          Attacks editing and notes use of material from
     Smollett's <u>History of England</u> whose political sympathies
     are assailed.

 17  [MURPHY, ARTHUR]. <u>An Ode to the Naiads of Fleet-Ditch</u>.
     London: M. Cooper, pp. iii, 11.
          Murphy denies connection with <u>Critical</u> and attacks it.

*18  VERITAS. <u>The Triumvirate</u>. London.
          Attacks <u>Critical Review</u>. Cited in Jones, 1942.4.

*19  [WOODHULL, MICHAEL]. <u>A Poetical Epistle to -----</u>. London.
          Attacks <u>Critical Review</u>. Cited in Jones, 1942.4.

1762

1  ANON.  Review of <u>Modern Part of an Universal History</u>, <u>Critical</u>
   <u>Review</u>, 13 (February), 107-20, (May), 381-92; 14 (October),
   241-249, (December), 401-10.
        Despite minor cavils, great praise for the entire pro-
   ject.  February and May reviews have been attributed to
   Smollett.

2  ANON.  Comment on <u>Critical</u>.  <u>Court Magazine</u> (February), p.
   270.
        Reviewers lack taste and fail to read books.

3  ANON.  Review of Robert Lloyd's Poems.  <u>Court Magazine</u> (March),
   p. 320.
        Abuses taste of <u>Critical</u> reviewers.

4  ANON.  "Advertisement for <u>Two Lyric Epistles; or Margery the</u>
   <u>Cook Maid to the Critical Reviewers</u>," <u>London Chronicle</u>, 11
   (April 29-May 1), 415.
        Attacks <u>Critical Review</u>.

5  ANON.  "Literary Remarks and Intelligence," <u>The Library: or,</u>
   <u>Moral and Critical Magazine</u>, 2 (May), 262.
        Praises humor, style, and sentiment in <u>Launcelot Greaves</u>,
   but complains about obscure nautical language and character
   of Capt. Crowe.

6  ANON.  Review of <u>Launcelot Greaves</u>, <u>Monthly Review</u>, 26 (May),
   391.
        One sentence review dismisses it as "unworthy" of
   Smollett.

7  ANON.  Review of <u>Launcelot Greaves</u>, <u>Critical Review</u>, 13 (May),
   427-29.
        Novel reveals Smollett's benevolence as well as comic
   talents, and it is not dependent upon knowledge of <u>Don</u>
   <u>Quixote</u>.  Highest praise for characterization, particularly
   of Capt. Crowe.

8  ANON.  Letter, <u>Court Magazine</u> (July), p. 503.
        Attacks <u>Critical Review</u>.

*9 ANON.  Review of Smollett's <u>History of England</u>, <u>Journal des</u>
   <u>Savants</u> (August).
        Cited in Joliat, 1935.5.

1762

10   ANON. Review of <u>Continuation of the Complete History of</u>
     <u>England</u>, <u>Critical Review</u>, 14 (August), 131-37.
          Praises style, discernment, and impartiality, and ap-
     plauds its success.

*11  ANON. <u>Dialogues of the Living</u>. London: J. Cooke, 148 pp.
          Includes attack on <u>Critical</u>. Cited in Jones, 1942.4.

*12  [BRIDGES, THOMAS]. <u>Homer Travestie: Being a New Translation</u>
     <u>of the First Four Books of the Iliad</u>. London: R. Marriner,
     231 pp.
          Attacks <u>Critical</u>. Cited in Jones, 1942.4.

13   CHURCHILL, CHARLES. <u>The Ghost</u>. London: William Flexney, 11.
     385ff.
          Attack on Smollett the critic.

*14  FREEMAN, GEORGE. <u>Day: an Epistle to Dr. Churchill</u>. London.
          Attacks <u>Critical</u>. Cited in Jones, 1942.4.

15   [GOLDSMITH, OLIVER]. "The Indigent Philosopher. Numb. 3.
     The State of Literature," <u>Lloyd's Evening Post</u> (January 29-
     February 1).
          Assesses Smollett's treatment of modern writers in his
     <u>Continuation of the History of England</u>. For attribution to
     Goldsmith and reprint, <u>see</u> Crane, 1927.8.

16   [GRIFFITHS, RALPH]. Review of <u>Modern Part of an Universal</u>
     <u>History</u>, <u>Monthly Review</u>, 27 (November), 358-63, (December),
     410-19.
          Finds work serviceable, but inferior to Hume's and
     Robertson's.

17   [LEMAN, TANFIELD]. Review of <u>Modern Part of an Universal His-</u>
     <u>tory</u>, <u>Monthly Review</u>, 27 (August), 81-94, (October), 275-
     80.
          Attacks editorial policies and generally criticizes
     writing.

*18  PLOUGHMAN, OXFORDSHIRE. <u>A Mirror for Critics</u>. London.
          Attacks <u>Critical Review</u>. Cited in Jones, 1942.4.

19   [RIDER, WILLIAM]. "Dr. Smollet [sic]," in <u>An Historical Ac-</u>
     <u>count of the Lives and Writings of the Living Authors of</u>
     <u>Great-Britain</u>. London: For the Author, pp. 11-12.
          Perhaps earliest general account. Praises <u>History of</u>
     <u>England</u>, <u>Roderick Random</u>, and <u>Fathom</u>, but critical of
     <u>Peregrine Pickle</u> and his dramas. Reprinted 1974.41.

20    SMOLLETT, TOBIAS. "Smollett's Account of the Birth of the
      Pretender," Scots Magazine, 24 (August), 402-3.
          Uses his account to fill out material in a history.

21    [WILKES, JOHN]. Political Controversy etc. London: S.
      Williams, 5 Vols., passim.
          Many attacks on Smollett and the Briton in collection of
      anti-ministerial and ministerial pamphlets. Reprinted
      1968.43.

## 1763

1     ALMON, JOHN. A Review of Lord Bute's Administration. London:
      I. Pridden, pp. 53-55.
          On Wilkes's controversy with Smollett's Briton.

2     ANON. Review of Modern Part of an Universal History, Critical
      Review, 15 (January), 1-11; 16 (August), 127-37, (Novem-
      ber), 360-70.
          Praises entire project and explains editorial plans.

*3    ANON. A Letter from the Cocoa-Tree to the Chiefs of the Oppo-
      sition. London.
          Assails Critical Review for Tory, Jacobite, and Scottish
      connections. Cited in Critical Review, 15 (1763), 68-69.

4     ANON. Peregrinations of Jeremiah Grant, Esq. London: G.
      Burnet, pp. 64-65.
          Smollett at least the equal of Fielding and Sterne.

*5    BISSET, C. Candid and Satisfactory Answers to the Several
      Criticisms of the Critical Reviewers etc. London.
          Attacks Critical Review. Cited in Jones, 1942.4.

6     CHURCHILL, CHARLES. The Author. London: W. Flexney et al.,
      11. 107ff., 1. 254.
          Personal attack on Smollett.

*7    KENNEDY, JOHN. Examination of Mr. Ferguson's Remarks on Mr.
      Kennedy's System of Astronomical Chronology in the Critical
      Review, May 1763. London.
          Attacks Critical. Cited in Critical Review, 16 (1763),
      339-52.

8     [KENRICK, WILLIAM]. Review of Translation of Voltaire's
      Works, Monthly Review, 29 (October), 273-82.

1763

Attacks Smollett's lending his name to dull production
for mercenary purposes.

9  [RUFFHEAD, OWEN]. Review of Continuation of the Complete History of England, Monthly Review, 28 (April), 249-56, (May),
359-69.
Smollett less biased than in his History and improved as
an historian despite evidence of hasty composition.

10  SMART, CHRISTOPHER. Poems. London: for the Author, and Sold
by Mr. Fletcher, and Mr. Laurence, preface.
Attack on the Critical Review.


1764

1  ANON. Review of Modern Part of an Universal History, Critical
Review, 17 (June), 401-9; 18 (October), 141-51 [bis].
Discusses editorial plans and praises entire project.

2  [BAKER, DAVID ERSKINE]. "Smollett, Tobias M.D.," in The Com-
panion to the Play-House. London: T. Becket and P. A.
Dehondt et al., II, under Smollett.
Fair and accurate account of his work, including minor
writing, to that time, with special praise for Roderick
Random. Reprinted with revision in 1782.2.

3  [GRIFFITHS, RALPH]. Review of Modern Part of an Universal
History, Monthly Review, 31 (October), 307-16.
Largely extracts.

4  [VERNON, FRANCIS]. A Letter to the Right Honourable Lord
Orwell ... and to P. Thicknesse, Lieutenant Governor of
Land-Guard Fort. London: n.p., pp. 18ff.
Condemns Smollett's failure to portray horrors of prison
life in Sir Launcelot Greaves.


1765

1  ANON. Review of Modern Part of an Universal History, Critical
Review, 19 (February), 130-36.
Praises editorial desire for completeness in the work.

2  ANON. Review of Smollett's Continuation of the Complete History of England, Vol. 5, Critical Review, 20 (October),
270-74.

Smollett judicious and non-partisan and accurate in a remarkable writing job.

3   [RAYNOR, JOHN]. Digest of the Law Concerning Libels. London: The Author, pp. 81, 127.
    Details of Knowles's libel case against Smollett.

1766

1   ANON. Review of Travels through France and Italy, Royal Magazine, 14 (May), 233.
    Introduction to excerpts praises book and Smollett's work.

2   ANON. Review of Travels through France and Italy, London Magazine, 35 (May), 243-49.
    Approves of Smollett's shrewd observations and style and didactic service in ridiculing English imitation of French.

3   ANON. "Extract from Dr. Smollett's Travels thro' France and Italy," British Magazine, 7 (May), 265-70.
    Selection on the character of French men.

4   ANON. Review of Travels through France and Italy, Critical Review, 21 (May), 321-29, (June), 401-6.
    Praises Smollett's rejection of nonsense, his understanding, independence, candidness, intelligence, and calls him "ingenious."

5   ANON. Review of Travels through France and Italy, Gentleman's Magazine, 36 (August), 368.
    Conclusion of four articles of paraphrase and quotation (May, June, July, August) praises work for its entertaining and didactic merits.

*6  ANON. Review of Travels through France and Italy, Journal Encyclopédique (September), pp. 55ff.
    Critical of treatment of French. Cited in Joliat, 1935.5.

7   ANON. "A Critical Examination of the Respective Merits of Voltaire, Rousseau, Richardson, Smollett, and Fielding," British Magazine, 7 (September), 463.
    Compares Smollett and Marivaux, cites Roderick Random as his only significant achievement, and ranks him below Fielding and Richardson.

1766

8    ANON.  Review of Samuel Sharp's <u>Letters from Italy</u>, <u>Critical</u>
     <u>Review</u>, 22 (October), 284–91.
        Couples Sharp's work and Smollett's <u>Travels</u> in their
     organization and purpose and applauds both.

9    ANON.  Review of Thicknesse's <u>Observations on the Customs and</u>
     <u>Manners of the French Nation</u>, <u>Critical Review</u>, 22 (Decem-
     ber), 430–34.
        Ridicules Thicknesse's book in comparison with Smollett's
     <u>Travels</u>, and denies that Smollett has been connected with
     the <u>Critical</u> for several years.

10   [BERKENHOUT, JOHN].  Review of <u>Travels through France and</u>
     <u>Italy</u>, <u>Monthly Review</u>, 34 (June), 419–29.
        Smollet provides an entertaining and instructive guide-
     book.

*11  CHASTELLUX.  Review of <u>Travels through France and Italy</u>, <u>Ga-</u>
     <u>zette Littéraire</u> (February), pp. 365ff.
        Severe attack.  Cited in Joliat, 1935.5.

12   FRIEND TO ROUSSEAU.  A Letter, <u>St. James's Chronicle</u> (Decem-
     ber 16–18).
        Praises Smollett's descriptive powers, "the English
     Cervantes."

13   HENDERSON, ANDREW.  <u>Life of William Augustus Duke of Cumber-</u>
     <u>land</u>.  London: J. Ridley et al., passim.
        Attack on Smollett and his work.

14   THICKNESSE, PHILIP.  <u>Observations on the Customs and Manners</u>
     <u>of the French Nation</u>.  London: Robert Davis et al., pp. 42–
     45, 71–72, 89–91, 104–5 and passim.
        Finds Smollett's <u>Travels</u> ill-tempered, prejudiced, and
     inaccurate, and berates the <u>Critical</u> for its Scots bias.


1767

1    ANON.  Review of <u>The History of Major Bromley and Miss Clissen</u>,
     <u>Monthly Review</u>, 37 (November), 394.
        Smollett, with Fielding, a standard to judge other nov-
     elists.

2    [CAMPBELL, ARCHIBALD].  <u>Lexiphanes, A Dialogue</u>.  London: J.
     Knox, pp. 136–37.
        Regrets necessity of Smollett's having to do hackwork as
     in his histories.

3   [CAMPBELL, ARCHIBALD].  The Sale of Authors, A Dialogue.
        London: Ptd. and Sold by Booksellers in London and West-
        minster, p. 128 and passim.
            Much of the book attacks reviews, including Critical,
        and one passage praises Smollett as a historian.

4   CANNING, GEORGE.  "On the Critical Reviewers" and "On the
        Tragedy of Elvira," in Poems by George Canning.  London:
        J. Dodsley et al., pp. 89-90.
            Attacks critical methods and Scottish bias of Smollett
        and the Critical Review.

5   GOLDSMITH, OLIVER.  Comment on "The Tears of Scotland," in The
        Beauties of English Poetry.  Selected by Oliver Goldsmith.
        London: William Griffin, II, 87.
            Praises feeling but not technique of Smollett's poem.


                            1768

1   ANON.  Review of Baretti's Account of the Manners and Customs
        of Italy, Political Register, 2 (May), 383.
            Applauds Baretti's defense of Italy against attacks by
        such travellers as Smollett.

2   BARETTI, JOSEPH.  An Account of the Manners and Customs of
        Italy, with Observations on the Mistakes of Some Travel-
        lers.  London: T. Davies et al., II, 285-86, 309.
            Amused by Smollett's style in Travels, but scoffs at his
        aesthetic judgments and numerous errors.

3   STERNE, LAURENCE.  A Sentimental Journey through France and
        Italy.  London: T. Becket and P. A. DeHondt, passim.
            Attacks Smollett as Smelfungus and makes various allu-
        sions to his Travels.

4   THICKNESSE, PHILIP.  Useful Hints to Those Who Make the Tour
        of France.  London: R. Davis et al., pp. 1-36 and passim.
            Vituperous attack on Smollett, his Travels, histories,
        and his Critical Review.


                            1769

1   [ALMON, JOHN].  Review of History of an Atom, Political Regis-
        ter, 4 (June), 389-90.
            Attacks work and finds it hard to believe low style is
        Smollett's but politics indicates it is.


                            21

1769

2    ANON.  Review of History of an Atom, London Chronicle, 15
         (April 8-11), 341.
             Preface to extracts suggests attribution to Smollett.

*3   ANON.  Review of History of an Atom, Lloyd's Evening Post and
         British Chronicle (April 14-17).
             Attributes work to Smollett.  Cited in Foster, 1953.7.

4    ANON.  Review of History of an Atom, Gentleman's Magazine, 39
         (April), 200-205.
             Although spirited and humorous, too coarse.

5    ANON.  Review of History of an Atom, Town and Country Maga-
         zine, 1 (May), 269.
             Brief note admires its wit and humor.

6    ANON.  Review of History of an Atom, Critical Review, 27 (May),
         362-69.
             Combines Rabelais and Swift to attack a decadent soci-
         ety with appropriate indelicacy.  Intelligent readers will
         recognize the objects of his satire.

7    ANON.  News Notice, London Chronicle, 15 (July 29-August 1),
         110.
             Erroneous report of Smollett's death in Italy.

8    ANON.  News Notice, London Chronicle, 15 (August 3-5), 122.
             Corrects false report of Smollett's death.

9    ANON.  "Essay on Ballads," London Magazine, 38 (November),
         580.
             Powerful emotional effect of Smollett's "Tears of
         Scotland."

*10  DE GOMICOURT, DAMIENS DE.  L'Observateur Littéraire à Londres,
         I, 348.
             Compares Smollett's histories unfavorably with Hume's.
         Cited in Joliat, 1935.5.

11   [HAWKESWORTH, JOHN].  Review of History of an Atom, Monthly
         Review, 40 (June), 441-55.
             Although spiritedly written, loses satiric effect
         through obscene and revolting details.

<u>1770</u>

1   JENNER, CHARLES.  <u>The Placid Man: or, Memoirs of Sir Charles</u>
    <u>Beville</u>.  London: J. Wilkie, I, 2.
        Criticizes Smollett's having turned from novelist to
    historian.

2   THICKNESSE, PHILIP.  "Of the <u>Critical Reviewers</u>," in <u>Sketches</u>
    <u>and Characters</u>.  Bristol: John Wheble, I, 123-24.
        Still attacking <u>Critical</u> as though Smollett were associ-
    ated with it.

<u>1771</u>

1   AMICUS.  Letter to the Editor, <u>Town and Country Magazine</u>, 3
    (October), 548.
        High praise for recently deceased Smollett as best nov-
    elist of his time.

2   ANON.  Review of <u>Humphry Clinker</u>, <u>London Magazine</u>, 40 (June),
    317-19.
        Acknowledges Smollett's deserved reputation, but objects
    to misleading title and weak plan of the novel.  Praises
    characterization, didacticism, and Scottish material.

3   ANON.  Review of <u>Humphry Clinker</u>, <u>Town and Country Magazine</u>,
    3 (June), 323.
        Lives up to reputation as a novelist, and despite maga-
    zine's policy gives extract from his excellent novel.

4   ANON.  Review of <u>Miss Melmoth: or, the New Clarissa</u>, <u>Critical</u>
    <u>Review</u>, 31 (June), 479.
        Smollett's novels as a standard of comedy.

*5  ANON.  Review of <u>Humphry Clinker</u>, <u>Everyman's Magazine</u>, 1
    (July), 33.
        Objects to partisan portrayal of Scotland and unfavor-
    able treatment of London.  Cited in Boucé, 1976.9.

6   ANON.  Review of <u>Humphry Clinker</u>, <u>Court and City Magazine</u>, 3
    (July), 310.
        Comment on extract praises characterization.  <u>See</u>, too,
    August number for extract (pp. 357-63).

7   ANON.  Review of <u>Humphry Clinker</u>, <u>Gentleman's Magazine</u>, 41
    (July), 317-21.

1771

Deplores coarseness and lack of story, but admires satire and characterization.

8    ANON.  Review of Humphry Clinker, Hibernian Magazine, 1
     (July), 324.
          Introduces extract with praise for the novel.

9    ANON.  Review of Humphry Clinker, Critical Review, 32 (August),
     81-88.
          Celebrates the imaginative creation of characters and
     scenes, fidelity to life, liberating humanism, and novelty
     and originality of the novel.

10   ANON.  Review of Humphry Clinker, Monthly Review, 45 (August),
     152.
          Single paragraph berates coarseness and places novel
     below Roderick Random and Peregrine Pickle and on a par
     with the History of an Atom.

*11  ANON.  Review of Humphry Clinker, Journal Encyclopédique (Oc-
     tober 15).
          Critical of its indelicacy, but praises liveliness and
     ingenuity.  Cited in Joliat, 1935.5.

12   ANON.  Obituary Notice, Scots Magazine, 33 (October), 558.
          Gives notice of Smollett's death at Pisa on September 17
     and identifies him as author of History of England.

13   ANON.  Obituary Notice, Town and Country Magazine, 3 (October),
     560.
          Laudatory obituary notice.

14   ANON.  "Critical Remarks on Humphry Clinker," Universal Maga-
     zine, 49 (November), 256-57.
          Misleading title and biased contrast of Scotland and
     England, but novel has great merit.

15   ANON.  Obituary of Duncan Rivers, Bailiff of Glasgow, Gentle-
     man's Magazine, 41 (December), 571.
          Supposed model for Strap in Roderick Random.

16   ANON.  "Extract of a Letter from an English Gentleman in Italy
     ...," Town and Country Magazine, 3 (December), 651.
          Describes Smollett's favorable reputation in Italy and
     mourns his death.

17    ANON.  "On the Report of the Death of Dr. Smollett," Royal
      Magazine, 25 (December), 656.
          Poem bemoans loss of Smollett (Roderick Random).

18    ANON.  Obituary Notice of Provost Buchanan," Annual Register,
      14 (1771), 146.
          Reputed original of Squire Gawky in Roderick Random.


                              1772

 1    ANON.  Review of The Contemplative Man, Monthly Review, 46
      (March), 264.
          Smollett's novels a standard for merit.

 2    ANON.  On Matt Bramble, Perth Magazine, 1 (July 3), 5.
          Epitome of character of Matt Bramble in Humphry Clinker.

 3    ANON.  "Smollett," in Letters Concerning the Present State of
      England.  London: J. Almon, p. 397.
          Extremely laudatory account of Smollett's life and work,
      especially Roderick Random.  Bemoans his need for hack work.

*4    MAYEUL-CHAUDON, L'ABBÉ.  Smollett as Historian.  Bibliothèque
      d'un Homme de Goût.  Avignon, II, 179.
          Compares Smollett's histories unfavorably with Hume's.
      Cited in Joliat, 1935.5.

 5    [STEVENSON, JOHN HALL].  Makarony Fables; Fables for Grown
      Gentlemen; Lyrick Epistles; and Several Other Poems.
      Dublin: Thomas Ewing, pp. 73-76, 251-60.
          Verse attacks on the Critical Review under Smollett and
      particular abuse of Smollett himself.  ("Queries to the
      Critical Reviewers" and "Two Lyric Epistles: or, Margery
      the Cook-Maid.")


                              1773

 1    ANON.  On Smollett's Monument, Weekly Magazine (Edinburgh), 21
      (September 9), 351.
          Describes monument erected to Smollett by James Smollett
      of Bonhill.

 2    ANON.  On Morality in Novels, Monthly Ledger, 1 (1773), 311.
          Smollett's novels have satisfactory moral effect.

1773

3    CAUTION. On Smollett's Lack of Moral Purpose, <u>Monthly Ledger</u>,
     1 (1773), 461.
         Deplores Smollett's lack of didacticism and failure to
     condemn vice in his novels.

4    [GRIFFITHS, RALPH]. Review of <u>Independence: an Ode</u>, <u>Monthly
     Review</u>, 49 (December), 500-502.
         Accepts it as Smollett's and praises style and senti-
     ments.


                            1774

1    ANON. Review of <u>Memoirs of an Unfortunate Lady of Quality</u>,
     <u>Monthly Review</u>, 51 (October), 322.
         Scoffs at pretended comparison with Smollett's <u>Peregrine
     Pickle</u>.

2    OGILVIE, JOHN. <u>Philosophical and Critical Observations on the
     Nature, Characters, and Various Species of Composition</u>.
     London: G. Robinson, I, 342-44.
         Praises <u>Roderick Random</u> and compares it to Fielding's
     work.


                            1775

1    ANON. "Some Account of the Life and Writings of the Late Dr.
     Smollett," <u>Westminster Magazine</u>, 3 (May), 225-28.
         General account regards <u>Peregrine Pickle</u>, <u>Humphry
     Clinker</u>, and <u>Roderick Random</u> as biographical sources.
     Ascribes Smollett's difficulties to his independent and
     generous nature and admires his intelligence and benevo-
     lence. Reprinted 1775.2.

2    ANON. "Some Account of the Life and Writings of the Late Dr.
     Smollett," <u>Annual Register</u>, 18 (1775), 45-50.
         Reprint of 1775.1. These are incorporated in <u>Plays and
     Poems</u>, 1777.2 and copied in <u>Encyclopaedia Britannica</u>,
     1783.3. For details <u>see</u> Boucé, 1971.6.

3    ARMSTRONG, JOHN. "An Inscription to the Memory of the Late
     Dr. Tobias Smollet [sic]," <u>Pennsylvania Magazine</u>, 1 (Janu-
     ary), 30.
         The Latin epitaph on Smollett's monument in Leghorn.

4    [HENDERSON, ANDREW]. <u>A Second Letter to Dr. Samuel Johnson...
     with An Impartial Character of Doctor Smollett</u>. London:

J. Henderson and J. Fox et al., pp. 12–14.
Severe account of Smollett's personality, character, and ability.

5    [LUXBOROUGH, LADY].  Letters Written by the Late Right Honour-
able Lady Luxborough, to William Shenstone, Esq.  London:
J. Dodsley, pp. 265–66, 290–91.
Two letters of 1751 speculate on authorship of Lady
Vane's "Memoirs" in Peregrine Pickle, criticize the novel,
and describe Smollett as a lawyer.

6    SHERIDAN, RICHARD BRINSLEY.  The Rivals.  London: John Wilkie,
pp. 5, 10.
Smollett's novels among those Lydia Languish reads in
secret.  Character of Mrs. Malaprop indebted to Humphry
Clinker.

## 1776

1    ANON.  "An Essay on Novel-Writing," Westminster Magazine, 4
(March), 129.
Smollett creates excellent humorous characters and sa-
tire, but is inferior to Richardson in celebrating virtue.

2    ANON.  Introduction to Smollett's "Ode to Independence," Pennsylvania Magazine, 3 (July), 325.
Praises poem's aesthetic qualities and celebration of
liberty.

3    ANON.  "A Criticism upon Modern Novels and Novel-Writers,"
Westminster Magazine, 4 (October), 522.
Smollett an inferior imitator of Fielding, but both are
superior to Richardson and Sterne.

*4   ANON.  Comparison of Humphry Clinker and Sebaldus, Revision
der Teutschen Literatur, II, 239; III, 204ff.
Humphry Clinker superior to the German novel.  Cited in
Price, 1932.22.

5    BEATTIE, JAMES.  "An Essay on Laughter and Ludicrous Composi-
tion," in Essays.  Edinburgh and London: William Creech and
E. & C. Dilly, pp. 321–486.
Refers to Smollett's humorous techniques and compares
Launcelot Greaves and Don Quixote as characters, noting
different kinds of treatment (pp. 350–51).

1776


6  HAWKINS, JOHN.  A General History of the Science and Practice
   of Music.  London: T. Payne and Son, V, 324.
      Handel's composition for Smollett's unperformed Alceste.

7  TOPHAM, EDWARD.  Letters from Edinburgh; Written in the Years
   1774 and 1775.  London: J. Dodsley, p. 184.
      Laments Smollett's need for hack writing.


1777

1  ANON.  Review of Smollett's Plays and Poems, Westminster Magazine, 5 (August), 435.
      Denigrates plays and suggests plagiarism in poetry.

2  ANON.  "The Life of T. Smollett, M.D.," in Plays and Poems
   Written by T. Smollett, M.D. with Memoirs of the Life and
   Writings of the Author.  London: T. Evans and R. Baldwin,
   pp. i–xxix.
      Highly favorable account sees novels as reflecting his
   life, drawing together Roderick, Peregrine, and Matt as
   stages in his own development.  Prints letters to Garrick
   and Wilkes.  Incorporates material from 1775.1 and copied
   in 1783.3.  Second edition 1784.1.

3  ANON.  "Observations on Dr. Smollett's 'Ode to Independence,'"
   in Plays and Poems Written by T. Smollett, M.D.  London:
   T. Evans and R. Baldwin, pp. 266–72.
      Detailed description of poem's sublime characteristics
   and an explication.

4  BACHAUMONT, LOUIS PETIT DE.  On Smollett's Travels, in Mém-
   oires Secrets pour Servir a L'Histoire de la Republique
   des Lettres en France.  London: John Adamsohn, III, 91.
      Angry about Smollett's treatment of French in his
   Travels.  Identifies him as an historian.

5  [ENFIELD, WILLIAM and JOHN LANGHORNE].  Review of Smollett's
   Translation of Fénelon's Telemaque, Monthly Review, 56
   (January), 70.
      Praises translation.

6  [GARRICK, DAVID].  Review of Frances Brooke's Excursion,
   Monthly Review, 57 (August), 142.
      Imitates theater episodes in Roderick Random, but
   Smollett himself later regretted using the material.

7   [N----].  Review of Smollett's Plays and Poems, Monthly Re-
    view, 57 (July), 77.
         Smollett's genius not in dramatic writing and only occa-
    sionally in his poetry.

8   THICKNESSE, PHILIP.  A Year's Journey through France, and Part
    of Spain.  London: W. Brown, I, 2-3; II, 166-67.
         Although entertaining in other work, Smollett disagree-
    able in his Travels because of his ill health and he lied.

9   W.  Review of Plays and Poems, London Review, 5 (March), 206-
    10.
         Praises Smollett's poetic abilities and suggests that
    the introductory life was written by Garrick.


                              1778

1   [BURNEY, FANNY].  "Author's Preface," in Evelina, or a Young
    Lady's Entrance into the World.  London: T. Lowndes, I,
    preface.
         Smollett praised for humor and bringing respectability
    to the novel.

2   THOMPSON, EDWARD.  "Bon-Hill," in The Muse's Mirrour.  London:
    J. Debrett, I, 54-56.
         Smollett one of the splendors emanating from Dumbarton.


                              1779

1   ANON.  Nocturnal Revels: or, The History of Kings-Place and
    Other Modern Nunneries.  London: M. Goadby, I, 22-23.
         Smollett's generous treatment of impoverished Samuel
    Derrick.


                              1780

1   ANON.  Essay on Scottish Writing, Mirror, no. 83 (February
    22), pp. 329-32.
         Smollett an exception to lack of humor in Scottish writ-
    ers because of his emigration to England.

2   DAVIES, THOMAS.  Memoirs of the Life of David Garrick, Esq.
    London: Thomas Davies, I, 280-87.
         Smollett's theatrical experiences, particularly with
    Garrick.  Includes Garrick letter of November 26, 1757.

1780

3   HOLCROFT, THOMAS. "Preface," in Alwyn: or the Gentleman Come-
    dian. London: Fielding and Walker, I, vi.
        Roderick Random a romance rather than a novel.

4   [HOLLIS, THOMAS]. Memoirs of Thomas Hollis, Esq., ed. Francis
    Blackburne et al. London: n.p., I, 210.
        Smollett's history Tory support of the monarchy.


                              1782

1   ANON. "Fire at Jamaica," London Chronicle, 52 (September 12-
    14), 262.
        Financial plight of Smollett's widow.

2   BAKER, DAVID ERSKINE. "Smollett, Tobias M.D.," in Biographia
    Dramatica, or, A Companion to the Playhouse, ed. Isaac
    Reed. London: Rivingtons et al., I, 424-25.
        Slight revision and expansion of 1764.2, but fails to
    mention Humphry Clinker.

3   KNOX, VICESIMUS. "On Novel Reading," in Essays: Moral and
    Literary. London: Charles Dilly, I, 69.
        Deplores Smollett's coarseness and humorous treatment of
    evil in Peregrine Pickle.


                              1783

1   ANON. Review of Fanny Burney's Cecilia, English Review, 1
    (January), 16.
        Importance of Smollett's nautical characters in creating
    a public for novels.

2   ANON. Review of Blair's Lectures on Rhetoric and Belles Let-
    tres, English Review, 2 (August), 92.
        Attacks Hugh Blair and James Beattie for treatment of
    Smollett, whose genius dwarfs theirs and whose kindness to
    fellow Scots deserved better from his countrymen.

3   ANON. "Smollet [sic] (Dr. Tobias)," in Encyclopaedia Britan-
    nica or, A Dictionary of Arts, Sciences, &c. 2nd ed.
    Edinburgh: J. Balfour and Co. et al., X, 8191-92.
        First appearance in Britannica. Reprint of 1775.2.

4   BEATTIE, JAMES. "On Fable and Romance," in Dissertations
    Moral and Critical. London and Edinburgh: W. Strahan et
    al., pp. 570-71.

Despite some praise for Smollett's humor and <u>Fathom</u> and <u>Greaves</u>, attacks novels as immoral, bombastic, and improbable.

5   BLAIR, HUGH.  "Metaphor," in <u>Lectures on Rhetoric and Belles Lettres</u>.  London: W. Strahan, T. Cadall; Edinburgh: W. Creech, I, 301-2n.
Severe criticism of Smollett's style in <u>History of England</u>.

## 1784

1   ANON.  "The Life of T. Smollett, M.D.," in <u>Plays and Poems Written by T. Smollett, M.D.</u>  London: T. Evans, pp. i-xxix.
Reprint of 1777.2.

2   ANON.  "Smollett (Dr. Tobias)," in <u>A New and General Biographical Dictionary</u>.  London: W. Strahan et al., XI, 458-62.
Brief sketch of life and career based on <u>Plays and Poems</u> of 1777.  Reprinted 1798.7.

3   H., G.  "To the Philological Society of London," <u>European Magazine</u>, 5 (March), 169-71.
Letters concerning Smollett's legal difficulties with Peter Gordon and Alexander Hume Campbell.

## 1785

1   ANON.  Review of <u>The Virtuous Villagers</u>, <u>Town and Country Magazine</u>, 17 (January), 31.
<u>Roderick Random</u> used as standard of achievement in the novel.

2   ANON.  "Literary Ladies," <u>Westminster Magazine</u>, 13 (March), 137.
<u>Humphry Clinker</u> vastly entertaining, but light reading.

3   ANON.  "Theatrical Journal," <u>European Magazine</u>, 7 (April), 284.
Attributes <u>The Israelites</u> to Smollett.

4   ANON.  Review of Clara Reeve's <u>The Progress of Romance</u>, <u>Critical Review</u>, 60 (July), 58.
Reviewer doubts that Reeve has read Smollett's novels.

1785

5    REEVE, CLARA. "Evening IX," in The Progress of Romance. Col-
chester: W. Keymer; London: G. G. J. and J. Robinson, II,
10.
      Despite exaggerations and improper scenes, Smollett's
novels are witty and generally moral. Reprinted 1930.15.

6    SCOTUS. "To the Philological Society of London," European
Magazine, 8 (November), 359-60.
      Presents Johnson's corrections for Latin memorial to
Smollett.

1786

1    ANON. Comments on Smollett, Yorkshire Magazine, 1 (January),
33.
      Smollett wasted talent on histories instead of applying
them more fully to his novels.

2    ANON. On Smollett's Reputation, Yorkshire Magazine, 1 (October), 303.
      Correspondent places Roderick Random in category of in-
ferior literature, but editor disagrees.

3    BOSWELL, JAMES. The Journal of a Tour to the Hebrides, with
Samuel Johnson, Ll.D. London: Charles Dilly, passim.
      References to Smollett's work and Johnson's revision of
Latin inscription for his memorial.

4    ICONOPHILOS. "A Series of Scottish Portraits Proposed,"
Edinburgh Magazine, 4 (December), 424.
      Recommends Smollett, who has been shamefully neglected.

5    PINKERTON, JOHN. "Tobias Smollet [sic]," in Ancient Scottish
Poems, Never before in Print...from the Ms. Collections of
Sir Richard Maitland. London: Charles Dilly; Edinburgh:
William Creech, I, cxxxviii-cxxxix.
      Rates novels with Fielding's, praises poetry, and la-
ments national neglect that forced Smollett into hack work.

1787

1    HAWKINS, JOHN. The Life of Samuel Johnson, Ll.D. London: J.
Buckland et al., pp. 215-16.
      Without mentioning Humphry Clinker, describes work as
booksellers' jobs and ridicules translation of Don Quixote
as plagiarism.

2    SMOLLETT, TOBIAS.  "The Unfortunate Lovers," <u>New Novelist's</u>
     <u>Magazine</u>, 1 (1787), 24-27.
          Publishes a story purportedly by Smollett.


## 1788

1    ANON.  Review of <u>The Adventures of Jonathan Corncob</u>, <u>General</u>
     <u>Magazine and Impartial Review</u>, 2 (January), 39.
          Resembles Smollett's work, but less concerned with de-
     cency.

2    ANON.  Review of <u>The West Indian</u>, <u>Critical Review</u>, 65 (Febru-
     ary), 150.
          Plagiarized from <u>Roderick Random</u>.

3    ANON.  Obituary Notice on Susannah Lady Viscountess Fane,
     <u>Gentleman's Magazine</u>, 58 (April), 368-69.
          Calls her memoirs the best part of <u>Peregrine Pickle</u> and
     claims Smollett merely inserted them in his work.  <u>See</u>
     1788.4 and 1788.5.

4    ANON.  Letter, <u>Gentleman's Magazine</u>, 58 (May), 379.
          Notes confusion of Lady Fane and Lady Vane in 1788.3 and
     describes Lady Vane's beauty and immorality.

5    ANON.  Corrected Obituary Notice on Lady Vane, <u>Gentleman's</u>
     <u>Magazine</u>, 58 (May), 461.
          Two accounts of the composition of Lady Vane's "Memoirs"
     in <u>Peregrine Pickle</u> attribute the writing to her.

6    ANON.  Review of <u>Henry and Isabella</u>, <u>Critical Review</u>, 65
     (June), 485.
          Contrasts Smollett's novels with those of Fanny Burney
     and new novelists.

7    ANON.  "An Account of the Life and Writings of Dr. John
     Shebbeare," <u>European Magazine</u>, 14 (August), 87.
          Shebbeare depicted as Ferret in <u>Sir Launcelot Greaves</u>.


## 1789

1    ANON.  Review of Robert Bage's <u>James Wallace</u>, <u>Critical Review</u>,
     67 (January), 76.
          Hero's adventures imitate those of <u>Roderick Random</u> by
     the "incomparable" Smollett.

1789

2    ANON. Review of <u>Life and Adventures of Anthony Leger, Esq.</u>,
     <u>or, The Man of Shifts</u>, <u>General Magazine and Impartial Re-</u>
     <u>view</u>, 3 (August), 362.
         Compares the novel with <u>Ferdinand Count Fathom</u>.

3    MYLIUS, W. C. S.   "Vorbericht," in <u>Peregrine Pickle</u>, trans.
     W. C. S. Mylius.  Berlin: F. Maurer, I, ix-xxix.
         Lauds Smollett's comic abilities and suggests his gen-
     eral popularity in Germany.


                                1790

1    ANON.  Review of <u>Radzivil, a Romance</u>, <u>Critical Review</u>, 69
     (January), 118.
         Suggests indebtedness to Gothic material in <u>Fathom</u>.

2    ANON.  "Matthew Bramble," <u>General Magazine and Impartial Re-</u>
     <u>view</u>, 4 (September), 397-98.
         Essay on Andrew Macdonald, who had used the pseudonym
     of "Matthew Bramble."

3    ANON.  "Short Account of the Author," in <u>The Miscellaneous</u>
     <u>Works of T. Smollett, M.D.</u>  Edinburgh: J. and J. Fairbairn,
     I, i-xi.
         Biographical sketch equating Smollett's novels with
     autobiography and based largely on 1777.2.


                                1791

1    ANON.  "Dr. Smollett," <u>European Magazine</u>, 19 (February), 94.
         Stresses Smollett's kindness despite his satire and
     praises forest scene in <u>Ferdinand Count Fathom</u>.

2    ANON.  Review of <u>The History of Tom Weston</u>, <u>English Review</u>,
     17 (April), 310.
         Welcomes attempt to renew the tradition of Smollett.

3    ANON.  Review of <u>The History of Tom Weston</u>, <u>Critical Review</u>,
     2nd ser., 1 (April), 470.
         Uses <u>Roderick Random</u> as well as Fielding's works.

4    ANON.  Review of <u>Gertrude; or, The Orphan of Llanfruist</u>,
     <u>Critical Review</u>, 2nd ser., 2 (June), 233.
         Notes effect of <u>Roderick Random</u> on conclusions of too
     many novels.


                                 34

5   ANON.  Review of <u>The Cypher; or, The World as It Goes</u>, <u>Critical Review</u>, 2nd ser., 2 (July), 356.
        Notes Smollett's great influence, but dissatisfied with his exaggerated characterization and loose narratives.

6   ANON.  "The Life of Dr. Tobias Smollett," in <u>The British Plutarch</u>.  Third Edition.  London: Charles Dilly, VIII, 117-28.
        General account based on the 1777.2 memoir in <u>Plays and Poems</u>.  Prints entire "The Tears of Scotland."

7   BOSWELL, JAMES.  <u>The Life of Samuel Johnson, Ll.D.</u>  London: Charles Dilly, 2 Vols., passim.
        Provides information on Johnson's relations with and opinions of Smollett.

8   [GARDEN, FRANCIS].  "Critical Remarks on Some of the Most Eminent Historians of England," <u>The Bee, or Literary Weekly Intelligencer</u>, 3 (May 25), 90-91.
        Praises Smollett's novels, but describes histories as plagiarized hack work.  <u>See</u> Lord Gardenstone.  Reprinted 1792.3.

9   [GARDEN, FRANCIS].  <u>Travelling Memorandums</u>.  Edinburgh: Bell & Bradfute, passim.
        Comments on Smollett's splenetic views in his <u>Travels</u>.  <u>See</u> Lord Gardenstone.

10  GARDENSTONE, LORD.  <u>See</u> Garden, Francis.

11  LACKINGTON, JAMES.  "Letter XXXIII," in <u>Memoirs of the First Forty-Five Years of the Life of James Lackington</u>.  London: James Lackington, p. 255.
        Describes popularity of <u>Roderick Random</u> and <u>Peregrine Pickle</u> with readers of the lower social order.

12  [NOORTHOUCK, JOHN].  Review of the <u>Labyrinths of Life</u>, <u>Monthly Review</u>, n.s. 5 (July), 338.
        Sees Smollett as one of the inventors of the novel.

13  WOODHOUSELEE, ALEXANDER FRASER TYTLER.  <u>Essays on the Principles of Translation</u>.  Edinburgh.
        <u>See</u> 1813.2.

## 1792

1   ARCTICUS. "Letter from Arcticus," The Bee, or Literary Weekly
      Intelligencer, 8 (May 2), 316.
        Smollett's humor best since Samuel Butler's Hudibras.

2   BOMBARDINION. See Garden, Francis.

3   [GARDEN, FRANCIS]. Miscellanies in Prose and Verse.   2nd ed.
      Edinburgh: J. Robertson, pp. 103, 222-23.
        Reprints material in 1791.8 and 1792.4.   See
      Gardenstone, Lord and Bombardinion.

4   [GARDEN, FRANCIS]. "On Smollet's [sic] Novels," The Bee, or,
      Literary Weekly Intelligencer, 7 (January 25), 130-32.
        Bemoans neglect of a novelist whose work, in its charac-
      ter portrayal, approaches, more closely than any other
      English writer's, Shakespeare's.  Reprinted 1792.3.  See
      Gardenstone, Lord and Bombardinion.

5   GARDENSTONE, LORD.  See Garden, Francis.

6   [NEWMAN, JEREMIAH WHITAKER].  "Smollet [sic], Tobias," in The
      Lounger's Common-Place Book; or, Alphabetical Anecdotes.
      London: n.p., pp. 129-36.
        Praises Smollett's heroic conduct in the Knowles case,
      and finds his novels more moving and exciting than
      Fielding's and Richardson's, attributing their coarseness
      to appropriate characterization and humor.  Particularly
      likes Peregrine Pickle, admires translation of Don Quixote,
      and excuses splenetic qualities of the Travels.  Reprinted
      with alterations 1793.2, 1794.6, and 1805.5.

7   YOUNG, ARTHUR.  Travels during the Years 1787, 1788, and 1789.
      Bury St. Edmund's: W. Richardson (London), p. 191.
        Opposition to Smollett in Nice because of his Travels.

## 1793

1   LUCIUS.  "On the Tendency of Novel-Reading," Universal Maga-
      zine, 93 (September), 165.
        Ridicules use of Roderick Random for didactic purposes.

2   [NEWMAN, JEREMIAH WHITAKER].  "Smollet [sic]," in The Loun-
      ger's Common-Place Book; or, Alphabetical Arrangement of
      Miscellaneous Anecdotes.  London: for the Author, II, 131.

Reprint of 1792.6 adds fact that Smollett attacked Mark Akenside in Peregrine Pickle.

## 1794

1   ANDERSON, ROBERT.  "The Life of Smollett," in The Works of the British Poets.  London: John & Arthur Arch; Edinburgh: Bell & Bradfute, and J. Mundell, X, 939-48.
      First of Anderson's lives is an authentic if brief assessment, which praises the novels and poetry and offers some analysis of the latter.  Volume published in 1795.

2   ANON.  Review of the Romance of the Cavern, Critical Review, 2nd ser., 10 (March), 349.
      Borrows most effective material from Ferdinand Count Fathom.

3   ANON.  Review of Things as They Are, or The Adventures of Caleb Williams, Critical Review, 2nd ser., 11 (July), 290.
      Review of William Godwin's novel uses Smollett's novels as a standard of achievement.

4   ANON.  "Dr. Tobias Smollet [sic]," Biographical Magazine, 1 (1794), n. pag.--alphabetical.
      Brief, uninformative biographical sketch.

5   ANON.  Literary and Critical Remarks, on Sundry Eminent Divines and Philosophers of the Last and Present Age.  London: B. Crosby, Appendix.
      Extracts from purported late letter by Smollett predicting calamatous revolutions because of colonialism and slavery and a revolution in France because of conditions there.  Reprinted 1795.2, 1795.3, and 1796.2.

6   [NEWMAN, JEREMIAH WHITAKER].  "Smollet [sic], Dr. Addition to His Article," in The Lounger's Common-Place Book, or, Alphabetical Arrangement of Miscellaneous Anecdotes.  London: for the Author, III, 83.
      Adds a laudatory account of The Regicide to 1792.6, 1793.2.

## 1795

1   ANON.  Review of Charlotte Smith's Montalbert, Monthly Mirror, 1 (December), 36.
      Smollett's satiric characterization worthy of imitation.

2   ANON.  Smollett's "Prophecy," <u>Rural Magazine: or Vermont Re-</u>
    <u>pository</u>, 1 (1795), 625.
        Reprint of 1794.5.

3   ANON.  "Tobias Smollet [<u>sic</u>]," in <u>Wonderful Prophecies: Being</u>
    <u>a Dissertation on the Existence, Nature, and Extent of the</u>
    <u>Prophetic Powers in the Human Mind</u>.  London: n.p., pp. 44-
    48.
        Reprint of 1794.5.

4   CUMBERLAND, RICHARD.  <u>Henry</u>.  London: Charles Dilly, I, 97-98.
        Novel characterizes Smollett's, Fielding's and
    Richardson's work.

5   DIBDIN, CHARLES.  <u>A Complete History of the Stage</u>.  London: C.
    Dibdin, V, 181-82.
        Notes on <u>The Regicide</u>, <u>The Reprisal</u>, and <u>The Israelite</u>.

6   D'ISRAELI, ISAAC.  "The Characters of Writers Not Discernable
    in Their Writings," in <u>An Essay on the Manners and Genius</u>
    <u>of the Literary Character</u>.  London: T. Cadell, Jr. and W.
    Davies, 140-41.
        Although a man of good character, Smollett unfortunately
    wrote scenes as lewd as those of Petronius.

7   SHAW, CUTHBERT.  "The Race," in <u>The Poetical Works of Cuthbert</u>
    <u>Shaw</u>.  <u>Works of the British Poets</u>, ed. Robert Anderson.
    Edinburgh: Mundell and Son, XI, 564-72.
        Scoffs at <u>The Regicide</u> and mocks Smollett as a grumbling
    critic, part of the Scottish tribunal on the <u>Critical Re-</u>
    <u>view</u>.  Originally published in 1766.

### 1796

1   ANDERSON, ROBERT.  "The Life of Smollett," in <u>The Miscellane-</u>
    <u>ous Works of Tobias Smollett, M.D.</u>  London: J. Mundell
    (Edinburgh), I, xiii-xxii.
        Greatly expanded version of the brief life of 1794.1.
    Anderson became an inveterate scholar of Smollett's biogra-
    phy and work, adding material in 1800, publishing a sepa-
    rate life in 1803, enlarging and altering his material
    (including appendix of original letters in 1806), printing
    further editions in 1811 and 1817, and culminating the
    whole in his most complete work in 1820.  An enthusiastic
    Scot, he stressed Smollett's Scottish background, identify-
    ing characters in the novels with real people, and respond-
    ing sympathetically to Smollett's personal problems.

2    ANON.  Smollett's "Prophecy," Morning Chronicle, January 6,
          No. 8168.
              Reprint of 1794.5.

*3   ANON.  On a Smollett Letter, La Feuille du Jour (April 30).
              Comment on purported Smollett letter praises his saga-
          city in his History of England.  Cited in Joliat, 1935.5.

4    ANON.  Review of Hannah Hewit; or The Female Crusoe, The
          Monthly Mirror, 2 (May), 35-38.
              Pillages from the works of Smollett.

5    ANON.  Review of Fanny Burney's Camilla, British Critic, 8
          (November), 527-28.
              Superiority of realistic novels of Fielding, Smollett,
          and Richardson.

6    ANON.  "Some Account of Dr. Tobias Smollett," Scots Magazine,
          58 (November), 725-27.
              Sees Roderick Random and Matt Bramble in Humphry Clinker
          as fundamentally autobiographical and praises his histo-
          ries.

7    McAULAY, ALEXANDER.  "Eminent Men," in The Statistical Account
          of Scotland.  Edinburgh: William Creech, XVII, 220-23.
              Sympathetic account praises Smollett's realistic charac-
          ters and admires his industry and notes his pride.


                              1797

1    [ALMON, JOHN].  "The Late Earl Temple," in Biographical,
          Literary, and Political Anecdotes.  London: T. N. Longman
          and L. B. Seeley, II, 9-12.
              Smollett's support of Lord Bute in the Briton.

2    ANON.  Review of Anderson's Life of Tobias Smollett, British
          Critic, 9 (March), 333.
              Praises Anderson's biography and its additional materi-
          al.

3    ANON.  "Progress of Literature in Scotland," Monthly Magazine,
          4 (November), 360.
              Smollett excelled in various literary genres and was
          among the outstanding Scotsmen of his century.

1797

4    ANON. "Smollett (Dr. Tobias)," in Encyclopaedia Britannica.
     Third Edition. Edinburgh: A. Bell and C. MacFarquhar,
     XVII, 556-58.
         Largely a repeat of 1783 edition, but adds details on
     Smollett's widow. Remains same in 4th, 5th, and 6th edi-
     tions.

5    [BECKFORD, WILLIAM]. Azemia. London: Sampson Low, pp. 14-15,
     27.
         Compares own fictional characters to those in Peregrine
     Pickle and Roderick Random. See Jenks, Jacquetta Agneta
     Mariana.

6    GODWIN, WILLIAM. "Of English Style," in The Enquirer: Reflec-
     tions on Education, Manners, and Literature. London: G. G.
     and J. Robinson, pp. 467-71.
         Because Smollett worked hastily and carelessly, he
     wasted his talent, and his writing lacks elegance and
     polish.

7    H., M. "On Novel-Writing," Monthly Magazine, 4 (September),
     180-81.
         Smollett's rendering of life and manners more important
     than offering models of virtue as instruction.

8    JENKS, JACQUETTA AGNETA MARIANA. See Beckford, William.

9    MOORE, JOHN. "The Life of T. Smollett, M.D.," in The Works of
     Tobias Smollett, M.D. London: B. Law et al., I, xcvii-
     cxcvi.
         Warm account, which includes some letters, but does not
     attempt scholarly detail. Sensibly evaluates Smollett's
     character, personality, and work, and appreciates his
     Scottish background. Moore distinguishes between his use
     of personal material and simple autobiographical character-
     ization in the novels and defends his work from charges of
     immorality. Published in same year in The Poetical Works
     of Tobias Smollett, M.D. London: C. Cooke, pp. 1-36.
     Several subsequent reprintings.


                              1798

1    ANON. Review of Moore's Edition of Smollett's Works, Euro-
     pean Magazine, 33 (February), 100-104.
         Pleased that edition will permit Smollett's genius to be
     appreciated and adds biographical material to Moore's
     account.

2  ANON.  Review of <u>Probable Incidents,</u> <u>Critical Review</u>, 2nd
     ser., 22 (March), 357-58.
        A poor imitation of <u>Roderick Random</u>.

3  ANON.  "The Wanderer," <u>European Magazine</u>, 33 (May), 309.
        Nostalgia for Smollett's realism and wit.

4  ANON.  "Smollet's [<u>sic</u>] Works, by Dr. Moore," <u>British Critic</u>,
     12 (July), 59-65.
        Smollett worthy of an edition.  High praise for "Ode to
     Independence."

5  ANON.  Review of <u>Henry Willoughby</u>, <u>Critical Review</u>, 2nd ser.,
     23 (August), 472.
        Influence of Smollett's style.

6  ANON.  <u>Impartial Strictures on a Poem Called "The Pursuits of
     Literature" and Particularly a Vindication of the Romance
     of "The Monk"</u>.  London: J. Bell, p. 42.
        Argues that <u>Ferdinand Count Fathom</u> and <u>Peregrine Pickle</u>
     are more harmful to public morals than M. G. Lewis's work.

7  ANON.  "Smollett (Tobias)," in <u>A New and General Biographical
     Dictionary</u>.  London: G. G. and J. Robinson et al., XIV, 47-
     51.
        Reprints with minor changes 1784.2, although Anderson's
     life, which it praises, had appeared in 1796.

8  BISSET, ROBERT.  On Fielding and Smollett, <u>The Historical,
     Biographical, Literary, and Scientific Magazine</u>, 1 (1798),
     55-56.
        Praises Smollett, but prefers Fielding.

9  DRAKE, NATHAN.  <u>Literary Hours</u>.  London: Longman et al., I,
     274 and II, 27, 37, 44.
        Praises terror scenes in <u>Ferdinand Count Fathom</u> and com-
     pares poetry with works by Dryden, Collins, Gray, Milton,
     and others.

<u>1799</u>

1  ANON.  "Biographical Memoir of Admiral Sir Charles Knowles,
     Bart.," <u>Naval Chronicle</u>, 1 (January-June), 120-21.
        Defends Knowles from Smollett's attack and accuses
     Smollett of ingratitude and political hack writing.

## 1800

1 ANDERSON, ROBERT. "The Life of Tobias Smollett, M.D.," in The
Miscellaneous Works of Tobias Smollett, M.D. Edinburgh:
Mundell, pp. xv-cxxix.
Adds material, chiefly from the work of John Moore
(1797.9) to 1796.1.

2 ANON. Review of The Neighbourhood, A Tale, Critical Review,
2nd ser., 30 (October), 230.
Poor imitation of Smollett's technique in characterization.

## 1801

1 ANON. "Epistolary," Port Folio, 1 (January 3), 2-3.
Eight letters to Smollett: Lord Shelburn, William Pitt,
Richardson, Hume, Boswell, John Armstrong, William Hunter.

2 ANON. Review of The Miser and His Family, Critical Review,
2nd ser., 32 (May), 106.
Contrasts use of nautical language with Smollett's.

3 ANON. Review of First Impressions, Critical Review, 2nd ser.,
32 (June), 232-33.
Praises Smollett's characterization.

4 ANON. "Literary Intelligence," Port Folio, 1 (September 19),
303.
Criticizes author of Wanderings of William for defending
swearing by citing Smollett as precedent.

5 ANON. "Preface," in The Wanderings of William, or The Incon-
stancy of Youth. Philadelphia: n.p., p. viii.
Praises Smollett's portraits of seamen, but objects to
his caricatures and repetition of nautical phrases.

*6 LA TOCNAYE. Promenades d'un Français en Angleterre, en Ecosse
et en Irlande. Brunswick, pp. 38ff.
Attacks Smollett's treatment of the French in his
Travels. Cited in Joliat, 1935.5.

7 MURPHY, ARTHUR. The Life of David Garrick, Esq. London: J.
Wright, I, 313-15; II, 299-301.
Describes Smollett's financial, though not artistic,
success with The Reprisal, and attributes his reconciliation with Garrick to Garrick's generosity.

8    RICHARDSON, WILLIAM.  The Maid of Lochlin: A Lyrical Drama
     with Legendary Odes, and Other Poems.  London: T. Maiden
     for Vernon and Hood et al., pp. 122-23.
         Smollett's spontaneous composition of "Tears of Scot-
     land."

9    WARNER, RICHARD.  The History of Bath.  London: G. G. and J.
     Robinson, p. 380, n. 23.
         Cites two editions of Essay on the External Use of
     Water.


                              1802

1    ANON.  Review of Old Nick, Critical Review, 2nd ser., 34
     (April), 449.
         Character derived from Narcissa's aunt in Roderick
     Random.

2    ANON.  "Miscellany," Port Folio, 2 (May 8), 138.
         Comments on reality of life in Roderick Random.

3    ANON.  "Miscellaneous Paragraphs," Port Folio, 2 (June 5),
     175.
         Attempts to identify characters in Peregrine Pickle.

4    D., J.  "The American Lounger," Port Folio, 2 (June 5), 169.
         Smollett among novelists concerned with ordinary charac-
     ters.

5    E., H.  "The American Lounger," Port Folio, 2 (June 19), 185-
     86.
         Compares Smollett, Fielding, and Richardson, and dis-
     approves of Smollett's morality and taste.


                              1803

1    ANDERSON, ROBERT.  The Life of Tobias Smollett, M.D.  Edin-
     burgh: Mundell, 242 pp.
         Anderson's first separately printed life.  Adds to and
     revises 1800.1.

2    ANON.  Review of Letters of a Solitary Wanderer by Charlotte
     Smith, Critical Review, 2nd ser., 37 (January), 55.
         Roderick Random based on Smollett himself.

1803

3    ANON. Review of <u>Peregrine, or The Fool of Fortune</u>, <u>Critical Review</u>, 2nd ser., 39 (October), 236.
Unfavorable review of imitation of <u>Peregrine Pickle</u>.

4    M., M. Letter, <u>European Magazine</u>, 44 (November), 335-36.
Ann Smollett's 1783 letter grateful for help, but distressed by general public neglect of her difficulties.

## 1804

1    ANON. "Letters to Dr. Smollett," <u>European Magazine</u>, 45 (March), 181-85.
Six letters: Pitt, Richardson, Hume, Boswell, Armstrong, and John Gray.

2    ANON. "Copy of a Letter from Dr. Tobias Smollett to ----, of New Jersey, North America," <u>European Magazine</u>, 4 (April), 244.
Letter to Richard Smith discusses work and denies that <u>Roderick Random</u> is autobiographical.

3    ANON. "Letters to Dr. Smollett," <u>European Magazine</u>, 45 (April), 257-59.
Four letters: Hunter, Armstrong, and one by Shelburn concerning Smollett.

4    ANON. Review of Anderson's <u>Life of Smollett</u>, <u>European Magazine</u>, 45 (April), 294-95.
Praises Smollett as man and writer.

5    ANON. Review of <u>A Picture from Life</u>, <u>Critical Review</u>, 3rd ser., 2 (July), 348.
Character imitated from <u>Peregrine Pickle</u>.

6    IRVING, DAVID. <u>The Lives of the Scottish Poets</u>. Edinburgh: J. & J. Robertson and P. Hill, S. Cheyne; London: Longman et al., I, 163-66.
Prints Anderson's evaluation of Smollett as a novelist and praises poetry as excellent.

## 1805

1    ALMON, JOHN. "Memoirs and Correspondence of John Wilkes," in <u>The Correspondence of the Late John Wilkes, with His Friends</u>. London: Richard Phillips, I, 46-51, 91-95.

Contrasts Smollett's published and private statements
about Wilkes and denigrates Smollett's work on the Briton.

2   ANON.  Review of Travellers in Switzerland, Anti-Jacobin Re-
    view, 21 (Appendix), 449.
        Praises literary qualities of Smollett's Travels.

3   BECKFORD, PETER.  Familiar Letters from Italy, to a Friend in
    England.  Salisbury: J. Eraston et al., I, 2; II, 70, 149.
        Several references to Smollett's opinions in his Travels.

4   Letters between the Rev. James Granger, M.A. and Many of the
    Most Eminent Literary Men of His Time, ed. J. P. Malcolm.
    London: Longman, Hurst, Rees, and Orme, pp. 315-16.
        Isabella Strange's 1763 letter ascribes engravings in
    Smollett's History of England to her husband.

5   [NEWMAN, JEREMIAH WHITAKER].  "Smollet [sic], Dr.," in The
    Lounger's Common-Place Book, or Miscellaneous Collections.
    3rd ed.  London: Longman et al., III, 191-99.
        Reprints with alterations 1794.6.  Less enthusiastic,
    particularly concerning the Knowles case and omits refer-
    ence to translation of Don Quixote.


## 1806

1   ANDERSON, ROBERT.  "The Life of Tobias Smollett, M.D.," in The
    Miscellaneous Works of Tobias Smollett, M.D.  Edinburgh:
    Mundell et al., 208 pp.
        Reprint with changes of 1803.1 adds appendix of letters.

2   ANDREOSSI, GENERAL.  "Observations on the Writings of Histori-
    ans," Monthly Magazine, 22 (December) 1, 443.
        Smollett's limited ability as an historian.

3   ANON.  "Original Letter from Dr. Smollet [sic]," Port Folio,
    2nd ser., 1 (April 5), 199.
        Introduces unpublished letter to Renner with encomium
    on Smollett's genius in Roderick Random.

4   ANON.  "Anecdotes of Anstey," Port Folio, 2nd ser., 1 (April
    5), 200.
        Falsely claims Anstey copied material for New Bath Guide
    from Humphry Clinker.

1806

5   ANON.  Review of <u>Nouveau Dictionaire Historique</u>, <u>Port Folio</u>,
        2nd ser., 1 (June 21), 381–82.
            Defends Smollett from unfair criticism in the French
        work.

6   ANON.  "The Sorrows of Werter," <u>Literary Magazine and American
        Register</u>, 6 (December), 451.
            <u>Peregrine Pickle</u> is a danger to morality.

7   [GRANT, ANNE].  <u>Letters from the Mountains; Being the Real
        Correspondence of a Lady, between the Years 1773 and 1803</u>.
        London: Longman et al., 3 Vols., passim.
            Favorable references to Smollett as "Smelfungus."  Ame-
        rican edition in 1809: Boston:  Greeough and Stebbins.

8   <u>Memoirs of the Life and Writings of the Honourable Henry Home
        of Kames</u>, ed. A. F. Tytler of Woodhouselee.  Edinburgh:  T.
        Cadell and W. Davies, I, 226–27, 434.
            Praises Smollett's comic talents.

*9  [WATSON, WILLIAM?].  "Life of Dr. Smollett," in <u>The Adventures
        of Peregrine Pickle</u>.  London: Silvester Doig and Andrew
        Stirling, Vol. I.
            Cited in 1949.12.  Also lists an 1811 edition.

10  WEST, JANE.  <u>Letters to a Young Lady</u>.  Troy and New York: O.
        Penniman and I. Riley, pp. 311, 320.
            Comments on caricature and the grotesque in Smollett.

11  WOOLL, JOHN.  <u>Biographical Memoir of the Late Reverend Joseph
        Warton</u>.  London: T. Cadell and W. Davies, p. 232.
            Smollett's relations with William Huggins and the ques-
        tion of log-rolling on the <u>Critical Review</u>.


                            <u>1807</u>

1   BRYDGES, SAMUEL EGERTON.  "Memoirs of Mrs. Charlotte Smith,"
        in <u>Censura Literaria</u>.  London: Longman et al., p. 81.
            On the immorality of <u>Peregrine Pickle</u>.

2   DERMODY, THOMAS.  "To Comic Romance," in <u>The Harp of Erin</u>.
        London: Richard Phillips, II, 94–100.
            Poem praises <u>Launcelot Greaves</u> as comic romance (pp. 97–
        98).

3   FORBES, WILLIAM.  <u>An Account of the Life and Writings of James
        Beattie, Ll.D.</u>  2nd ed.  Edinburgh: Arch. Constable;

London: Longman et al., II, 172, 375.
Verbosity and ornateness of Latin inscription on
Smollett's memorial and Johnson's preference of Smollett
above Fielding.

4    HAMILTON, LADY ANNE.  The Epics of the Ton.  London: C. and R.
      Baldwin, p. 6.
      Suggests scandalous appeal of Peregrine Pickle.


                              1808

1    [COOKE?].  "Smollet [sic], (Dr. Tobias)," in Thespian Diction-
      ary or Dramatic Biography of the Present Age.  London:
      James Cundee, under "SM."
      Lists some works and brief biographical details.
      Ascribes The Israelites to Smollett.

2    GILLILAND, THOMAS.  "Smollet [sic], Dr. Tobias," in The Dra-
      matic Mirror.  London: C. Chapple, I, 579-80.
      Brief account attributes The Israelites to Smollett.

3    GREGORY, GEORGE.  "Fictitious Narrative," in Letters on Liter-
      ature, Taste, and Composition.  London: Richard Phillips,
      II, 72-73.
      Praises Smollett's humor, but deplores morality and
      rates him an imitator of Fielding.  Humphry Clinker a dull
      narrative.

4    MANGIN, EDWARD.  An Essay on Light Reading.  London: James
      Carpenter, pp. 30-50.
      Smollett's indecency more reprehensible than Fielding's,
      and Roderick Random, Peregrine Pickle, and Ferdinand Count
      Fathom endanger the morals of youth.

5    MURRAY, HUGH.  "Smollet [sic]," in Morality of Fiction: or, An
      Inquiry into the Tendency of Fictitious Narratives.  Edin-
      burgh: A. Constable and J. Anderson; London: Longman et
      al., pp. 106-8.
      Smollett coarser than Fielding.  Sees Roderick Random
      and Humphry Clinker as autobiographical, and praises the
      humor and ludicrous characterization in the latter.

6    ROWLANDSON, THOMAS.  Thirteen Etchings Illustrative of Strik-
      ing Passages in Tom Jones and Joseph Andrews: Also Specimen
      of a New Edition of Smollett's Works.  Edinburgh: Cornelius
      Elliot; London: John Murray, unpaged.

1808

Smollett's Miscellaneous Works to include 30 copper
plates; gives sample marriage scene from Humphry Clinker.

7 A Series of Letters between Mrs. Elizabeth Carter and Miss
Catherine Talbot, from the Year 1741 to 1770. London: F.
C. and J. Rivington, I, 166.
1748 Talbot letter abjures vulgarity but praises realism
of Roderick Random.


1809

1 ANON. Review of Warburton's Letters, Edinburgh Review, 13
(January), 356-57.
Attributes Warburton's unfavorable views of Smollett to
jealousy over sales of their works.

2 [PEGGE, SAMUEL]. Anonymiana; or, Ten Centuries of Observa-
tions on Various Authors and Subjects. London: John
Nichols and Son, pp. 287-88.
Suggests originals of characters in Ferdinand Count
Fathom and Peregrine Pickle.

3 [SCOTT, WALTER]. Review of Richard Cumberland's John de
Lancaster, Quarterly Review, 1 (May), 337-38.
Smollett's superior ability to render nautical life.

4 [WARBURTON, WILLIAM]. Letters from a Late Eminent Prelate to
One of His Friends. New York: E. Sargeant, p. 207.
Attack in 1759 on Smollett as an historian.


1810

1 ANON. Obituary of M'Callum, Gentleman's Magazine, 80 (June),
597.
Served with Smollett at Carthagena in 1741.

2 ANON. "Life of T. Smollett, M.D.," in The Poetical Works of
T. Smollett, M.D. Charlestown (Mass.): Asahel Brown, pp.
3-55.
Unenthusiastic derivative account of Smollett's life and
work. Inaccurate in details and uses writing as autobiography.

3 BARBAULD, ANNA LAETITIA. "Smollet [sic]," in The Expedition
of Humphry Clinker. The British Novelists. London: F. C.
and J. Rivington et al., XXX, i-xviii.

Harsh treatment of Smollett's character and writing. Although praising his humor and robustness, regards him as a vulgar and coarse hack. Sees material as journalistic and autobiographical.

4   CHALMERS, ALEXANDER. "The Life of Tobias Smollett, M.D.," in The Works of the English Poets from Chaucer to Cowper. London: J. Johnson et al., XV, 543-53.
General biographical and critical account unwilling to overlook lack of morality and decency in writing and emphasizes his quarrelsome character. While praising his poetry, condemns his novels, histories, and dramas. Reprinted without acknowledgement in 1822.9.

5   DRAKE, NATHAN. Essays, Biographical, Critical, and Historical, Illustrative of the Rambler, Adventurer, and Idler. London: W. Suttaby, II, 353-57.
Finds Smollett's Briton inferior to Arthur Murphy's Auditor.

6   EDITOR. Note to "A Letter to a Young Lady on Novels and Novel Reading," European Magazine, 58 (July), 21.
Notes failure to discuss the important category of such humorous novels as Smollett's.

7   [MORE, HANNAH]. Coelebs in Search of a Wife. 5th American ed. Boston: J. West et al., II, 6.
Fictional character objects to unchristian conduct of Smollett's "worthless" heroes. First published in 1808.

8   MUDFORD, WILLIAM. "The Life of Tobias Smollett, M.D." and "Critical Observations," in The British Novelists. London: W. Clarke et al., I, 3-4; I (Peregrine Pickle), 5-6; I (Humphry Clinker), i-iv; II (Roderick Random), i-iv; II (Ferdinand Count Fathom), i-iv; II (Launcelot Greaves), i-iv.
Inaccurate biographical sketch suggests illness impaired Smollett's mind and affected his Travels. Individual evaluations offer little worthwhile, noting characters in Peregrine Pickle, attacking lack of verisimilitude in Fathom, dismissing Launcelot Greaves, praising Random and Clinker, but without illumination.

9   [SCOTT, WALTER]. Review of Maturin's Fatal Revenge, Quarterly Review, 3 (May), 341.
Praises Smollett's ability to create credible characters despite their oddities.

## 1811

1   ANDERSON, ROBERT. "The Life of Tobias Smollett, M.D.," in The
    Miscellaneous Works of Tobias Smollett, M.D. Edinburgh:
    Mundell.
        Reprint of 1806.1.

2   ANON. "Critical Comments on Sterne, Smollett, and Fielding,"
    Port Folio, n.s. 6 (November), 412-31.
        Smollett's novels reflect his character and personality,
    combining the splenetic and fiercely independent, but also
    some surprising sensibility if not tenderness.

3   GARNETT, T. Observations on a Tour through the Highlands.
    London: John Stockdale, I, 26-31.
        Describes Smollett's birthplace and monument and praises
    his "Ode to Leven Water."

4   [HODGSON, FRANCIS]. Review of Salmagundi, Monthly Review, 2nd
    ser., 65 (August), 418.
        Washington Irving's humor exaggerates Smollett's farce.

5   [SEWARD, ANNA]. Letters of Anna Seward Written between the
    Years 1784 and 1807. Edinburgh: Archibald Constable, II,
    185.
        Compares Smollett unfavorably with Sterne.

## 1812

1   BAKER, DAVID ERSKINE. "Smollett, Tobias, M.D.," in Biographia
    Dramatica, or, A Companion to the Playhouse, ed. by Isaac
    Reed and revised by Stephen Jones. London: Longman et al.,
    I, Part II, 677-78.
        Poor revision and expansion of 1782.2. Now includes
    Humphry Clinker, but regards it as inferior. Ascribes His-
    tory of an Atom to Smollett.

2   [CROKER, JOHN WILSON]. Review of Maria Edgeworth's Tales of
    Fashionable Life, Quarterly Review, 7 (June), 331-32.
        Criticizes immoral example set in Peregrine Pickle.

3   D'ISRAELI, ISAAC. "Authors by Profession," in Calamaties of
    Authors. London: John Murray; Edinburgh: W. Blackwood, I,
    17-23.
        Deplores conditions under which Smollett, despite his
    genius, was forced to work in order to survive.

4   IRVING, WASHINGTON.  "Preface," in A History of New York from
    the Beginning of the World to the End of the Dutch Dynasty.
    2nd ed.  New York: Inskeep and Bradford, I, xxi.
        Hopes to be as successful as Smollett's History of
    England. First edition in 1809. See Knickerbocker, Diedrich.

5   KNICKERBOCKER, DIEDRICH.  See Irving, Washington.

6   MUDFORD, WILLIAM.  A Critical Examination of the Writings of
    Richard Cumberland.  London: Sherwood, Neely, Jones, I,
    171.
        Cumberland's Captain Ironsides indebted to Smollett's
    nautical characters.

7   NICHOLS, JOHN.  Literary Anecdotes of the Eighteenth Century.
    London: for the Author, III, 465; VIII, 229, 412, 497, 574;
    IX, 118, 261, 480.
        Details about Smollett's work, relationships, and repu-
    tation.


                            1813


1   STEPHENS, ALEXANDER.  Memoirs of John Horne Tooke.  London: J.
    Johnson, I, 355-56.
        Smollett sacrificed novelistic talents for polemical
    journalism and histories.

2   WOODHOUSELEE, LORD ALEXANDER FRASER TYTLER.  Essays on the
    Principles of Translation.  3rd ed.  Edinburgh: Archibald
    Constable; London: Longman et al., pp. 256-59 and 282-319.
        First edition 1791.13. Finds merit in Smollett's trans-
    lation of Gil Blas, but too formal and stilted; Don
    Quixote, although too imitative of Jarvis's translation and
    inferior to Motteux's, also has merit.


                            1814


1   AIKIN, JOHN and WILLIAM JOHNSTON.  "Smollett, Tobias, M.D.,"
    in General Biography.  London: John Stockdale et al., IX,
    177-78.
        Acknowledges Smollett's talent, but condemns his per-
    sonality, taste, and coarseness.  Praises his poetry, but
    not his satires.  Article by Aikin.

2   ANON.  "On Novel-Writing and Reading," The Ladies' Monthly
    Museum, n.s. 16 (January), 27.

1814

An unfamiliarity with Smollett signifies an incomplete
education.

3   ANON. Review of Fanny Burney's The Wanderer, Critical Review,
    4th ser., 5 (April), 406.
        Laments disappearance from the novel of such richly ec-
    centric characters as Bowling, Trunnion, Lismahago.

4   [CROKER, JOHN WILSON]. Review of Walter Scott's Waverley,
    Quarterly Review, 11 (July), 355.
        Attacks manners and morals in Peregrine Pickle.

5   DUNLOP, JOHN C. History of Fiction. Edinburgh: James
    Ballantyne and Co.; London: Longman et al., III, 106, 467-
    68.
        Praises multiple point of view and characterization in
    Humphry Clinker and the sailors in Smollett's novels.
    Launcelot Greaves a poor imitation of Don Quixote. Re-
    printed 1888.2.


                            1815

1   ANON. "Standard Novels and Romances," Edinburgh Review, 24
    (February), 320-38.
        Compares Smollett and Fielding, discusses relative mer-
    its of Smollett's individual novels, rating Roderick Random
    best and offering some praise of Ferdinand Count Fathom.

2   ANON. Review of Alicia De Lacy, Critical Review, 5th ser., 2
    (July), 103-4.
        Smollett important to development of the novel, but his-
    torical material absent from his fiction, although he was
    an historian.

3   CREECH, WILLIAM. Edinburgh Fugitive Pieces. Edinburgh: John
    Fairbairn et al., pp. 154-55, 277, 341-43.
        Praises Smollett's histories and novels despite his
    coarseness.

4   [MACKINTOSH, JOHN?]. Review of Godwin's Lives of Edward and
    John Philips, Edinburgh Review, 25 (October), 485.
        Praises Smollett's humor.

5   [SCOTT, WALTER]. Review of Jane Austen's Emma, Quarterly Re-
    view, 14 (October), 188, 191.
        Influences of Smollett's work and difference between it
    and later novels.

## 1816

1 ANON. "View of the Present State of Polite Learning," Porti-
co, 1 (March), 210-11.
    Praises Smollett's novels, particularly Roderick Random
and Peregrine Pickle.

2 ANON. Review of Scott's The Antiquary, Critical Review, 5th
ser., 3 (May), 487.
    Compares Scott's and Smollett's humor and characteriza-
tion.

3 ANON. "Introduction," in The Miscellaneous Works of Tobias
Smollett, M.D. Dublin: J. Christie, pp. i-xvi.
    Summarizes without adding to Anderson's biographical
work.

4 CANDIDUS. "Observations on Novel Reading," Christian Observer, 15 (December), 785.
    Despite genius, Smollett's and Fielding's novels are
immoral.

5 MILLIN, A. L. Voyage en Savoie, en Piémont, A Nice, et a
Gènes. Paris: C. Wassermann, II, 107, 118.
    Critical of Smollett's unjust treatment of Nice in his
Travels.

## 1817

1 ANDERSON, ROBERT. "The Life of Tobias Smollett, M.D.," in
Miscellaneous Works of Tobias Smollett, M.D. Edinburgh:
Mundell.
    Reprint of 1806.1.

2 ANON. Review of Six Weeks at Long's. Literary Gazette, no.
5 (February 22), p. 69.
    Attacks novelist for describing Smollett's novels as
"labored."

3 ANON. Review of Millin's Voyage en Italie. Edinburgh Review,
29 (November), 209.
    Defends Smollett's description of Nice in his Travels.

4 BARRETT, EATON STANNARD. Six Weeks at Long's. London: For
Author, I, x-xi.
    Criticizes Smollett's labored style of wit.

5 CANDIDIOR. Letter, Christian Observer, 16 (April), 230.
    Sharp criticism of Smollett's immorality.

1817

6  EXCUBITOR. "On the Influence of the Literature of Fiction,"
   Christian Observer, 16 (June), 372.
   The indecency of Smollett's novels.


### 1818

1  ANON. "Novel Writing," British Review, and London Critical
   Journal, 11 (February), 40-42.
   Attacks indecency in Smollett's novels. Sees his characters as indistinguishable from each other and from the
   author.

2  ANON. "Italy," Gentleman's Magazine, 88 (September), 267.
   Smollett's tomb covered with laurel branches left by
   visitors.

3  ANON. Brambleton Hall, a Novel, Being a Sequel to the Cele-
   brated Humphrey [sic] Clinker, by Tobias Smollet [sic].
   London: T. H. Green et al., xix-162 pp.
   A good imitation of Smollett's style.

4  M., J. "Smollett's Tomb," Literary Gazette, no. 86 (September
   12), p. 591.
   Description of Smollett's tomb and its inscriptions.

5  THRASEA. "The Tendency of Novels," Northumberland and Newcastle Monthly Magazine, 1 (July), 247.
   Deplores effect of Smollett's novels on impressionable
   young readers.


### 1819

*1  ANON. Review of Edition of Continuation of the History of
   England, Journal des Debats (September 8).
   Favorable treatment. Cited in Joliat, 1935.5.

2  ANON. "Smollett's Tomb," European Magazine, 76 (December),
   512.
   Describes tomb and many visitors. Suggests James Hay
   Beattie as author of the English inscription.

3  BRUNTON, ALEXANDER. "Memoir," in Emmaline with Some Other
   Pieces by Mary Brunton. Edinburgh: Manners and Miller et
   al.; London: John Murray, p. lxxvi.
   Scott best novelist since Fielding and Smollett.

4   CAMPBELL, THOMAS. "Tobias Smollett," in Specimens of the
      British Poets. London: John Murray, VI, 218-24.
         Sensible and balanced account of life and work is aware
      of dangers of using novels as autobiography. Praises the
      poetry and is enthusiastic about the novels.

5   HAZLITT, WILLIAM. "On the English Novelists," in Lectures on
      the English Comic Writers. London: Taylor and Hessey, pp.
      229-33.
         Smollett more modern than Fielding, but deficient in in-
      sight into characters and tied to his own times. Apprecia-
      tive of Smollett's humor, but notes vulgarity and weak
      plots. Rates Roderick Random best, praises Humphry Clinker
      and scenes in Ferdinand Count Fathom.


                              1820

1   ANDERSON, ROBERT. "The Life of Tobias Smollett, M.D.," in
      Miscellaneous Works of Tobias Smollett, M.D. Sixth edi-
      tion. Edinburgh: Stirling & Slade et al., I, 1-203.
         Anderson's most complete biography of Smollett and his
      best work. Includes long appendix of letters (pp. 163-
      203). See works by Anderson: 1794, 1796, 1800, 1803, 1806,
      1811, 1817.

2   ANON. Review of The Mystery, or Forty Years Ago, Literary
      Gazette, no. 160 (February 12), p. 97.
         Praises its humor by comparing it to Smollett's work.

*3  ANON. Review of Edition of Continuation of the History of
      England, Journal de Paris (August 15).
         Praises Smollett's careful treatment of his material.
      Cited in Joliat, 1935.5.

4   B., W. "Extract of a Letter to Major Cartwright," Saturday
      Register, 1 (April 15), 216-18.
         Misquotes Lismahago in Humphry Clinker to make a radical
      argument for social reform.

5   BYERLEY, THOMAS and JOSEPH CLINTON ROBERTSON. The Percy Anec-
      dotes. London: T. Boys, 22 Vols., passim. Indexed.
         Popular anecdotes such as Smollett's generosity to a
      beggar. See Percy, Sholto and Reuben.

6   HUNT, LEIGH. "Neapolitan Revolution," Examiner, No. 657 (July
      30), p. 481.
         Uses feast in Peregrine Pickle as allusion.

1820

7   PERCY, SHOLTO and REUBEN. See Byerley, Thomas and Joseph
    Clinton Robertson.

8   WILLIAMS, H. W. "Dr. Smollet's [sic] Diploma," in Travels in
    Italy, Greece, and the Ionian Islands. Edinburgh:
    Archibald Constable, I, 198-99.
        Reports destruction of Smollett's diploma from Aberdeen
    and indicates his posthumous popularity attested to by
    visitors to his tomb.

1821

1   ANON. Essay on Washington Irving, Port Folio, 5th ser., 11
    (March), 134-35.
        Conjectures on Smollett's response had he seen America.

2   ANON. Review of Ballantyne Library Edition of Smollett's Nov-
    els, Literary Gazette, no. 235 (July 21), pp. 449-51.
        Paraphrases Scott's essay, but strongly approves of the
    novels.

3   ANON. Review of Rouge et Noir, Eclectic Review, n.s. 16 (Oc-
    tober), 473-74.
        Compares satire of Byron, Smollett, and Swift.

4   ANON. "Stephensiana--No. 1," Monthly Magazine, 52 (October
    1), 236-37.
        Anecdote about Smollett as a doctor.

*5  ANON. Review of Edition of Continuation of the History of
    England, Constitutionnel (October 24).
        Smollett's abilities as an historian enhance his reputa-
    tion. Cited in Joliat, 1935.5.

6   DAVIS, WILLIAM. A Journey Round the Library of a Bibliomani-
    ac. London: W. Davis, pp. 29-30.
        Because Smollett followed Jarvis's translation of Don
    Quixote too closely it is inferior to Motteux's.

7   EGAN, PIERCE. Life in London. London: Sherwood et al., pp.
    3-4, 6.
        Praises Smollett's animated style and characterization.

8   NODIER, CHARLES. Promenade de Dieppe aux Montagnes d'Ecosse.
    Paris: J. N. Barba, p. 183.
        On Smollett's monument at Dumbarton. Trans. 1822.
    Edinburgh: W. Blackwood.

9   SCOTT, WALTER.  "Prefatory Memoir," in <u>Ballantyne's Novelist's
    Library</u>.  London: Hurst, Robinson and Co., II.
        First appearance of Scott's life of Smollett is an en-
    thusiastic treatment of the man and his work, stressing his
    Scottish heritage.  For factual information depends largely
    on Moore and Anderson, but attempts to set forth Smollett's
    personality.  Places Smollett on the same level as Fielding
    and both far above their followers.  Reprinted many times:
    1833, 1835, 1836, 1841, 1843, 1852, 1879, 1906, 1925, etc.
    <u>See</u>, particularly, 1st American ed.: 1825.6.


                            1822

1   ANON.  "Sketches on the Road," <u>London Magazine</u>, 5 (January),
    64-65.
        Describes Smollett's monument in Leghorn and praises his
    "Ode on Independence."

2   ANON.  "A New Edition of <u>Don Quixote</u>," <u>Blackwood's Magazine</u>,
    11 (June), 657, 659.
        Scoffs at Smollett's notes, but praises sketch of
    Cervantes's life in his edition of <u>Don Quixote</u>.

3   ANON.  Review of John Galt's <u>The Provost</u>, <u>Literary Gazette</u>,
    no. 283 (June 22), p. 386.
        Compares death scene with that of Trunnion in <u>Peregrine
    Pickle</u>.

*4   HEINE, HEINRICH.  <u>Briefe aus Berlin</u>.
        Compares Smollett and Sterne.  Cited in Price, 1932.22.

5   MACKENZIE, HENRY.  <u>An Account of the Life and Writings of John
    Home, Esq</u>.  Edinburgh: Archibald Constable, pp. 56, 134,
    137.
        Home's opinion of Smollett, and Smollett's friendship
    with Home and other Scotsmen in London.

6   PAULDING, JAMES KIRK.  "Letter XXIX" and "Letter XXX," in <u>A
    Sketch of Old England</u>.  New York: Charles Wiley, II, 149-
    50, 157.
        Smollett's work lacks developed narrative and character-
    ization, but has emotional and imaginative appeal.  Disap-
    proves of the type of travel book to which Smollett's
    belongs.

1822

7   SINGER, S. W. "The Life of Tobias Smollett, M.D.," in The
    British Poets. Chiswick: P. Whittingham for J. Carpenter
    et al., LXVI, 197-214.
      Brief sketch dependent on Scott's work praises
    Smollett's writing and places his poetry in the first rank.
    Emphasizes biographical connections of his work. For re-
    prints and abridgments, see Boucé, 1971.6.

8   WALPOLE, HORACE. Memoirs of the Last Ten Years of the Reign
    of George the Second. London: John Murray, II, 419-21.
      Savage attack on Smollett's character, politics, and
    work.

9   WALSH, ROBERT JR. "The Life of Dr. Tobias Smollett," in The
    Works of the British Poets, with Lives of the Authors.
    Philadelphia: Samuel F. Bradford for John Laval, XXXIII,
    325-36.
      Unacknowledged abridgment of Chalmers, 1810.4.


1823

1   ANON. "Dr. Smollett," The Emmet, 1 (April 5), 5-6.
      Smollett's youth in Glasgow and suggestions for origi-
    nals of characters in Roderick Random. Two volume collec-
    tion of the work appeared in 1824. Reprint of essay in
    Knapp, 1949.12.

2   ANON. "Anecdotes of Provost Buchanan, The Squire Gawky of
    Smollett, &c.," The Emmet, 2 (October 4), 9-10.
      Forcefulness of Smollett's characters comes from their
    dependence on real persons, particularly in Roderick
    Random. Essay reprinted in Knapp, 1949.12.

3   LOCKHART, JOHN G. "Letters of Timothy Tickler," Blackwood's
    Magazine, 14 (August), 226-27.
      Smollett a social satirist like Fielding and others.


1824

1   ANON. Review of Ballantyne's Novelist's Library, Blackwood's
    Magazine, 15 (April), 407-08, 414.
      Attacks Smollett's translation of Don Quixote and finds
    Scott a superior novelist.

2   ANON. Review of Washington Irving's Tales of a Traveller,
    Westminster Review, 2 (October), 345.

Weak imitation of Smollett and Goldsmith whose works are fading.

3   ANON. "Life of Tobias Smollett, M.D.," in The Miscellaneous Works of Tobias Smollett, M.D. with a Life of the Author. London: Otridge and Rackham et al., I, vii-xi.
    Brief, inaccurate, and unsympathetic sketch of life and work.

4   FERRIER, SUSAN E.   The Inheritance.   Edinburgh: William Blackwood; London: T. Cadell, II, 116.
    Fictional characters discuss impurity of Smollett's works.

*5   [GUIRAUD, ALEXANDRE?].   Review of Sir Launcelot Greaves, Le Drapeau Blanc (June 10).
    Favorable review because of its Toryism.   Cited in Joliat, 1935.5.

6   SCOTT, WALTER.   Life of Smollett, in Fielding und Smollett. Zwei Biographi von Walter Scott, trans. W. U. Lindau. Leipzig: Rein'sche Buchhandlung, pp. 61-126.
    German translation of 1821.9.

7   SCOTT, WALTER.   "Prefatory Memoir to Smollett," Museum of Foreign Literature and Science, 5 (July to December), 209-38.
    Reprint of 1821.9.

8   WADD, WILLIAM.   "Tobias Smollett," in Nugae Chirurgicaes or, a Biographical Miscellany.   London: John Nichols and Son, p. 259.
    Admires Smollett's independence and pride although they probably cost him greater worldly success.

9   WATT, ROBERT.   Bibliotheca Britannica, or A General Index to British and Foreign Literature.   Edinburgh: Archibald Constable; London: Longman et al., Part 1, II, 866f. and v.; Part 2, II, under "S."
    Laudatory biographical and bibliographical account relates work to life, praises poetry and writing in Critical Review.   Fails to mention Humphry Clinker, but gives list of selected editions of Smollett and some works, particularly attacks, on him.

## 1825

1  BRYDGES, [SAMUEL] EGERTON. <u>Recollections of Foreign Travel on</u>
    <u>Life, Literature, and Self-Knowledge</u>. London: Longman et
    al., I, 40-41.
        Smollett's novels among those being printed but not
    read.

2  CHAMBERS, ROBERT. "House of Mrs. Smollett," in <u>Traditions of</u>
    <u>Edinburgh</u>. Edinburgh: W. & C. Tait, I, 270-80.
        Information on Smollett's family, portraits of him, and
    memorials for him. Identifies originals for characters in
    <u>Humphry Clinker</u>. Reprints in 1912, London: W. and R.
    Chambers; Philadelphia: J. B. Lippincott.

3  DAVIS, WILLIAM. "Key to Smollett's <u>History and Adventures of</u>
    <u>an Atom</u>," in <u>A Second Journey Round the Library of a Bibli-</u>
    <u>omaniac</u>. London: W. Davis, pp. 115-18.
        Comments on the novel and offers a key to its characters
    and places, but presents no supporting evidence.

4  EGAN, PIERCE. <u>The Life of an Actor</u>. London: C. S. Arnold, p.
    131.
        Compares his fictional hero with Smollett's Peregrine
    Pickle.

5  LEFEBVRE-CAUCHY. "Smollett (Tobie-George)," in <u>Biographie</u>
    <u>Universelle (Michaud) Ancienne et Moderne</u>. Paris: Madame
    C. Desplaces et al., XLII, 494-98.
        Expresses disagreement with favorable treatment of
    Smollett by Robert Anderson and Walter Scott. Reprint
    1854-65.

6  SCOTT, WALTER. "Smollett," in <u>Lives of the Novelists</u>. Phila-
    delphia: H. C. Carey & I. Lea et al., pp. 81-141.
        First American publication of 1821.9.

7  TENNEY, TABITHA. <u>Female Quixotism</u>. Boston: J. P. Peaslee,
    II, 131-32.
        Effect of reading <u>Roderick Random</u> on a fictional charac-
    ter. First publication in 1808.

## 1826

1  ANON. Review of <u>Naval Sketch-Book</u>, <u>Blackwood's Magazine</u>, 19
    (March), 354.

Praises Smollett's treatment of nautical life and characters.

2   ANON.  Review of <u>Recollections of a Pedestrian</u>, <u>Gentleman's</u>
    <u>Magazine</u>, 96 (June), 531-32.
        Extract from 1826.3.

3   [BOSWELL, THOMAS ALEXANDER].  <u>Recollections of a Pedestrian</u>.
    London: Sanders and Otley, II, 26-27.
        Smollett's <u>Travels</u> contributed to popularity of Nice.

4   [LOCKHART, JOHN G.].  <u>Review of Scott's Lives of the Novel-</u>
    <u>ists</u>, Quarterly Review, 34 (September), 349-78.
        Generally appreciates Smollett's art as a novelist.

5   [SCOTT, WALTER].  Review of John Galt's <u>The Omen</u>, <u>Blackwood's</u>
    <u>Magazine</u>, 20 (July), 52.
        Notes changes in subject matter since Smollett's novels.


## 1827

1   ANON.  Review of <u>Truth</u>, <u>Westminster Review</u>, 7 (April), 343.
        Smollett's novels superior to doctrinal novels in their
    ability to please.

2   GOODHUGH, WILLIAM.  <u>The English Gentleman's Library Manual: or</u>
    <u>a Guide to the Formation of a Library of Select Literature</u>.
    London: William Goodhugh and Goodhugh, p. 47.
        Successful publishing and advertising methods for the
    <u>History of England</u>.

*3  VOGT, W. H. VON.  Biographical-Critical Introduction, in
    <u>Peregrine Pickle</u> (German translation).  Magdeburg: F.
    Rubach.
        Cited in Joliat, 1935.5.


## 1828

1   BLACKSTONE, WILLIAM.  "The King <u>vs</u>. Dr. Smollet [<u>sic</u>]," in
    <u>Reports of Cases Determined in the Several Courts of West-</u>
    <u>minster-Hall from 1746 to 1779</u>.  Second edition.  Rev. by
    C. H. Elsley.  London: S. Sweet et al., I, 268.
        Smollett's trial for libel of Admiral Knowles.

2   HUNT, LEIGH.  "Recollections of the Author's Life," in <u>Lord</u>
    <u>Byron and Some of His Contemporaries; with Recollections</u>

1828

of the Author's Life, and of His Visit to Italy. London:
Henry Colburn, pp. 400, 475.
   Comments on Smollett's characters and style.

3  LOCKHART, JOHN G. Life of Robert Burns. Edinburgh: Constable
and Co. and Hurst, Chance, pp. 21, 247, 300.
   Comments on Smollett's yielding to British prejudices
against Scots and on Burns's early reading of Smollett.

4  NICHOLS, JOHN. Illustrations of the Literary History of the
Eighteenth Century. London: J. B. Nichols and Son, V, 776.
   1767 letter approving of Smollett's Travels, but object-
ing to its use of words of foreign extraction. See 1848.3.


1829

1  ANON. Review of Devereux, Southern Review, 4 (November), 379-
81.
   Objects to Smollett's coarseness and failure to develop
plots, but praises characterization and effectiveness, particularly in Humphry Clinker.

2  COBBETT, WILLIAM. Advice to Young Men and (Incidentally) to
Young Women. London: B. Bensley for the Author, p. 49.
   Belittles Smollett's History of England as a romance.

3  FAULKNER, THOMAS. "Dr. Smollett," in An Historical and Topo-
graphical Description of Chelsea and Its Environs.
Chelsea: T. Faulkner et al., I, 266-72 and I and II, passim. Indexed.
   Praises all the novels, suggesting major characters are
autobiographical.

4  GLASCOCK, WILLIAM. Sailors and Saints; or, Matrimonial Ma-
noeuvres. Second edition. London: Henry Colburn, I, 89.
   Fictional character praises Smollett's realistic sailors.


1830

1  ANON. Review of Translation of Cooper's Work, Revue de Paris,
22 (December 31), 62.
   Smollett's influence on James Fenimore Cooper.

2  [DANIEL, GEORGE]. "Remarks. Humphry Clinker," in Cumberland's
Minor Theater. London: John Cumberland, IV, 2-6.

Praises Smollett's translations, poetry, and nautical
characters, sees him using autobiographical material, and
deplores his coarseness.

3   WARNER, RICHARD. Literary Recollections. London: Longman et
    al., II, 17.
        Erroneously asserts Anstey's New Bath Guide had borrowed
    from Humphry Clinker.


## 1831

1   [ALLEN, JOHN]. Review of Lingard's History of England, Edin-
    burgh Review, 53 (March), 16-17.
        Attributes success of Smollett's History of England to
    its being bound with Hume's work.

2   ANON. Review of Scott's Waverley Novels, North American Re-
    view, 32 (April), 404-5.
        Grateful Smollett kept his coarse art from treating
    Scotland in fiction, but would have been superior to Scott
    in depicting British cruelty to Jacobites.

3   ANON. Review of Cooper's The Water Witch, North American Re-
    view, 32 (April), 514.
        Compares Richardson's and Smollett's kinds of realism.

4   ANON. "The Novels of the Season," Fraser's Magazine, 4 (Au-
    gust), 11.
        Smollett's novels require editing for refined tastes.

5   ANON. Review of The Youth and Manhood of Cyril Thornton,
    Southern Review, 8 (November), 45.
        Compares Smollett with Fielding and rates him very fav-
    orably, particularly in imagination, humor, and pathos.

6   G., W. N. "Naval Novels," Metropolitan Magazine, 1 (August),
    370-76.
        Despite importance to the genre, not a great nautical
    novelist because of exaggeration in Peregrine Pickle and
    Roderick Random.

7   ROSCOE, THOMAS. Memoir of Smollett, in The Expedition of
    Humphry Clinker. London: Cochrane and Pickersgill.
        Apparently first of Roscoe's memoirs of Smollett. See
    1836.5.

## 1832

1 ANON. Review of <u>Newton Forster; or, The Merchant Service</u>, <u>Westminster Review</u>, 16 (April), 392.
Frederick Marryat carries on Smollett's work against the impressment of sailors.

2 ANON. Review of <u>English Literature of the Nineteenth Century</u>, <u>North American Review</u>, 35 (July), 188–89.
Scott's novelistic skills superior to Smollett's.

3 BUCKE, CHARLES. <u>On the Life, Writings, and Genius of Akenside: with Some Account of His Friends</u>. London: James Cochrane, pp. 41–43.
Anecdote about Smollett and comment on his portrait of Akenside in <u>Peregrine Pickle</u>.

4 CRUIKSHANK, GEORGE. <u>Illustrations of Smollett, Fielding, and Goldsmith</u>. London: Charles Tilt, passim.
Illustrations for scenes in <u>Humphry Clinker</u>, <u>Roderick Random</u>, <u>Peregrine Pickle</u>, and <u>Launcelot Greaves</u> with texts.

5 GENEST, JOHN. <u>Some Account of the English Stage from the Restoration in 1660 to 1830</u>. Bath: H. E. Carrington, IV, 479–80; VI, 362.
Account and evaluation of <u>The Reprisal</u> and suggestion that <u>The Israelites</u> is Smollett's.

6 MARRYAT, FREDERICK. "On Novels and Novel Writing," <u>Metropolitan Magazine</u>, 5 (November), 234.
Implies that Smollett's nautical novels are inferior to depiction of sea life by marine painters.

7 PLANCHE, GUSTAVE. Article on Fielding, <u>Revue des Deux Mondes</u>, 5 (January 31), 339.
Smollett a follower of Fielding.

8 TAYLOR, JOHN. <u>Records of My Life</u>. London: Edward Bull, II, 409. Rumors that Dennis McKerchier wrote Lady Vane's memoirs for <u>Peregrine Pickle</u>.

## 1833

1 ANON. Review of <u>The Port-Admiral</u>, <u>Quarterly Review</u>, 49 (April and July), 485.
Smollett's treatment of nautical characters excels that of his imitators and successors.

2   ANON.  Review of <u>Select Works of Tobias Smollett</u>, <u>Knicker-</u>
    <u>bocker Magazine</u>, 2 (October), 315.
        Delighted by the new availability of Smollett's writ-
    ings.

3   CHAMBERS, ROBERT.  "House of Smollett's Relations," in <u>Reeki-</u>
    <u>ana: Minor Antiquities of Edinburgh</u>.  Edinburgh: William
    and Robert Chambers, pp. 231–33.
        Describes Smollett's ill health during stay with rela-
    tives in 1766 and suggests models for characters in <u>Humphry</u>
    <u>Clinker</u>.

4   [MACAULAY, THOMAS B.].  Review of Walpole's Letters to Horace
    Mann, <u>Edinburgh Review</u>, 58 (October), 255/257.
        Compares Smollett's portrait of Duke of Newcastle in
    <u>Humphry Clinker</u> with Walpole's and objects to novel's
    coarseness.

5   MOORE, OLIVER.  <u>The Staff Officer; or, The Soldier of Fortune</u>.
    Philadelphia: E. L. Carey & A. Hart, II, 72.
        Fictional character takes Smollett's coarse but enter-
    taining novels on a long voyage.

6   SCOTT, MICHAEL.  <u>Tom Cringle's Log</u>.  Philadelphia: E. L. Carey
    & A. Hart, II, 59ff. and 85ff.
        Uses names of Smollett's characters, imitates and uses
    their characteristics.


                            <u>1834</u>

1   ANON.  "State of the British Stage," <u>Westminster Review</u>, 20
    (January), 153.
        Triumphs of Smollett in <u>Humphry Clinker</u> should not dis-
    suade other novelists from trying.

2   ANON.  Review of Maria Edgeworth's <u>Helen</u>, <u>North American Re-</u>
    <u>view</u>, 39 (July), 171.
        Criticizes Smollett's immoral delight in sordidness.

3   ANON.  "Novel Writing," <u>American Quarterly Review</u>, 16 (Decem-
    ber), 503–4.
        Smollett, with Fielding, raised realistic novels to
    their highest level.

4   [CRABBE, GEORGE].  <u>Poetical Works of the Rev. George Crabbe</u>
    <u>with His Letters and Journals, and His Life, by His Son</u>.

1834

        London: John Murray, I, 243.
        Thomas Campbell describes self as "Smollettite."

5    GLASCOCK, WILLIAM N. "Strictures on Smollett," in <u>Naval Sketch Book, Second Series</u>. London: Whittaker & Co., I, 121-40.
        Vagueness and exaggeration make Smollett's nautical fiction unreliable as portrait of reality. While satisfactory on shipboard medical conditions, lacks feeling for nature.

6    HUNT, LEIGH. "Thieves, Ancient and Modern," in <u>The Indicator</u>. London: Henry Colburn, I, 152.
        Unappealing character of Ferdinand Count Fathom.

7    LOWNDES, WILLIAM THOMAS. <u>The Bibliographer's Manual</u>. London: William Pickering, IV, 1701-2.
        Unreliable bibliographical details of Smollett's works and some secondary material.

8    MÉZIÈRES, LOUIS. "Smollett," in <u>Histoire Critique de la Littérature Anglaise</u>. Paris: Baudry, à la Librairie Européenne, II, 161-217.
        Balanced discussion of three major novels and relation to Le Sage and Scarron. Ranks Smollett among the great novelists of his time, particularly praising his industry and imagination.

9    [RANDOLPH, JOHN]. <u>Letters of John Randolph, to a Young Relative</u>. Philadelphia: Carey et al., p. 191.
        Recollects youthful joy of reading <u>Humphry Clinker</u>.

1835

1    CHAMBERS, ROBERT. "Tobias George Smollett," in <u>A Biographical Dictionary of Eminent Scotsmen</u>. Glasgow, Edinburgh, London: Blackie and Son, IV, 268-78.
        General account presents interesting information on Smollett's childhood, memorials written for him, and wife's condition after his death. Publishes a letter of 1744. Reprints in 1870, 1875 (according to Boucé, 1971.6), and one in 1856, IV, 293-303.

2    [COLERIDGE, SAMUEL TAYLOR]. <u>Specimens of the Table Talk of the Late Samuel Taylor Coleridge</u>. London: John Murray, II, 297.
        Praises Marryat's <u>Peter Simple</u> as closest thing to Smollett's work.

3    MACKINTOSH, JAMES.  Memoirs of the Life of Sir James
     Mackintosh, ed. Robert James Mackintosh.  London: Edward
     Moxon, II, 104-5.
          Approves of Mrs. Barbauld's derogatory comments on
     Ferdinand Count Fathom, but questions whether Smollett is
     less read because of his coarseness.

4    VALERY, M.  Voyages Historiques et Litteraires en Italie.
     Bruxelles: Louis Hanman, p. 377.
          Describes Smollett's tomb in Livorno.


                              1836

1    ANON.  Review of Dickens's Pickwick Papers, Athenaeum, no. 475
     (December 3), p. 841.
          Comparison of Dickens and Smollett stresses their vul-
     garity.

2    ANON.  Anecdotes of Books and Authors.  London: Orr and Smith,
     p. 163.
          Anecdote on Smollett's generosity to a beggar.

3    COLERIDGE, SAMUEL TAYLOR.  Letters, Conversations, and Recol-
     lections.  New York: Harper & Brothers, pp. 40, 92.
          Smollett's characters superior to Scott's.

4    CUNNINGHAM, G. G.  "Tobias Smollett," in Lives of Eminent and
     Illustrious Englishmen.  Glasgow: A Fullarton, V, 299-302.
          Derivative but favorable account of his abilities.

5    ROSCOE, THOMAS.  "A Memoir of the Author," in The Expedition
     of Humphry Clinker.  New York: Harper & Brothers, pp. v-
     xxxiii.
          Emphasizes abilities, but notes failures and balances
     fine personal qualities with temperamental deficiencies.
     First printed 1831.7.  Reprinted with additions 1841.2.


                              1837

1    ANON.  Review of Dickens's Boz and Pickwick, Westminster Re-
     view, 27 (July), 213.
          Dickens should work in same vein as Smollett.

2    CHAMBERS, ROBERT.  "Smollett," in History of the English Lan-
     guage and Literature.  Hartford: Edward Hopkins, pp. 163-64.
          Although a greater humorist, Smollett inferior to
     Fielding.

1837

3  [HAYWARD, ABRAHAM?].  Review of Dickens's Work, Quarterly Re-
     view, 59 (October), 484.
         Dickens lacks Smollett's exuberant, vital style.

4  LOCKHART, JOHN G.  Memoirs of the Life of Sir Walter Scott,
     Bart.  Philadelphia: Carey et al., II, 207, 699.
         Discusses Smollett's death and Scott's comments on his
     work.

5  [MONTAGU, LADY MARY WORTLEY].  The Letters and Works of Lady
     Mary Wortley Montagu, ed. Lord Wharncliffe.  2nd ed.
     London: Richard Bentley, III, 104, 199.
         Letters of 1755 and 1760 praise Smollett, but express
     some displeasure with Ferdinand Count Fathom and his wasted
     effort as an historian and translator.

## 1838

1  ANON.  "Art in Fiction," Monthly Chronicle, 1 (March), 50.
         Smollett fails to arouse passions and lacks sentiment.

2  ANON.  Review of Dickens's Oliver Twist, Literary Gazette (No-
     vember 24), 741.
         Smollett among novelists still dominant.

3  [LISTER, THOMAS HENRY].  Review of Dickens's Early Works,
     Edinburgh Review, 68 (October), 76, 86.
         Comic affinities and similar narrative techniques of
     Dickens and Smollett, but Dickens less coarse.

*4  PARTINGTON, CHARLES F.  "Smollett, Tobias," in British Cyclo-
     paedia of Biography.  London: Wm. S. Orr and Co., II.
         Brief account taken chiefly from Scott.  Cited in Boucé,
     1971.6.

*5  PRINCE, PHILIP.  Tobias Smollett, in Parallel Universal His-
     tory.  London, p. 438.
         Brief biographical sketch.  Cited in Boucé, 1971.6.  Re-
     printed 1842.5.

6  QUÉRARD, J.-M.  "Smollett (Tobias)," in La France Littéraire,
     ou Dictionnaire Bibliographique.  Paris: Didot Freres, IX,
     198.
         Praises Smollett and gives bibliography of French trans-
     lations.

## 1839

1  ANON.  Review of Marryat's <u>Diary in America</u>, <u>Edinburgh Review</u>,
    70 (October), 149.
       Smollett a poor historian.

2  ANON.  Review of <u>Reports of the Society for the Suppression of
    Mendacity</u>, <u>Quarterly Review</u>, 64 (October), 349.
       Prefers Smollett's vigorous style to that of sentimental
    novelists.

3  D.  "Confessions of a Novel Reader," <u>Southern Literary Messen-
    ger</u>, 5 (March), 183.
       Smollett's talent makes his immorality dangerous.

## 1840

1  THACKERAY, WILLIAM MAKEPEACE.  "Fielding's Works, <u>The Times</u>
    (September 2).
       Contrasts weak picaresque structure of <u>Roderick Random</u>
    with that of <u>Tom Jones</u>.  Reprinted in <u>Critical Papers in
    Literature</u>, London: Macmillan, p. 207 in 1904.

2  [THACKERAY, WILLIAM MAKEPEACE].  "On Some French Fashionable
    Novels," in <u>The Paris Sketch Book</u>.  London: John Macrone,
    I, 173.
       <u>Roderick Random</u> inferior to <u>Pickwick Papers</u>.

## 1841

1  MÉZIÈRES, M. L.  "Smollett," in <u>Histoire Critique de la Lit-
    térature Anglaise</u>.  Paris: A. Allouard, II, 161-217.
       Detailed discussion of Smollett's major novels describes
    his greater appeal in England than on the Continent, la-
    ments his failure with plot, warns against his morality,
    and finds Henry Mackenzie a superior novelist.

2  ROSCOE, THOMAS.  "Life and Works of Tobias Smollett," in <u>Mis-
    cellaneous Works of Tobias Smollett</u>.  London: Henry G.
    Bohn, pp. vii-xl.
       Expanded version of 1836.5 includes more quotations from
    sources like Anderson, Moore, and Scott.  Many reprints:
    1844, 1848, 1849, 1850, 1851, 1852, 1853, 1857, 1858, 1860,
    1863, 1868, 1869, 1871, 1881, 1889, 1894.

1841

1 WARD, ROBERT PLUMER. <u>De Clifford, or, The Constant Man</u>.
London: H. Colburn, pp. 254-55.
Fictional character deplores Smollett's seductive im-
morality.

## 1842

1 ANON. "Smollett, Tobias," in <u>Encyclopaedia Britannica</u>. 7th
ed. Edinburgh: Adam and Charles Black, XX, 425-28.
Alters earlier editions with additions from Scott and
others and presents a remarkably favorable account of
Smollett and his work. Reprinted in eighth edition.

2 [DE LEON, EDWIN]. "Modern Fiction," <u>Southern Literary Messen-
ger</u>, 8 (May), 344.
Smollett's coarse but accurate depiction of life and
society.

3 KNIGHT, CHARLES. <u>London</u>. London: Charles Knight, II, 353-54.
Smollett's young heroes related to loose society of
their time.

4 [POE, EDGAR ALLAN]. Review of Lorrequer's <u>Charles O'Malley</u>,
<u>Graham's Magazine</u>, 20 (February), 187.
Dickens's genius superior to Smollett's talent.

5 PRINCE, PHILIP. "Tobias Smollett," in <u>Parallel Universal His-
tory</u>. 2nd ed. London: n.p., II, 548-49.
Expanded edition of 1838.5 is sympathetic to Smollett.

6 TIMPERLEY, C. H. <u>Encyclopaedia of Literary and Typographical
Anecdote</u>. London: Henry G. Bohn, pp. 696, 703, 704, 778,
822.
Genuine and apocryphal anecdotes about the <u>Critical Re-
view</u>, <u>History of England</u>, and Smollett's associations.

## 1843

1 [LOCKHART, JOHN G.]. Review of Theodore Hooke's <u>Peregrine
Bruce</u>, <u>Quarterly Review</u>, 72 (May), 105-6.
Compares Hooke's and Smollett's techniques.

2 SMYTH, WILLIAM. "Sir Robert Walpole" and "George II," in
<u>Lectures on Modern History</u>. Cambridge: J. and J. J.
Deighton; London: William Pickering, II, 214, 217.

Smollett's histories prejudiced by Tory and Scottish sympathies. Reprinted 1854.2.


## 1844

1    CHAMBERS, ROBERT. Cyclopaedia of English Literature. Edin-
     burgh: William and Robert Chambers, II, 64-66, 165-67, 191.
         General account praises poetry, treats novels, with the
     exception of Humphry Clinker, generally unfavorably, and
     dismisses his histories. First of many printings: see
     1857-60, London: Chambers and 1902-4, Philadelphia: J. B.
     Lippincott.

*2   VIVOLI, GIUSEPPE. Annali di Livorno. Livorno.
         Humphry Clinker written at Villa Gamba where Smollett
     died. Cited in N&Q, 9th ser., 1 (April 11, 1898), 310.


## 1845

1    ALISON, ARCHIBALD. "British History during the Eighteenth
     Century," Blackwood's Magazine, 57 (March), 353-68.
         Smollett unqualified as a historian. Reprinted 1850.1.

2    CRAIK, GEORGE L. "Richardson, Fielding, Smollett," in Sketch-
     es of the History of Literature and Learning in England.
     London: Charles Knight, V, 155-58.
         Heightened by his talent, Smollett's novels are tran-
     scriptions of life and experience.

3    FAULKNER, THOMAS. The History and Antiquities of Brentford,
     Ealing, and Chiswick. London: Payne and Foss et al., p.
     352.
         Severe judgment of Critical Review and translation of
     Don Quixote.

4    [LYTTELTON, LORD GEORGE]. Memoirs and Correspondence of
     George, Lord Lyttelton, ed. Robert Phillmore. London:
     James Ridgeway, I, 342.
         Disapproves of Smollett's novels.

5    [MARTIN, THEODORE]. "Nights in the Martello," Tait's Edin-
     burgh Magazine, 12 (April), 239.
         Compares Dickens's and Smollett's realism.

6    WALPOLE, HORACE. Memoirs of the Reign of King George the
     Third, ed. Denis le Marchant. Philadelphia: Lea &

1846

Blanchard, I, 112 and II, 337.
Smollett a party writer in the Briton and Humphry
Clinker. Editorial notes defend Smollett.


### 1846

1   ANON. Review of Cary's Lives of the English Poets, Gentleman's Magazine, n.s. 26 (October), 347-48.
Offers a few notes of additional information.

2   CARY, HENRY FRANCIS. "Tobias Smollett," in Lives of English
Poets. London: Henry G. Bohn, pp. 119-46.
Undocumented account identifies some characters in novels, suggests parts of Fathom and Greaves are translations.
Praises Smollett's industry and grotesque characters, but
finds Humphry Clinker lacks zest of earlier novels, and
minimizes importance of Smollett's poetry. Originally published in London Magazine according to Boucé, 1971.6.

3   CHASLES, PHILARÈTE. "Fielding et Richardson," in Le Dix-
Huitième Siècle en Angleterre. Paris: Librairie D'Amyot,
I, 370-71.
Compares Smollett unfavorably with Fielding.

4   DICKENS, CHARLES. "Leghorn," in Pictures from Italy. London:
Bradbury & Evans, p. 155.
Smollett's tomb gives importance to Leghorn.


### 1847

1   HUNT, LEIGH. "A Novel Party," in Men, Women, and Books. A
Selection of Sketches, Essays, and Critical Memoirs, etc.
New York: Harper & Brothers, I, 87-101.
Smollett's characters gather at a fictional party with
those of Richardson, Fielding, and Goldsmith.

2   SANDFORD, DANIEL K. On the Rise and Progress of Literature.
Glasgow, Edinburgh, and London: Blackie & Son, p. 191.
Praises Smollett's "descriptive humour."


### 1848

1   [DE QUINCEY, THOMAS]. Review of Forster's Life of Goldsmith,
North British Review, 9 (May-August), 194.

1850

Smollett's work too brutal and coarse for nineteenth-
century audience.

2    FORSTER, JOHN.  The Life and Adventures of Oliver Goldsmith.
     London: Bradbury & Evans; Chapman & Hall, passim.  Indexed.
          Interesting facts about Smollett's publications and his
     personal and literary relationships with Goldsmith.  Many
     reprints: 1855, 1873, 1903, 1927, 1928.

3    NICHOLS, JOHN BOWYER.  Illustrations of the Literary History
     of the Eighteenth Century.  London: J. B. Nichols and Son,
     VII, 228, 268.
          Smollett's controversy with James Grainger and Thomas
     Percy.  Work is a continuation of 1828.4.

4    THACKERAY, WILLIAM MAKEPEACE.  Vanity Fair. A Novel without a
     Hero.  London: Bradbury & Evans, p. 80.
          Fictional characters (Ch. 10) compare Smollett's and
     Hume's histories and read Humphry Clinker.

1849

1    ANON.  Review of Dickens's Dombey and Son, North American Re-
     view, 69 (October), 386.
          Regrets vulgarity, but praises Smollett's novels.

2    IRVING, WASHINGTON.  Oliver Goldsmith: A Biography.  New York:
     George P. Putnam, pp. 85-87, 129.
          An expanded version of Irving's 1840 account of
     Smollett's relations with Goldsmith.  Irving regards
     Smollett as a powerful hack writer.

3    TICKNOR, GEORGE.  On Don Quixote, in History of Spanish Liter-
     ature.  New York: Harper and Brothers, III, 419, 421.
          Smollett's translation too reliant on Jarvis's and Sir
     Launcelot Greaves is a poor imitation of Don Quixote.
     Among many reprints: 1863 and 1866.

1850

1    ALISON, ARCHIBALD.  "British History during the Eighteenth
     Century," in Essays, Political, Historical, and Miscellane-
     ous.  Edinburgh and London: William Blackwood and Sons,
     pp. 322-23.
          Reprint of 1845.1.

1850

2   [CAMPBELL, THOMAS]. <u>Life and Letters of Thomas Campbell</u>, ed.
      William Beattie. London: Hall, Virtue, I, 57, 163.
        Campbell's great appreciation of Smollett's novels.

3   COOPER, J. FENIMORE. "Preface," in <u>The Red Rover</u>. New York
      and London: D. Appleton, p. vii.
        Smollett's popularity forces nautical novelists to in-
      novate.

4   HUNT, LEIGH. <u>The Autobiography of Leigh Hunt</u>. London: Smith,
      Elder, III, 126, 132-33.
        Smollett's well-written <u>Travels</u> accurate about Venus de
      Medici.

<u>1851</u>

1   ANON. "Recent Works of Fiction," <u>North British Review</u>, 15
      (August), 422, 423.
        Compares Smollett and Fielding, deplores their "indeli-
      cacy," but cites influence on Thackeray and Dickens.

2   FRANCIS, JOHN. "Old Hewson and Smollett's 'Strap,'" <u>N&Q</u>, 3
      (February 15), 123.
        Suggests Hugh Hewson, a hair-dresser, as original of
      Smollett's character in <u>Roderick Random</u>. <u>See</u> 1853.2.

3   HUNT, LEIGH. "Smollett," in <u>Table Talk</u>. London: Smith, Elder
      and Co., pp. 43-44.
        Excuses coarseness and praises Smollett's character and
      style.

4   MILLS, ABRAHAM. "Tobias George Smollett," in <u>The Literature</u>
      <u>and Literary Men of Great Britain and Ireland</u>. New York:
      Harper & Brothers, II, 514-18.
        Cannot recommend Smollett's novels because of their
      coarseness and immorality, but praises his poetry and finds
      <u>History of England</u> his most important work.

5   READE, CHARLES. <u>Peregrine Pickle: A Biographical Play</u>.
      Oxford: Henry Slatter for the Author, 78 pp.
        Closet drama based on Smollett's novel.

6   WORDSWORTH, CHRISTOPHER. <u>Memoirs of William Wordsworth</u>.
      London: Edward Moxon, II, 459.
        William Wordsworth's praise of Smollett's prose style.

1852

1   The Grenville Papers, ed. William James Smith.  London: John
    Murray, II, 270-71.
        In 1764 claims Smollett received a pension or government
    position for his political writing.

2   MASSON, DAVID.  Review of Lord Cockburn's Life of Lord
    Jeffrey, North British Review, 17 (August), 284-85.
        Smollett among illustrious Scots who affected British
    literature.  Reprinted 1856.3.

3   SHAW, THOMAS B.  "Smollett," in Outlines of English Litera-
    ture.  Philadelphia: Blanchard and Lea, pp. 266-71.
        Places Smollett below Richardson and Fielding, but
    praises use of the grotesque and narrative ability.

1853

1   COLERIDGE, SAMUEL TAYLOR.  "On the Distinctions of the Witty,
    the Droll, the Odd, and the Humorous," in The Complete
    Works of Samuel Taylor Coleridge, ed. Professor Shedd.  New
    York: Harper & Brothers, Publishers, IV, 277.
        In A Course of Lectures, 1818, the characteristics of
    humor in Smollett's characters.

2   D., H. G.  "Smollett's Strap," N&Q, 7 (March 5), 234.
        Challenges identification of Hugh Hewson as Strap.  See
    1851.2.

3   ELIOT, GEORGE.  See Evans, Mary Ann.

4   EVANS, MARY ANN.  "The Progress of Fiction as an Art," West-
    minster Review, n.s. 4 (October), 355-56.
        Deplores Smollett's coarseness as sign of lack of re-
    finement in his period.  See Eliot, George.

5   HILLARD, GEORGE STILLMAN.  "Smollett," in Six Months in Italy.
    Boston: Ticknor et al., 374-78.
        Despite vigorous style, Travels is monotonous because of
    its querulousness.  London edition by John Murray.  Earlier
    publication in 1844.

6   ROSE, HUGH JAMES.  "Smollett, (Tobias)," in A New General Bio-
    graphical Dictionary.  London: B. Fellowes et al., XII, 61-
    62.

1853

Unreliable, unfriendly, and inadequate sketch of life
and work.

7   SPALDING, WILLIAM. The History of English Literature. New
York: D. Appleton, pp. 337, 348.
Smollett's novels immoral and histories without value.

8   THACKERAY, WILLIAM MAKEPEACE. "Hogarth, Smollett, and
Fielding," in The English Humourists of the Eighteenth Century. London: Smith, Elder, pp. 242-50.
While fully appreciative of Smollett's humor and characterization, sees him as drawing wholly from experience and
without much inventive power. Numerous reprints.


1854

1   GILFILLAN, GEORGE. "Thackeray," in A Third Gallery of Portraits. Edinburgh: James Hogg; London: R. Groombridge &
Sons, pp. 273-74.
While praising Humphry Clinker, terror scene in Fathom,
and the poetry, generally low estimate of Smollett's work.

2   SMYTH, WILLIAM. "Sir Robert Walpole" and "George II," in Lectures on Modern History. London: H. G. Bohn, II, 208-9,
279.
Reprint of 1843.2.

3   STOBO, ROBERT. Memoirs of Major Stobo, of the Virginia Regi-
ment. Pittsburgh: John S. Davidson, passim.
Adventures suggesting Lismahago in Humphry Clinker.
Neville B. Craig's introduction relates the character only
vaguely to the original.


1855

1   BROUGHAM, LORD HENRY. "Robertson," in Men of Letters of the
Time of George III. Edinburgh: Adam and Charles Black, p.
246.
Robertson's low estimate of Smollett as an historian.

2   GILFILLAN, GEORGE. "Life of Tobias Smollett," in Poetical
Works of Johnson, Parnell, Gray, and Smollett. Edinburgh:
James Nichol, pp. 211-17.
Apart from Roderick Random and Humphry Clinker, poor
opinion of the novels, which, although displaying

originality, are coarse. Reprinted 1878 in Cassell's Library Edition of British Poets, London.

3  LAWRENCE, EUGENE. "Tobias Smollet [sic]," in The Lives of the British Historians. New York: C. Scribner, I, 385-95.
    Describes Smollett as a Tory and Jacobite, irascible and misanthropic, and finds novels autobiographical, coarse, and ill-natured. Condemns his carelessness as an historian.

4  LAWRENCE, FREDERICK. "Smollett and Fielding," in The Life of Henry Fielding. London: Arthur Hall, Virtue, pp. 307-11.
    Their antagonism emanated from politics and Fielding's friendships.


### 1856

1  [ADAMS, JOHN]. Works of John Adams. Boston: Little, Brown and Company, X, 80-81.
    1813 letter from Thomas McKean finds Peregrine Pickle morally instructive.

2  MACAULAY, THOMAS B. The History of England from the Accession of James II. Philadelphia: E. H. Butler, I, 279.
    Smollett's nautical characters were the rude types of his period.

3  MASSON, DAVID. "Scottish Influence in British Literature," in Essays, Biographical and Critical: Chiefly on English Poets. Cambridge: Macmillan, pp. 393-94.
    Reprint of 1852.2.

4  TALFOURD, T. NOON. "On British Novels and Romances, etc.," in Critical and Miscellaneous Writings. Boston: Phillips, Sampson, p. 7.
    Roderick Random belongs to the romance tradition.

5  [WATSON, ELKANAH]. Men and Times of the Revolution; or Memoirs of Elkanah Watson, ed. Winslow C. Watson. 2nd ed. New York: Dana, p. 474.
    Enthusiastic youthful reading of Smollett and high praise for his artistry.

## 1857

1    TOWNSEND, G. H.  "Memoirs of the Author," in The Adventures of
     Roderick Random.  London.
         Cited in 1887.1.

2    UNEDA.  "Letters from Dr. Armstrong to Smollett," N&Q, 2nd
     ser., 3 (April 25), 326-27.
         Two letters to Smollett abroad.


## 1858

1    ANON.  Review of G. S. Hillard's Six Months in Italy, Quarter-
     ly Review, 103 (April), 357.
         Smollett's Travels ill-tempered and written by a sick
     man.

2    [HANNAY, JAMES].  "Tobias Smollett," Quarterly Review, 103
     (January), 66-108.
         Sympathetic and balanced account with new information,
     particularly about Scottish background, and with compari-
     sons with work of other Scots.  Suggests originals for
     characters.  Comparison with Fielding shows Smollett's
     strengths but acknowledges his inferiority.  Reprinted in
     Living Age, n.s. 20 (March), 641-95.

3    JEAFFRESON, J. CORDY.  "Tobias Smollett," in Novels and Novel-
     ists from Elizabeth to Victoria.  London: Hurst and
     Blackett, I, 148-79.
         Strongly compassionate account applauds his courage and
     honesty and presents balanced view of the novels.  Although
     rating him below Fielding, praises abilities to entertain
     and lauds Humphry Clinker.

4    MAHON, LORD.  See Stanhope, Philip Henry Stanhope, 5th Earl.

5    [SCHIMMELPENNINCK, MARY ANNE].  Life of Mary Anne
     Schimmelpenninck, ed. Christiana C. Hankin.  London:
     Longman et al., I, 12.
         Smollett's corrupting influence on youthful readers.

6    STANHOPE, PHILIP HENRY STANHOPE, 5th EARL.  "Novel-Reading,"
     in History of England, from the Peace of Utrecht to the
     Peace of Versailles.  5th ed.  London: John Murray, VII,
     324-25.
         Smollett licentious.  See Mahon, Lord.

## 1859

1  IRVING, JOSEPH. <u>Some Account of the Family of Smollett of</u>
   <u>Bonhill</u>. Dumbarton: for the Author, 24 pp.
       For a description of this rare work, <u>see</u> 1879.3.

2  M.4. "Thomas Maude," <u>N&Q</u>, 2nd ser., 8 (November 12), 407.
       Are Maude and his patron, Duke of Bolton, depicted in
   Smollett's novels? See 1862.4.

3  MASSON, DAVID. "Novels of the Eighteenth Century," <u>in</u> <u>British</u>
   <u>Novelists and Their Styles</u>. Boston: Gould and Lincoln, pp.
   111-14, 134-51.
       General sketch compares Smollett to contemporaries, par-
   ticularly Fielding to whom he is remarkably similar. Re-
   fuses to rate Smollett beneath Fielding and prefers both
   for their strong masculinity to Richardson. Published in
   Cambridge: Macmillan, pp. 104-7, 128-45.

4  [SARGENT, W.]. "Some Inedited Memorials of Smollett," <u>Atlan-</u>
   <u>tic Monthly</u>, 3 (June), 693-703.
       Maintains Smollett's continued and deserved popularity
   despite coarseness and presents, annotates, and analyzes
   Smollett's letter to Richard Smith and letters to and about
   Smollett.

5  THOMSON, JOHN. <u>An Account of the Life, Lectures, and Writings</u>
   <u>of William Cullen, M.D.</u> Edinburgh: W. Blackwood, I, passim. Indexed.
       Smollett's relations with doctors, particularly John
   Hunter.

## 1860

1  CARLYLE, ALEXANDER. <u>Autobiography</u>, ed. John Hill Burton.
   Edinburgh: Blackwood, pp. 186, 189-91, 264-66, 337-40, 346-
   47, 358.
       Personal reminiscences of Smollett in Scotland and
   London, which give some insight into his personality, temperament, and beliefs. Reprinted 1861.3, 1910.4. New
   edition 1973.11.

2  TAYLOR, TOM. "Introduction," in <u>Autobiographical Recollec-</u>
   <u>tions of the Late Charles Robert Leslie, R.A.</u> London: John
   Murray, I, lxv-lxvi, lxxvi.
       On Leslie's painting of "The Reading of the Will Scene
   in <u>Roderick Random</u>" (1846).

## 1861

1   ANON. Review of Carlyle's Autobiography, Edinburgh Review,
       113 (January), 166-67, 175.
          Smollett less important than Hume and ludicrous in pre-
       siding over a levee of hack writers.

2   ANON. "Boswell, Soame Jenyns, Lyttelton, and Smollett," N&Q,
       2nd ser., 12 (July 20), 48.
          Question and answer on Smollett's parody of Lyttelton.

3   Autobiography and Correspondence of Mary Granville, Mrs.
       Delany, ed. Lady Augusta Waddington Hall Llanover.  London:
       Richard Bentley, II, 6, 7; III, 16, 34, 216, 220, 223.
          Generally unfavorable comments on Smollett's novels, but
       approves of his intentions in Ferdinand Count Fathom.

4   CARLYLE, ALEXANDER. Autobiography, ed. John Hill Burton.
       Boston: Ticknor and Fields, pp. 152, 154-56, 215-16, 275-
       76, 282, 291.
          Reprint of 1860.1.  American edition.

5   [MONTAGU, LADY MARY WORTLEY]. The Letters and Works of Lady
       Mary Wortley Montagu, ed. Lord Wharncliffe.  Third edition.
       London: Henry G. Bohn, 2 Vols., passim.  Indexed.
          Various responses to Smollett's novels.  For modern edi-
       tion, see 1965.25.

## 1862

1   BEWICK, THOMAS. A Memoir of Thomas Bewick.  Newcastle-on-
       Tyne: Jane Bewick; London: Longman et al., p. 86.
          Love of Smollett's work and anecdote about occurrence
       at his monument.

2   HUNT, LEIGH. The Correspondence of Leigh Hunt, ed. Thornton
       Leigh Hunt.  London: Smith, Elder, I, 80-81, 148; II, 83.
          Dislikes Travels and coarseness, but praises Smollett's
       honesty and independence, Roderick Random, and terror
       scenes in Ferdinand Count Fathom.

3   L., A. "Shebbeare, Smollett, and Lady Vane," N&Q, 3rd ser.,
       1 (March 22), 232.
          Questions and comments on relationship of the trio to
       Peregrine Pickle.  Provides information on John Hill and
       Daniel McKercher.

4   OXONIENSIS. "Thomas Maude," N&Q, 3rd ser., 2 (September 6),
     198.
         Maude the original of Capt. Whiffle in Roderick Random.
     Response to 1859.2.

5   SOUTHEY, ROBERT. The Doctor, ed. J. W. Warter.  London:
     Longman et al., p. 45.
         Humorous praise for Smollett.

6   THOMSON, KATHERINE. "Tobias Smollett," in The Literature of
     Society. London: Tinsley Brothers, II, 249-54.
         Sympathetic to Smollett the man, but criticizes the
     work, except for Humphry Clinker, for its coarseness.  Sees
     it as autobiographical.  See Wharton, Grace.

7   WHARTON, GRACE.  See Thomson, Katherine.


                              1863

1   ANDERSON, WILLIAM. "Smollett," in The Scottish Nation, etc.
     Edinburgh and London: A. Fullarton, III, 483-85.
         Highly laudatory account provides bibliographical and
     genealogical materials.  Reprinted 1880.1.

2   TAINE, H. "Les Romanciers," in Histoire de la Littérature
     Anglaise.  Paris: Librairie de l'Hachette et Cie, III, 319-
     24.
         Savage attack on Smollett's work as coarse, vulgar, un-
     imaginative, and offensive to French readers.  Trans. H.
     Van Laun in 1871, Edinburgh: Demonston and Douglas, II,
     176-79.

3   THACKERAY, WILLIAM MAKEPEACE. "De Juventute," in Roundabout
     Papers.  New York: Harper & Brothers, p. 105.
         Childhood reading of Roderick Random and Peregrine
     Pickle.  Originally published in Cornhill Magazine.


                              1864

1   DE L'ISLE, H. "Tobie Smollett," L'Intermédiaire des Chercheurs
     et Curieux, 1 (November 20), 308.
         Was Smollett author of a travel book with prophecy of
     revolution?  See 1864.4.

1864

2  [JAMES, HENRY].  Review of Senior's Essays on Fiction, North
   American Review, 205 (October), 585.
      Characteristics of Smollett's fiction.

3  LYTTON, EDWARD BULWER.  Comparison of Smollett and Fielding,
   in Caxtoniana: A Series of Essays on Life, Literature, and
   Manners.  New York: Harper & Brothers, pp. 391-92.
      Praises Smollett, but finds him inferior to Fielding and
   with limited influence.

4  MASSON, G. et al.  "Tobie Smollett," L'Intermédiaire des Chercheurs et Curieux, 1 (December 20), 364-65.
      Five replies (by Masson, T. de L., B. R., A. H. H., J.
   D.) to 1864.1 indicate considerable knowledge of Smollett
   and his work.


                              1865

1  ANON.  Review of Taine's History of English Literature, Edinburgh Review, 121 (April), 319.
      Strongly critical of Taine's attack on Smollett.

2  K.  "Smollett's Characters," N&Q, 3rd ser., 8 (November 11),
   393.
      Recalls character key to Roderick Random and Peregrine
   Pickle and seeks information on them and Advice and Reproof.

3  KNIGHT, CHARLES.  "Andrew Millar; Cadell and Strahan," in
   Shadows of the Old Booksellers.  London: Bell and Daldy,
   pp. 222-23.
      Failure of Complete History and subsequent tying of for-
   tunes of Continuation to Hume's work.

4  KNIGHT, CHARLES.  "The Third Epoch," in Passages of a Working
   Life during Half a Century.  London: Bradbury & Evans, III,
   12.
      Laments passing of interest in Roderick Random.

5  MARRYAT, FREDERICK.  The Dog Fiend; or, Snarleyyow.  New ed.
   London: George Routledge and Sons, p. 12.
      Smollett's portrait of naval life historically accurate.

6  TAYLOR, BAYARD.  "On Leven's Banks," in Views A-Foot; or
   Europe Seen with Knapsack and Staff.  New York: G. P.
   Putnam et al., p. 45.

On neglect of Smollett's monument and local associations with Smollett.

7  TURNER, CHARLES EDWARD.  "Our First Novelists," in Our Great Writers.  St. Petersburg: A. Münx, II, 147-49.
   Compares Smollett unfavorably with Fielding and criticizes formlessness, derivativeness, and coarseness.


1867

1  C., R.  "Smollett's Humphry Clinker," N&Q, 3rd ser., 11 (June 15), 491.
   Suggests Mr. R--- C--- in Humphry Clinker was Robert Cullen.  See 1867.2.

2  C., X.  "Humphry Clinker," N&Q, 3rd ser., 11 (May 4), 353-54.
   Asks identity of Mr. R--- C--- in Humphry Clinker.  See 1867.1.

3  CHAMBERS, ROBERT.  Smollett: His Life and a Selection from His Writings.  London and Edinburgh: W. & R. Chambers, vi + 221 pp.
   Enthusiastic account presents much information not in Moore and Anderson, stressing importance of Scots background, analyzing all the novels, and offering considerable detail on other publications.  Prints memoir from a manuscript of Sir James Smollett, novelist's grandfather, and material from Smollett's putative prophecy.  Reprinted 1956.3.

4  MARTIN, THEODORE.  "Early Taste for Reading," in Memoir of William Edmonstoune Aytoun.  Edinburgh and London: William Blackwood and Sons, p. 11.
   Aytoun's childhood delight in reading Humphry Clinker despite mother's protests.


1868

1  ANON.  "Don Quixote," Westminster and Foreign Quarterly Review, 89 (April 1), 299-327.
   Smollett grossly vulgarized Cervantes's work by introducing spirit of Le Sage in his translation and by depending upon a corrupt French text.  Popularity of Smollett's translation injured reputation of the original in England.

1868

2   RATHERY, E. J. B.   "Smollett (Tobias-George)," in Nouvelle
      Biographie Générale, ed. Hoefer.   Paris: Firmin Didot
      Frères, Fils et Cie, XLIV, 82-83.
         Accurate for its time sketch, using Plays and Poems,
      Scott, and Anderson.

3   WRIGHT, THOMAS.   Caricature History of the Georges.   London:
      J. C. Hotten, pp. 211, 217, 233, 264, 271-73, 283, 287-88.
         Revision of England under the House of Hanover (1848)
      discusses Smollett chiefly as a periodical writer and an
      object of satire in contemporary prints and literature.


                            1869


1   ANON.   "A Nocturnal Adventure," in Episodes of Fiction; or,
      Choice Stories from the Great Novelists, with Biographical
      Introductions.   New York: Virtue & Yorston, p. 73.
         Introduces episode from Peregrine Pickle with conven-
      tional praise in general account of Smollett and his work.

2   CRAIK, GEORGE L.   "Richardson. Fielding. Smollett," in A Com-
      pendious History of English Literature.   New York: Charles
      Scribner's Sons, II, 296-98.
         Smollett's novels, depending on autobiographical reali-
      ty, are strong in humor, weak in craftsmanship, and coarse.

3   [HUTTON, R. H.].   "Mr. Dickens's Moral Services to Litera-
      ture," Spectator, 42 (April 17), 475.
         Compares Smollett, Swift, and Fielding, whose coarseness
      was a natural part of their art.


                            1870


1   HERBERT, DAVID.   "Life of Tobias George Smollett," in The
      Works of Tobias Smollett.   Edinburgh: William P. Nimmo, pp.
      7-40.
         Vigorous and entertaining account makes use of earlier
      biographies, but seriously attempts to separate fact from
      legend.   Without overpraising Smollett, evaluates writing
      in its own terms, eschewing customary comparison with
      Fielding, and, while making customary comments about epi-

sodic plots, discounts the coarseness in Smollett's realism. Particularly admires Humphry Clinker. Reprinted in
1871, 1873, 1874, 1883.

2   PROWSE, W. J.   "Smollett at Nice," Macmillan's Magazine, 21
      (April), 527-33.
         Faults in Smollett's Travels are superficial, the result
      of illness and Philistinism. Although coarse, the work is
      honest, precise, and, apart from aesthetic judgment, per-
      ceptive in its observations.

3   [ROBINSON, HENRY CRABB]. Diary, Reminiscences, and Corres-
      pondence of Henry Crabb Robinson, ed. Thomas Sadler.
      Boston: Fields, Osgood, I, 308; II, 114.
         Ranks Smollett outside the classics of Richardson and
      Fielding.


                              1871

1   COLLIER, WILLIAM FRANCIS.   "Tobias Smollett," in A History of
      English Literature in a Series of Biographical Sketches.
      London, Edinburgh, New York: T. Nelson and Sons, pp. 316-
      20.
         Stresses coarseness and rates him below Richardson and
      Fielding, but praises nautical characters and Humphry
      Clinker.

2   ELIOT, GEORGE.   See Evans, Mary Ann.

3   EVANS, MARY ANN.   "Chapter XXX," in Middlemarch. A Study of
      Provincial Life. Edinburgh and London: William Blackwood
      and Sons, II, 113.
         Fictional character praises humor and light reading of
      Roderick Random and Humphry Clinker. See Eliot, George.

3   FORSYTH, WILLIAM.   "Chapter IX," in The Novels and Novelists
      of the Eighteenth Century. New York: D. Appleton, pp. 278-
      303.
         Coarse and vulgar, Smollett fails to relate humorous
      scenes to any development in his novels. While Humphry
      Clinker is his most entertaining work, it is a travelogue
      with a dull story. Reprinted 1970.16.

1871

5    JAMES, HENRY.  "A Passionate Pilgrim," <u>Atlantic Monthly</u>, 27
     (March), 364.
         Fictional character puns on Smollett's picaresque char-
     acters.


<u>1872</u>

1    BROWNE, JAMES P.  "Preface," in <u>The Works of Tobias Smollett,</u>
     <u>M.D.</u>  London: Bickers and Son et al., I, v-xxxviii.
         Balanced evaluation makes continued comparisons with
     Fielding, but not to diminish Smollett's achievement.  Sur-
     veys prior criticism and presents John Moore's work (pp.
     73-152).

2    CHAMBERS, WILLIAM.  "Efforts at Self-Education," in <u>Memories</u>
     <u>of the Chambers Brothers</u>, ed. Derek Maggs.  London: Galahad
     Press, p. 24.
         Reprints parts of 1872.3.

3    CHAMBERS, WILLIAM.  <u>Memoir of Robert Chambers with Autobio-</u>
     <u>graphic Reminiscences of William Chambers</u>.  Edinburgh and
     London: W. & R. Chambers, pp. 61, 103-4.
         On the success and general appeal of Smollett's work in
     the nineteenth century.  Reprinted in New York: Scribner et
     al., pp. 55, 95.  Reprinted in part 1872.2.

4    CLARKE, CHARLES COWDEN.  "On the Comic Writers of England,"
     <u>Gentleman's Magazine</u>, n.s. 8 (May), 563, 565-75.
         Compares Smollett's humor with Fielding's wit.  Objects
     to Smollett's vulgarity and coarseness, but praises style,
     <u>Roderick Random</u>, Gothic scenes in <u>Fathom</u>, and character of
     Lismahago in <u>Humphry Clinker</u>.

5    CLEVELAND, CHARLES D.  "Tobias Smollet [<u>sic</u>], 1721-1771," in
     <u>A Compendium of English Literature</u>.  New York and Chicago:
     A. S. Barnes, pp. 606-8.
         Praises poetry, attacks histories, and finds novels li-
     centious, applauding decline in their popularity.

6    FIELDS, JAMES T.  <u>Yesterdays with Authors</u>.  Boston: James R.
     Osgood, p. 239.
         Dickens's preference of Smollett over Fielding.

7    WILSON, DANIEL.  <u>Memorials of Edinburgh in the Olden Time</u>.
     Second edition.  Edinburgh: Thomas C. Jack; London:
     Simpkin, Marshall, pp. 199, 289.

Smollett's 1766 visit to Edinburgh and effect on Humphry Clinker.

## 1873

1   COPPÉE, HENRY. "Tobias George Smollett," in English Literature, Considered as an Interpretation of English History. Second edition. Philadelphia: Claxton et al., pp. 292–95.
Uninformative, derivative account stresses historical value of the novels.

2   FORSTER, JOHN. The Life of Charles Dickens. Philadelphia: J. B. Lippincott, I, 128; III, 22.
Attributes Smollett's realism to autobiography and notes influence of Peregrine Pickle on Pickwick.

3   HANNAY, JAMES. "Sea Novels—Captain Marryat," Cornhill Magazine, 27 (February), 171–76.
Smollett, father of nautical novel, used autobiographical material and picaresque for Roderick Random and Peregrine Pickle.

4   MORLEY, HENRY. "From Anne to Victoria," in A First Sketch of English Literature. London: Cassell, pp. 832–38.
Comparison with Fielding finds Smollett inferior, but important to development of the novel.

## 1874

1   BASCOM, JOHN. "The Novelists," in Philosophy of English Literature. New York: G. P. Putnam's Sons, p. 199.
Smollett's coarse and grotesque work a low point in English literature.

2   DUANE, WILLIAM. "Letter of Smollett," N&Q, 5th ser., 1 (May 16), 384.
Replies to American Richard Smith (1763) about his work.

3   FORSTER, JOHN. The Works and Life of Walter Savage Landor. London: Chapman and Hall, I, 499.
1856 comment on dissatisfaction with Humphry Clinker.

4   [GRANVILLE, A. B.]. Autobiography of A. B. Granville, M.D., F.R.S., ed. Paulina B. Granville. London: Henry S. King, I, 273.

1874

        Appreciates depiction of nautical life in Roderick Random.

5    WORDSWORTH, DOROTHY. Recollections of a Tour Made in Scotland, ed. J. C. Shairp. 2nd ed. New York: G. P. Putnam's Sons, p. 63.
        Smollett's memorial and Coleridge's criticism of its Latin inscription.

1875

1    [MACREADY, WILLIAM CHARLES]. Macready's Reminiscences, ed. Frederick Pollack. New York: Harper & Bros., p. 316.
        Describes painting of scene from Roderick Random (1845).

2    PRÖHLE, HEINRICH. "Die Büchse," Archiv für Litteraturgeschichte, 4 (1875), 344.
        Quotes poem praising Peregrine Pickle above German novels.

3    SMITH, GEORGE BARNETT. "Tobias Smollett," Gentleman's Magazine, n.s. 14 (May), 729-37.
        Despite coarseness, Smollett superior to Richardson and just below Fielding, rates along with Dickens and Le Sage. Praises poetry, but will not overrate it.

1876

1    DORAN, JOHN. "Smollett in Italy," in "Mann" and Manners at the Court of Florence, 1740-1786. London: Richard Bentley and Son, II, 217-18.
        Describes final days and calls novels "anything but works of fiction."

2    GIBSON, T. H. "Smollett at Chelsea," London Magazine, 2 (1876), 98-103.
        Cited in 1887.1.

3    STEPHEN, LESLIE. History of English Thought in the Eighteenth Century. New York: G. P. Putnam's Sons, I and II, passim. Indexed.
        Generally unfavorable comments on Smollett's art and thought.

4    TREVELYAN, GEORGE OTTO. The Life and Letters of Lord Macaulay. New York: Harper & Brothers, I, 198-99, 293; II, 37, 267.

Severe comment on Smollett's histories and other references. Published in London by Longman's, Green: I, 216,
328; II, 35-36, 316. Reprints in 1878 and 1909.

5   WILSON, JAMES GRANT. "Tobias G. Smollett," in The Poets and
    Poetry of Scotland. New York: Harper & Brothers, I, 201-3.
    General account lavishly praises poetic talent.


## 1877

1   [BROWNING, ELIZABETH BARRETT]. Letters of Elizabeth Barrett
    Browning Addressed to Richard Hengist Horne, ed. S. R.
    Townshend Mayer. London: Richard Bentley and Son, I, 242.
    Victor Hugo's influence on Dickens neglected because of
    stress given to Smollett's (1844 letter).

2   GRIMM, FRIEDRICH MELCHIOR. Correspondance Littéraire, Philo-
    sophique et Critique, ed. Maurice Tourneux. Paris: Garnier
    Frères, II, 267; IV, 177, 472; V, 189; VII, 241; VIII, 93;
    X, 14.
    Unfavorable comments on Smollett's novels (particularly
    their coarseness and vulgarity) and his History of England.

3   [HOLMES, OLIVER WENDELL]. "Reflections," Scribner's Monthly,
    14 (August), 446-48.
    Verse criticism of Peregrine Pickle.

4   [MARTINEAU, HARRIET]. Harriet Martineau's Autobiography, ed.
    Maria Weston Chapman. London: James R. Osgood, II, 326.
    Revolted by Smollett's work.

5   STEPHENS, FREDERICK GEORGE. Catalogue of Prints and Drawings
    in the British Museum Division I. Political and Personal
    Satires. London: By Order of the Trustees, III, IV, pas-
    sim.
    Describes satiric prints involving Smollett, particular-
    ly in connection with the Briton.


## 1878

1   L'ESTRANGE, A. G. "Smollett," in History of English Humour.
    London: Hurst and Blackett, II, 123-26.
    Smollett lacks genuine humor and work is coarse, inde-
    cent, and violent. Nautical material best because auto-
    biographical.

1878

2   WILSON, DANIEL. <u>Reminiscences of Old Edinburgh</u>. Edinburgh:
      David Douglas, I, 233–34, 237–41.
          Describes Smollett's stay in Edinburgh in 1766 and pur-
      ported real persons in <u>Humphry Clinker</u>.


1879

1   [DICKENS, CHARLES]. <u>The Letters of Charles Dickens</u>, ed. His
      Sister-in-Law and His Eldest Daughter. New York: Charles
      Scribner's Sons, I, 26, 416–17.
          1839 and 1854 letters indicate fondness for Smollett and
      place <u>Humphry Clinker</u> first.

2   FITZPATRICK, W. J. <u>The Life of Charles Lever</u>. London:
      Chapman and Hall, I, 317; II, 194–95.
          Suggestive comparison of lives and works of Smollett and
      Lever.

3   IRVING, JOSEPH. "Family of Smollett of Bonhill," in <u>The Book
      of Dumbartonshire</u>. Edinburgh and London: W. and A. K.
      Johnston, II, 175–208.
          In addition to family genealogy to early sixteenth cen-
      tury, comments favorably on novels, despite their coarse-
      ness, corrects earlier biographies, and describes portraits
      of Smollett. Reprints 1859.1, which appeared in second
      edition in 1860.

4   TROLLOPE, ANTHONY. "Novel-Reading," <u>The Nineteenth Century</u>,
      5 (January), 30.
          Smollett less gifted and coarser than Fielding.


1880

1   ANDERSON, WILLIAM. "Smollett, Dr. Tobias George," in <u>The
      Scottish Nation</u>. Edinburgh and London: A. Fullarton, pp.
      483–85.
          Reprint of 1863.1.

2   ANON. Smollett Letter, <u>Athenaeum</u>, 1 (1880), 578.
          1750 letter to Francis Hayman on difficulty producing
      <u>The Regicide</u>.

3   DOBSON, AUSTIN. "An Inedited Letter from Smollett," <u>N&Q</u>, 6th
      ser., 1 (April 24), 330.
          Comment on Smollett's <u>Travels</u> and 1763 letter to
      Alexander Reid on his poor health.

## 1881

1  ANON.  A Reading Diary of Modern Fiction.  New York: F.
   Leypoldt, p. 13.
      Smollett's novels for mature readers only.

2  BELJAME, ALEXANDRE.  Le Public et les Hommes de Lettres en
   Angleterre au Dix-Huitième Siècle.  Paris: Librairie
   Hachette et Cie, passim.
      Uses Humphry Clinker in discussing authorship in the
   eighteenth century.  Second edition in 1897 adds index.
   Trans. 1948.2.

3  CONWAY, MONCURE D.  Thomas Carlyle.  New York: Harper & Brothers, pp. 31-32.
      Carlyle's delight in Smollett's novels.

4  DeQUINCEY, THOMAS.  The Works of Thomas DeQuincey.  Globe Edition.  Boston: Houghton, Mifflin, III, 617-18; V, 348.
      Berates Smollett's indecency and bestiality, but notes
   Wordsworth's enjoyment of his novels.

5  RAMSAY, JOHN.  "Armstrong and Smollett," in Scotland and
   Scotsmen in the Eighteenth Century, ed. Alexander Allardyce.
   Edinburgh and London: William Blackwood and Sons, I, 311-
   12.
      Smollett a "naturalised Englishman."  Note states that
   Ramsay wrote part of inscription for Smollett's monument.

## 1882

1  The Friendships of Mary Russell Mitford as Recorded in Letters
   from Her Literary Correspondents, ed. A. G. L'Estrange.
   New York: Harper & Brothers, p. 409.
      Smollett among few fiction writers pleasing to Mitford's
   father's good taste.

2  GRANT, JAMES.  Cassell's Old and New Edinburgh.  London,
   Paris, Melbourne: Cassell, 3 Vols., passim.  Indexed.
      Describes Smollett, wife, and sister and background ma-
   terial for Humphry Clinker.  Engraving of house where
   Smollett stayed in 1766.

3  [HOOD, THOMAS].  The Works of Thomas Hood, ed. His Son and
   Daughter.  London: Ward, Lock, & Co., VII, 3; X, 21, 351,
   377.
      Hood's favorable comments on Smollett in the 1840s.

1882

4   ROSIÈRES, RAOUL.  "La Littérature Anglaise en France de 1750
    à 1800," Revue Politique et Littéraire de la France et de
    l'Étranger, 3rd ser., 4 (August 12), 237.
        Peregrine Pickle among important novels translated into
    French in 1750s.

5   TUCKERMAN, BAYARD.  "Smollett," in A History of English Prose
    Fiction from Sir Thomas Malory to George Eliot.  New York:
    G. P. Putnam's Sons, pp. 211-17.
        Major interest in Smollett's coarse picaresque novels is
    historical.

6   WARD, ADOLPHUS WILLIAM.  "The Future of Dickens's Fame," in
    Dickens.  English Men of Letters, ed. John Morley.  New
    York: Harper & Brothers, pp. 196-98.
        Although admiring and using Smollett's work, Dickens
    wrote more in Fielding's manner.

1883

1   FILON, AUGUSTIN.  "Roderick Random, et l'Oeuvre de Smollett,"
    in Histoire de la Littérature Anglaise.  Paris: Librairie
    Hachette et Cie, pp. 376-78.
        Unfavorable comparison with Fielding that praises only
    Humphry Clinker.

2   LANIER, SIDNEY.  The English Novel and the Principle of Its
    Development.  New York: Charles Scribner's Sons, pp. 177-
    79.
        Sketchy account of Smollett's works ignores Sir
    Launcelot Greaves, deplores his coarseness, but admires
    Humphry Clinker.

3   MORRISON, J. COTTER.  Macaulay.  New York: Harper & Brothers,
    p. 172.
        Macaulay's pleasure in reading Smollett's novels.

4   NICOLL, HENRY J.  "Tobias Smollett," in Landmarks of English
    Literature.  London: John Hogg, pp. 222-29.
        Smollett had little inventiveness and created from per-
    sonal experience.  Yet grudgingly expresses admiration for
    him and his work, particularly nautical characters and
    poetry.

5   PERRY, THOMAS SERGEANT.  English Literature in the Eighteenth
    Century.  New York: Harper & Brothers, pp. 144, 217, 351.

Praises realism and cites views on poor authors and the Gothic.

6    SIGMA.  "Tobias Smollett," N&Q, 7th ser., 5 (January 21), 58.
       Possible genealogy of Smollett family.

7    WERSHOVEN, F. J.  Smollett et Lesage.  Berlin: n.p., 33 pp.
       Detailed account of Smollett's use of Lesage's work in
       novels.


                                1884

1    COOPER, SUSAN FENIMORE.  "Introduction," in J. F. Cooper's The
       Pilot.  Boston and New York: Houghton, Mifflin, p. xiv.
       Reports Cooper's discussion of Smollett as a nautical
       novelist.

2    GROOME, FRANCIS H.  "Bonhill," in Ordnance Gazeteer of Scot-
       land.  Edinburgh: Thomas C. Jack, I, 173-74.
       Connection of Smollett family to town in Dumbartonshire.

3    HAWTHORNE, JULIAN.  Nathaniel Hawthorne and His Wife.  Boston
       and New York: Houghton, Mifflin; Riverside Press,
       Cambridge, I, 105.
       1819 Hawthorne letter on reading Roderick Random and
       Fathom.

4    MACLEOD, DONALD.  "Tobias George Smollett, M.D." and "Vale of
       Leven Poets," in Dumbarton, Vale of Leven and Lochlomond:
       Historical, Legendary, Industrial, and Descriptive.
       Dumbarton: Bennett & Thomson; Glasgow: John Menzies, et al.,
       pp. 98-102 and 158-59.
       Memorial poem, details of his youth and his memorial,
       and praise for "Dumbarton's foremost literary man."

5    NASH, JAMES.  Guide to Nice.  London: n.p., p. 110.
       Praises description of Nice in Smollett's Travels.

*6   PROESCHOLDT, L.  "Einleitung," in T. G. Smollets Werke.
       Stuttgart: W. Spemann, I.
       Cited in 1935.5.

7    [WRAXALL, NATHANIEL WILLIAM].  Historical and Posthumous Mem-
       oirs of Sir Nathaniel William Wraxall, 1772-1784, ed. Henry
       B. Wheatley.  New York: Scribner and Welford; London:
       Bickers and Son, I, 37.
       Places Smollett in second line of novelists.

## 1885

1    ANDERSON, P. J.  "Smollett's Medical Degree," N&Q, 6th ser.,
     11 (June 20), 487.
     Marischal College and University, Aberdeen, lists
     Smollett's degree in 1750.

2    BABEAU, ALBERT.  "Un Anglais de Mauvaise Humeur--Smollett," in
     Les Voyageurs en France.  Paris: Didier et Cie, pp. 212-34.
     Despite Smollett's unfairness and exaggeration in his
     Travels, finds him a talented writer whose views are worth
     having.

3    MORLEY, HENRY.  "Introduction," in El Ingenioso Hidalgo Don
     Quixote de la Mancha.  London: George Routledge and Sons,
     p. xix.
     Smollett's translation drawn from Motteux's.

4    WARD, C. A.  "Query," N&Q, 6th ser., 12 (October 31), 349.
     Asks for documentation of Smollett's residence in May-
     fair, 1746.

5    WELSH, CHARLES.  "Smollett and the British Magazine," in A
     Bookseller of the Last Century.  London: Griffith et al.,
     pp. 39-40.
     Smollett's editing, his character, and relations with
     Goldsmith.

6    WILLIS, NATHANIEL PARKER.  "Love in the Library," in Prose
     Writings of Nathaniel Parker Willis, ed. Henry A. Beers.
     New York: Charles Scribner's Sons, p. 31.
     Fictional character in Edith Linsey describes attrac-
     tions of Peregrine Pickle to boys of 14.

## 1886

1    ANON.  "The Growth of the English Novel," Quarterly Review,
     163 (July), 34-64.
     Compares Smollett to major contemporaries, and praises
     his style and diversified portraits of life, but objects
     to his coarseness.

2    [CARLYLE, THOMAS].  Early Letters of Thomas Carlyle, ed.
     Charles Eliot Norton.  London and New York: Macmillan, pp.
     23, 68, 193.

In 1815, 1818, and 1822 comments on caricature of Akenside in Peregrine Pickle and poor continuation of Hume's history.

3    GRIFFINHOOFE, HARRY G.  "Smollett," N&Q, 7th ser., 1 (February 27), 178.
     Evidence for Smollett residences in 1744, 1746.  See 1885.4.

## 1887

1    ANDERSON, JOHN P.  "Bibliography," in David Hannay, Life of Tobias George Smollett, 1887.4, pp. i-x.
     List of Smollett's works--six sections.  Secondary works on biography, criticism, etc.  Chronological list of Smollett's Works.  Reprinted 1970.2.

2    BOURNE, H. R. FOX.  "Wilkes and Junius," in English Newspapers. Chapters in the History of Journalism.  London: Chatto & Windus, I, 154-62.
     Denigrates Smollett's political journalism in his Briton.

3    GILCHRIST, ANN.  Her Life and Writings, ed. Herbert H. Gilchrist.  London: T. Fisher Unwin, p. 63.
     Carlyle's delight in Roderick Random.

4    HANNAY, DAVID.  Life of Tobias George Smollett.  Great Writers, ed. Eric C. Robertson.  London: Walter Scott, 163 pp.
     Part of renewed interest in Smollett, Hannay's biography suffers somewhat from Victorian attitudes and emphasis on autobiographical character of Smollett's fiction, but offers important material on naval background, particularly the expedition to Carthagena, in Smollett's novels.  Includes Anderson's bibliography, 1887.1.  Reprinted 1971.28.

5    LEE, WILLIAM.  "Roderick Random in the North," Monthly Chronicle of North-Country Lore and Legend, 1 (October), 340-43.
     Smollett drew almost wholly from life and Roderick Random, Peregrine Pickle, and Matt Bramble were self-portraits.

6    MINTO, WILLIAM.  "Smollett, Tobias George (1721-71)," in Encyclopaedia Britannica.  9th ed.  Edinburgh: Adam and Charles Black, XXII, 183-85.

1887

        Follows Walter Scott and offers very favorable account of Smollett's work, finding his influence greater than Fielding's.

7    ORMSBY, JOHN. "Introduction," in The Ingenious Gentleman Don Quixote of La Mancha by Miguel de Cervantes Saavedra. New York: Dodd, Mead, I, 9.
        Smollett's translation taken largely from Jarvis's.

8    STEBBING, WILLIAM. "The Eighteenth Century," in Some Verdicts of History Reviewed. London: John Murray, pp. 6–7.
        Regrets circumstances that forced Smollett to do hack work.

9    STEVENSON, ROBERT LOUIS. "The English Admirals," in Virginibus Puerisque and Other Papers. 2nd ed. New York: Charles Scribner's Sons, p. 183.
        Smollett's powerful portrait of naval life in Roderick Random. Original in 1881.

10    WOLCOTT, FRED. "Tobias Smollett, M.D.," N&Q, 7th ser., 4 (December), 507.
        Announces preparation of a Smollett edition.

11    WOTTON, MABEL E. "Tobias Smollett," in Word Portraits of Famous Writers. London: Richard Bentley & Son, pp. 289–90.
        Quotes three sources on his physical characteristics.

## 1888

1    ANON. Review of Hannay's Life of Smollett, Athenaeum, no. 3189 (December 8), pp. 767–69.
        Ranks Smollett high among his contemporaries and attributes his coarseness to his times.

2    DUNLOP, JOHN C. History of Fiction. London: George Bell and Sons, II, 320, 478, 575–76.
        Reprints 1814.5. Adds note on influence of Lesage.

3    EVERITT, GRAHAM. See Richardson, William Rodgers.

4    FITZ-PATRICK, W. J. "Tobias Smollett," N&Q, 7th ser., 5 (February 18), 133.
        Obituary notice from Dublin Pantheon (1809) on Hugh Hewson, supposed original of Strap in Roderick Random.

5   FRITH, W. P.  "Subjects from Goldsmith, Smollett, and
    Molière," in My Autobiography and Reminiscences.  New York:
    Harper & Brothers, pp. 146-47.
        Roderick Random as source for one of his paintings.

6   GOSSE, EDMUND.  "Smollett," in A History of Eighteenth Century
    Literature.  London and New York: Macmillan, pp. 258-64.
        Smollett's journalistic novels fail to engage the read-
    er.  Their characters are unamiable, plots disorganized,
    and manner coarse.  Praises parts of Peregrine Pickle, all
    of Humphry Clinker, and stresses influence on Dickens.

7   MACDONNELL, JOHN.  "The King against Edmonds and Others," in
    Reports of State Trials, N.S. (1820-1858).  London: n.p.,
    I, Cols. 785-948.
        Speech for radical defendant uses Smollett as an author-
    ity for support of his position.

8   PERA, FRANCESCO.  Curiosità Livornesi Inedite o Rare.  Livorno:
    R. Giusti, p. 316.
        Account of Smollett's death.

9   [RAMSAY, JOHN].  "Armstrong and Smollett," in Scotland and
    Scotsmen in the Eighteenth Century from the Mss. of John
    Ramsay, ed. Alexander Allardyce.  Edinburgh and London:
    William Blackwood and Sons, I, 311-12.
        Despite feeling for Scotland, Smollett more English
    than Scottish.

10  RICHARDSON, WILLIAM RODGERS.  "Doctors and Patients: An Essay
    on 'Humbug,'" in Doctors and Doctors: Some Curious Chapters
    in Medical History and Quackery.  London: Swan Sonnenschein,
    Lowrey, pp. 280-84.
        Too proud and intellectually superior to succeed in
    practice, Smollett expresses his disappointment in angry
    and accurate, if exaggerated, portraits of doctors.  See
    Everitt, Graham.

11  SEILHAMER, GEORGE O.  History of the American Theatre: Before
    the Revolution.  Philadelphia: Globe Printing House, p.
    154.
        Performance of The Reprisal in Pennsylvania in 1767.

12  [SHARPE, CHARLES KIRKPATRICK].  Letters from and to Charles
    Kirkpatrick Sharpe, Esq., ed. Alexander Allardyce.  Edin-
    burgh and London: William Blackwood and Sons, II, 518.
        1839 letter berates immorality in Smollett's novels,
    except Humphry Clinker.

1888

13 WATTS, HENRY EDWARD. "Introduction," in <u>The Ingenious Gentle-</u>
<u>man Don Quixote of La Mancha by Miguel de Cervantes</u>
<u>Saavedra</u>. London: Bernard Quaritch, I, 12-13.
    Smollett's translation a derivative hack job, but praise
for <u>Humphry Clinker</u> and suggestion of affinity to Cervantes.


<u>1889</u>

1 BAGEHOT, WALTER. "The Waverley Novels," in <u>Works of Walter</u>
<u>Bagehot</u>, ed. Forrest Morgan. Hartford: Travelers Insurance
Company, II, 199.
    Smollett, a panoramic novelist, attempts a broad de-
scription of life. Originally in <u>National Review</u> (April,
1858).

2 [BURNEY, FANNY]. <u>The Early Diary of Frances Burney 1768-1778</u>,
ed. Annie Raine Ellis. London: George Bell and Sons, I,
94, 275n.; II, 231.
    Fanny dislikes Smollett's style and language in his <u>His-</u>
<u>tory</u>, and Charles Burney attacks his grossness as a novel-
ist.

3 CLEMENS, SAMUEL L. <u>A Connecticut Yankee in King Arthur's</u>
<u>Court</u>. New York: Charles L. Webster, p. 56.
    <u>Roderick Random</u> reflects low morality and conduct of its
period. <u>See</u> Twain, Mark.

4 FITZ-PATRICK, W. J. "Strap in <u>Roderick Random</u>," <u>N&Q</u>, 7th
ser., 8 (November 9), 377.
    Repeats identification (1888.4) of Hewson as Strap.

5 FURNIVALL, F. J. "Strap in <u>Roderick Random</u>," <u>N&Q</u>, 7th ser.,
8 (November 2), 348.
    Cites Obituary Notice in <u>Annual Register</u> (1772, p. 166)
identifying Duncan Rivers as Strap.

6 [HONE, PHILIP]. <u>The Diary of Philip Hone</u>, ed. Bayard
Tuckerman. New York: Dodd, Mead, I, 353-54; II, 17.
    Comments of 1839 and 1840 on paintings using Smollett's
work as subject and on decline of his reputation.

7 MARTIN, BENJAMIN ELLIS. <u>Old Chelsea. A Summer-Day's Stroll</u>.
London: T. Fisher Unwin, pp. 24, 80, 94, 138-42.
    Smollett's residence and experiences in Chelsea.

8 S., S. "Strap in <u>Roderick Random</u>," <u>N&Q</u>, 7th ser., 8 (December 14), 475.

Supports claim that Hewson was Strap and presents a key to other characters.

9  SCHUYLER, EUGENE. "Smollett in Search of Health," in Italian Influences. New York: Charles Scribner's Sons, pp. 220-44.
Regrets neglect of the Travels. Despite some coarseness, Smollett was an entertaining, informative, accurate, and commonsensical observer whose aesthetic judgments are independent and honest. Printed, too, in The Nation, 48 (May 23), 423-25 and (May 30), 444-45. Reprinted 1901.4.

10  TWAIN, MARK. See Clemens, Samuel L.


## 1890

1  BARRIE, J. M. "Brought Back from Elysium," Contemporary Review, 57 (June), 846-54.
Smollett's ghost among a group of literary figures debating the characteristics of the novel.

2  CARNARVON, EARL OF. "Memoir of Lord Chesterfield," in Letters of Philip Dormer Fourth Earl of Chesterfield to His Godson and Successor. Oxford: Clarendon Press; New York: Macmillan and Co., p. xxxviii, n.1.
Smollett no longer of interest as a literary figure.

3  PEET, WILLIAM H. "Booksellers' Sales in the Eighteenth Century," N&Q, 7th ser., 9 (April 19), 301-2.
Sales prices for copyrights to Peregrine Pickle and Roderick Random in 1766.

4  PÉRONNE, JOHANNES. Über Englische Zustände im XVIII. Jahrhundert nach den Romanen von Fielding und Smollett. Berlin: W. & S. Loewenthal, 51 pp.
Comparison of the political and social portraits and attitudes in the works of the two novelists. Comment on Smollett restricted to Roderick Random.

5  TELFER, J. BUCHAN. "Smollett's Death and Burial," N&Q, 7th ser., 9 (May 24), 408.
Offers some putative information, but asks for documentation.

## 1891

1  ALLIBONE, S. AUSTIN. "Smollett, Tobias Goerge, M.D.," in
   Critical Dictionary of English Literature and British and
   American Authors. Philadelphia: J. B. Lippincott, II,
   2165-67.
       Unfriendly account of Smollett's work. Includes primary
   and secondary bibliographical material.

2  [AMES, NATHANIEL, Father and Son]. The Essays, Humor and
   Poems of Nathaniel Ames, Father and Son, of Dedham, Massachusetts, from their Almanacks 1726-1775, ed. Sam Briggs.
   Cleveland: n.p., pp. 391, 399.
       Almanack for 1768 uses Smollett's Travels for humorous
   comment on American customs.

3  ANON. "Smollett in the South," All the Year Round, 68 (May
   2), 420-24.
       Smollett's Travels truly informative, scholarly, and
   generally temperate considering discomforts he encountered.

4  BAYNE, THOMAS. "Smollett and Dibdin," N&Q, 7th ser., 12 (September 12), 205.
       Parallel death scenes in Charles Dibdin's Tom Bowling
   and Smollett's Peregrine Pickle.

5  PEACH, R. E. M. Bath, Old and New. London: Simpkin,
   Marshall; Bath: G. Mundy, pp. 231-34.
       Assuming 1761 publication date insists Bath portions of
   Humphry Clinker are autobiographical and attributes
   Smollett's hostility to political opposition to Fielding
   and Ralph Allen.

6  REPPLIER, AGNES. "Fiction in the Pulpit," in Points of View.
   Boston and New York: Houghton, Mifflin. Riverside Press,
   Cambridge, pp. 109-10.
       Scoffs at notion of moral purpose in Humphry Clinker.

7  WHEATLEY, HENRY B. and PETER CUNNINGHAM. London Past and
   Present. Its History, Associations, and Traditions.
   London: John Murray, I, 380, 439, 520.
       Places associated with Smollett.

1892

1   ANDERSON, P. J. "Aberdeen University Graduates: Arbuthnot,
    Smollett, Wolcot," <u>Scottish Notes and Queries</u>, 6 (Decem-
    ber), 107.
       Smollett's M.D. at Marischal College and University,
    1750.

2   ANON. "Smollett in the South," <u>Living Age</u>, 5th ser., 77
    (February 20), 507-10.
       Same as 1891.3.

3   BEAVER, ALFRED. <u>Memorials of Old Chelsea: A New History of
    the Village of Palaces</u>. London: Elliot Stock, pp. 90-92,
    236, 252, 302.
       Smollett's friendships, experiences, and writing in
    Chelsea.

4   BLACK, WILLIAM GEORGE. "Smollett's <u>Roderick Random</u>," <u>N&Q</u>,
    8th ser., 2 (December 10), 463-64.
       Argues that Duncan Niven was the original of Strap.

5   CESARESCO, COUNTESS EVELYN MARTINENGO. "Introduction," in
    <u>Glimpses of Italian Society in the Eighteenth Century.
    From the "Journey" of Mrs. Piozzi</u>. London: Seeley, p. 2.
       Smollett's <u>Travels</u> of no consequence.

6   DICKENS, CHARLES. <u>The Works of Charles Dickens</u>. Roxburgh
    Edition. Boston: Estes & Lauriat, XVI, iv-v; XXXVI, 80-81,
    92, 134-35, 242; XXXIX, 178-80.
       Dickens and his fictional characters in <u>Nicholas
    Nickleby</u> (1838-39), <u>David Copperfield</u> (1849-50), and the
    <u>Uncommercial Traveller</u> (1860-68) indicate their familiarity
    and identification with Smollett's work.

7   DOBSON, AUSTIN. "Old Vauxhall Gardens," in <u>Eighteenth Cen-
    tury Vignettes</u>. New York: Dodd, Mead, p. 232.
       Smollett's treatment of Vauxhall in <u>Humphry Clinker</u>.

8   HUTTON, LAURENCE. "Tobias Smollett," in <u>Literary Landmarks
    of London</u>. 8th ed. New York and London: Harper & Broth-
    ers, pp. 280-82.
       Relationship of places to Smollett's life and work.
    First edition in 1885.

9   LEE, A. COLLINGWOOD. "Goethe and Smollett," <u>N&Q</u>, 8th ser.,
    2 (December 31), 533.

1892

No resemblance between the Smollett and Goethe passages
cited by Moseley in 1892.13.

10   MASSON, DAVID.  "Literary History of Edinburgh," in Edinburgh
Sketches & Memories.  London and Edinburgh: Adam and
Charles Black, p. 425.
Considers Smollett an emigre writer in England rather
than a Scot.

11   MAYHEW, A. L.  "The Pseudo-Smollett," Academy, 42 (October 8),
313-14.
Describes modern editions of Gil Blas ascribed as
Smollett translations, but actually the inferior work of
Benjamin Heath Malkin.

12   [MORRISON, ALFRED].  Catalogue of the Collection of Autograph
Letters and Historical Documents Formed between 1865 and
1882 by Alfred Morrison.  London: n.p., VI, 146-47.
Describes 1753 editorial contract of Smollett and prints
(with facsimile) 1754 letter to Dr. George Macaulay.

13   MOSLEY, B. D.  "Goethe and Smollett," N&Q, 8th ser., 2 (December 10), 466.
Smollett as a source for Goethe.  See 1892.9.

14   RICHARDSON, ABBY SAGE.  "The Novelists Smollett and Sterne,"
in Familiar Talks on English Literature.  Chicago: A. C.
McClurg, p. 304.
Smollett coarse, but praised by Dickens.

15   STEPHEN, LESLIE.  "Fielding's Novels" and "Sterne," in Hours
in a Library.  London: Smith, Elder, II, 177-79, 201-2;
III, 151.
Compares Smollett unfavorably with Fielding and Dickens
and disparages his Travels.

16   SYDNEY, WILLIAM CONNOR.  England and the English in the Eigh-
teenth Century.  London: Ward & Downey.  2 Vols., passim.
Indexed.
Smollett's work as illustrative of fashions and manners.


1893

1   CRAWFORD, F. MARION.  The Novel: What It Is.  New York:
Macmillan, p. 38.
Women embarrassed by Peregrine Pickle, but not at the
same thing in French.

2   ESPINASSE, FRANCIS. <u>Literary Recollections and Sketches</u>. New
    York: Dodd, Mead, p. 227.
        Carlyle's delight in Smollett for whom a good biography
    is needed.

3   GRIFFINHOOFE, H. G. "Smollett's <u>Roderick Random</u>," <u>N&Q</u>, 8th
    ser., 3 (January 7), 12.
        Lewis, a Chelsea bookbinder, not Duncan Niven, was
    Strap.

4   HIPWELL, DANIEL. "The Widow of Tobias Smollett, M.D. (1721–
    1771)," <u>N&Q</u>, 8th ser., 4 (November 25), 426.
        <u>London Chronicle</u> notice of 1782 on her need for funds.

5   MOSELEY, B. D. "Goethe and Smollett," <u>N&Q</u>, 8th ser., 3 (Janu-
    ary 21), 55–56.
        Reasserts Smollett as source. <u>See</u> 1892.9 and 13.

6   ORMSBY, JOHN. "Introduction," in <u>The Ingenious Gentleman Don
    Quixote of La Mancha by Miguel de Cervantes Saavedra</u>. New
    York: Harvard Publishing Company, I, Part 1, p. 9.
        Smollett's translation based on Jarvis's.


<u>1894</u>

1   ANON. "Sir Walter Scott," <u>Scottish Review</u>, 23 (1894), 227.
        Speaks of "prurient incidents in Smollett's career."

2   DOBSON, AUSTIN. "The Topography of <u>Humphry Clinker</u>," and
    "Ranelagh," in <u>Eighteenth Century Vignettes. Second
    Series</u>. New York: Dodd, Mead, pp. 138–67, 281–82.
        Condemns Smollett's coarseness, but tours places visited
    in <u>Humphry Clinker</u>, and praises "Ode to Leven Water."

3   GLAISTER, JOHN. <u>Dr. William Smellie and His Contemporaries</u>.
    Glasgow: Maclehose, pp. 111–18.
        Smollett's relations with Smellie, particularly his
    <u>Treatise on Midwifery</u>.

4   KNIGHT, JOSEPH. <u>David Garrick</u>. London: Kegan Paul, Trench,
    Trübner, passim. Indexed.
        Smollett's reciprocation for Garrick's generosity in
    producing <u>The Reprisal</u>. Reprinted in New York in 1969.

5   PROTHERO, ROWLAND E. with G. G. BRADLEY. "School Prizes," in
    <u>The Life and Correspondence of Arthur Penrhyn Stanley</u>.

1894

New York: Charles Scribner's Sons, I, 65.
Thomas Arnold's great fondness for Humphry Clinker.

6   RALEIGH, WALTER.  "The Eighteenth-Century Novel," in The
    English Novel.  London: John Murray, pp. 183-90.
        Regarding Smollett's works as based on experience rather
    than literary sources for their picaresque romances, finds
    them without the intellectual qualities or artistic skills
    of Fielding's novels.

7   RANDALL, JOHN.  "Smollett's Humphry Clinker," N&Q, 8th ser.,
    6 (December 22), 486-87.
        Supports Humphry as proper spelling of character's name.

8   SAUNDERS, BAILEY.  Life and Letters of James Macpherson.
    London: Swan Sonnenschein; New York: Macmillan, pp. 214-16,
    224, 236.
        Poorly informed comments on Smollett's journalism and
    histories.


                              1895

1   COLLINS, JOHN CHURTON.  "Lord Chesterfield's Letters," in
    Essays and Studies.  London and New York: Macmillan, pp.
    210-12.
        Rebukes Lord Carnarvon's judgment that Smollett's repu-
    tation is negligible and argues about reason for quarrel
    with Chesterfield.  See 1890.2.

2   [EDGEWORTH, MARIA].  Life and Letters of Maria Edgeworth, ed.
    Augustus J. C. Hare.  Boston and New York: Houghton,
    Mifflin, II, 371, 373.
        1821 letters compare J. F. Cooper and Smollett and com-
    ment on Smollett's ill-natured Travels.

3   ISAACS, J. H.  "Life of Smollett," in Roderick Random.  Bohn's
    Novelist's Library.  London: G. Bell & Sons, pp. i-xv.
        Brief laudatory description of Smollett and bibliograph-
    ical notes on his works and specific bibliography of
    Roderick Random.  Reprints in 1911, 1915.

4   PEACH, R. E. M.  The Life and Times of Ralph Allen.  London:
    D. Nutt, p. 221.
        Smollett's perceptive and accurate views of evils of
    Bath.

5   RANDALL, JOHN.  "Smollett's Death," N&Q, 8th ser., 8 (December
    7), 446.
        Prints obituary notices from London Evening-Post and
    Westminster Journal and London Political Miscellany, which
    disagree on date and place of death.

6   SAINTSBURY, GEORGE.  "Introductions," in The Works of Tobias
    Smollett.  12 Vol.  London: Gibbings, I, xi-xxxvii; IV, xv-
    xxiii; VIII, xi-xix; X, ix-xvi; XI, vii-xvi.
        Introductions to each of Smollett's five novels.  That
    for Roderick Random gives general account of his life and
    work as well as particular discussion of the novel.  Ap-
    plies customary Victorian values to Smollett and his work--
    deploring coarseness and vulgarity, comparing him unfavor-
    ably with Fielding, stressing use of autobiographical ma-
    terial, and praising only abilities as a story-teller and
    painter of grotesque characters.  Reprints in 1900, 1902,
    1928.  See reprint in 1925.9.

7   SWALLOW, J. ALBERT.  "Tobias Smollett," in Methodism in the
    Light of the English Literature of the Last Century.
    Erlangen and Leipzig: A. Diechert'sche Verlagsbuchhe, pp.
    146-51.
        Smollett's treatment of Methodism in Humphry Clinker,
    the History and Adventures of an Atom, and the Travels.


                              1896

1   DUNCAN, ALEXANDER.  Memorials of the Faculty of Physicians and
    Surgeons of Glasgow, 1599-1850.  Glasgow: Maclehose, p.
    120.
        Record of Smollett's apprenticeship as a surgeon.

2   JUSSERAND, J. J.  "Smollett," in Histoire Abrégee de la Lit-
    térature Anglaise.  Paris: Librairie Ch. Delagrave, pp.
    203-4.
        Smollett vindictive and mean-spirited; novels are weakly
    picaresque.

3   NICKLIN, J. A.  "An Eighteenth Century Saga," Gentleman's
    Magazine, 280 (May), 453-58.
        Although acknowledging Fielding's superiority, argues
    for Smollett's merits in characterization, action, and
    realism, and questions failure to resurrect his reputation
    in a period that has overcome its objections to coarseness.

## 1897

1    CAINE, HALL. "A Recollection," in My First Book. London: Chatto & Windus, p. 65.
      Reading Smollett's novels aloud with D. G. Rossetti.

2    CARLYLE, THOMAS. Sartor Resartus in Works. London: Chapman and Hall, I, 140.
      Character comments on Smollett's ironical description of ending war.

3    DUFFIELD, PITTS. "Tobias George Smollett (1721-1771)," in Warner's Library of the World's Best Literature. New York: The International Society, Vol. 34, 13575-79.
      An overrated novelist, a competent hack-writer without originality, who, like a reporter, draws on own experience.

4    LANG, ANDREW. The Life and Letters of John Gibson Lockhart. London: J. C. Nimmo; New York: C. Scribner's Sons, I, 72-73, 78.
      Praises opening of Roderick Random and contrasts treatment of nautical characters with neglect of clerical characters.

5    LANG, ANDREW. Pickle the Spy or the Incognito of Prince Charles. London, New York, Bombay: Longman's, Green, pp. 24, 147, 164 and passim.
      Smollett's Jacobitism and his appeal to Scots who used names of his heroes as aliases.

6    MALCOLM, ALEXANDER. "Letter XIII," in Letters of an Invalid from Italy, Malta, and the South of France. London: William Clowes & Sons, pp. 156-58.
      On Smollett's residence in Leghorn and high praise for his genius.

7    MEREDITH, GEORGE. An Essay on Comedy and the Uses of the Comic Spirit. New York: Charles Scribner's Sons, p. 89.
      Comic quality of the supper scene in Peregrine Pickle.
   First published in New Quarterly Magazine, April, 1877.

*8    SCHWINGER, RICHARD. Friedrich Nicolais Roman "Sebaldus Northanker," Literarhistorische Forschungen, 2 (1897), xiv + 272 pp.
      Includes Smollett's influence on Nicolais. Cited in 1932.22.

9    SMEATON, OLIPHANT. Tobias Smollett. Famous Scots Series.
     New York: Charles Scribner's Sons, 156 pp.
         Popular and sympathetic biographical and critical ac-
     count, which offers no authentication of its material and
     may indeed be inventive in some of its details. Stressing
     Smollett's integrity and independence (though besmirched
     by political journalism), argues strongly against the no-
     tion that his art is limited to merely copying from life or
     dependent on autobiographical material for its effective-
     ness.


                              1898


1    ANDERSON, PETER JOHN. Fasti Academiae Mariscallanae Aberdon-
     ensis. Aberdeen: New Spalding Club, II, 116.
         For "Doctors of Medicine," June, 1750, Smollett listed
     as novelist and historian.

2    [BYRON, LORD GEORGE GORDON]. The Works of Lord Byron, ed.
     Ernest Hartley and Rowland E. Prothero. Revised edition.
     London: John Murray. Poetry, II, 40, 203; VI, 210. Let-
     ters and Journals, I, 198; II, 155, 248; III, 172; IV, 153,
     276, 366, 381; V, 25, 216; VI, 156.
         Comments by Byron from 1808 to 1822 and in Childe Harold
     and Don Juan indicate his familiarity with and admiration
     for Smollett's poetry and novels and his use of Smollett's
     example as authority for frank expression.

3    CARLYLE, THOMAS. History of Friedrich II. of Prussia, Called
     Frederick the Great. London: Chapman and Hall, IV, 187-88,
     191-92, 386.
         Admires Smollett and his nautical characters and his
     personal toughness. Uses fictional character of
     "Smelfungus" as a commentator. Originally published in
     1858-65.

4    CARMICHAEL, MONTGOMERY. "Smollett: His Death and Burial,"
     N&Q, 9th ser., 1 (April 16), 309-11.
         Horace Mann's date of Smollett's death (September 17,
     1771) is accurate and he died at Villa Gamba at Antignano
     and is buried in Leghorn.

5    [HANNAY, DAVID]. "Smollett and the Old Sea-Dogs," Blackwood's
     Magazine, 164 (August), 231-43.
         Despite caricature, Smollett's portrait of nautical life
     is faithful to reality. Compares it with other fiction and
     factual accounts. Reprinted 1910.10.

1898

6    KENT, WILLIAM.  <u>Memoirs and Letters of James Kent, Ll.D.</u>
     Boston: Little, Brown, p. 240.
        High praise for Smollett's novels.

7    SECCOMBE, THOMAS.  "Smollett, Tobias George," in <u>Dictionary of</u>
     <u>National Biography</u>, ed. Sidney Lee.  New York: Macmillan
     Company; London: Smith, Elder, LIII, 174-84.
        Sympathetic account of life and writing, using original
     material and presenting a detailed primary and secondary
     bibliography.

8    TELFER, J. BUCHAN.  "Smollett, His Death and Burial," <u>N&Q</u>, 9th
     ser., 1 (March 12), 201-2.
        Questions date of death and place of burial.

9    [WHITEFOORD, CALEB].  <u>The Whitefoord Papers</u>, ed. W. A. S.
     Hewins.  Oxford: Clarendon Press, pp. 132, 148-49.
        William Burnet's 1757 letter describes savage reviewing
     methods of the <u>Critical</u> and 1770 Smollett letter concerns
     politics.


                              1899

1    CROSS, WILBUR L.  "Tobias Smollett," in <u>The Development of the</u>
     <u>English Novel</u>.  New York and London: Macmillan, pp. 63-69
     and passim.
        Compares Smollett and Fielding's work; discusses pica-
     resque and realism in the novels.  Stresses importance of
     Smollett's nautical characters and notes influence on
     Gothic and romances.

2    GRAHAM, HENRY GREY.  <u>The Social Life of Scotland in the Eigh-</u>
     <u>teenth Century</u>.  London: Adam and Charles Black, I, 44,
     112; II, 208-9.
        Smollett's observations on contemporary life.

3    HENLEY, W. E.  "Introduction," in <u>The Works of Tobias Smollett</u>.
     Westminster: Archibald Constable and Co.; New York: Chas.
     Scribner's Sons, I, v-xlviii.
        Severe criticism.  Derivative biographical material
     attacks Smollett's pride, scurrility, and temper.  Treat-
     ment of his writing praises only as prelude to rebuke--
     stressing its farcical and coarse characteristics, mocking
     Roderick and Peregrine as ruffians, and reserving approval
     largely for realizing characterization through dialogue.
     Work includes bibliographical accounts by Thomas Seccombe.
     Reprinted without changes in 1921.

4   SECCOMBE, THOMAS. "Tobias Smollett," in <u>The Age of Johnson</u>.
    Handbooks of English Literature, ed. Hales. London: George
    Bell and Sons, pp. 131-32, 170-78, passim.
        General account marvels at Smollett's energy, style, ob-
    servation, and eccentric characterizations, but regrets the
    brutality of early novels. Finds <u>Humphry Clinker</u> his mas-
    terpiece and compares him favorably with Fielding.

5   TEXTE, JOSEPH. <u>Jean-Jacques Rousseau and the Cosmopolitan
    Spirit in Literature</u>, tr. J. W. Matthews. London:
    Duckworth & Co.; New York: Macmillan Company, passim.
    Indexed.
        Uncongeniality of Smollett's writing for the French.

*6  WILSON, FRANK. "Dickens in Seinen Beziehungen zu den Humoris-
    ten Fielding und Smollett." Diss., Leipzig, 1899.
        Cited in McNamee, <u>Dissertations in English and American
    Literature</u>.


                              <u>1900</u>

1   ANON. "Musings without Method," <u>Blackwood's Magazine</u>, 167
    (May), 697-99.
        Inferior to Fielding and mercenary, Smollett wrote in a
    lively style, dealt with harsher aspects of reality, and
    offered effective dialogue.

2   FLETCHER, W. J. "The Traditional 'British Sailor,'" <u>The Nine-
    teenth Century</u>, 48 (September), 423-35.
        Entertaining nautical portraits fail to probe inner
    reality of Smollett's characters.

3   [GRAY, THOMAS]. <u>The Letters of Thomas Gray Including the Cor-
    respondence of Gray and Mason</u>, ed. Duncan C. Tovey.
    London: George Bell and Sons, I, 92, 212, 285; II, 7, 302.
        Letters and notes comment generally unfavorably on
    Smollett's work.

4   HAWTHORNE, NATHANIEL. <u>The Writings of Nathaniel Hawthorne</u>.
    Boston and New York: Houghton, Mifflin. The Riverside
    Press, Cambridge, XI, 353-54; XXI, 183; XXII, 410.
        <u>Our Old Home</u> (1860-63) deplores moral climate in the
    England of Smollett's novels; <u>Notes of Travel</u> (1858 and
    1860) describes Hawthorne's reading of <u>Roderick Random</u> and
    his visit to Smollett's grave in Leghorn.

1900

5   LOCKHART, JOHN G.  Memoirs of Sir Walter Scott.  London and
        New York: Macmillan, I, 30; V, 354.
            Scott's reading of Smollett's work and concern about
        manner of his death.

6   STODDARD, FRANCIS HOVEY.  The Evolution of the English Novel.
        New York: Macmillan, passim.  Indexed.
            Relates Smollett's novels to eighteenth-century realis-
        tic concerns.


                            1901

1   FOX, R. HINGSTON.  William Hunter, Anatomist, Physician, Ob-
        stetrician (1718-1783) etc.  London: H. K. Lewis, pp. 45,
        48.
            Smollett's role as author of works for John and William
        Hunter.

2   LANG, ANDREW.  "Smollett," Anglo-Saxon Review, 9 (June), 123-
        38.
            Stresses Smollett's use of autobiographical material and
        ascribes limitations to Smollett's Scottishness, tempera-
        ment, and circumstances.  Dislikes coarseness, saving kind
        words for Humphry Clinker, which presents Smollett's admir-
        able side.  Reprinted 1905.3.

3   SCHNEIDER, ARNO.  "Smollett," in Die Entwickelung des Seero-
        mans in England im 17. und 18. Jahrhundert.  Leipzig:
        Druck Von August Pries, pp. 27-54.
            Analyzes techniques, particularly of characterization,
        in Roderick Random and Peregrine Pickle, which are related
        to Smollett's nautical experiences.

4   SCHUYLER, EUGENE.  "Smollett in Search of Health," in Italian
        Influences.  New York: Charles Scribner's Sons, pp. 220-44.
            Reprint of 1889.9.

5   SCUDDER, HORACE ELISHA.  James Russell Lowell.  Boston and New
        York: Houghton, Mifflin, Riverside Press, Cambridge, I, 32.
            Lowell's Familiarity with Smollett's works.

6   SECCOMBE, THOMAS.  "Smelfungus Goes South," Cornhill Magazine,
        n.s. 11 (August), 192-210.
            Intelligent appraisal of Smollett's abilities as a
        travel writer compares his works to Fielding's, Johnson's,
        and Sterne's and defends it against criticism of Walpole
        and Sterne and charges against his aesthetic judgment.

Sees relationship of Travels and Humphry Clinker as third
stage of Smollett's artistic development.

7    WILLIAMS, C. F. ABDY.  Handel.  London: J. M. Dent and Sons,
     passim.  Indexed.
         Smollett's relations with Handel.


<u>1902</u>

1    ANON.  "Tobias George Smollett," The Practitioner, 68 (Febru-
     ary), 195-98.
         Unsympathetic account notes points of medical interest.
     Reprinted in part 1906.1.


2    ANON.  One Hundred Books Famous in English Literature.  New
     York: The Grolier Club of the City of New York, pp. 112-13.
         Thackeray quotation and title-page facsimile of Humphry
     Clinker.


*3   BRANDL, LEOPOLD.  Engels "Herr Lorenz Stark" and Smollett's
     Humphrey [sic] Clinker.  Prog. Wien, 22 pp.
         Smollett's influence.  Cited in 1932.22.


4    BURTON, RICHARD.  "The Vigorous Dr. Smollett," The Dial, 32
     (February 1), 81-83.
         Henley's edition indicates change of taste.  Smollett
     still readable and an important influence on development of
     the novel.


5    DOBSON, AUSTIN.  "The Covent-Garden Journal," in Side-Walk
     Studies.  London: Chatto and Windus, passim.  Indexed.
         Antagonistic literary relations of Smollett and
     Fielding.


6    ELWIN, WHITWELL.  Some XVIII Century Men of Letters, ed.
     Warwick Elwin.  London: John Murray, II, 146, 179, 340,
     341, 344, 349, 351, 355.
         Smollett's relationships to Grub St. and contemporaries.


7    MAYNADIER, G. H.  "Introductions," in The Works of Tobias
     Smollett.  Cambridge, Mass.: University Press; Boston: Old
     Corner Bookstore.  John Wilson and Son, I, xv-xxvii; IV,
     xv-xxviii; VIII, xiii-xxi; X, xi-xviii; XI, vii-xxi.
         Dismissing History of an Atom as filth, provides back-
     ground and discussion for other five novels, disapproving
     generally the coarseness, citing relationships to autobio-
     graphical details, noting picaresque weaknesses in

1902

structure of early work, praising characterization.
Humphry Clinker best; Fathom poorest, but interesting for
romantic characteristics and improvement in technique.
Favorable comment for Launcelot Greaves. Reprinted in
1905, 1907, 1908, 1911.

8    MILLAR, J. H. "Smollett," in The Mid-Eighteenth Century.
Periods of European Literature, IX, ed. George Saintsbury.
New York: Charles Scribner's Sons, pp. 157-62 and passim.
Very unfavorable, although acknowledging gift for cari-
cature and praising Humphry Clinker.

9    MÖBIUS, HANS. "The Adventures of Ferdinand Count Fathom," in
The Gothic Romance. Leipzig: Grimme & Trömel, pp. 14-18.
As an introduction to the genre in the eighteenth cen-
tury.

10   PASTON, GEORGE. See Symonds, Emily Morse.

11   PEARCE, J. W. "Otway's Orphan: Smollett's Count Fathom," MLN,
17 (November), 230.
Cites similarities and suggests Otway as source.

12   POE, EDGAR ALLAN. "Marginalia," in Complete Works of Edgar
Allan Poe, ed. James A. Harrison. New York: Thomas Y.
Crowell, XVI, 62.
Smollett's use of vulgar colloquialism.

13   SYMONDS, EMILY MORSE. "The Monthly Review," in Side-Lights
on the Georgian Period. London: Methuen, pp. 148, 154-55.
Antagonism between Griffiths's Monthly and Smollett's
Critical Review. See Paston, George.


1903

1    ANON. "Doctors in British Fiction," British Medical Journal,
1 (January 3), 40-41.
Smollett's caricature of the medical profession in his
novels.

2    BAYNE, THOMAS. "Squire Gawkie," N&Q, 9th ser., 12 (September
12), 205.
James Buchanan original of Gawkie in Roderick Random.

3    BECKER, GUSTAV. "Die Bedeutung des Wortes 'romantic' bei
Fielding und Smollett," Archiv für das Studium der Neuren

Sprachen und Litteraturen, n.s. 10 (March), 56-66.
Smollett's use of and attitude toward the term romantic.

4   BESANT, WALTER. London in the Eighteenth Century. London:
    Adam & Charles Black; New York: Macmillan, pp. 113, 297,
    366, 404, 597.
    Smollett's observations on London life and experiences
    there.

5   BUTLER, SAMUEL. The Way of All Flesh. London: Grant
    Richards, passim.
    Several references to Smollett's fiction.

6   KENT, HENRY W. "Tobias George Smollett," in Bibliographical
    Notes on One Hundred Books Famous in English Literature.
    New York: The Grolier Club of the City of New York, pp.
    130-31.
    Bibliographical details and publisher's account book on
    first edition of Humphry Clinker.

7   [LAMB, CHARLES and MARY LAMB]. The Works of Charles and Mary
    Lamb, ed. E. V. Lucas. London: Methuen, I, 83; II, 61,
    173; V, 75; VI, 209.
    Charles Lamb's favorable comments, from 1801 to 1833, on
    Smollett's work in essays, poetry, and letters.

8   LEUSCHEL, MAX. Autobiographisches in Smollett's "Roderick
    Random". Inaugural-Dissertation. Leipzig: Buchdruckerei
    von Heinrich John, 75 pp.
    Believes Smollett's works profited from use of autobio-
    graphical material and systematically investigates rela-
    tionships of details of his life to development of events
    and characters in Roderick Random.

9   MILLAR, J. H. A Literary History of Scotland. London: T.
    Fisher Unwin, passim. Indexed.
    Unfavorable comments or limited praise--finds few Scot-
    tish elements in Smollett's work.

10  PEMBERTON, T. EDGAR. The Life of Bret Harte. London: C.
    Arthur Pearson, pp. 4-5.
    Smollett's novels part of Harte's childhood reading.

11  [RUSKIN, JOHN]. The Works of John Ruskin, ed. E. T. Cook and
    Alexander Wedderburn. London: George Allen; New York:
    Longmans, Green, I, 417-18; V, 374; XII, 119; XXVII, 619;
    XXXV, 144; XXXVI, 431.

1903

> From earliest letters and publications, displays close familiarity with Smollett's work, but is appalled by its soulless, indecent portrayal of characters and episodes.

12  WALPOLE, HORACE.  The Letters of Horace Walpole, Fourth Earl of Orford, ed. Mrs. Paget Toynbee.  Oxford: Clarendon Press, IV, 236, 263; VI, 257; VII, 372; VIII, 184.
    Letters of 1759, 1765, 1770, and 1772 express hostility to Smollett, his criticism, politics, and history.

## 1904

1  BARBEAU, A.  "Authors at Bath," in Life & Letters at Bath in the XVIIIth Century.  London: William Heinemann; New York: Dodd, Mead, pp. 186-202 and passim.
    Smollett's treatment of Bath in his works is misanthropic, coarse, brutal, and pessimistic and creates a false picture.  Compares Smollett's description with that of other writers.  Published in French: Paris: Alphonse Picard & Fils.

2  [COWPER, WILLIAM].  The Correspondence of William Cowper, ed. Thomas Wright.  London: Hodder and Stoughton, III, 262.
    1788 letter praises Smollett's translation of Don Quixote.

3  LOWELL, JAMES RUSSELL.  The Complete Writings of James Russell Lowell.  Boston and New York: Houghton, Mifflin, The Riverside Press, Cambridge, I, 161; VII, 164; XV, 154.
    Journals, lectures, and letters show familiarity and fondness for Smollett's work, though deploring its coarseness.

4  [SHARPE, CHARLES KIRKPATRICK].  Letters of Sir Walter Scott and Charles Kirkpatrick Sharpe to Robert Chambers etc., ed. C. E. S. Chambers.  Edinburgh: W. & R. Chambers, pp. 20-23.
    In 1824 Sharpe offers anecdotes and information about Smollett and his family and models for characters in Humphry Clinker.

5  STEPHEN, LESLIE.  English Literature and Society in the Eighteenth Century.  London: Gerald Duckworth, pp. 148-49.
    Smollett an elevated hack-writer.

## 1905

1    FITZMAURICE-KELLY, JAMES.  "Cervantes in England," <u>Proceedings of the British Academy</u>, 11 (1905), 16-18.
     Smollett's imitations of <u>Don Quixote</u> are inferior, but preface to his translation is important.

2    HUME, MARTIN.  <u>Spanish Influence on English Literature</u>.
     London: Eveleigh Nash, pp. 181-82.
     Praises Smollett's scholarship in his translation of <u>Don Quixote</u> and notes his importance for the picaresque in English.

3    LANG, ANDREW.  "Smollett," in <u>Adventures among Books</u>.  London, New York, Bombay: Longmans, Green, pp. 173-210.
     Reprint of 1901.2.

4    NEWCOMER, ALPHONSO GERALD.  "Smollett," in <u>English Literature</u>.
     Chicago, Atlanta, New York: Scott, Foresman, pp. 201-3.
     Objects to coarseness and brutality, but praises nautical characters and <u>Humphry Clinker</u>.

5    SMYTH, ALBERT HENRY.  "Introduction," in <u>The Writings of Benjamin Franklin</u>, ed. A. H. Smyth.  London and New York: Macmillan, I, 171.
     Franklin's writing sometimes even coarser than Smollett's.

6    THAYER, HARVEY WATERMAN.  <u>Laurence Sterne in Germany</u>.  New York: Columbia University Press, passim.  Indexed.
     Comments on German responses comparing Sterne and Smollett.

## 1906

1    ANON.  "Some Medical Worthies of Bath," <u>The Practitioner</u>, 76 (January), 115.
     Smollett's temperament and "Essay on the External Use of Water" led to departure from Bath.  Reprints part of 1902.1.

2    BECKER, GUSTAV.  "Tobias Smollett," in <u>Die Aufnahme des Don Quijote in die Englische Literatur (1605-c.1770)</u>.  Berlin: Mayer & Müller, pp. 19-23.
     Relates Smollett's translation to those of Jarvis and Motteux and lists its eighteenth-century editions.

1906

3    GOSSE, EDMUND.  "Smollett," in English Literature, an Illus-
     trated Record. From Milton to Johnson.  London: William
     Heinemann; New York: Macmillan, III, 323-26.
         Unsympathetic account, with Cruikshank illustrations,
     portrait of Smollett, and facsimile of a letter.

4    [MONTAGU, ELIZABETH].  Elizabeth Montagu. The Queen of the
     Blue-stockings. Her Correspondence from 1720 to 1761, ed.
     Emily J. Climenson.  London: John Murray, II, 2.
         1752 letter praises Peregrine Pickle.

5    PARSONS, MRS. CLEMENT.  Garrick and His Circle.  New York: G.
     P. Putnam's Sons; London: Methuen, pp. 173, 250, 339-40.
         Comments on Smollett's relations with Garrick, his ex-
     cessive naturalism, and his unfair treatment of Methodism.

6    PLARR, VICTOR G.  "Unpublished Letters to William Hunter,"
     Chambers's Journal, 6th ser., 9 (January 1), 57-59.
         Five letters (1762-67) from Smollett.  Provides material
     on their relationship, Smollett's role in Hunter's Commen-
     taries, his health, finances, and travels.

7    RANGER.  "Tobias Smollett," The Bookman, 29 (March), 241-43.
         Conventional comments on picaresque and coarseness, but
     sympathetic treatment of man and his writing.


                                1907

1    ADAMS, HENRY.  The Education of Henry Adams.  Washington: n.
     p., p. 12.
         Peregrine Pickle on bookshelf of grandfather, the presi-
     dent.

2    ALLINGHAM, WILLIAM.  A Diary, ed. H. Allingham and D. Radford.
     London: Macmillan, p. 212.
         In 1872, Carlyle's low estimate of translation of Don
     Quixote and praise for sentiment in Humphry Clinker.

3    ANON.  "Smollett," in Enciclopedia Universal Illustrada Euro-
     peo-Americana.  Barcelona: Espasa, LVI, 1067.
         Not altogether accurate sketch and chronology.

4    BALL, MARGARET.  Sir Walter Scott as a Critic of Literature.
     New York: Columbia University Press, pp. 73, 74, 156.
         Scott's praise of Smollett excessive.

5   [BROWN, JOHN]. Letters of Dr. John Brown, ed. his son and D.
    W. Forrest. London: Adam and Charles Black, p. 276.
        1882 letter, Smollett unreadable, but perhaps more
    humorous than the superior Fielding.

6   CHANDLER, FRANK WADLEIGH. "Tobias Smollett," in The Litera-
    ture of Roguery. Boston and New York: Houghton, Mifflin,
    pp. 309-20.
        Smollett dependent on the picaresque formula, but lacks
    skill in techniques and work differs from continental mod-
    els.

7   FITZMAURICE-KELLY, JAMES. "Introduction," in The Adventures
    of Gil Blas de Santillana. World's Classics. London:
    Oxford University Press, Humphrey Milford, p. xxvi n.
        Questions authenticity of Smollett's authorship of
    translation.

8   FORD, DOUGLAS. "Chapter XIII," in Admiral Vernon and the
    Navy: a Memoir and Vindication. London: T. Fisher Unwin,
    pp. 271-77 and passim.
        Argues inaccuracy and unfairness of Smollett's treatment
    in Roderick Random and his history of Vernon's conduct and
    competency at battle of Carthagena.

9   NICOLL, W. ROBERTSON AND THOMAS SECCOMBE. "The Eighteenth-
    Century Novel," in A History of English Literature. New
    York: Dodd, Mead, II, 663-70.
        Favorable account and balanced comparison with work of
    Fielding.

10  SECCOMBE, THOMAS. "Introduction," in Smollett's Travels
    through France and Italy. London: Oxford University Press,
    pp. v-lx.
        Discounts artistry and construction and regards Travels
    as loose collection of actual letters put together to make
    money. Relates it to Smollett's life and sees its impor-
    tance in understanding Smollett's personality and in its
    shrewd observations on human nature. Reprints in 1919,
    1935.

11  TUCKER, T. G. The Foreign Debt of English Literature.
    London: George Bell and Sons, pp. 173, 177, 224.
        Influences on Roderick Random and Peregrine Pickle.

## 1908

1  BARNOUW, A. J.  "The Spiritual Quixote and Smollett," N&Q,
   10th ser., 9 (February 1), 88.
       Elizabeth Wolff's 1798 Dutch translation bears
   Smollett's name as author of Spiritual Quixote.

2  COLQUHOUN, ARCHIBALD R.  Dan to Beersheba: Work and Travel in
   Four Continents.  London: William Heinemann, pp. 1-2.
       Describes relations between Smolletts and Colquhouns and
   suggests an original for "the old Admiral" in Humphry
   Clinker.

3  CONANT, MARTHA PIKE.  The Oriental Tale in England in the
   Eighteenth Century.  New York: Columbia University Press,
   pp. 203, 252, 262, 263, 285.
       Relation of Humphry Clinker and the Atom to orientalism
   and ascription of the Orientalist to Smollett.

4  DOYLE, ARTHUR CONAN.  Through the Magic Door.  New York:
   McClure, pp. 140-43.
       Places Smollett below Fielding and Richardson, and re-
   gards merits as primitive and humor strong but gross.
   London publication in 1907 by Smith, Elder.

5  GRAHAM, HENRY GREY.  "Tobias Smollett," in Scottish Men of
   Letters in the Eighteenth Century.  London: Adam and
   Charles Black, pp. 297-317.
       Highly colored account draws heavily from Chambers and
   Moore and presents Smollett as rough and crude and writing
   as a reflection of actual experiences.

6  HOWELLS, W. D.  "A Week at Leghorn," in Roman Holidays and
   Others.  New York and London: Macmillan, pp. 257-58.
       Mixed reaction to work praises Travels and Humphry
   Clinker and emphasizes influence of his literary method.
   Describes Smollett's tomb.

7  JACKSON, HOLBROOK.  "Tobias Smollett," in Great English Novelists.  London: Grant Richards, pp. 87-107.
       Least important of the early novelists, Smollett uses
   picaresque for moral purposes. Doubts that his novels can
   be regarded as autobiography and stresses importance of
   his influence as a nautical novelist.

8  WICKLEIN, ERNST.  "Die Vorrede zum Roderick Random," in Das
   "Ernsthafte" in dem Englischen Komischen Roman des XVIII.

Jahrunderts und seine Quellen.  Dresden: Max Emil Fischer,
pp. 51-53.
    Roderick Random chiefly an imitation of satiric tech-
nique of Gil Blas.


## 1909

1   BURTON, RICHARD.  "Smollett, Sterne and Others," in Masters of
    the English Novel. A Study of Principles and Personalities.
    New York: Henry Holt, pp. 73-84.
        Acknowledges Smollett's importance, particularly his in-
    fluence on Dickens, but compares him unfavorably with
    Fielding and condemns his violence and coarseness.

2   DICKENS, CHARLES.  "The Holly-Tree" and "The Lazy Tour of Two
    Idle Apprentices," in Christmas Stories.  London: J. M.
    Dent; New York: E. P. Dutton, pp. 97, 661.
        Stories from Household Words and All the Year Round ex-
    press Dickens's fondness for Smollett's work.

3   HANNAY, DAVID.  A Short History of the Royal Navy 1217-1815.
    London: Methuen, II, 82, 85, 118.
        Smollett's accurate, although exaggerated, nautical por-
    traits.

4   ROBINSON, CHARLES NAPIER and JOHN LEYLAND.  "Smollett and the
    Naval Novel," in The British Tar in Fact and Fiction.
    London and New York: Harper & Brothers, pp. 266-83 and
    passim.
        Acknowledges Smollett's accuracy, but cautions that he
    exaggerates through caricature in his creation of original
    characters and grotesque types of seamen.


## 1910

1   ARCHER, H. G.  "Alfieri in England: Original of Hawser
    Trunnion," N&Q, 11th ser., 2 (November 26), 421.
        Admiral Hoare the original of the Commodore in Peregrine
    Pickle.

2   BENJAMIN, LEWIS.  "Laurence Sterne and the Demoniacs," Book-
    man, 30 (February), 643.
        Character of William Hewett or Hewitt depicted in
    Humphry Clinker.  See Melville, Lewis.

1910

3    BLACKIE, JOHN STUART.  Notes of a Life, ed. A. Stodart Walker.
     Edinburgh and London: William Blackwood and Sons, p. 4.
     Reading Smollett's work as a youth.

4    CARLYLE, ALEXANDER.  Autobiography, ed. John Hill Burton.
     London and Edinburgh: T. N. Foulis, passim.  Indexed.
     Reprint with additions of 1860.1.

5    CHRISTIE, JOHN.  "Smollett's History of England," N&Q, 11th
     ser., 2 (August 13), 129.
          William Bisset supposedly wrote parts of Smollett's
     work.

6    CHRISTIE, JOHN.  "Smollett's History of England," N&Q, 11th
     ser., 2 (September 24), 256.
          William Bisset one of the continuators of Smollett's
     work.

7    DIBELIUS, WILHELM.  "Tobias Smollett," in Englische Roman-
     kunst.  Die Technik des Englischen Romans im Achtzehnten
     und zu Anfang des Neunzehnten Jahrhunderts.  Berlin: Mayer
     & Müller, I, 159-213.
          Long, but rather elementary discussion emphasizes epi-
     sodic plots and caricature and considers satire, didacti-
     cism, and sources.

8    [EMERSON, RALPH WALDO].  Journals of Ralph Waldo Emerson, ed.
     E. W. Emerson and W. E. Forbes.  Boston and New York:
     Houghton, Mifflin, The Riverside Press, Cambridge, IV, 93.
          Emerson's 1836 view of Smollett as too restricted to
     common sense, nothing spiritual.

*9   GALLI, I.  La Réalisme Pittoresque chez Le Sage et Ses Pré-
     décesseurs Immediats.  Grenoble.
          Cited in 1948.7.

10   HANNAY, DAVID.  "Smollett and the Old Sea-Dogs," in Ships and
     Men.  Edinburgh and London: William Blackwood and Sons,
     pp. 16-38.
          Reprint of 1898.5.

*11  HAPPEL, FRIEDRICH.  "Tobias Smollett und der Humor."  Diss.,
     Marburg, 1910.
          Cited in McNamee, Dissertations in English and American
     Literature.

12   HILL, N. W.  "Smollett's History of England," N&Q, 11th ser.,
     2 (November 12), 393.

Thomas Smart Hughes wrote seven volumes in continuation of Smollett's History.

13 MEIKLE, HENRY W. "The Learning of the Scots in the Eighteenth Century," Scottish Historical Review, 7 (April), 293.
Eighteenth-century pamphlet suggests Smollett might have done a great history if not connected with the booksellers.

14 MELVILLE, LEWIS. See Benjamin, Lewis.

15 ROBERTS, W. "Smollett's 'Hugh Strap,'" N&Q, 11th ser., 2 (July 9), 26.
Sources for claims of Hewson and Lewis as originals of Strap.

16 SCOTT, W. "Smollett's History of England," N&Q, 11th ser., 2 (September 10), 213.
Publication details of Smollett's History, the Continuation, and additions after Smollett's death.

17 WHITMORE, CLARA H. Woman's Work in English Fiction from the Restoration to the Mid-Victorian Period. New York and London: G. P. Putnam's Sons. The Knickerbocker Press, pp. 8, 23, 24, 88, 101, 179.
Smollett as a standard of realistic novelists and his relationship to later writers.

## 1911

1 BEACH, JOSEPH WARREN. The Comic Spirit in George Meredith. London: Longman's, Green, and Co., passim. Indexed.
Comparisons of Smollett's and Meredith's techniques.

2 KÜNZIG, FERDINAND. Washington Irving und Seine Beziehung zur Englischen Literatur des 18. Jahrhunderts. Heidelberg: Inaug.-Diss., passim.
Reflections and sources of Smollett's work in Irving's.

3 MASSON, DAVID. Memories of Two Cities: Edinburgh and Aberdeen. Edinburgh and London: Oliphant et al., p. 33.
Impression left by Smollett's last visit to Edinburgh in 1766.

4 SECCOMBE, THOMAS. "Smollett, Tobias George," in Encyclopaedia Britannica. 11th ed. Cambridge: Cambridge University Press, XXV, 278-80.

1911

        Written at a low point in Smollett's reputation, a re-
markably sympathetic account, presenting a fair judgment
of his work and offering interesting insights into his personality and its relationship to his background.

5    WHITE, FREDERICK CHARLES. "Dr. Thomas Arnold and Humphry
      Clinker," N&Q, 11th ser., 4 (October 28), 348.
         Cites source giving Arnold's praise and requests others.

6    WILLIAMS, HAROLD. "Tobias Smollett (1721-71)," in Two Centu-
      ries of the English Novel. London: Smith, Elder, pp. 78-91
      and passim.
         Despite favorable comment on Humphry Clinker, generally
    unsympathetic account regarding Smollett's novels as a
    retrogression in the genre.

### 1912

1    [COWPER, WILLIAM]. Letters of William Cowper, ed. J. G.
      Frazer. London: Macmillan, II, 159.
         1788 letter admiring Smollett's humor.

2    JERROLD, WALTER. "Quin, Foote, Bannister, Colman," in A Book
      of Famous Wits. London: Methuen, pp. 102-3.
         Smollett's portrait of Quin in Humphry Clinker is accu-
    rate.

3    LANG, ANDREW. "Tobias Smollett," in History of English Liter-
      ature from "Beowulf" to Swinburne. London, New York, et
      al.: Longmans, Green, pp. 467-70.
         Unfavorable comparison with Fielding particularly notes
    failures in form and taste.

4    MILLAR, JOHN HEPBURN. Scottish Prose of the Seventeenth &
      Eighteenth Centuries. Glasgow: James Maclehose and Sons,
      p. 245.
         Praises Smollett, but notes little of his work is re-
    lated to Scotland.

5    WATT, FRANCIS. "Closes and Houses," in Edinburgh and the
      Lothians. New York: Frederick A. Stokes; London: Methuen,
      pp. 85-86.
         Realistic scenes in Humphry Clinker related to
    Smollett's living in Edinburgh in 1766.

1913

1 BOYNTON, PERCY H. "Johnson's London," in London in English
 Literature. Chicago: University of Chicago Press, pp. 159,
 171, 191.
  Smollett's social attitudes in his novels.

2 CHILD, HAROLD. "Fielding and Smollett," in Cambridge History
 of English Literature: The Age of Johnson, ed. A. W. Ward
 and A. R. Waller. Cambridge: Cambridge University Press,
 X, 20-45.
  Emphasizes relationship between Smollett's life and
 work, influence of the picaresque, and compares his novels,
 not unfavorably, with Fielding's.

3 FISCHER, ALBIN. Autobiographisches in Smolletts "Humphry
 Clinker". Coburg: A. Robtentscher, 108 pp.
  General discussion of Smollett's work and early biogra-
 phies, and then emphasizes relationship between Matt
 Bramble and Smollett and the effect of autobiography on
 his literary technique in the novel.

4 LYTTON, EARL OF. The Life of Edward Bulwer First Lord Lytton.
 London: Macmillan, II, 394-95.
  1861 letter praises vigorous writing generally and
 humorous characters in Humphry Clinker.

5 MEDWIN, THOMAS. Life of Percy Bysshe Shelley. London:
 Humphrey Milford, Oxford University Press, p. 25.
  Smollett's realism not to Shelley's taste.

6 MURRAY, DAVID. "Robert & Andrew Foulis and the Glasgow
 Press," Records of the Glasgow Bibliographical Society, 2
 (1913), 6, 53, 64.
  Smollett's relations with the Foulises and other Scots.

7 [NORTON, CHARLES ELIOT]. Letters of Charles Eliot Norton, ed.
 Sara Norton and M. A. De Wolfe Howe. Boston and New York:
 Houghton Mifflin. The Riverside Press, Cambridge, I, 459,
 469-70.
  Thomas Carlyle's praise of Smollett's work and his read-
 ing of the novels and Travels.

8 SAINTSBURY, GEORGE. "The Four Wheels of the Novel Wain," in
 The English Novel. London: J. M. Dent & Sons; New York:
 E. P. Dutton, pp. 115-25 and passim.
  Smollett's three major novels related to his experiences
 and influence of Le Sage. Praises nautical characters and

1913

          offers favorable comment on <u>Launcelot Greaves</u>, but places Smollett well below Fielding.

9    SHAW, BERNARD. "The New Element," in <u>The Quintessence of Ibsenism</u>. London: Constable, p. 176.
          Effect of change of taste on readability of Smollett's savage humor and <u>Humphry Clinker</u>.

10   STIRLING, A. M. W. <u>Letter-Bag of Lady Elizabeth Spencer-Stanhope</u>. London and New York: John Lane, p. 18.
          Lord Henry Paulet the original of Captain Whiffle in <u>Roderick Random</u>.

11   WATT, FRANCIS. "Men of Letters in Edinburgh," in <u>The Book of Edinburgh Anecdote</u>. New York: Charles Scribner's Sons, p. 153.
          On Smollett and his mother and influence of Edinburgh visit on Win Jenkins in <u>Humphry Clinker</u>.

12   WILLIAMS, BASIL. <u>The Life of William Pitt: Earl of Chatham</u>. London: Longmans, Green, I and II, passim. Indexed.
          Smollett as historian.

### 1914

1    BLACK, GEORGE F. "List of Works in the New York Public Library Relating to Scotland," <u>BNYPL</u>, 18 (December), 1561-62.
          Lists forty works and gives bibliographical data.

2    FULLERTON, WILLIAM MORTON. "Introduction," in <u>The Adventures of Gil Blas of Santillane</u>. London: George Routledge and Sons; New York: E. P. Dutton, pp. xxvii-xxviii.
          Smollett among those inspired by Le Sage's work.

3    GREEN, ROBERT M. "Tobias Smollett: Physician and Novelist," <u>Boston Medical and Surgical Journal</u>, 171 (October 22), 635-38.
          Laudatory, somewhat inaccurate, account suggests Smollett as greatest of the eighteenth-century novelists and considers influence of medical training on his writing.

4    JERROLD, WALTER. <u>Douglas Jerrold, Dramatist and Wit</u>. London, New York, Toronto: Hodder and Stoughton, I, 22.
          Jerrold's childhood reading of Smollett.

5    MAIER, WALTER. <u>Christopher Anstey und der "New Bath Guide": Ein Beitrag zur Entwicklung der Englischen Satire im 18.</u>

Jahrundert. Anglistische Forschungen, Heft 39. Heidelberg:
Carl Winter's Universitätsbuchhandlung, pp. 177-82 and passim.
    Relates Anstey's work and Humphry Clinker and cites
parallel passages.

6    MEAD, WILLIAM EDWARD. The Grand Tour in the Eighteenth Century. Boston and New York: Houghton Mifflin, passim.
Indexed.
    Smollett's ill-tempered Travels.

7    MURRAY, DAVID. "Bibliography: Its Scope and Methods with a
View of the Work of a Local Bibliography Society," Records
of the Glasgow Bibliographical Society, 1 (1914), 60, 90.
    Smollett's observations of golf and Scots abroad.


## 1915

1    LÜCKER, HEINZ. Die Vewendung der Mundart im Englischen Roman
des 18. Jahrhunderts (Fielding, Smollett). Darmstadt: K.
F. Bender, passim.
    Considerable discussion and lists of various dialectical
elements in Smollett's five novels.

2    MAUGHAM, W. SOMERSET. Of Human Bondage. Garden City: Grosset
& Dunlap, p. 615.
    Fictional character shows knowledgeability by identify-
ing Smollett as the author of Peregrine Pickle.

3    TATLOCK, JOHN S. P. "Pygmalion and Peregrine," Nation, 100
(February 18), 197.
    Parallels between Shaw's play and chapter in Peregrine
Pickle.

4    VIGO, PIETRO. Livorno. Bergamo: Istituto Italiano D'Arti
Grafiche, p. 116.
    Comment on Smollett's writing and death in Italy.

5    [WESLEY, JOHN]. The Journal of the Rev. John Wesley, A.M.,
ed. Nehemiah Curnock. London: The Epworth Press, VI, 229-
30.
    In 1779 ridicules treatment of Methodism in History of
England.

## 1916

1   CLARK, J. SCOTT and JOHN PRICE ODELL. "Tobias George
    Smollett," in A Study of English and American Writers.
    Chicago and New York: Row, Peterson, III, 229-37.
        Emphasizes Smollett's brutality, coarseness, exaggera-
    tion, lack of unity, but notes his kindness.

2   HOLTHAUSEN, F. "Smollett und Jean Paul," Archiv für das Stu-
    dium der Neueren Sprachen, 135 (1916), 402-3.
        Smollett's influence on work of Jean Paul (Johann Paul
    Friedrich Richter).

3   PHELPS, WILLIAM LYON. "Fielding, Smollett, Sterne," in The
    Advance of the English Novel. New York: Dodd, Mead, pp.
    65-70.
        Praises vitality and the humor of Humphry Clinker, but
    critical of structure and vulgarity and lack of feeling.

## 1917

1   BARSTOW, MARJORIE LATTA. Wordsworth's Theory of Poetic Dic-
    tion. Yale Studies in English, 57, ed. Albert S. Cook.
    New Haven: Yale University Press; London: Humphrey Milford,
    Oxford University Press, p. 93.
        Wordsworth's indebtedness to Smollett.

2   BENNETT, ARNOLD. "Censorship by the Libraries," in Books and
    Persons: Being Comments on a Past Epoch 1908-1911. London:
    Chatto & Windus, p. 192.
        Smollett's novels kept from Glasgow's lending libraries.

3   BLEACKLEY, HORACE. Life of John Wilkes. London and New York:
    John Lane; Toronto: S. B. Gundy, passim. Indexed.
        Smollett's personal relations with Wilkes and an attack
    on the Briton.

4   BROWNE, J. H. BALFOUR. "Reading," in Recollections Literary
    and Political. London: Constable, pp. 52-53.
        Praises Roderick Random and Travels, but not Humphry
    Clinker.

## 1918

1   CROSS, WILBUR L. The History of Henry Fielding. New Haven:
    Yale University Press, I-III, passim. Indexed.

Various details on Smollett's relations with Fielding and comments on estimates of their works by contemporaries and later writers.

2   CROSS, WILBUR L.  "Smollett, Tobias George," in The Encyclopedia Americana.  New York: Encyclopedia Americana Corpora-
tion, XXV, 138-39.
Unsympathetic treatment, although admiring range and satire.

3   DOUGHTY, KATHARINE F.  "The Attack on Carthagena, 1741,"
United Service Magazine, n.s. 58 (October), 40-52.
Smollett a reliable observer of the battle.

4   GOAD, CAROLINE.  "Richardson, Sterne, and Smollett" and
"Tobias George Smollett," in Horace in the English Literature of the Eighteenth Century.  Yale Studies in English,
58.  New Haven: Yale University Press, pp. 213-32 and 534-
43.
Contrasts Smollett's deep concern with absence in Sterne
and Richardson and describes his knowledgeable use of
Horace.  Appendix cites particular use of Horace.

5   WHITEFORD, ROBERT NAYLOR.  "Samuel Richardson, Henry Fielding,
Sarah Fielding, and Tobias Smollett," in Motives in English
Fiction.  New York and London: G. P. Putnam's Sons.  The
Knickerbocker Press, pp. 109-18 and passim.
Detailed description of the relationships and parallels
of Smollett's novels to earlier and later fiction.

## 1919

1   BEATTY, JOSEPH M. JR.  "The Political Satires of Charles
Churchill," SP, 16 (October), 303-33.
Comments on Smollett, the Briton, and the Critical Re-
view.

2   MOORE, GEORGE.  Avowals.  New York: Boni and Livewright, pp.
25-26.
Imaginary dialogue between Moore and Edmund Gosse about
Smollett's work.

3   PILATTE, DR., Ed.  Smollett: Lettres de Nice sur Nice et Ses
Environs (1763-1765).  Traduites et Précédeés d'un Aperçu
Biographique.  Nice: Imprimerie de l'Eclaireur, 185 pp.
General account of Smollett and notes on selected let-
ters.

1919

4    RIVINGTON, SEPTIMUS. The Publishing Family of Rivington.
     London: Rivingtons, pp. 42-45.
        Composition, publication, and enormous sale of History
     of England. Smollett's letter to Richard Smith.

5    SMITH, G. GREGORY. Scottish Literature: Character & Influ-
     ence. London: Macmillan, passim. Indexed.
        Various comments, particularly on Critical Review and
     History of England.

6    WATERS, W. G. "Englishmen in Italy: Smollett," Anglo-Italian
     Review, 4 (May), 31-45.
        Favorable assessment of Travels praises its scholarship
     and most of its aesthetic judgments, but confuses dates of
     Smollett's works.


                              1920

1    BIRON, H. C. "Smelfungus," The National Review, 75 (May),
     344-53.
        Good-natured general assessment of Smollett and his
     work, undisturbed by its coarseness and predicting a re-
     vival of interest.

2    HUFFMAN, CHARLES HERBERT. The Eighteenth-Century Novel in
     Theory and Practice. Dayton, Virginia: Ruebush-Kieffer,
     passim. Indexed.
        Contrasts Smollett's critical statements and practices
     and relates contradiction to Smollett's personality. Re-
     printed in 1969 by Folcroft Press: Folcroft, Pa.


                              1921

1    ANON. "Tobias Smollett, 1721-1771," TLS, March 17, pp. 165-
     66.
        Bicentennial tribute evaluates novels, assesses realism,
     and traces influence and reputation in the nineteenth cen-
     tury. Discusses translations and history.

2    BIRKHEAD, EDITH. The Tale of Terror: A Study of the Gothic
     Romance. London: Constable, pp. 23-25 and passim. In-
     dexed.
        Gothic characteristics of Ferdinand Count Fathom and
     relation to later fiction.

*3   BÜGE, KARL.  "Untersuchungen über Smolletts Roman <u>Adventures</u>
      <u>of Sir Launcelot Greaves</u> Insbesondere über Seine Technik
      und Seine Quellen."  Diss., Königsberg, 1921.
           Cited in McNamee, <u>Dissertations in English and American</u>
      <u>Literature</u>.

 4   C___N, H.  "Pope: Smollett," <u>N&Q</u>, 12th ser., 9 (July 16), 48.
           <u>Peregrine Pickle</u> borrows language from the <u>Dunciad</u>.

 5   CHANCELLOR, E. BERESFORD.  "Smollett as a Traveler," <u>Fort-</u>
      <u>nightly Review</u>, n.s. 109 (March), 478-88.
           Praises Smollett's achievement, particularly in <u>Humphry</u>
      <u>Clinker</u>, but concentrates on the <u>Travels</u>, careful, scholar-
      ly, and marked by Smollett's independence and common sense.

 6   CHANCELLOR, E. BERESFORD.  "Tobias Smollett," <u>Chambers's Jour-</u>
      <u>nal</u>, 7th ser., 11 (March 19), 241-44.
           A great, if somewhat neglected, writer, as a general
      account of his life and work indicates.

 7   CROSS, WILBUR L.  "Smollett--Two Centuries After," <u>Literary</u>
      <u>Review of the New York Evening Post</u>, 1 (May 14), 1-2.
           Favorable account of Smollett and his work repeats much
      of the standard criticism.

 8   HENLEY, WILLIAM ERNEST.  "Smollett," in <u>Essays</u>.  London:
      Macmillan, pp. 47-95.
           Reprint of Henley's introduction to Smollett's <u>Works</u>,
      1899.3.

 9   JAMES, HENRY.  "Fiction and Sir Walter Scott," in <u>Notes and</u>
      <u>Reviews</u>.  Cambridge, Mass.: Dunster House, p. 10.
           Smollett a didactic novelist.  Originally in <u>North</u>
      <u>American Review</u> (October 1864).

10   KELLY, JOHN ALEXANDER.  "English Culture," in <u>England and the</u>
      <u>Englishman in German Literature of the Eighteenth Century</u>.
      New York: Columbia University Press, pp. 41-42.
           General approval of Smollett's novels in Germany.

11   VAN DOREN, CARL.  <u>The American Novel</u>.  New York: Macmillan,
      passim.  Indexed.
           Smollett's novels in early America and comparisons with
      work of James Fenimore Cooper.

1922

1   BRYCE, THOMAS H. <u>William Hunter and His Museum</u>. Glasgow:
    Maclehose, Jackson, passim.
      Material, including correspondence, on Smollett's rela-
    tions with Hunter.

2   HOWE, P. P. <u>The Life of William Hazlitt</u>. New York: George H.
    Doran, passim. Indexed.
      Hazlitt's reading and opinion of Smollett's work.

3   HUSE, WILLIAM WOODMAN JR. "Pickle and Pickwick," <u>Washington
    University Studies</u>, 10, Humanistic Series, (October), 143-
    54.
      Dickens's indebtedness to <u>Peregrine Pickle</u> for <u>Pickwick</u>
    with parallels in plot and technique.

4   MELVILLE, HERMAN. <u>The Works of Herman Melville</u>. Standard
    edition. London et al.: Constable, II, 347; V, 177; VI,
    57-58.
      In <u>Omoo</u> (1847), <u>Redburn</u> (1849), and <u>White Jacket</u> (1850),
    characters read Smollett, praise work, and describe charac-
    ters.

*5  OLIVE, M. "The Elements of Caricature in Smollett's Novels."
    Thesis, University of Paris (Sorbonne), 1922.
      Cited in Cordasco, 1948.7.

6   THALER, ALWIN. "The Playwrights," in <u>Shakespere [sic] to
    Sheridan: A Book about the Theatre of Yesterday and To-Day</u>.
    Cambridge, Mass.: Harvard University Press, pp. 62, 66.
      Smollett's relations with Garrick and his description of
    Rich in <u>Roderick Random</u>.

7   TINKER, CHAUNCEY BREWSTER. <u>Nature's Simple Plan: A Phase of
    Radical Thought in the Mid-Eighteenth Century</u>. Princeton:
    Princeton University Press, p. 73.
      Smollett's treatment of primitivism in <u>Humphry Clinker</u>.

8   WICHELNS, HERBERT A. "Burke's <u>Essay on the Sublime</u> and Its
    Reviewers," <u>JEGP</u>, 21 (December), 645-61.
      Treatment in <u>Critical Review</u> compared with others.

1923

1   BINKLEY, HAROLD COOK.  "Letter Writing in English Literature."
    Diss., Harvard University, 1923.
        Epistolary technique in Humphry Clinker and the Travels.

2   BOAS, RALPH PHILIP and BARBARA M. HAHN.  "The Age of Johnson,"
    in Social Backgrounds of English Literature.  Boston:
    Atlantic Monthly Press, p. 189.
        Smollett's novels coarse journalism appropriate to his
    age.

3   BUCHAN, JOHN.  "Smollett and Sterne," in A History of English
    Literature.  London, New York, et al.: Thomas Nelson &
    Sons, pp. 345-47.
        Emphasizes episodic technique, autobiographical charac-
    teristics, and coarseness of Smollett's novels.

4   [CARLYLE, THOMAS].  Letters of Thomas Carlyle to John Stuart
    Mill, John Sterling, and Robert Browning, ed. Alexander
    Carlyle.  London: T. Fisher Unwin, p. 155.
        In 1837 Carlyle will read Pickwick because it has been
    compared to Smollett's work.

5   DRINKWATER, JOHN.  "Tobias Smollett," in The Outline of Liter-
    ature. A Plain Story Simply Told, ed. John Drinkwater.  New
    York and London: G. P. Putnam's Sons.  The Knickerbocker
    Press, II, 495-97.
        Account of Smollett's life and work praises his poetry
    and Humphry Clinker.

6   HARRISON, FREDERIC.  "Tobias Smollett," in De Senectute. More
    Last Words.  London: T. Fisher Unwin, pp. 152-56.
        Repelled by Smollett's personality, coarseness and vul-
    garity of his work, weaknesses of his plots, but praises
    caricatures and portrait of society and Launcelot Greaves
    and Humphry Clinker.

7   MARR, GEORGE S.  "The Adventurer and Other Periodicals," in
    The Periodical Essayists of the Eighteenth Century.
    London: James Clarke, pp. 163-64.
        Critical Review a precursor to reviews of the next cen-
    tury.  Reprinted New York: Augustus M. Kelley, 1971.

8   [MONTAGU, ELIZABETH].  Mrs. Montagu, "Queen of the Blues":
    Her Letters and Friendships from 1762 to 1800, ed. Reginald
    Blunt.  London et al.: Constable, I, 324-25, 327.

131

1923

Mrs. Montagu's and Smollett's views in his Travels con-
trasted.

*9 SCHUDT, E. Das Ausland in Smolletts Romanen. Giessen.
Cited in Cordasco, 1948.7.

*10 SHAVER, ALICE. "Autobiography in Smollett's Roderick Random
and Peregrine Pickle and Dickens' David Copperfield and
Oliver Twist." M.A. thesis, University of Alberta, 1923.
Cited in Canadian Graduate Theses in the Humanities and
Social Sciences, 1921-1946.

1924

1 LEGOUIS, E. and L. CAZAMIAN. "Smollett," in Histoire de la
Littérature Anglaise. Paris: Librairie Hachette, pp. 838-
42 and passim.
Emphasizes autobiographical characteristics of the novels and compares him unfavorably with Fielding. Sees
Humphry Clinker yielding to taste for sentiment. Trans.
1927, New York: Macmillan.

*2 MÜHLBERG, E. "Tobias Smolletts History and Adventures of an
Atom und Charles Johnstones Chrysal or the Adventures of a
Guinea. Zwei Polit. Satire des 18 Jahrhundert Ein Beitrag
zur Geschichte des Engl. Satire." Diss., Hall, 1924.
Cited in Cordasco, 1948.7.

3 PARTRIDGE, ERIC. The French Romantics' Knowledge of English
Literature (1820-1848). Paris: Librairie Ancienne Édouard
Champion et al., p. 28.
Smollett's history recommended reading in 1824.

4 PERRIN, W. G. "Tobias George Smollett," Mariner's Mirror, 10
(January), 94.
Additions and corrections to DNB account of Smollett's
naval experiences.

5 POTTLE, FREDERICK A. "A North Briton Extraordinary," N&Q,
147 (October 11), 259-61.
Doubts Smollett's authorship of two pamphlets in 1765
and 1769.

6 POTTLE, FREDERICK A. "A North Briton Extraordinary: Boswell
and Corscia," N&Q, 147 (December 6), 403-4.
Again Smollett connection unlikely. See 1924.5.

7   ROBERTS, MORLEY.  W. H. Hudson. A Portrait.  New York: E. P.
     Dutton, pp. 221/244.
        Unfavorable comment on Atom and attributes Smollett's
     concern for dirt to medical training.

8   TUPPER, CAROLINE F.  "Essays Erroneously Attributed to
     Goldsmith," PMLA, 39 (June), 325-42.
        "Belles Lettres" essays in British Magazine are
     Smollett's.

9   WILLIS, EOLA.  The Charleston Stage in the XVIII Century with
     Social Settings of the Time.  Columbia, S.C.: The State
     Company, pp. 71, 74.
        Charleston production of The Reprisal in 1773.

10  WYNDHAM, MAUD.  Chronicle of the Eighteenth Century Founded on
     the Correspondence of Sir Thomas Lyttelton and His Family.
     Boston: Houghton Mifflin Company, 2 Vols., passim.  In-
     dexed.
        Smollett as historian, his parody of Lyttelton's ode,
     and his literary portraits of Lyttelton and the Duke of
     Newcastle.

11  YVON, PAUL.  La Vie d'un Dilettante.  Horace Walpole (1717-
     1797).  Essai de Biographie Psychologique et Littéraire.
     Paris: Les Presses Universitaires de France; London:
     Oxford University Press, passim.  Indexed.
        Walpole's unfavorable attitude toward Smollett as his-
     torian, novelist, and man.

## 1925

1   BIRKHEAD, EDITH.  "Sentiment and Sensibility in the Eighteenth-
     Century Novel," Essays and Studies, 11 (1925), 104-5, 109.
        Smollett's influence on Henry Brooke and Susan Ferrier.

2   BISSELL, BENJAMIN.  "The Indian in Fiction," in The American
     Indian in English Literature of the Eighteenth Century.
     Yale Studies in English, 68.  New Haven: Yale University
     Press, pp. 104-6.
        Lismahago's Indian captivity realistically treated in
     Humphry Clinker and Smollett's description of religion
     satirizes Christianity.  Reprinted 1968, Hamden, Conn.:
     Archon Books.

1925

3   BRAWLEY, BENJAMIN. "Smollett and Sterne," in A New Survey of
    English Literature. New York: F. S. Crofts, pp. 195-96.
        Conventional comments on picaresque and social criti-
    cism.

4   BUCK, HOWARD SWAZEY. A Study in Smollett: Chiefly "Peregrine
    Pickle," with a Complete Collation of the First and Second
    Editions. New Haven and London: Yale University Press;
    Humphrey Milford, Oxford University Press, xii + 216 pp.
        Study of Peregrine Pickle and other work, including
    Roderick Random and The Regicide, as they relate to
    Smollett's life. Details Smollett's quarrels with Garrick,
    Fielding, etc., and provides account of Smollett's revi-
    sions for second edition. Sees Memoirs of a Lady of
    Quality written by Lady Vane, corrected by Shebbeare, re-
    vised by Smollett, and then Lady Vane. Collates first and
    second editions (but see 1975.6). Reprinted 1973.9.

5   CROSS, WILBUR L. The Life and Times of Laurence Sterne. New
    Haven: Yale University Press; London: Humphrey Milford,
    Oxford University Press, 2 Vols., passim. Indexed.
        Relations between Smollett and Sterne, particularly
    Travels and A Sentimental Journey.

6   DEINHARDT, MARGRETH. "Beziehungen der Philosophie zu dem
    Grossen Englischen Roman des Achtzehnten Jahrhunderts."
    Diss., Hamburg, 1925, pp. 68-82.
        Smollett's characterization, values, and philosophy in
    terms of Mandeville, Shaftesbury, and Samuel Clarke.

7   DRINKER, CECIL K. "Doctor Smollett," Annals of Medical His-
    tory, 7 (Spring), 31-47.
        Informal survey of Smollett's fictional and non-fic-
    tional treatment of medical practices and theory and of his
    relations with contemporary doctors.

8   GRAHAM, R. B. CUNNINGHAME. Doughty Deeds: An Account of the
    Life of Robert Graham of Gartmore, Poet & Politician, 1735-
    1797. London: William Heinemann, pp. 66, 85-86, 115, 135.
        Moral and social climate in Smollett's novels. Prints
    1771 letter to Smollett and part of one in 1773 to Mrs.
    Smollett.

9   SAINTSBURY, GEORGE. "Introductions," in The Works of Tobias
    Smollett. London: The Navarre Society, I, xi-xxxvii; IV,
    xv-xxiii; VIII, xi-xix; X, ix-xvi; XI, vii-xvi.
        Reprint of 1895.6.

10   SWINBURNE, ALGERNON CHARLES. "Charles Dickens," in The Complete Works of Algernon Charles Swinburne, ed. Edmund Gosse
and Thomas J. Wise. London: W. Heinemann; New York: G.
Wells, XIV, 64.
     In 1913 essay comments on Dickens's borrowing from
Smollett.

11   WHITRIDGE, ARNOLD. Tobias Smollett: A Study of His Miscellaneous Works. New York: n.p., x + 129 pp.
     Although much of Whitridge's work on Smollett as poet,
historian, dramatist, journalist, political and travel
writer has been superseded by later scholarship, his readable monograph offers a great many details and some interesting analytical commentary. Appendix prints seven letters, four previously unpublished, from Smollett to John
Wilkes. Reprinted 1968.47.


## 1926

1   ANON. "Tobias Smollett," Medical Journal and Record, 124
(July 7), 42-43.
     Laudatory and sympathetic account, but unreliable in
dates and details.

2   BENJAMIN, LEWIS S. The Life and Letters of Tobias Smollett
(1721-1771). London: Faber and Gwyer, 319 pp.
     Unscholarly, uncritical, inaccurate, and poorly written
biography, not to be trusted for either its facts or judgments. Reprinted 1966.2. See Melville, Lewis.

3   BINZ-WINIGER, ELIZABETH. "Tobias Smollett," in Erziehungsfra-
gen in den Romanen von Richardson, Fielding, Smollett,
Goldsmith und Sterne. Zürich: Thomas & Hubert, pp. 34-61.
     Smollett's concern for narrative overshadows his treat-
ment of ideas, although novels deal with problems of edu-
cating children. Sees Roderick Random as autobiographical.

4   BOYD, ERNEST. "Introduction," in The Adventures of Ferdinand
Count Fathom. The Rogues' Bookshelf, ed. Ernest Brennecke,
Jr. New York: Greenberg, pp. v-x.
     Attributes decline of interest to general neglect of
eighteenth-century writers and to Victorian squeamishness,
but defends Smollett's realism and stresses merits of
picaresque.

5   BROOKS, VAN WYCK. "Introduction," in William Godwin's The
Adventures of Caleb Williams. The Rogues' Bookshelf, ed.

1926

Ernest Brennecke, Jr. New York: Greenberg, p. viii.
Godwin's general indebtedness to Smollett.

6 COLLINS, A. S. "The Growth of the Reading Public during the
Eighteenth Century," RES, 2 (July), 290/292-93; (October),
431.
Relates Smollett's journalism and novels to the new
audience.

7 DOUGHTY, OSWALD. "The English Malady of the Eighteenth Century," RES, 2 (July), 263.
Smollett's comments on and use of the splenetic in his
work.

8 FOSTER, JAMES R. "The Minor English Novelists, 1750-1800."
Diss., Harvard University, 1926.
Turning away from the Fielding-Smollett tradition.

9 FREEMAN, JOHN. Herman Melville. English Men of Letters. New
York: Macmillan, p. 88.
Compares Melville's White Jacket and Smollett's nautical
treatment.

10 HIRST, FRANCIS W. Life and Letters of Thomas Jefferson. New
York: Macmillan, p. 28.
Smollett among the few of Jefferson's favorite novel-
ists.

11 MELVILLE, LEWIS. See Benjamin, Lewis S.

12 NOYES, EDWARD S. The Letters of Tobias Smollett, M.D. Cambridge, Mass.: Harvard University Press, xix + 260 pp.
65 complete letters, 5 fragments, and 2 memoranda.
Lists two letters for which no text has been discovered.
Covers 1735 through 1771 and offers important information
on early life, later financial difficulties, friendships,
health, character, and work. Provides extensive annotation. Reprinted 1969.20.

13 NOYES, EDWARD S. "A Note on Peregrine Pickle and Pygmalion,"
MLN, 41 (May), 327-30.
Compares Smollett's episode with Shaw's play. Shaw
letter acknowledges likeness, but denies his reading of the
novel.

14 PHILLIPS, M. and W. S. TOMKINSON. English Women in Life and
Letters. Oxford: Oxford University Press, Humphrey Milford,

136

pp. 108-9, 117-20, 146-48, 266-67.
Portrayal of women in Humphry Clinker.

15   PONS, E.  "Le 'Voyage' Genre Littéraire au XVIIIe Siècle,"
     Bulletin de la Faculté des Lettres de Strasbourg, 4
     (March), 206-7.
     Smollett's unfavorable treatment of France in his
     Travels.

16   READ, HERBERT.  "Tobias Smollett," in Reason and Romanticism.
     London: Faber and Gwyer, pp. 187-205.
     Sensible general reassessment praises Smollett's inde-
     pendent mind and character and literary style and contrasts
     his rationalism with rising taste for sensibility.  Re-
     printed 1938.9.

17   ROOSEVELT, THEODORE.  The Works of Theodore Roosevelt.  Na-
     tional Edition.  New York: Charles Scribner's Sons, XIX,
     515.
     1906 letter on Smollett's treatment of nautical life in
     Roderick Random, though not certain it is not Humphry
     Clinker.

18   ROSS, ERNEST C.  "Tobias George Smollett," in The Development
     of the English Sea Novel from Defoe to Conrad.  Ann Arbor,
     Michigan: Edwards Brothers, pp. 9-13.
     Smollett's use of experience, caricature, and picaresque
     in his contribution to the genre.  Reprinted 1969,
     Folcroft, Pa.: Folcroft Press.

19   SMITH, HAMILTON JEWETT.  Oliver Goldsmith's "The Citizen of
     the World."  Yale Studies in English, 71.  New Haven: Yale
     University Press, p. 17.
     Goldsmith's puff for Launcelot Greaves to boost British
     Magazine.

20   SQUIRE, J. C.  "Smollett," Living Age, 328 (February), 379-81.
     Deplores coarseness of Smollett's readable, rambling
     picaresques, but calls Humphry Clinker a masterpiece.

21   TURBERVILLE, A. S.  English Men and Manners in the Eighteenth
     Century.  Oxford: Clarendon Press, passim.  Indexed.
     Describes Smollett's coarseness and sees characters and
     descriptions as exaggerated but representative portraits.

1927

1 BLANCHARD, FREDRIC T.  Fielding the Novelist: A Study in Historical Criticism.  New Haven: Yale University Press;
London: Humphrey Milford, Oxford University Press, passim.
Indexed.
        Smollett's relationships with his contemporaries and his
   later influence.  Describes contemporary and nineteenth-
   century estimates of Smollett's work.

2 BUCK, HOWARD SWAZEY.  Smollett as Poet.  New Haven and London:
   Yale University Press and Oxford University Press, xiv +
   93 pp.
        Records publication details of Smollett's poetry and
   relates his verse to his life and novels.  Persuasively
   argues his authorship of "Ode to Independence," adds three
   poems to the canon, and provides twenty lines from the
   libretto of his lost opera, Alceste.

3 CASKEY, JOHN HOMER.  "Gil Blas," in The Life and Works of
   Edward Moore.  Yale Studies in English, 75.  New Haven:
   Yale University Press, pp. 74-78.
        Suggests Smollett's participation in periodical attacks
   on Moore's play produced after Smollett's translation.  Re-
   printed 1973, Hamden, Conn.: Archon Books, Shoe String
   Press.

4 COLLINS, A. S.  Authorship in the Days of Johnson, Being a
   Study of the Relation between Author, Patron, Publisher and
   Public 1726-1780.  London: George Routledge & Sons, passim.
   Indexed.
        Information on publication details of History of
   England, Critical Review, and Peregrine Pickle.  Reprinted
   1973, Clifton, N.J.: Augustus M. Kelley.

5 CROSS, WILBUR L.  "Fielding and Smollett," Yale Review, 16
   (July), 798-800.
        Prospects for improved fortunes of Smollett's reputation
   and description of his importance as precursor to modern
   satirists.

6 ERNLE, ROWLAND EDMOND P. (Lord Ernle).  "Tobias Smollett," in
   The Light Reading of Our Ancestors.  London: Hutchinson,
   pp. 227-32 and passim.
        Dislikes Smollett's coarseness and compares him unfavor-
   ably with Fielding and Richardson, but notes importance for
   Gothic and nautical novels.

7   FOSTER, JAMES R.  "The Abbé Prevost and the English Novel,"
    <u>PMLA</u>, 42 (June), 444, 451.
        Smollett's vulgarity repelled French critics.

8   [GOLDSMITH, OLIVER].  <u>New Essays by Oliver Goldsmith</u>, ed.
    Ronald S. Crane.  Chicago: University of Chicago Press,
    passim.  Indexed.
        Possible Goldsmith essay on Smollett's discussion of
    writers in <u>Continuation of the Complete History of England</u>.
    Crane's comments weigh Smollett's possible contributions to
    the <u>British Magazine</u>.

9   HEARN, LAFCADIO.  "The Prose of the Age of Johnson," in <u>A His-</u>
    <u>tory of English Literature</u>.  Tokyo: Hokuseido Press, pp.
    423-25.
        Acknowledges Smollett's appeal to young readers and in-
    fluence on nautical novels, but finds him disagreeable and
    his work ugly and brutal.

10  HODGES, H. W.  "Introduction," in <u>Roderick Random</u>.  Everyman's
    Library, no. 790.  London: Dent; New York: Dutton, pp. v-
    xiv.
        Unsympathetic to Smollett's personality and dissatisfied
    with his coarseness and narrative structures, but some fav-
    orable and perceptive comment, particularly on nautical
    characters in <u>Roderick Random</u> and <u>Peregrine Pickle</u>.

11  HUSSEY, CHRISTOPHER.  <u>The Picturesque: Studies in a Point of</u>
    <u>View</u>.  London: Frank Cass and Co.; New York: G. P. Putnam's
    Sons, pp. 232, 261.
        Smollett's attitude toward painting in <u>Humphry Clinker</u>.

12  [MACKENZIE, HENRY].  <u>The Anecdotes and Egotisms of Henry</u>
    <u>Mackenzie, 1745-1831</u>, ed. Harold William Thompson.  London:
    Oxford University Press, Humphrey Milford, p. 58.
        Use of Scottish material in <u>Humphry Clinker</u>.

*13 MURRAY, PHYLLIS MARJORIE.  "The English Novel of the Sea from
    Smollett to Conrad."  M.A. Thesis, McGill University, 1927.
        Cited in <u>Canadian Graduate Theses in the Humanities and</u>
    <u>Social Sciences, 1921-1946</u>.

14  NOYES, EDWARD S.  "Another Smollett Letter," <u>MLN</u>, 42 (April),
    231-35.
        1762 letter to John Moore on contributions to and pro-
    prietorship of <u>Critical Review</u>.

1927

15  ODELL, GEORGE C. D.  Annals of the New York Stage.  New York:
    Columbia University Press, I, 154.
        New York performance of The Reprisal in 1768.

16  PRIESTLEY, J. B.  "The Eighteenth Century," in The English
    Novel.  Benn's Essex Library, ed. E. G. Hawke.  London:
    Ernest Benn, pp. 32-33.
        Smollett entertaining, but superficial and inferior to
    Fielding.

17  RAILO, EINO.  The Haunted Castle: A Study of the Elements of
    English Romanticism.  London: Routledge & Kegan Paul, pp.
    67, 303.
        "Romantic" characteristics in Smollett's fiction.  Re-
    printed 1964, New York: Humanities Press.

18  STEIN, HAROLD.  "Smollett's Imprisonment," TLS, May 5, p. 318.
        Dates of imprisonment and amount of fine in Knowles
    case.  On release date, however, see 1949.12.


                              1928

1  BRIGHTFIELD, MYRON F.  Theodore Hook and His Novels.  Cambridge, Mass.: Harvard University Press; London: Humphrey
   Milford, Oxford University Press, pp. 262-67 and passim.
       Compares plot, characterization, and comedy in Hook's
   novels to those in Smollett.

2  BUCK, HOWARD SWAZEY.  "A Roderick Random Play, 1748," MLN, 43
   (February), 111-12.
       Weak attempt to capitalize on success of the novel.

3  DOWNS, BRIAN W.  Richardson.  London: Frank Cass, passim.
   Indexed.
       Worthwhile comments on Richardson's connection with
   printing of Smollett's work, their opinions of each other's
   writing, and comparisons of their novels.  Reprinted 1969,
   New York: Barnes & Noble, Inc.

4  ELTON, OLIVER.  "Fielding and Smollett," in A Survey of
   English Literature, 1730-1780.  New York: Macmillan;
   London: Edward Arnold, I, 204-16.
       Despite disapproval of Smollett's coarseness, asserts
   his moral purpose and reformist zeal and admires his vigor-
   ous style and journalistic talents.  Favorable to poetry,
   Travels, Launcelot Greaves, and particularly Humphry
   Clinker.

                              140

5   FAIRCHILD, HOXIE NEALE.  "Early Romanticism," in The Noble
    Savage: A Study in Romantic Naturalism.  New York: Columbia
    University Press, pp. 88-89.
        Treatment of American Indian in Humphry Clinker opposed
    to sentimental primitivism.  Reprinted 1961, New York:
    Russell & Russell.

6   HARDY, FLORENCE EMILY.  "Observations on Many Things," in The
    Early Life of Thomas Hardy, 1840-1891.  London: Macmillan,
    p. 301.
        Hardy's reading of Smollett in 1890.

7   HEIDLER, JOSEPH BUNN.  "The History, from 1700 to 1800, of
    English Criticism of Prose Fiction," University of Illinois
    Studies in Language and Literature, 13 (May), passim.  In-
    dexed.
        Compares Smollett's theories of fiction with those of
    his contemporaries and discusses his prefaces.  Comments on
    structure of his novels and on critical theory in the
    Critical Review.

8   KNAPP, LEWIS M.  "The Final Period of Tobias Smollett." Diss.,
    Yale University, 1928.
        Detailed account of Smollett's later years, but, as
    Knapp acknowledges, requires correction.  See 1949.12.

*9  KRÁSENSKY, OTTOKAR.  Goethes Verhältnis zu den Hauptvertretern
    des Sentimentalen Englischen Romans des 18. Jahrhunderts,
    Richardson, Fielding, Smollett, Sterne und Goldsmith.
    Diss., Vienna.
        Cited in 1932.22.

10  McKILLOP, ALAN D.  "Notes on Smollett," PQ, 7 (October), 368-
    74.
        Three notes: Smollett's authorship of "The Tears of
    Scotland"; relations with Samuel Richardson; controversies
    with Churchill.

11  MUIR, EDWIN.  "Novels of Action and Character," in The Struc-
    ture of the Novel.  London: The Hogarth Press, pp. 27-32.
        Techniques and function of characterization in
    Smollett's novels and comparison with other novelists.

12  ODELL, GEORGE C. D.  Annals of the New York Stage.  New York:
    Columbia University Press, III, 115; IV, 228.
        1824 play based on Peregrine Pickle and 1838 based on
    Humphry Clinker.

1928

13  SCOTT, TEMPLE. <u>Oliver Goldsmith Bibliographically and Bio-
graphically Considered</u>. New York: The Bowling Green Press,
pp. 25-26, 61, 63-64, 68-69.
Relationship of Goldsmith and Smollett, particularly on
<u>British Magazine</u>.

14  WIERSTRA, FRANS DIRK. <u>Smollett and Dickens</u>. Den Helder:
University of Amsterdam, 117 pp.
Detailed discussion of Dickens's indebtedness to
Smollett's novels and relationship of their methods of
characterization, style, plots, and structures.

1929

1  BAKER, ERNEST A. <u>The History of the English Novel</u>. London:
H. F. & G. Witherby, III, 46, 178.
Sources for <u>Ferdinand Count Fathom</u> and <u>Peregrine Pickle</u>.

2  BOAS, RALPH PHILIP and BARBARA M. HAHN. "The Age of Johnson,"
in <u>Social Backgrounds of English Literature</u>. Boston:
Little, Brown, p. 189.
Appalled by Smollett's coarseness and brutality.

3  DEVONSHIRE, M. G. "Smollett," in <u>The English Novel in France,
1830-1870</u>. London: University of London Press, pp. 86-87.
General neglect of Smollett in France during the period.

4  ELLISON, LEE MONROE. "Elizabethan Drama and the Works of
Smollett," <u>PMLA</u>, 44 (September), 842-62.
Smollett indebted to Shakespeare's realistic comedies,
but lacks Shakespeare's humanizing spirit. His language,
content, and characterization find parallels and sources
in the humours comedies of Ben Jonson.

5  FORD, FORD MADOX. "The English Novel. Historical: Towards
Flaubert," <u>Bookman</u>, 68 (February), 675, 681.
Admires Smollett but acknowledges lack of appeal to
Anglo-Saxon taste because of his vulgarity. Reprinted
1930.4.

*6  HASKELL, GLEN. "Picaresque Elements in Smollett's Novels,"
Diss., Syracuse University, 1929.
Cited in 1942.4.

7  KNAPP, CHARLES. "The Classical Element in Smollett, <u>Roderick
Random</u>," <u>Classical Weekly</u>, 23 (October 14 and 21), 9-11,
17-19.

Clear classical allusions or antecedents in passages of Roderick Random.

8   KNAPP, LEWIS M.   "Smollett's Admirers in Eighteenth Century America," Williams Alumni Review, 22 (December), 114-15.
        Prints correspondence with Richard Smith and suggests Smollett's popularity in eighteenth- and nineteenth-century America.

9   KOHLER, MAX J.   "Scott, Smollett, and the Jews," The American Hebrew, 125 (June 7), 136.
        Treatment of the Jew in Ferdinand Count Fathom remarkable for the period.

10  MACHEN, ARTHUR.   "Introduction," in Humphry Clinker.  New York: Modern Library, Random House, pp. v-xii.
        Appreciative essay prefers Smollett to Fielding.  Attracted by vigorous early novels, but concedes greater likeability of Humphry Clinker.

11  MYERS, J. A.   "Tuberculous Physicians and Their Contributions --Tobias Smollett," Hygeia. The Health Magazine, 7 (May), 504-7.
        General account drawn from secondary sources, but relates Smollett's irascibility to his tuberculosis and admires his courage in adversity.

12  PROPER, COENRAAD BART ANNE.   "Tobias Smollett," in Social Elements in English Prose Fiction between 1700 and 1832.  Amsterdam: H. J. Paris, pp. 62-68.
        Smollett's attacks on injustice, particularly in Roderick Random, paved the way for social novelists.

13  REYNOLDS, GEORGE F.   "Tobias Smollett (1721-1771)," in English Literature in Fact & Story.  New York: Century, p. 219.
        Unfavorable comments on novels, except for Humphry Clinker.

14  SOUTHEY, ROBERT.   Journal of a Tour in Scotland in 1819, ed. C. H. Herford.  London: John Murray, p. 250.
        Approves of creation of monument to Smollett at Leven.


### 1930

1   BAKER, ERNEST A.   "Smollett," in The History of the English Novel.  London: H. F. & G. Witherby, IV, 197-239.

       Dated criticism, but a detailed description of
Smollett's novels and their relationship to contemporary
developments in the genre.

2    CHARNWOOD, LADY DOROTHEA. <u>An Autograph Collection and the
Making of It</u>. London: Ernest Benn, p. 257.
       Contains single signature by Smollett.

3    CRUSE, AMY. <u>The Englishman and His Books in the Early Nineteenth Century</u>. London: George G. Harrap, passim. Indexed.
       Attitudes of such people as Francis Place, Hazlitt, and
Lamb toward Smollett's work.

4    FORD, FORD MADOX. "Towards Flaubert," in <u>The English Novel
from the Earliest Days to the Death of Joseph Conrad</u>.
London: Constable, passim. Indexed.
       Reprint of 1929.5.

5    GRAHAM, WALTER. <u>English Literary Periodicals</u>. New York:
Thomas Nelson & Sons, pp. 177-79, 212-15 and passim.
       Smollett's work in <u>British Magazine</u> and <u>Critical Review</u>.
Falsely attributes "The Unfortunate Lovers" to Smollett.

6    HABEL, URSULA. "Fielding und Smollett," in <u>Die Nachwirkung
des Picaresken Romans in England (Von Nash bis Fielding und
Smollett)</u>. Breslau und Oppeln: Priebatsch's Buchhandlung,
pp. 37-72.
       Analyzes picaresque characteristics of Smollett's novels
and compares work to Fielding's.

7    [HAZLITT, WILLIAM]. <u>The Complete Works of William Hazlitt</u>,
ed. P. P. Howe. London and Toronto: J. M. Dent and Sons,
IV, 80, 138; VI, 115-17, 127; VII, 37, 194; IX, 68, 140;
X, 64; XII, 36, 221-23, 303; XVII, 101, 161, 184; XVIII,
245-46, 298; XX, 58.
       In addition to comments from <u>Lectures on the English
Comic Writers</u>, many that indicate close knowledge of
Smollett's work and use of it for essays.

8    HENDERSON, PHILIP. "Note," in <u>The Adventures of Peregrine
Pickle</u>. Everyman's Library, ed. Ernest Rhys. London &
Toronto: J. M. Dent; New York: E. P. Dutton & Co., I, vii-
viii.
       Unfavorable treatment of Smollett's work and note on
composition, publication, and reception of <u>Peregrine
Pickle</u>. Bibliography, pp. ix-x.

9   KELLEY, CORNELIA PULSIFER.  The Early Development of Henry
      James.  University of Illinois Studies in Language and
      Literature, 15.  Urbana, Illinois, pp. 27, 46, 100, 118.
          James's general dislike of Smollett's fiction.

10  KETTON-CREMER, R. W.  The Early Life and Diaries of William
      Windham.  London: Faber & Faber, p. 47.
          Eighteenth-century pamphlet by Windham's father attacked
      Smollett's proposal for translating Don Quixote.

11  KNAPP, LEWIS M.  "Ann Smollett, Wife of Tobias Smollett,"
      PMLA, 45 (December), 1035-49.
          Favorable description of Mrs. Smollett's character of-
      fers some details of their marital relationship and cor-
      rects belief that she died impoverished and neglected.

12  McKILLOP, ALAN D.  "Smollett's First Comedy," MLN, 45 (June),
      396-97.
          1752 auction catalogue lists The Absent Man as
      Smollett's.

13  MATHESON, P. E.  German Visitors to England 1770-1795 and
      Their Impressions.  The Taylorian Lecture 1930.  Oxford:
      Clarendon Press, pp. 24-25.
          High praise for Smollett's nautical figures.

14  POSTGATE, RAYMOND.  "The Hell-Fire Club and the North Briton,"
      in "That Devil Wilkes."  London: Constable, pp. 23-55.
          Controversy between the Briton and North Briton.

15  REEVE, CLARA.  The Progress of Romance.  New York: Facsimile
      Text Society.
          Reprint of 1785.5.


                              1931

*1  BELL, L. R.  "Realism in the Novels of Smollett."  M.A.
      Thesis, University of Toronto, 1931.
          Cited in Canadian Graduate Theses in the Humanities and
      Social Sciences, 1921-1946.

2   [BURNS, ROBERT].  The Letters of Robert Burns, ed. J. DeLancey
      Ferguson.  Oxford: Clarendon Press, I, 113, 236, 244; II,
      29, 52.
          Letters of 1787, 1788, 1790, 1791 on Burns's reading of
      Smollett's novels, praise of his humor and "Ode to Inde-
      pendence."

1931

3 [EDGEWORTH, MARIA]. <u>Maria Edgeworth: Chosen Letters</u>, ed. F.
  V. Barry. Boston and New York: Houghton Mifflin, pp. 98,
  298.
      Suggests importance of Smollett's <u>Travels</u> to early nine-
  teenth-century travellers and compares Cooper and Smollett.

4 FORD, JEREMIAH D. M. and RUTH LANSING. "Translations," in
  <u>Cervantes. A Tentative Bibliography</u>. Cambridge, Mass.:
  Harvard University Press, pp. 46-52.
      Bibliographical information on thirty-nine eighteenth
  and nineteenth-century editions of translations of <u>Don
  Quixote</u> using Smollett's work.

5 GRAY, CHARLES HAROLD. <u>Theatrical Criticism in London to 1795</u>.
  New York: Columbia University Press, passim. Indexed.
      Characteristics of dramatic criticism in <u>Critical Review</u>
  and <u>British Magazine</u>.

6 GRAY, ERNEST WESTON. "The Fielding-Smollett Tradition in the
  English Novel from 1750 to 1835." Diss., Harvard Univer-
  sity, 1931.
      Traces characteristics of Smollett's novels in works of
  Fanny Burney, Walter Scott, Pierce Egan, Frederick Marryat,
  Dickens, and others and finds Smollett's influence greater
  than Fielding's after 1800.

7 HUNTER, A. C. "Les Livres de Smollett Détenus par la Douane
  à Boulogne en 1763," <u>Revue de Littérature Comparée</u>, 11
  (October), 736-37.
      List of the books Smollett took abroad on his travels.

8 [KEATS, JOHN]. <u>Letters of John Keats</u>, ed. Maurice Buxton
  Forman. London: Humphrey Milford, Oxford University Press,
  I, 81-82; II, 426-27.
      Letters of 1818 and 1819 describe anti-romantic charac-
  ter of Smollett's fiction and sketch continuation of
  <u>Humphry Clinker</u>.

9 KNAPP, LEWIS M. "A Rare Satire on Smollett," <u>TLS</u>, October 8,
  p. 778.
      Pamphlet, perhaps the "first separately published satire
  on Tobias Smollett."

10 KNAPP, LEWIS M. "Smollett's <u>Roderick Random</u>," <u>TLS</u>, January 8,
   p. 28.
      Early printings and editions indicate its success,
   1748-58.

11   KNAPP, LEWIS M.   "Smollett's Verses and Their Musical Settings
      in the Eighteenth Century," MLN, 46 (April), 224-32.
           Musical settings by Oswald and others for successful
      songs based on "Tears of Scotland" and lyrics from Roderick
      Random, Peregrine Pickle, and The Reprisal.

12   KNIGHT, GRANT C.   "Tobias Smollett," in The Novel in English.
      Richard R. Smith, pp. 53-63.
           Although praising Smollett's energy and nautical materi-
      al, severely criticizes his brutality and coarseness as
      destructive of the genre.

13   LONGAKER, MARK.   English Biography in the Eighteenth Century.
      Philadelphia: University of Pennsylvania Press, pp. 67, 84,
      87, 88.
           Smollett's novels autobiographical.

14   NORWOOD, LUELLA FREDERICKA.   "A Descriptive Bibliography with
      Notes, Bibliographical and Biographical of the Creative
      Works of Tobias Smollett, M.D., 1746-1771, with the Post-
      humous 'Ode to Independence,' 1773."  Diss., Yale Univer-
      sity, 1931.
           Fullest descriptive and annotated bibliography of
      Smollett's creative works, but with limited information on
      the Travels and the Atom.

15   RICHARDSON, LYON N.   A History of Early American Magazines,
      1741-1789.  London: Thomas Nelson and Sons, pp. 190, 192.
           Smollett material in Pennsylvania Magazine, 1775-76.

16   SADLEIR, MICHAEL.   Bulwer: A Panorama.  Boston: Little, Brown,
      pp. 172, 286.
           Bulwer's familiarity with and desire to imitate
      Smollett's novels.

17   WATSON, HAROLD FRANCIS.   The Sailor in English Fiction and
      Drama, 1550-1800.  New York: Columbia University Press, pp.
      156-57, 164-69, 172.
           Characteristics and sources of Smollett's nautical mate-
      rial in The Reprisal and novels, especially Roderick
      Random.

18   WILSON, DAVID ALEC.   Carlyle to Threescore-and-Ten (1853-
      1865).  New York: E. P. Dutton; London: Kegan Paul et al.,
      pp. 360/446.
           Carlyle's delight in Roderick Random and Humphry
      Clinker.

1932

1    BEACH, JOSEPH WARREN. The Twentieth Century Novel, Studies in
     Technique. New York and London: Appleton-Century-Crofts,
     passim. Indexed.
         Discusses structure of Smollett's novels and compares
     work with those of later novelists.

2    BOYD, JAMES. "Tobias Smollett," in Goethe's Knowledge of
     English Literature. Oxford: Clarendon Press, pp. 124-25.
         Goethe's limited knowledge of Smollett's work, but fa-
     miliar with Roderick Random, the Travels, and particularly
     Humphry Clinker.

3    BUCK, HOWARD SWAZEY. "A New Smollett Anecdote," MLN, 47 (Feb-
     ruary), 90-91.
         Smollett's unfortunate, accidental brawl with a butcher.

4    BUCK, HOWARD SWAZEY. "Smollett and Dr. Akenside," JEGP, 31
     (January), 10-26.
         Caricature of Akenside as physician in Peregrine Pickle,
     accurate in general and in many particulars, was motivated
     by Akenside's ludicrous public character and conduct and
     his anti-Scottish sentiments.

5    CHAPPELL, EDWIN. "Run Upon," TLS, April 21, p. 291.
         Pepys used phrase earlier than Smollett. See 1932.24
     and 27.

6    COLLINS, NORMAN. "Tobias George Smollett," in The Facts of
     Fiction. New York: E. P. Dutton; London: V. Gollancz, pp.
     56-69.
         Lively, but misinformed and sometimes misleading popu-
     larized account of the man and his work.

*7   DeLURY, HELEN BERTRAND. "The Treatment of Women in the Novels
     of Fielding and Smollett." M.A. Thesis, University of
     Toronto, 1932.
         Cited in Canadian Graduate Theses in the Humanities and
     Social Sciences, 1921-1946.

8    GRIERSON, H. J. C. "Introduction," in Sir Walter Scott Today:
     Some Retrospective Essays and Studies. London: Constable,
     passim. Indexed.
         Compares Scott and Smollett and explains what Grierson
     regards as Scott's overestimation of Smollett.

9   HALLENBECK, CHESTER T.  "A Colonial Reading List," Pennsyl-
    vania Magazine of History and Biography, 56 (October), 289-
    340.
        Includes Smollett's books borrowed from a Pennsylvania
    subscription library from 1762 to 1787.

10  HARVEY, PAUL.  "Smollett, Tobias George," in The Oxford Com-
    panion to English Literature.  Oxford: Clarendon Press, p.
    730.
        Uncritical account of Smollett's career.

11  [HUME, DAVID].  The Letters of David Hume, ed. J. Y. T. Greig.
    Oxford: Clarendon Press, 2 Vols., passim.  Indexed.
        Letters concern Hume's unsuccessful attempt to gain
    Smollett a diplomatic post, Robert Stobo (supposed original
    of Lismahago), and Smollett's financial success with his
    history.

12  KNAPP, LEWIS M.  "Elizabeth Smollett, Daughter of Tobias
    Smollett," RES, 8 (July), 312-15.
        All the available information on Smollett's daughter.

13  KNAPP, LEWIS M.  "A Sequel to Smollett's Humphry Clinker,"
    TLS, October 6, p. 716.
        Describes Brambleton Hall, published in 1818, but ap-
    parently also in 1810.

14  KNAPP, LEWIS M.  "Smollett's Early Years in London," JEGP,
    31 (April), 220-27.
        Smollett during residences in London from 1744 to 1750,
    the crucial years leading to the beginning of his literary
    career.

15  KNAPP, LEWIS M.  "Smollett and Le Sage's The Devil upon
    Crutches," MLN, 47 (February), 91-92.
        Evidence of Smollett's correcting a translation in 1759
    and perhaps having done the translation ten years earlier.

16  KNAPP, LEWIS M.  "Smollett's Works as Printed by William
    Strahan, with an Unpublished Letter of Smollett to
    Strahan," Library, 4th ser., 13 (December), 282-91.
        Strahan's publication of Smollett's work and their per-
    sonal relationship.  Letter of 1759 assures Strahan of
    Smollett's friendship.

17  LAWRENCE, ALEXANDRE.  "L'Influence de Lesage sur Smollett,"
    Revue de Littérature Comparée, 12 (July-September), 533-45.

1932

Without denying Smollett's originality, details the considerable indebtedness and affinities of Roderick Random to
Gil Blas.

18  LEAVIS, Q. D.  Fiction and the Reading Public.  London: Chatto
& Windus, passim.  Indexed.
Relates Smollett's work to reading tastes in late eighteenth and nineteenth centuries and argues superiority of
his prose style to Scott's.  Reprinted 1965.

19  LOVETT, ROBERT MORSE and HELEN SARD HUGHES.  "Tobias George
Smollett," in The History of the Novel in England.  Boston:
Houghton Mifflin, The Riverside Press, Cambridge, pp. 76-
85.
Old-fashioned criticism sees Smollett's work as part of
the decline after Fielding and Richardson and stresses his
reportorial ability and indebtedness to predecessors.

20  MAXWELL, CONSTANTIA.  "Dr. Tobias Smollett," in The English
Traveller in France, 1698-1815.  London: George Routledge
& Sons, pp. 77-96.
Stresses Smollett's disagreeable comments, but considers
his observations on the French more interesting and acute
than those of any of his contemporaries except Arthur
Young.

21  PARRY, ELSIE A.  "When Literature Went to Sea," Bookman, 75
(June and July), 243-48.
Smollett as model for nautical novelists prior to
Cooper.

22  PRICE, LAWRENCE MARSDEN.  The Reception of English Literature
in Germany.  Berkeley: University of California Press, passim.  Indexed.
Since the eighteenth century, Smollett's work aroused
far less interest in Germany than that of the other major
novelists.

23  PURCELL, J. M.  "A Note on Smollett's Language," MLN, 47 (February), 93-94.
Cites two uncommon usages by Smollett.

24  PURCELL, J. M.  "A Note on Smollett's Language," TLS, April
14, p. 271.
Two words from Roderick Random whose use antedate listing in O.E.D.  See 1932.5 and 27.

*25   ROBERTS, W. E.   "The Social and Political Satire in the Novel
      of the Eighteenth Century (1740-1780), with Special Refer-
      ence to Fielding and Smollett."  M.A. Thesis, University of
      Wales, 1932.
           Cited in Retrospective Index to Theses of Great Britain
      and Ireland. 1716-1950, I.

26   SITWELL, EDITH.   Bath.   London: Faber & Faber, pp. 258-60 and
      passim.
           Smollett's harsh treatment attributed to the city's un-
      willingness to accept him as a doctor.

27   STEWART-BROWN, R.   "Run Upon," TLS, April 28, p. 311.
           Antedates phrase discussed in 1932.5 and 24.

28   TOMPKINS, J. M. S.   "Old Patterns in the Novel," The Popular
      Novel in England, 1770-1800.   London: Constable, pp. 43-46
      and passim.
           Discusses Gothic elements in Ferdinand Count Fathom and
      Smollett's use of pictorial art and his journalistic and
      picaresque influence on minor novelists.

## 1933

1    ALLEN, ROBERT J.   The Clubs of Augustan London.   Cambridge,
      Mass.: Harvard University Press, pp. 144-45, 165, 185.
           Club life as it appears in Smollett's novels.

2    [BENNETT, ARNOLD].   The Journal of Arnold Bennett 1896-1928.
      New York: The Viking Press, pp. 261, 263.
           Smollett's practical knowledge and particular observa-
      tions in his Travels.

3    BIRSS, JOHN HOWARD.   "A Letter to Tobias Smollett," N&Q, 164
      (May 6), 315-16.
           Offers information about publication history of
      Smollett's response to letter from the American Richard
      Smith.

4    BIRSS, JOHN HOWARD.   "Note on Smollett Letter No. 37," N&Q,
      165 (September 16), 189.
           Unlocated letter No. 37 in Noyes actually No. 6.

5    BISSELL, FREDERICK OLDS JR.   Fielding's Theory of the Novel.
      Cornell Studies in English, 22.   Ithaca, New York: Cornell
      University Press, passim.   Indexed.

1933

        Influence of Scarron and Elizabethans on Smollett and his use of "history" to signify "fictitious biography."

6    [CHURCHILL, CHARLES]. <u>Poems of Charles Churchill</u>, ed. James Laver. London: Eyre and Spottiswoode, I, xxiii, xxvi, 50, 57, 85; II, 267, 271.
        Churchill's attacks on Smollett in 1761, 1762, and 1763. Laver's notes comment on relationship of the two men.

7    COOK, ELIZABETH CHRISTINE. <u>Reading the Novel</u>. Boston: Little, Brown, pp. 10, 31, 35, 168.
        Famous American readers of Smollett's novels.

8    KENT, ELIZABETH EATON. <u>Goldsmith and His Booksellers</u>. Ithaca, New York: Cornell University Press; London: Humphrey Milford, Oxford University Press, passim. Indexed.
        Smollett on the <u>Critical Review</u>, <u>British Magazine</u>, and his <u>History of England</u>.

9    KNAPP, LEWIS M. "More Smollett Letters," <u>MLN</u>, 48 (April), 246-49.
        Records one lost letter; prints letters to William Hunter and Robert Cotton.

*10    McCLELLAND, JOHN. "The Course of Realism in the English Novel from Addison and Steele through Sir Walter Scott." Diss., Stanford University, 1933.
        Praises Smollett's eccentric characters, emphasizes lack of form, and concentrates on journalistic contributions to the novel. Cited in <u>Abstracts of Dissertations, Stanford University</u>, 9 (1934), 52-54.

11    PARSONS, COLEMAN O. "Smollett's Influence on Sheridan's <u>The Rivals</u>," <u>N&Q</u>, 164 (January 21), 39-41.
        Similarities between material in <u>The Rivals</u> and <u>Ferdinand Count Fathom</u> and <u>Humphry Clinker</u>.

12    RATH, JOSEPH. "Smollett," in <u>Die Personenbeschreibung der Humoristischen Charaktere in der Erzählenden Literatur von Addison bis Dickens</u>. Quakenbrück: Robert Kleinert, pp. 24-32.
        Smollett's caricature, use of the picaresque, and Rabelaisian humor, chiefly in <u>Roderick Random</u> and <u>Humphry Clinker</u>.

13    SINGER, GODFREY FRANK. <u>The Epistolary Novel: Its Origin, Development, Decline, and Residuary Influence</u>. Philadelphia:

University of Pennsylvania Press, pp. 107–8 and passim.
Generalized and not altogether accurate comment on the
epistolary technique in Humphry Clinker.

14    TURBERVILLE, A. S.  Johnson's England: An Account of the Life
& Manners of His Age.  Oxford: Clarendon Press, 2 Vols.,
passim.  Indexed.
Essays by various hands on warfare, law, medicine, and
prisons treat Smollett's novels as though they were autobiographical and historical.

1934

1    BAKER, ERNEST A.  The History of the English Novel.  London:
H. F. & G. Witherby, V, passim.  Indexed.
Compares Smollett's novels with those of subsequent
minor eighteenth-century novelists and discusses influence.

2    BIRSS, JOHN HOWARD.  "A Letter of Tobias G. Smollett," N&Q,
166 (March 17), 189.
1839 catalogue description of undiscovered letter to
Earl of Buchan.

3    [BOSWELL, JAMES].  Boswell's Life of Johnson together with
Boswell's Journal of a Tour to the Hebrides and Johnson's
Diary of a Journey into North Wales, ed. George Birkbeck
Hill; rev. L. F. Powell.  Oxford: Clarendon Press, 6 Vols.,
passim.  Indexed.
In addition to Boswell's and Johnson's comments on
Smollett, offers informative notes on his life and work.

4    DOUBLET, GEORGE.  "Les Consuls de la Nation Britannique a
Nice, aux XVIIe et XVIIIe Siècles," in E. R. Blanchet, Les
Anglais dans le Comté de Nice et en Provence depuis le
XVIIIme Siècle.  Nice: Musée Masséna, pp. 39–60.
Smollett's experiences in Nice during the consulship of
John Buckland.

5    EDGAR, PELHAM.  The Art of the Novel from 1700 to the Present
Time.  New York: Macmillan, passim.  Indexed.
Enthusiastic discussion of epistolary technique in
Humphry Clinker and of Smollett's use of detail in his
fiction.

6    ELWIN, MALCOLM.  Charles Reade.  London: Jonathan Cape, pp.
32, 219.

Compares Smollett and Reade and notes Smollett's influence.

7    HILL, CHARLES JARVIS. "The Literary Career of Richard Graves. The Author of the Spiritual Quixote," Smith College Studies in Modern Languages, 16 (October, 1934-April, 1935), passim. Indexed.
     Comments on relationship of Graves's and Smollett's works and notes attribution of Dutch edition of Spiritual Quixote to Smollett.

8    HOOKER, EDWARD NILES. "The Discussion of Taste, from 1750 to 1770, and the New Trends in Literary Criticism," PMLA, 49 (June), 577-92.
     Compares aesthetic values in Critical Review with other contemporary judgments.

9    HOOKER, EDWARD NILES. "The Reviewers and the New Criticism, 1754-1770," PQ, 13 (April), 189-202.
     Compares attitude in Critical Review toward unorthodox works with judgments in rival periodicals.

10   JONES, CLAUDE E. "Tobias Smollett on the 'Separation of the Pubic Joint in Pregnancy,'" Medical Life, 41 (June), 302-5.
     Smollett's particular medical knowledge and his aid to William Smellie's Treatise on Midwifery.

11   KNAPP, LEWIS M. "The Naval Scenes in Roderick Random," PMLA, 49 (June), 593-98.
     Adds to known details of Smollett's naval experiences, compares his and contemporary writing on the subject, and examines his use of fact in scenes in Roderick Random.

12   **MARSHALL, RODERICK.** Italy in English Literature 1755-1815: Origins of the Romantic Interest in Italy. Columbia University Studies in English and Comparative Literature, no. 116. New York: Columbia University Press, pp. 78-81 and passim. Indexed.
     Smollett's treatment of Italy in his Travels refuted by Baretti and character of Huet in Humphry Clinker identified.

13   MAUGHAM, SOMERSET. "Tobie Smollett à Nice, 1763-1765," tr. into French E. R. Blanchet, in 1934.4, pp. 13-22.
     Account of Smollett's stay in Nice and attitudes expressed in his Travels.

1934

14    MEHROTRA, K. K.  <u>Horace Walpole and the English Novel</u>. A Study
      of the Influence of "The Castle of Otranto" 1764-1820.
      Oxford: Basil Blackwell, pp. 2, 7, 36, 45.
           Walpole's unfavorable view of Smollett and the relation-
      ship of <u>Ferdinand Count Fathom</u> to the Gothic.

15    MIRSKY, D. S.  "Tendencies of the Modern Novel--Russia," <u>Fort-
      nightly Review</u>, n.s. 135 (March), 290.
           Interest in Smollett's <u>Peregrine Pickle</u> in Communist
      Russia; Mirsky's long essay on Smollett for a translation.

16    NANGLE, BENJAMIN C.  <u>"The Monthly Review" First Series 1749-
      1789.  Index of Contributors and Articles</u>.  Oxford:
      Clarendon Press, pp. 42, 156, 181, 199.
           Smollett's relations with Ralph Griffiths and his work
      on the journal.

17    RAO, ANANDA VITTAL.  "Politics, 1750-1760. The Antipathy of
      Smollett and Johnson towards Lyttelton," in <u>A Minor Augus-
      tan being the Life and Works of George, Lord Lyttelton,
      1709-1773</u>.  Calcutta: The Book Company, pp. 226-35.
           Calls Smollett's conduct intemperate and unwarranted in
      unfriendly literary relations with Lyttelton.

18    ROBERTS, W.  "A Shelf of Eighteenth-Century Novels," <u>The
      Book-Collector's Quarterly</u>, 15 (July-Sept.), 21.
           Smollett less influential than Fielding.

19    ROSENBACH, A. S. W.  "The Libraries of the Presidents of the
      United States," <u>Proceedings of the American Antiquarian
      Society</u>, n.s. 44 (October), 338, 344, 352.
           Smollett's works in the Presidents' libraries.

20    SMITH, WARREN HUNTING.  <u>Architecture in English Fiction</u>.  Yale
      Studies in English, 83.  New Haven: Yale University Press;
      London: Humphrey Milford, Oxford University Press, pp. 70,
      89-90, 92, 168-69.
           Attitudes toward architecture in <u>Humphry Clinker</u> unim-
      pressive.

21    WILSON, DAVID ALEC and DAVID WILSON MacARTHUR.  <u>Carlyle in Old
      Age (1865-1881)</u>.  London: Kegan Paul et al., pp. 57, 243.
           Delights in <u>Roderick Random</u> and questions impurities in
      Smollett's work.

1935

1   BABCOCK, R. W.  "The Idea of Taste in the Eighteenth Century,"
    <u>PMLA</u>, 50 (September), 922-26.
        Subject of taste in Smollett's <u>Critical Review</u>.

2   BLOOR, R. H. U.  "Richardson, Fielding, and Smollett," in <u>The
    English Novel from Chaucer to Galsworthy</u>. London: Ivor
    Nicholson and Watson, pp. 160-64.
        Praises Smollett's narratives and appeal to the senses,
    but finds him inferior to his contemporaries and unreflec-
    tive.

3   GRANT, A. J.  "Smollett and Billiards," <u>TLS</u>, November 16, p.
    746.
        Questions Smollett's knowledge of the game as described
    in <u>Peregrine Pickle</u>.

4   GREEN, F. C.  "The Novel," in <u>Minuet: A Critical Survey of
    French and English Literary Ideas in the Eighteenth Cen-
    tury</u>. London: J. M. Dent & Sons, pp. 348-64 and passim.
        Compares Smollett's caricature and invective to Le
    Sage's dispassionate irony, and describes Smollett's ina-
    bility to universalize his art and his sacrifice of tech-
    nique to satiric purposes.

5   JOLIAT, EUGÈNE.  <u>Smollett et la France</u>. Bibliothèque de la
    Revue de Littérature Comparée, 105.  Paris: Librairie An-
    cienne Honoré Champion, 279 pp.
        Judicious and detailed study of Smollett in relation to
    France discusses French influence, Smollett's chauvinistic
    treatment of the French, and the incompatibility of his
    literary attitudes and characteristics with French taste
    and standards.  Although his novels and histories were
    translated into French, he did not enjoy the popularity and
    reputation of his major contemporaries.  Appendix lists and
    describes translations in France, Germany, Holland, and
    other European nations.  Reprinted 1974.25.

6   JONES, CLAUDE E.  "Introduction," in <u>An Essay on the External
    Use of Water by Tobias Smollett</u>, ed. C. E. Jones.  Balti-
    more: The Johns Hopkins Press, 82 pp.
        Introduction describes Smollett's contribution to our
    knowledge of eighteenth-century medicine through his non-
    fiction and fiction.  Jones reprints Smollett's rare essay
    and provides brief annotation.  Originally printed in <u>Bul-
    letin of the Institute of the History of Medicine</u>, 3 (Janu-
    ary), 31-82.

7   JONES, CLAUDE E.   "A Smollett Letter," <u>MLN</u>, 50 (April), 242-
    43.
        With a copy of his translation of <u>Don Quixote</u> and ac-
    knowledging gift of translation of <u>Orlando Furioso</u>.  Re-
    cipient was William Huggins: <u>see</u> 1936.22.

8   KAHRL, GEORGE M.   "The Influence of Shakespeare on Smollett,"
    in <u>Essays in Dramatic Literature: The Parrott Presentation
    Volume</u>, ed. Hardin Craig.  Princeton: Princeton University
    Press, pp. 399-420.
        Considers Smollett's knowledge and use of Shakespeare
    and describes his interest as being in stage productions
    rather than printed texts.  Argues that Smollett employed
    Shakespeare's dramatic rather than literary elements.

9   KNAPP, LEWIS M.   "The Publication of Smollett's <u>Complete His-
    tory</u>...and <u>Continuation</u>," <u>Library</u>, 4th ser., 16 (December),
    295-308.
        In addition to pertinent publication information on the
    histories (including the rare fifth volume), discusses use
    of modern advertising methods and publication in separate
    numbers to increase sales.

10  KNAPP, LEWIS M.   "Smollett and the Case of James Annesley,"
    <u>TLS</u>, December 28, p. 899.
        Likenesses between anonymous tract on Annesley case and
    Smollett's treatment in <u>Peregrine Pickle</u>.

11  LEISERING, WALTER.  <u>Das Motiv des Einsiedlers in der Englis-
    chen Literatur des 18. Jahrhunderts und der Hochromantik</u>.
    Würzburg: Richard Mayr, passim.  Indexed.
        References to hermits and recluses in Smollett's work.

12  LINN, JAMES WEBER and HOUGHTON WELLS TAYLOR.   "The Picaresque:
    <u>Peregrine Pickle</u>," in <u>A Forward to Fiction</u>.  New York and
    London: D. Appleton-Century, pp. 117-21.
        Picaresque characteristics in the novel close to origi-
    nals in the genre.

13  MONK, SAMUEL H.   <u>The Sublime: A Study of Critical Theories in
    XVIII-Century England</u>.  New York: Modern Language Associa-
    tion of America, p. 90.
        Relates terror passages in <u>Fathom</u> to emotional appeal of
    sublime.

14  OSGOOD, CHARLES G.   "Smollett (1721-1771)," in <u>The Voice of
    England: A History of English Literature</u>.  New York and
    London: Harper & Brothers, pp. 338-40.

1935

Conventional criticism emphasizes discursiveness and
coarseness, but approves liveliness of the novels.

15  SMALL, MIRIAM ROSSITER.  Charlotte Ramsay Lennox: An Eigh-
teenth-Century Lady of Letters.  Yale Studies in English,
85.  New Haven: Yale University Press, passim.  Indexed.
Relates Smollett's works to Don Quixote and later eigh-
teenth-century novels and compares Female Quixote and
Launcelot Greaves as different ways of profiting from
Cervantes's work.  Reprinted 1969, Hamden, Conn.: Archon
Books.

16  [STERNE, LAURENCE].  Letters of Laurence Sterne, ed. Lewis
Perry Curtis.  Oxford: Clarendon Press, passim.  Indexed.
Sterne's comments on Smollett.  Curtis's notes compare
their travel books and discuss their personal relations.

17  VAN DER VEEN, H. R. S.  "Smollett," in Jewish Characters in
Eighteenth-Century English Fiction and Drama.  Groningen-
Batavia: J. B. Wolters' Uitgevers-Maatschappij, pp. 37-50.
After early anti-semitic depictions, Smollett offers
favorable, although unrealistic, Jewish character in
Fathom.  Tries unsuccessfully to account for the change,
which did not endure in later work.

18  WILLIAMS, STANLEY T.  The Life of Washington Irving.  New
York: Oxford University Press, I, 79, 82, 114, 440; II,
269-70, 282, 290.
Borrowings and echoes from Smollett's work in Irving's.

19  WOODWORTH, MARY KATHERINE.  The Literary Career of Sir Samuel
Egerton Brydges.  Oxford: Basil Blackwell, p. 129.
High regard for "Ode to Independence."

1936

1  ALLHUSEN, E. L.  "Peregrine Pickle," TLS, February 29, p. 188.
Questions reason for title change in French translation,
1753.

2  BECK, CARL.  "Tobias Smollett," American Journal of Surgery,
n.s. 32 (May), 383-89.
Enthusiastic account predicts new popularity in a period
amenable to realism.  Admires humor, vividness, intellect,
and artistry.

3   BERESFORD, G. C.  Schooldays with Kipling.  London: Victor
    Gollancz, p. 244.
        Kipling's boyhood reading of Smollett.

4   BLACK, FRANK GEES.  "The English Epistolary Novel from 1740 to
    1800."  Diss., Harvard University, 1936.
        Use of varied points-of-view, travel, and no respondents
    in epistolary technique of Humphry Clinker.

5   CARMICHAEL, MONTGOMERY.  "Tobias Smollett a Livorno," Liburni
    Civitas: Rassegna di Attività Municipale, 9, no. 2, 114–
    23.
        Details on Smollett's residence in Livorno.

6   CHESTERTON, G. K.  "Introduction," in The Adventures of
    Peregrine Pickle.  Oxford: Limited Editions Club, Oxford
    University Press, I, v–x.
        Discusses moral characteristics of the novel, Smollett's
    natural treatment of his subject matter, and fact that it
    must be understood as an eighteenth-century novel.  Re-
    printed 1950.3.

7   [COLERIDGE, SAMUEL TAYLOR].  Coleridge's Miscellaneous Criti-
    cism, ed. Thomas Middleton Raysor.  London: Constable, pp.
    55, 329, 433, 443.
        Comments chiefly on characterization and humor in
    Smollett's novels.

8   CURTISS, PHILIP.  "A College for One," Harper's Magazine, 172
    (May), 660.
        Taste for Smollett is a sign of literary sophistication.

9   CURTOYS, W. F. D.  "Tobias Smollett's Influence on Dickens,"
    Dickensian, 32 (September), 249–54.
        Offers conventional biographical and picaresque criti-
    cism and notes general parallels with Dickens's work, but
    contrasts tone and stresses Smollett's unpleasantness com-
    pared with Dickens's ultimate concern for goodness in life.

10  [DENNIE, JOSEPH].  Letters of Joseph Dennie 1768–1812, ed.
    Laura Green Pedder.  University of Maine Studies, 2nd ser.,
    36.  Orono, Maine: University Press, pp. xx, xxi, 31–32,
    40, 144, 198.
        Dennie's delight in Smollett's work.

11  ESHER.  "Smollett: Humphry Clinker, 1771–2," Bibliographical
    Notes and Queries, 2 (April), 3.
        Response to 1936.28 describes own copy of first edition.

1936

12  EWING, J. C.  "Brash and Reid.  Booksellers in Glasgow and
      Their Collection of Poetry Original and Selected," <u>Records
      of the Glasgow Bibliographical Society</u>, 12 (1936), 8.
         Smollett's poems in 1796 anthology.

13  G., G.  "Smollett: <u>Humphry Clinker</u>, 1771-2," <u>Bibliographical
      Notes and Queries</u>, 2 (April), 3.
         Response to 1936.28 poses further questions about early
      editions of the novel.

14  GARNETT, DAVID.  "Richardson, Fielding, and Smollett," in <u>The
      English Novelists: A Survey of the Novel by Twenty Contem-
      porary Novelists</u>, ed. Derek Verschoyle.  New York:
      Harcourt, Brace, pp. 71-82.
         Smollett, far inferior to others, capable of simple and
      crude humor, but little more.

15  HOOKER, EDWARD NILES.  "The Reviewers and the New Trends in
      Poetry, 1754-1770," <u>MLN</u>, 51 (April), 207-14.
         Attitudes on poetry in <u>Critical Review</u> compared to those
      in rival periodicals.

16  KAHRL, GEORGE M.  "Travel and the Prose Fiction of Tobias
      Smollett, M.D."  Diss., Harvard University, 1936.
         Relates Smollett's novels to his own travels, to his and
      others' travel-writings, and discusses significant influ-
      ences of travel literature on his style, humor, and atti-
      tudes.  <u>See</u> 1945.2.

17  KNAPP, LEWIS M.  "An Important Smollett Letter," <u>RES</u>, 12 (Jan-
      uary), 75-77.
         1759 letter on health, work on <u>Critical</u>, and politics.

18  McKILLOP, ALAN D.  <u>Samuel Richardson: Printer and Novelist</u>.
      Chapel Hill: University of North Carolina Press, passim.
      Indexed.
         Personal and literary relations of Smollett and
      Richardson and their later reputations.

19  MURRY, JOHN MIDDLETON.  "Metamorphosis," in <u>The Autobiography
      of John Middleton Murry. Between Two Worlds</u>.  New York:
      Julian Messner, p. 41.
         Childhood familiarity with titles of Smollett's books
      because of their funny names.

20  NORTH, ALFRED.  "Pigtails and Pitch," <u>Times. London</u>, September
      16, p. 8.
         Hugh Hewson original of Strap in <u>Roderick Random</u>.

21    NORWOOD, LUELLA F.  "Smollett: Humphry Clinker," Bibliograph-
      ical Notes and Queries, 2 (May), 3.
           Response to 1936.28 gives information on a pirated
      "second edition" in 1771, differing from Warburton's four.

22    POWELL, L. F.  "William Huggins and Tobias Smollett," MP, 34
      (November), 179-92.
           Correspondence indicates close personal and literary
      ties.

23    PUTNEY, RUFUS D. S.  "Lesage and Smollett. With a List of
      English Editions, Translations, and Imitations of the Works
      of Alain-René Lesage."  Diss., Yale University, 1936.
           Influence of Le Sage's work on Smollett greatest in
      first two novels, then declines.  Argues for Smollett as
      translator of Le Diable Boiteux as well as Gil Blas.

24    SHEPPERSON, ARCHIBALD BOLLING.  The Novel in Motley: A History
      of the Burlesque Novel in English.  Cambridge, Mass.:
      Harvard University Press, passim.  Indexed.
           Smollett's use of the burlesque and burlesques of his
      work.

25    STREETER, HAROLD WADE.  "A Renewal of the Picaresque Novel:
      Tobias Smollett," in The Eighteenth Century English Novel
      in French Translation: A Bibliographical Study.  New York:
      Publications of the Institute of French Studies, pp. 70-76.
           Gives French translations of Smollett's work in eigh-
      teenth and early nineteenth centuries.  Unfavorable recep-
      tion because of vulgarity, attack on French in Travels, and
      decline of interest in picaresque.

26    STRONG, L. A. G.  "Introduction," in The Expedition of Humphry
      Clinker.  London, New York, et al.: Thomas Nelson & Sons,
      pp. v-xiv.
           Simple, uninformative account of Smollett's life and
      career and description of Humphry Clinker, which especially
      praises characterization of Matthew Bramble.

27    UTTER, ROBERT PALFREY and GWENDOLYN BRIDGES NEEDHAM.  Pamela's
      Daughters.  New York: Macmillan, passim.  Indexed.
           Smollett, opposed to sentimental novel, admires rakish,
      but fundamentally good, heroes.  Weak depiction of women,
      except Emilia in Peregrine Pickle.  Study traces develop-
      ment from the French of Tabitha in Humphry Clinker.

1936

28   WARBURTON, T.  "Smollett: Humphrey [sic] Clinker, 1771-2,"
     Bibliographical Notes and Queries, 2 (January), 7.
           Notes variants in four editions. See replies above.

29   WILLIAMS, BLANCHE COLTON.  George Eliot.  New York: Macmillan,
     p. 170.
           Eliot and G. H. Lewes's disappointment in Humphry
     Clinker.


                              1937

1    ALLEN, B. SPRAGUE.  Tides in English Taste (1619-1800). A
     Background for the Study of Literature.  Cambridge, Mass.:
     Harvard University Press, 2 Vols., passim.  Indexed.
           Compares Smollett's aesthetic tastes and interests with
     those of his contemporaries.

2    BROWN, SAMUEL HORTON.  "Tobias George Smollett, Physician,"
     General Magazine and Historical Chronicle. University of
     Pennsylvania, 39 (April), 252-55.
           Assesses Smollett's medical interests and knowledge.

3    CRAIGIE, WILLIAM.  Northern Words in Modern English.  Society
     for Pure English Tract, 50.  Oxford: Clarendon Press, pp.
     334, 338, 339, 340.
           Use of Scottish words in Humphry Clinker.

4    GRANT, M. H.  "Gainsborough and Smollett," TLS, October 9, p.
     735.
           John Taylor was painter referred to in Humphry Clinker.

5    HEILMAN, ROBERT B.  America in English Fiction: 1760-1800: The
     Influences of the American Revolution.  Louisiana State
     University Studies, no. 33.  Baton Rouge: Louisiana State
     University Press, passim.  Indexed.
           American material in the Atom, Humphry Clinker, and
     Launcelot Greaves.

*6   NEEDHAM, GWENDOLYN BRIDGES.  "The 'Old Maid' in the Life and
     the Fiction of Eighteenth-Century England."  Diss., Univer-
     sity of California, Berkeley, 1937.
           Smollett's use of the "old maid" as a type character.
     Cited in California University, Graduate Division, Pro-
     grammes of Final Public Examinations.

7    POWELL, L. F.  "Gainsborough and Smollett," TLS, October 16,
     p. 759.

Further argument for Taylor as painter in <u>Humphry Clinker</u>.

8    RICE-OXLEY, L. "Gainsborough and Smollett," <u>TLS</u>, October 2, p. 715.
        Supports argument for John Taylor as landscape painter in <u>Humphry Clinker</u>.

9    ROBERTS, KENNETH. <u>Northwest Passage</u>. Garden City, New York: Doubleday, Doran & Company, p. 506.
        Fictional character comments on accuracy of portrait of Sir William Johnson in the <u>Atom</u>.

10    ROBERTS, W. "Gainsborough and Smollett," <u>TLS</u>, September 18, p. 675.
        Suggests Gainsborough as landscape painter, "Mr. T---," praised in <u>Humphry Clinker</u>.

11    ROBERTS, W. "Gainsborough and Smollett," <u>TLS</u>, September 25, p. 695.
        Rejects John Taylor and weakly defends earlier argument for Gainsborough as painter in <u>Humphry Clinker</u>.

12    UNDERWOOD, E. ASHWORTH. "Medicine and Science in the Writings of Smollett," <u>Proceedings of the Royal Society of Medicine</u>, 30 (June), 961-74.
        Sensible account offers valuable detailed information on Smollett's use of medical knowledge in his writing.

13    WARNER, JAMES H. "Eighteenth-Century English Reactions to the <u>Nouvelle Héloise</u>," <u>PMLA</u>, 52 (September), 803-19.
        Compares responses in <u>Critical Review</u> to that in rival periodicals.

14    WRIGHT, RICHARDSON LITTLE. <u>Revels in Jamaica, 1682-1838; Plays and Players</u> etc. New York: Dodd, Mead, passim. Indexed.
        Performances of Smollett's plays in the West Indies.

## 1938

1    BAYNE-POWELL, R. <u>Eighteenth-Century London Life</u>. New York: E. P. Dutton, pp. 66, 195, 322, 328, 367-68.
        Smollett's social attitudes and an anecdote about the <u>Critical Review</u>.

1938

2   DAICHES, DAVID.  Literature and Society.  London: Victor
    Gollancz, pp. 134, 138, 156, 206.
        Praises Smollett's realism, but ranks him below
    Fielding.

3   FORD, FORD MADOX.  "Fielding and Smollett," in The March of
    Literature from Confucius' Day to Our Own.  New York: The
    Dial Press, pp. 571-79.
        High praise for Smollett's novels approves realistic
    humor and rates him above Fielding.

4   JOLIAT, EUGÈNE.  "Millin's Use of Smollett's Travels," Revue
    de Littérature Comparée, 18 (July-September), 510-14.
        Aubin-Louis Millin copied from Smollett for his book in
    1807-11, which is evidence of Smollett's accuracy and per-
    ception in his descriptions of Nice.

5   JONES, CLAUDE E.  "A Smollett Note," N&Q, 174 (February 26),
    152.
        A Smollett letter of 1759 suggests his authorship of a
    poem in British Magazine.

6   OTIS, WILLIAM BRADLEY and MORRIS H. NEEDLEMAN.  "Tobias George
    Smollett," in A Survey-History of English Literature.  New
    York: Barnes & Noble, pp. 396-99.
        Deplores coarseness and indecency and compares him un-
    favorably to Fielding.

7   PRICE, LAWRENCE M.  "Smollett, Jünger, and Stephanie der
    Jüngere," Monatshefte für Deutschen Unterricht, 30 (March-
    April), 157-62.
        Eighteenth-century German plays based on Peregrine
    Pickle and Humphry Clinker.  Price discusses dramatic pos-
    sibilities of Smollett's novels and terms under which a
    German audience was willing to accept them.

8   PURCELL, J. M.  "Smollett on Oats as Food for Scots," PMLA,
    53 (June), 629.
        Bramble's comment supports view that Johnson regarded
    the practice as contemptuous.

9   READ, HERBERT.  "Tobias Smollett," in Collected Essays in
    Literary Criticism.  London: Faber and Faber, pp. 234-46.
        Reprint of 1926.16.

10  SLAGLE, KENNETH CHESTER.  The English Country Squire in English
    Prose Fiction from 1700-1800.  Philadelphia: University of

Pennsylvania Press, passim.  Indexed.
Many references to Smollett's work on the subject.

11    SMART, GEORGE K.  "Private Libraries in Colonial Virginia,"
      <u>AL</u>, 10 (March), 35, 37.
          Frequent presence of <u>Peregrine Pickle</u>, <u>Roderick Random</u>,
      <u>History of England</u>, and less often <u>British Magazine</u>.


<u>1939</u>

1     ANDERSON, CHARLES R.  "<u>White Jacket</u> as Romance," in <u>Melville</u>
      <u>in the South Seas</u>.  Columbia University Studies in English
      and Comparative Literature, no. 138.  New York: Columbia
      University Press, pp. 402-5, 490.
          Melville's particular indebtedness to <u>Roderick Random</u>.

2     BÉLANGER, JEAN.  "Note sur <u>Roderick Random</u> et L'Expédition de
      Carthagène," <u>EA</u>, 3 (July-September), 250-51.
          New material throws further light on Smollett's partici-
      pation in and description of the event.

3     CLARK, T. BLAKE.  <u>Oriental England: A Study of Oriental Influ-</u>
      <u>ences in Eighteenth Century England as Reflected in the</u>
      <u>Drama</u>.  Shanghai: Kelly & Walsh, pp. 95-96, 120.
          Discusses <u>History and Adventures of an Atom</u> and <u>The</u>
      <u>Israelites</u>, play falsely attributed to Smollett.

4     DAVIS, ROSE MARY.  "'Object of Every Aspiring Pen,'" in <u>The</u>
      <u>Good Lord Lyttelton. A Study in Eighteenth Century Politics</u>
      <u>and Culture</u>.  Bethlehem, Pa.: Times Publishing Company, pp.
      219-22 and passim.
          Smollett's generally unfriendly literary relations with
      Lyttelton.  Largely follows 1925.4.

5     JOLIAT, EUGÈNE.  "Smollett, Editor of Voltaire," <u>MLN</u>, 54
      (June), 429-36.
          Smollett annotated the prose in important translation of
      the <u>Works</u>.

6     KINNE, WILLARD AUSTIN.  <u>Revivals and Importations of French</u>
      <u>Comedies in England, 1749-1800</u>.  New York: Columbia Univer-
      sity Press, passim.  Indexed.
          Influence of Smollett's work on plays of his time.

*7    MARTZ, LOUIS L.  "Tobias Smollett's Association with Travel-
      Books."  Diss., Yale University, 1939.
          <u>See</u> 1942.5.

1939

8  MODDER, MONTAGU FRANK. "The Eighteenth Century," in The Jew
   in the Literature of England to the End of the 19th Century. Philadelphia: Jewish Publication Society of America,
   pp. 58-62.
        Smollett's unsympathetic treatment of the Jew in all but
   Ferdinand Count Fathom, at the time of the Jewish Naturalization Act.

9  NOBBE, GEORGE. The North Briton: A Study in Political Propaganda. New York: Columbia University Press, passim. Indexed.
        Smollett's journalistic failure in the Briton in support
   of Lord Bute and the Treaty of Paris.

*10 PARKER, ALICE. "Views of Crime and Punishment in Fielding and
   Smollett." Diss., Yale University, 1939.
        Cited in McNamee, Dissertations in English and American
   Literature.

*11 SARCHET, HELEN COOKE. "Women in English Fiction of the Mid-
   Eighteenth Century from 1740 to 1771." Diss., University
   of Minnesota, 1939.
        Some discussion of Smollett's attitudes toward women in
   his novels. Cited in Minnesota University. Summaries of
   Ph.D. Theses, 2 (1943), 146-49.

12 [SHENSTONE, WILLIAM]. The Letters of William Shenstone, ed.
   Marjorie Williams. Oxford: Basil Blackwell, passim. Indexed.
        Unfavorable comments about Smollett, particularly his
   character, in controversies with Shenstone's friends.

13 TAYLOR, W. D. "Tobias Smollett, M.D., Aberdeen, 1750,"
   Aberdeen University Review, 26 (March), 125-35.
        Emphasizes his attitudes toward Scotland and the Scot-
   tish material and background of his writing.

14 TOBIN, JAMES E. "Tobias George Smollett (1721-1771)," in
   Eighteenth Century English Literature and Its Cultural
   Background: A Bibliography. New York: Fordham University
   Press, pp. 157-58.
        Lists 13 works and editions of Smollett and 47 secondary
   items.

15 [WORDSWORTH, WILLIAM and DOROTHY]. Letters of William and
   Dorothy Wordsworth. The Later Years, ed. Ernest De
   Selincourt. Oxford: Clarendon Press, I, 65.

William's 1822 letter shows familiarity with Smollett's work.

## 1940

1   ASPINALL-OGLANDER, CECIL. Admiral's Wife, Being the Life and Letters of the Hon. Mrs. Edward Boscawen from 1719 to 1761. New York et al.: Longmans, Green, pp. 77, 78-79, 141.
     Contemporary response to Roderick Random and use of Smollett's history.

*2   BOEGE, FREDERICK WILLIAM. "Smollett's Reputation as a Novelist." Diss., Princeton University, 1940.
     See 1947.1.

3   BROWN, HERBERT ROSS. The Sentimental Novel in America 1789-1860. Durham, N.C.: Duke University Press, passim. Indexed.
     Attitudes toward Smollett in America and use of his nautical characters in American sentimental novels.

4   DIGEON, AURÉLIEN. "Un Grand Conteur: Tobias Smollett," in Le Roman Anglais au Dix-Huitième Siècle. Études d'Aujourd-'hui, no. 3. Paris: Henri Didier, pp. 53-60.
     Generally favorable discussion of Smollett's narrative techniques.

5   DYSON, H. V. D. and JOHN BUTT. "The Age of Johnson," in Augustans and Romantics 1689-1830. Introductions to English Literature, ed. Bonamy Dobrée. London: The Cresset Press, III, 63-64.
     Conventional comparison with Fielding and dissatisfaction with coarseness, emphasizing novels as "source books."

6   GALLAWAY, FRANCIS. Reason, Rule, and Revolt in English Classicism. New York: Charles Scribner's Sons, passim. Indexed.
     General comments on Smollett's social and aesthetic values.

7   GALLAWAY, W. F. JR. "The Conservative Attitude toward Fiction, 1770-1830," PMLA, 55 (December), 1041-59.
     Includes some critical responses to Smollett's novels.

8   SHEPHERD, T. B. Methodism and the Literature of the Eighteenth Century. London: The Epworth Press, pp. 219-24 and passim. Indexed.

1940

Smollett's attitude toward Methodism in Humphry Clinker had softened from views in the History of England.

9  TRANGER, WILMER KOHL. "Pedagogues and Pupils: A Study in Eighteenth-Century Fiction." Diss., Harvard University, 1940.
   Discusses educative process as treated in Smollett's novels.

10  VIETS, HENRY R. "Smollett, the War of Jenkins' Ear, and an Account of the Expedition to Carthagena, 1743," Medical Library Association Bulletin (Boston), 28 (June), 178-81.
   Compares historical account and Smollett's fictional treatment.

11  VINCENT, H. P. "Tobias Smollett's Assault on Gordon and Groom," RES, 16 (April), 183-88.
   Describes Smollett's generosity to fellow Scots and details incident in which he assaulted Peter Gordon and Edward Groom, provoked by their ingratitude and insolence.

12  WORK, JAMES AIKEN. "Introduction," in Sterne's The Life and Opinions of Tristram Shandy, Gentleman. New York: The Odyssey Press, passim.
   Relates style of Tristram Shandy to parody of Smollett's technique and contrasts Sterne's humor and characterization to Smollett's.

## 1941

1  CRAIGIE, WILLIAM A. "Coach and Four," in Completing the Record of English. Society for Pure English, Tract No. 58. Oxford: Oxford University Press, p. 285.
   Smollett's use of the term in Humphry Clinker.

2  GOVE, PHILIP BABCOCK. The Imaginary Voyage in Prose Fiction. New York: Columbia University Press, pp. 165, 175, 320, 357.
   References to Smollett in text and checklist.

3  KAHRL, GEORGE M. "Captain Robert Stobo," Virginia Magazine of History and Biography, 49 (April and July), 141-51, 254-68.
   Biographical sketch of Stobo, whom Smollett knew personally and respected, but turned into the eccentric Lismahago in Humphry Clinker.

1941

4  MACKENZIE, AGNES MURE.  Scotland in Modern Times, 1720-1939.
   London and Edinburgh: W. & R. Chambers, p. 34.
         Contrasts Smollett and Henry Mackenzie and sees Smollett
   in the English tradition.

5  MARTZ, LOUIS L.  "Smollett and the Expedition to Carthagena,"
   PMLA, 56 (June), 428-46.
         Compares Smollett's treatment in his Compendium of Au-
   thentic and Entertaining Voyages to that in Roderick Random
   and concludes that he turned his material to satiric purposes in his fiction to maintain the tone of the narrative
   and to express his indignation with the military.

6  MARTZ, LOUIS L.  "Tobias Smollett and the Universal History,"
   MLN, 56 (January), 1-14.
         Smollett had major editorial duties, but not complete
   responsibility and wrote considerable portions.  Addendum
   cites evidence for reviews by Smollett, including his own
   work, in the Critical.

7  MATTHIESSEN, F. O.  American Renaissance: Art and Expression
   in the Age of Emerson and Whitman.  New York et al.: Oxford
   University Press, pp. 207, 389.
         Hawthorne's interest in Smollett and Melville's use of
   his work in White Jacket.

8  NORWOOD, LUELLA F.  "The Authenticity of Smollett's 'Ode to
   Independence,'" RES, 17 (January), 55-64.
         Overlooked evidence for authenticity of ascription to
   Smollett.

9  NORWOOD, LUELLA F.  "Tobias George Smollett (1721-1771)," in
   Cambridge Bibliography of English Literature, ed. F. W.
   Bateson.  New York and Cambridge: Macmillan, and Cambridge
   University Press, II, 523-27.
         Bibliographies of Smollett's work, collected editions,
   individual publications, questionable attributions, and
   biographical and critical secondary works.

10 SAMPSON, GEORGE.  "Fielding and Smollett," in The Concise
   Cambridge History of English Literature.  Cambridge: University Press, pp. 507-9 and passim.
         General account of Smollett's life and career and con-
   tribution to the novel.

11 STAUFFER, DONALD A.  The Art of Biography in Eighteenth Century England.  Princeton: Princeton University Press, 2
   Vols., passim.  Indexed.

Smollett's work in relation to biography and description
of some biographies of Smollett. Reprinted 1970, New York:
Russell & Russell.

12  WELLEK, RENÉ. The Rise of English Literary History. Chapel
Hill: University of North Carolina Press, pp. 70, 152.
Contributions to literary history in British Magazine
and preface to Roderick Random.

13  [WORDSOWRTH, DOROTHY]. Journals of Dorothy Wordsworth, ed. E.
De Selincourt. London: Macmillan, I, 244-45, 334; II,
351.
Smollett's Latin scholarship, poetry, and romanticism in
Ferdinand Count Fathom. Comment on inscription on his
monument in Scotland.

## 1942

1  BOWEN, ELIZABETH. English Novelists. London: Collins, pp.
18-20.
Brief account emphasizes picaresque and autobiographical.

2  FOSTER, JAMES R. "Smollett's Pamphleteering Foe Shebbeare,"
PMLA, 57 (December), 1053-1100.
Shebbeare's personal, literary, and political relation-
ships with Smollett.

3  GEROULD, GORDON HALL. The Patterns of English and American
Fiction, a History. Boston: Little, Brown, pp. 92-98 and
passim. Indexed.
Emphasizes episodic structure, gross caricature, and
lack of invention in Smollett's works, but praises powers
of observation and eccentric characters.

4  JONES, CLAUDE E. Smollett Studies. University of California
Publications in English, 9, no. 2. Berkeley and Los
Angeles: University of California Press, xi + 133 pp.
Two essays. "Smollett and the Navy" discusses accuracy
of his description of naval conditions and analyzes technique with nautical characters. "Smollett and 'Critical
Review'" details editorial labors and contributions to its
success. Appendices include reviews, letters, a story and
poem, and a list of attacks on the Critical. Reprinted
1970.23.

5   MARTZ, LOUIS L.  The Later Career of Tobias Smollett.  Yale
    Studies in English, no. 97.  New Haven: Yale University
    Press, xi + 213 pp.
        Richly detailed study of Smollett's work after 1753 in-
    vestigates Smollett's journalistic and editorial efforts in
    relation to development of his later prose style and ana-
    lyzes the distinctive characteristics of the Travels and
    Adventures of an Atom, especially against their contempor-
    ary cultural background.  Discusses in detail effect of
    compilation of The Present State of All Nations on Humphry
    Clinker.  An excellent example of historical scholarship
    put to the use of sensitive stylistic and intellectual
    criticism.  Reprinted 1968.28.

6   PARKER, ALICE.  "Tobias Smollett and the Law," SP, 39 (July),
    545-58.
        Smollett's legal entanglements and their relationship to
    his personality and novels.

7   PRITCHETT, V. S.  "Books in General," The New Statesman and
    Nation, 23 (February 28), 145.
        Discusses characteristics of Smollett's realism and
    caricature and praises his Travels and the Trunnion materi-
    al in Humphry Clinker.  Reprinted 1953.14.

8   SYPHER, WYLIE.  Guinea's Captive Kings: British Anti-Slavery
    Literature of the XVIIIth Century.  Chapel Hill: University
    of North Carolina Press, passim.  Indexed.
        Smollett's attitudes toward blacks and slavery.

9   [THRALE, HESTER LYNCH].  Thraliana: The Diary of Mrs. Hester
    Lynch Thrale (Later Mrs. Piozzi), 1776-1809, ed. Katherine
    C. Balderston.  Oxford: Clarendon Press, I, 248, 328-29.
        Mrs. Thrale's preference of Smollett over Fielding, but
    not Richardson or Rousseau.

10  WELLEK, RENÉ and AUSTIN WARREN.  Theory of Literature.  New
    York: Harcourt, Brace, pp. 99, 229.
        Smollett linked with Fielding in narrative techniques.

## 1943

1   ALLISON, R. S.  Sea-Diseases.  London: J. Bale Medical Publi-
    cations, pp. 65, 117-19.
        Smollett's picture of nautical life in Roderick Random.

1943

*2   CORDASCO, FRANCESCO. <u>Smollett en España</u>. Madrid.
       Cited in Cordasco, 1947.2. No other evidence.

3    HARTLEY, LODWICK. <u>This Is Lorence: A Narrative of the Rever-</u>
       <u>end Laurence Sterne</u>. Chapel Hill: University of North
       Carolina Press, passim. Indexed.
          Smollett's and Sterne's travel accounts and their rela-
       tionship.

4    JONES, HOWARD MUMFORD. "Introduction," in <u>The Expedition of</u>
       <u>Humphry Clinker</u>. Everyman's Library, No. 975. London: J.
       M. Dent & Sons; New York: E. P. Dutton & Co., pp. v-xi.
          Cautious praise of Smollett's achievement notes final
       triumph of his genius over his personality and cites im-
       portance of his broad picture of eighteenth-century life.

5    KNAPP, LEWIS M. "Smollett's Friend Smith," <u>TLS</u>, October 9,
       p. 492.
          Information on Robert (Bob) Smith and his friendship
       with Smollett.

6    MEIKLE, HENRY W. "New Smollett Letters--I," <u>TLS</u>, July 24, p.
       360.
          Four letters to Alexander Carlyle on <u>The Regicide</u>,
       <u>Alceste</u>, and an unidentified comedy, and Smollett's delight
       with response to <u>Roderick Random</u>.

7    MEIKLE, HENRY W. "New Smollett Letters--II," <u>TLS</u>, July 31, p.
       372.
          Three letters to Carlyle on theatrical efforts and sup-
       posed plagiarism in <u>Tom Jones</u>.

8    RANDOLPH, MARY CLAIRE. "Diamond-Satires in the Eighteenth
       Century," <u>N&Q</u>, 185 (July 31), 62-65.
          Background for comments in <u>Humphry Clinker</u> on the "dia-
       mond-satires" engraved on inn-windows in Scotland.

9    TAYLOR, JOHN TINNON. <u>Early Opposition to the English Novel:</u>
       <u>The Popular Reaction from 1760 to 1830</u>. New York: King's
       Crown Press, passim. Indexed.
          Reactions to Smollett's fiction, particularly attacks
       on moral grounds.

10   WAGENKNECHT, EDWARD. "Smollett and the Novel of Humors," in
       <u>Cavalcade of the English Novel</u>. New York et al.: Holt,
       Rinehart and Winston, pp. 69-77 and passim.

Fairly sympathetic account of Smollett's novels relates their structure to the picaresque and characters to Elizabethan humours and praises eccentric and nautical characters.

## 1944

1   BOWEN, ELIZABETH. "English Novelists," in Romance of English Literature, ed. W. J. Turner. New York: Hastings House, p. 241.
    Smollett's oversensitiveness to social conditions leads to his coarseness and imbalance.

*2   CORDASCO, FRANCESCO. Ensayo sobre las Obras de Smollett y la Gil Blas de Lesage. Salamanca.
    Cited in Cordasco, 1947.2. No other evidence.

3   EAVES, THOMAS CARY DUNCAN. "Graphic Illustration of the Principal English Novels of the Eighteenth Century." Diss., Harvard University, 1944.
    Discusses illustrations of Roderick Random, Peregrine Pickle, and Humphry Clinker, but notes Smollett's work elicited less interest from contemporary artists than those of Goldsmith, Fielding, and Sterne.

4   ENGEL, CLAIRE-ELIANE. "English Novels in Switzerland in the XVIIIth Century," Comparative Literature Studies, 14-15 (1944), 7.
    Swiss reader finds Fathom has verisimilitude despite some unbelievable events.

5   HOUPT, CHARLES THEODORE. "London Physician (1750-1770)," in Mark Akenside: A Biographical and Critical Study. Philadelphia: University of Pennsylvania Press, pp. 126-29, 131-33.
    Traces Smollett's personal, professional (medical), and literary relationships with Akenside. Reprinted 1970, New York: Russell & Russell.

6   KNAPP, LEWIS M. "Dr. John Armstrong, Littérateur, and Associate of Smollett, Thomson, Wilkes, and Other Celebrities," PMLA, 59 (December), 1019-58.
    Gives details of Smollett's close personal and literary relationship from 1750 on with Armstrong and their collaboration on the Critical Review.

1944

7    KNAPP, LEWIS M.  "Rex versus Smollett: More Data on the
     Smollett-Knowles Libel Case," MP, 41 (May), 221-27.
         Details of the trial and Smollett's conduct (including
     appeal to Lord Mansfield) in the Knowles' case.

8    KNAPP, LEWIS M.  "Smollett and the Elder Pitt," MLN, 59
     (April), 250-57.
         Smollett's assessment of Pitt was balanced and consis-
     tent.

9    KNAPP, LEWIS M.  "Smollett's Letter to Philip Miller," TLS,
     June 24, p. 312.
         Smollett's active role as editor of the Critical and his
     probable friendship with the botanist.

10   PANE, REMIGIO UGO.  English Translations from the Spanish,
     1484-1943.  New Brunswick, N.J.: Rutgers University Press,
     pp. 69-70, 126-27.
         Lists editions of Smollett's translations of Gil Blas
     and Don Quixote and of translations based on them.

11   POWELL, WILLIAM C.  "Christopher Anstey: Bath Laureate."
     Diss., University of Pennsylvania, 1944 (printed in Phila-
     delphia), pp. 96-98.
         Influence of New Bath Guide on Humphry Clinker grossly
     exaggerated.


                              1945

*1   BRITTON, WEBSTER E.  "The Educative Purpose of Smollett's Fic-
     tion."  Diss., University of Michigan, 1945.
         Cited in McNamee, Dissertations in English and American
     Literature.

2    KAHRL, GEORGE M.  Tobias Smollett Traveler-Novelist.  Chicago:
     University of Chicago Press, xxiv + 165 pp.
         Meticulous study of relationship of Smollett's prose
     fiction to his personal and literary interests in travel.
     Considers importance of Scottish background to attitudes
     expressed in his fiction.  Demonstrates significance of
     travel interests to structure, style, and characterization
     of the novels and explores his compilations and editions of
     travel literature and journalistic treatment of the sub-
     ject.  Emphasizes the artistic rather than autobiographical
     nature of the Travels.  Reprinted 1968.22.

3   KNAPP, LEWIS M.   "Smollett and Garrick," in Elizabethan Stud-
    ies and Other Essays in Honor of George F. Reynolds.   Uni-
    versity of Colorado Studies, 2 (1945), 233-43.
        Existing evidence on their relationship makes it impos-
    sible to offer any absolute judgment on where responsibili-
    ty lay in the differences between Smollett and Garrick.

4   PUTNEY, RUFUS.   "The Plan of Peregrine Pickle," PMLA, 60 (De-
    cember), 1051-65.
        Argues effectively that the structure relates to
    Smollett's aim, a satire on high society, and even interpo-
    lated material reinforces view of social corruption.
    Smollett builds around the relationship of Peregrine and
    Emilia, and his narrative describes Peregrine's growth.

5   RICHMOND, H. W.   "The Naval Officer in Fiction," Essays and
    Studies, 30 (1945), 7-25.
        Smollett's generally unfavorable portrait of officers
    resulted from his subordinate position to them and his dis-
    satisfaction with conditions of his job aboard ship.

6   SUTHERLAND, JAMES.   "Some Aspects of Eighteenth-Century
    Prose," in Essays on the Eighteenth Century Presented to
    David Nichol Smith.   Oxford: Clarendon Press, pp. 107-9.
        Literary style of eighteenth-century Scotsmen.

7   [THACKERAY, WILLIAM MAKEPEACE].   The Letters and Private
    Papers of William Makepeace Thackeray, ed. Gordon N. Ray.
    Cambridge, Mass.: Harvard University Press, I, 48; II, 144;
    IV, 186.
        Letters and diary (1829, 1844, 1860), sympathetic com-
    ments on Smollett, his history, and Peregrine Pickle.

8   WOLF, EDWARD C. J.   "Rowlandson and Eighteenth Century Prose,"
    in Rowlandson and His Illustrations of Eighteenth Century
    English Literature.   Copenhagen: Einar Munksgaard, pp. 115-
    46, 169-70, and passim.
        Compares Smollett's and Rowlandson's caricatures and
    discusses Rowlandson's illustrations of Smollett's work.

9   YOSELOFF, THOMAS.   "Continental Interlude," in A Fellow of
    Infinite Jest.   New York: Prentice-Hall, Inc., pp. 156-57.
        Questions whether Smollett and Sterne met in Montpelier,
    and attributes Sterne's attack on Smollett to unfavorable
    reviews of Tristram Shandy in the Critical Review.

1946

1   CRAIGIE, WILLIAM A.  "c. 1767. Smollett, Humphrey [sic]
    Clinker, Letter of July 13," in The Critique of Pure
    English from Caxton to Smollett.  Society for Pure English,
    Tract No. 65.  Oxford: Clarendon Press, pp. 163-64.
        Extract from letter defending Scottish use of English.

2   DUNBAR, HOWARD HUNTER.  The Dramatic Career of Arthur Murphy.
    New York: The Modern Language Association of America.  Re-
    volving Fund Series, pp. 46, 110-11, 151, 152.
        Compares Murphy's and Smollett's use of malapropism and
    discusses the Briton.  Reprinted 1966, New York: Kraus.

3   EMERY, JOHN PIKE.  Arthur Murphy: An Eminent English Dramatist
    of the Eighteenth Century.  Philadelphia: University of
    Pennsylvania Press for Temple University Publications, pp.
    83-84.
        Smollett's work on the Briton.

4   FRIEDMAN, ARTHUR.  "Goldsmith's Contributions to the Critical
    Review," MP, 44 (August), 23-52.
        Evaluates evidence for Goldsmith's contributions during
    the period Smollett was editor of the Critical Review.

5   HEILMAN, ROBERT B.  "Falstaff and Smollett's Micklewhimmen,"
    RES, 22 (July), 226-28.
        Smollett borrowed from Shakespeare for character in
    Humphry Clinker, but turned comic into satirical.

6   JONES, CLAUDE E.  "Contributors to the Critical Review 1756-
    1785," MLN, 61 (November), 433-41.
        Details on some contributors during years Smollett was
    editor.

7   JONES, CLAUDE E.  "Smollett's Peregrine Pickle: A Note," N&Q,
    190 (May 18), 213.
        Letter in newspaper from Daniel Mackercher denies that
    narrative of Mr. M---e in Peregrine Pickle is memoir of his
    life.

8   L., E.  "Quotation from Smollett," N&Q, 191 (July 13), 18.
        Query about reference to Smollett in an edition of
    Voltaire.

9   McCULLOUGH, BRUCE.  "The Picaresque Novel: Tobias George
    Smollett," in Representative English Novelists: Defoe to
    Conrad.  New York and London: Harper & Brothers, pp. 58-68.

Unfavorable account of Smollett's use of the picaresque, primarily in Roderick Random.

10  MALCOLM, CHARLES A.  The Bank of Scotland, 1695-1945.  Edinburgh: R. & R. Clark, pp. 26, 168.
    Role of Smollett's grandfather in the Bank of Scotland.

11  NORWOOD, LUELLA F.  "Imposition of a Half-Sheet in Duodecimo," Library, 5th ser., 1 (December), 242-44.
    Printing and binding methods of two copies of the first edition of Humphry Clinker.

12  NORWOOD, LUELLA F.  "Smollett's 'Ode to Independence,'" Colby Library Quarterly, 1st ser., no. 15 (June), pp. 233-37.
    Publication history of the poem and evidence for Smollett's authorship.

13  NOTESTEIN, WALLACE.  The Scot in History.  New Haven: Yale University Press, pp. 217, 243.
    Despite some Scottish ties, Smollett in the English tradition.

14  OPPENHEIMER, JANE M.  New Aspects of John and William Hunter. New York: Henry Schuman, pp. 146-47, 167.
    Smollett letter of 11 August 1763 probably to William rather than, as supposed, to John Hunter.

15  PUTNEY, RUFUS D. S.  "Smollett and Lady Vane's Memoirs," PQ, 25 (April), 120-26.
    Smollett wrote her memoirs from information she supplied him.

16  SAINTSBURY, GEORGE.  "Smollett," in The Peace of the Augustans: A Survey of Eighteenth Century Literature as a Place of Rest and Refreshment.  Oxford World Classics, no. 506. New York et al.: Oxford University Press, pp. 131-40.
    Epitomizes Victorian reaction that delighted in his narrative powers, but lamented coarseness, vulgarity, and brutality of his fictional world even in Humphry Clinker in parts.  Originally published in 1916.

17  WEINSTOCK, HERBERT.  Handel.  New York: Alfred A. Knopf, pp. 284-86, 291.
    Discusses Smollett's Alceste and attributes Rich's failure to produce it to an earthquake scare.

18  WILLIAMS, MARJORIE.  Lady Luxborough Goes to Bath.  Oxford: Basil Blackwell, passim.  Indexed.

1946

Considerable use of Humphry Clinker to discuss Lady
Luxborough's visit to Bath.

19  WINTERICH, JOHN T. and DAVID A. RANDALL. "The Pursuit of the
    Point," in A Primer of Book-Collecting. Revised and En-
    larged. New York: Greenberg, pp. 152, 156.
        Discusses the two "first" editions of Humphry Clinker.

20  YOUNG, PERCY M. "Observations on Music by Tobias Smollett,"
    Music & Letters, 27 (January), 18-24.
        Smollett's common-man's attitudes toward music generally
    and his use of various forms of the period in his work.


                            1947

1   BOEGE, FRED W. Smollett's Reputation as a Novelist. Prince-
    ton Studies in English, 27. Princeton: Princeton Univer-
    sity Press, 175 pp.
        Detailed account of the phases of Smollett's reputation
    in England and the United States from 1748 through 1940.
    Although concerned primarily with the novels, includes some
    information about his other works. Reveals the enormous
    variation in critical attitudes, ranging from the highly
    appreciative to the most derogatory, and associates the
    changes to alterations in conventions and taste. Treatment
    from 1800 on is necessarily more selective than with earli-
    er material. Reprinted 1969.2.

2   CORDASCO, FRANCESCO. Smollett Criticism, 1925-1945: A Compi-
    lation. Brooklyn: Long Island University Press, 9 pp.
        Seventy-three items arranged chronologically. Neither
    "exhaustive," as Cordasco claims, nor accurate, the work
    should be used with utmost caution. For some corrections
    and additions, see Boucé, 1971.7. Reprinted 1970.11.

3   MacCARTHY, B. G. The Later Women Novelists 1744-1818. Oxford:
    B. H. Blackwell, Cork University Press, pp. 32-33, 101,
    108, 135-36.
        Smollett's attitude toward women; his anticipation of
    the Gothic; the structure of his novels; and comparisons
    with the work of Fanny Burney and Ann Radcliffe.

4   MACK, EDWARD C. "Pamela's Stepdaughters: The Heroines of
    Smollett and Fielding," College English, 8 (March), 293-
    301.
        Smollett's heroines represent the eighteenth-century
    norm in manners, appearance, abilities, and marriages, but

deviate from the model in their suggestion of sensuality.
Comparison of treatment with Fielding's.

5   MOTT, FRANK LUTHER.  Golden Multitudes: The Story of Best
    Sellers in the United States.  New York: Macmillan, pp. 59-
    60, 316-17.
        Popularity of History of England and Roderick Random in
    eighteenth-century America.

6   OPPENHEIMER, JANE M.  "A Note on William Hunter and Tobias
    Smollett," Journal of the History of Medicine and Allied
    Sciences, 2 (Autumn), 481-86.
        Details of their friendship and of Smollett's medical
    interests.

7   PRITCHETT, V. S.  "The Shocking Surgeon," in The Living Novel.
    London: Chatto & Windus, pp. 18-23.
        Attributes Smollett's brutality and coarseness to his
    shocked sensitivities to eighteenth-century life.  Also
    makes interesting comparison to James Joyce, comments in-
    telligently on Rowlandson's illustrations, and particularly
    praises the Travels.

8   WILLCOCKS, M. P.  A True-Born Englishman: Being the Life of
    Henry Fielding.  London: George Allen & Unwin, passim.  In-
    dexed.
        Unfavorable description of Smollett and relationship to
    Fielding.

<u>1948</u>

1   BARTON, MARGARET.  Garrick.  New York: Macmillan, pp. 157-58,
    160.
        Reasonably discusses Smollett's relations with Garrick.

2   BELJAME, ALEXANDRE.  Men of Letters and the English Public in
    the Eighteenth Century, 1660-1744, Dryden, Addison, Pope,
    ed. Bonamy Dobrée, trans. E. O. Lorimer.  London: Kegan
    Paul et al., passim.  Indexed.
        Reprint of 1881.2.

3   CORDASCO, FRANCESCO.  "The Ascription of 'A Sorrowful Ditty
    ...' to Smollett Affirmed," N&Q, 193 (October 2), 428.
        Reference in Shenstone letter reinforces argument for
    Smollett's authorship.

1948

4    CORDASCO, FRANCESCO. "J. P. Browne's Edition of Smollett's
     Works," N&Q, 193 (October 2), 428-29.
        Browne's work no mere reprint of Moore's and deserves
     high commendation.

5    CORDASCO, FRANCESCO. "A Peregrine Pickle Play, 1929," N&Q,
     193 (April 3), 142-43.
        Kate Parsons's The Commodore Marries produced unsuccess-
     fully in New York.

6    CORDASCO, FRANCESCO. "Robert Anderson's Edition of Smollett,"
     N&Q, 193 (December 11), 533.
        Bibliographical information on the six editions (1796-
     1820). Calls third most valuable.

7    CORDASCO, FRANCESCO. Smollett Criticism, 1770-1924: A Bibli-
     ography, Enumerative and Annotated. Brooklyn: Long Island
     University Press, [vi] + 28 pp.
        Twelve sections cover 305 items of bibliography, biogra-
     phy and general criticism, plays and poems, translations,
     historical writings, the Atom, the Travels, and the five
     novels. Casual annotation. Requires utmost caution in
     use. See Boucé, 1971.7, for some corrections and additions.
     Reprinted 1970.11.

8    CORDASCO, FRANCESCO. "Smollett and His Detractor, Hugh Blair:
     with an Unpublished Smollett Letter," N&Q, 193 (July 10),
     295-96.
        Smollett blames James Macpherson for Blair's attack on
     Smollett. Letter is a forgery: see 1952.8.

9    CORDASCO, FRANCESCO. "Smollett and Petronius," MLQ, 9 (Decem-
     ber), 415-17.
        Ineffectively argues Smollett's use of the Satyricon in
     all his novels except Humphry Clinker.

10   CORDASCO, FRANCESCO. "Smollett and the Translation of the
     Don Quixote--A Critical Bibliography," N&Q, 193 (September
     4), 383-84.
        List of 18 items in which the translation attributed to
     Smollett is discussed.

11   CORDASCO, FRANCESCO. "Smollett and the Translation of the
     Don Quixote: Important Unpublished Letters," N&Q, 193
     (August 21), 363-64.
        Three letters ascribing the translation chiefly to
     Isaiah Pettigrew. The three letters are forgeries. See
     1952.8.

12  CORDASCO, FRANCESCO.  "Smollett and the Translation of
    Fénelon's <u>Telemachus</u>," <u>N&Q</u>, 193 (December 24), 563.
        1776 translation ascribed to Smollett actually a reissue
    of John Hawkesworth's of 1768.

13  CORDASCO, FRANCESCO.  "Smollett's Creditor Macleane Identi-
    fied," <u>N&Q</u>, 193 (April 3), 141-42.
        Supports Noyes's suggestion that Laughlin Macleane was
    creditor Smollett described in his letters.

14  COWIE, ALEXANDER.  <u>The Rise of the American Novel</u>.  New York
    et al.: American Book Company, passim.  Indexed.
        The reading and influence of Smollett's work in America.

15  DEUTSCH, OTTO ERICH.  "Poetry Preserved in Music: Bibliograph-
    ical Notes on Smollett and Oswald, Handel, and Haydn," <u>MLN</u>,
    63 (February), 73-88.
        On Smollett's relationship with the composer James
    Oswald, and discusses his earliest printed poem and pub-
    lishes the lyrics of <u>Alceste</u> preserved with Handel's music.

16  JONES, CLAUDE E.  "Poetry and the <u>Critical Review</u>, 1756-1785,"
    <u>MLQ</u>, 9 (March), 17-36.
        Principles of poetry reviews during years Smollett was
    editor.

17  KLINE, JUDD.  "Three Doctors and Smollett's Lady of Quality,"
    <u>PQ</u>, 27 (July), 219-28.
        "Dr. S----" in Lady Vane's memoirs in <u>Peregrine Pickle</u>
    was neither Smollett nor Shebbeare, but rather Dr. Peter
    Shaw, a London physician.

18  LINSALATA, CARMINE ROCCO.  "Tobias Smollett's Translation of
    <u>Don Quixote</u>," <u>Library Chronicle of the University of Texas</u>,
    3 (Fall), 55-68.
        Parallel passages from Smollett's and Jarvis's transla-
    tions demonstrate that Smollett plagiarized.

19  McKILLOP, ALAN D.  "Tobias George Smollett (1721-1771)," in
    <u>English Literature from Dryden to Burns</u>.  New York: Apple-
    ton-Century-Crofts, pp. 271-75 and passim.
        Brief biographical and critical sketch emphasizes the
    episodic structure and autobiographical relationships of
    his novels.

20  MARLOW, LOUIS.  <u>Sackville of Drayton</u>.  London: Home & Van
    Thal, p. 127.

1948

Discusses accuracy of Smollett's historical description
of public response to Sackville's disgrace at Minden.

21   MOORE, ROBERT ETHERIDGE. "Hogarth and Smollett," in <u>Hogarth's</u>
<u>Literary Relationships</u>. Minneapolis and London: University
of Minnesota Press, Geoffrey Cumberlege, and Oxford University Press, pp. 162-95.
     Recounts Smollett's appreciation of Hogarth and their
emotional and temperamental affinities. Considers
Smollett's indebtedness to Hogarth's prints, but distin-
guishes his didacticism from Hogarth's comedy and contrasts
Smollett's caricature and Hogarth's characterization. Reprinted 1969.18.

*22  SCOTT, W. A. G. "Smollett's Reputation and Influence in the
Eighteenth Century, Chiefly as a Novelist." B. Litt.
Thesis, Oxford University, 1948.
     Cited in <u>Retrospective Index to Theses of Great Britain</u>
<u>and Ireland, 1716-1950</u>, Vol. 1.

23   SHERBURN, GEORGE. "The Restoration and Eighteenth Century
(1660-1789)," in <u>A Literary History of England</u>, ed. Albert
C. Baugh. New York: Appleton-Century-Crofts, III, 961-64
and passim.
     Praises narrative and descriptive abilities, but empha-
sizes weak episodic picaresque structures. Suggests later
experimentation leads to triumph of <u>Humphry Clinker</u>.
Briefly describes <u>Travels</u> and periodical writing. Reprinted 1967.44.

24   [WALPOLE, HORACE and THOMAS GRAY]. <u>Horace Walpole's Corres-</u>
<u>pondence with Thomas Gray</u> etc., ed. W. S. Lewis et al., 2.
<u>Yale Edition of Horace Walpole's Correspondence</u>, ed. W. S.
Lewis. New Haven: Yale University Press, XIV, 48.
     Gray's 1751 letter attacks <u>Peregrine Pickle</u>.

25   WIMSATT, W. K. JR. <u>Philosophic Words: A Study of Style and</u>
<u>Meaning in the "Rambler" and "Dictionary" of Samuel</u>
<u>Johnson</u>. New Haven: Yale University Press, pp. 114, 117.
     Style in <u>Humphry Clinker</u> combines commonly coarse lan-
guage and gross materials of a physician's experience.


<u>1949</u>

1    CORDASCO, FRANCESCO. "Smollett and the Death of King William
III," <u>MLN</u>, 64 (January), 21-23.

Smollett's source was Nicholas Tindal's translation of
Histoire d'Angleterre and Macaulay followed Smollett's
description. But see 1952.14.

2    CORDASCO, FRANCESCO. "Smollett and the Translation of the Gil
     Blas," MLQ, 10 (March), 68-71.
          Questions extent to which Smollett was the translator
     and notes confusion of later publications issued as
     Smollett's.

3    CORDASCO, FRANCESCO. "Smollett's 'Register of the Weather,'"
     N&Q, 194 (April 16), 163.
          Inclusion in Travels derives from such publications in
     eighteenth-century magazines.

4    CORDASCO, FRANCESCO. "Two Notes on Smollett," N&Q, 194 (De-
     cember 24), 557-58.
          Further information on Laughlin Macleane as Smollett's
     creditor and, from Percy's Anecdotes, story of Smollett's
     generosity and identification of Hugh Hewson as Strap in
     Roderick Random.

*5   EASTWOOD, W. "Smollett as Critic of Social Conditions in
     Eighteenth Century England." M.A. Thesis, Sheffield Uni-
     versity, 1949.
          Cited in Retrospective Index to Theses of Great Britain
     and Ireland, 1716-1950, Vol. 1.

6    FOSTER, JAMES R. "The Great and Near-Great," in History of
     the Pre-Romantic Novel in England. New York and London:
     Modern Language Association of America and Oxford Univer-
     sity Press, pp. 120-30.
          Smollett's opposition to sentimentalism yields somewhat
     in Launcelot Greaves and virtually succumbs in Humphry
     Clinker.

7    GALLUP, DONALD C. "Baretti's Reputation in England," in The
     Age of Johnson: Essays Presented to Chauncey Brewster
     Tinker, ed. Frederick W. Hilles. New Haven and London:
     Yale University Press, p. 370.
          Antagonism between Baretti and Smollett.

8    GLÄTTLI, WALTER. "Smollett," in Die Behandlung des Affekts
     der Furcht in Englischen Roman des 18. Jahrhunderts.
     Zürich: Juris-Verlag, pp. 83-95.
          Compares Smollett's treatment of fear in his novels with
     that of his contemporaries.

1949

9    GRAHAM, W. H. "Smollett's Humphrey [sic] Clinker," Contemporary Review, 176 (July), 33-38.
        Weak general account of the novel treats it as travelogue and identifies Bramble and Smollett.

10    GREEN, DAVID BONNELL. "Keats and Smollett," N&Q, 194 (December 24), 558-59.
        Suggests several allusions to Humphry Clinker in Keats's letters underscore his admiration of the novel.

11    KNAPP, LEWIS M. "Smollett's Self-Portrait in The Expedition of Humphry Clinker," in 1949.7, pp. 149-58.
        Sensible discussion of Smollett's use of personal experiences for details and of resemblances of his character and social criticism to those of Matt and Jerry. Notes features of Bramble that are an exact portrait of Smollett.

12    KNAPP, LEWIS M. Tobias Smollett: Doctor of Men and Manners. Princeton: Princeton University Press, xiii + 362 pp.
        The definitive biography. Together with Knapp's edition of the letters in 1970, presents the fullest, most scrupulously exact account of Smollett's life and details of his publications. Particularly successful in separating facts from the apocrypha and myths with which Smollett's life, personality, and reputation had become distorted in the nineteenth century, and offers a well-balanced portrait of the man. Literary criticism, however, is limited to a single chapter that generally evaluates his contribution to the development of the novel. Reprinted 1963.17.

13    McCUTCHEON, ROGER P. "Richardson, Fielding, Smollett, Sterne," in Eighteenth-Century English Literature. Home University Library, 212. New York: Oxford University Press, pp. 67-70.
        Unfavorable account emphasizes autobiographical and picaresque, but describes Humphry Clinker as one of the great novels of its period.

14    MAGILL, FRANK N. and DAYTON KOHLER. "Humphry Clinker," "Peregrine Pickle," and "Roderick Random," in Masterplots. New York: Salem Press, pp. 394-97, 731-34, 841-44.
        Brief criticism, general information, and plot summaries. Reprinted in various works by Magill.

15    MONTAGUE, EDWINE and LOUIS L. MARTZ. "Fanny Burney's Evelina," in 1949.7, pp. 171-72.
        Compares literary techniques with those of Humphry Clinker.

16    MOORE, ROBERT E.  "William Hogarth: The Golden Mean," in
        1949.7, pp. 386-87.
            Compares Hogarth's and Smollett's methods of characteri-
        zation.

17    OPPENHEIMER, JANE M.  "John and William Hunter and Some Con-
        temporaries in Literature and Art," Bulletin of the History
        of Medicine, 23 (January-February), 21-47.
            Smollett's professional and personal relationships with
        the Hunters and their friends.

18    ROSATI, SALVATORE.  "Smollett, Tobias George," in Enciclopedia
        Italiane di Scienze, Lettere ed Art.  Rome: Instituto della
        Enciclopedia Italiana, XXXI, 981.
            Traditional but favorable account stresses comparison
        with Fielding.

*19   SAMARIN, R.  "Afterword," in Roderick Random.  Moscow, pp.
        531-39.
            Cited in Korte, 1969.15.

20    SHERWOOD, IRMA Z.  "The Novelists as Commentators," in 1949.7,
        pp. 118, 121.
            Criticizes Smollett's intrusive narrative voice and ex-
        traneous inset in Roderick Random.

21    SITWELL, OSBERT.  "Introduction," in Travels through France
        and Italy.  London: John Lehmann, pp. v-xi.
            Praises liveliness, style, and shrewd observations of
        manners and customs, but discounts artistic taste as phi-
        listine and aesthetic comments as tedious and jejune.

22    TODD, WILLIAM B.  "The Number and Order of Certain Eighteenth-
        Century Editions."  Diss., University of Chicago, 1949.
            Includes discussion of bibliographical problems pre-
        sented by first edition of Humphry Clinker.


                              1950


1     ARVIN, NEWTON.  Herman Melville.  The American Men of Letters
        Series.  New York: William Sloane Associates, pp. 78, 80,
        117-18.
            Acknowledges Melville's indebtedness to Smollett, but
        contrasts their artistic techniques.

1950

2  CALDER-MARSHALL, ARTHUR. "Introduction," and "Biographical
   Note," in <u>Tobias Smollett: Selected Writings</u>, ed. Arthur
   Calder-Marshall. London: The Falcon Press, pp. 7-15.
        Brief assessment of Smollett's work attempts some psy-
   chological probing of the artistic impulse that gives it
   its special quality.

3  CHESTERTON, G. K. "The Romance of a Rascal," in <u>The Common
   Man</u>. New York: Sheed and Ward, pp. 42-49.
        Reprint of 1936.6. Drops sentence expressing bewilder-
   ment by the novel.

4  CORDASCO, FRANCESCO. <u>Letters of Tobias George Smollett: A
   Supplement to the Noyes Collection with a Bibliography of
   Editions of the Collected Works</u>. Madrid: Imp. Avelino
   Ortega, Cuesta de Sancti-Spiritus, vii + 46 pp.
        Contains 31 letters discovered after Noyes's edition.
   Five--numbers 19, 26, 29, 30, 31--Cordasco acknowledged as
   forgeries (<u>see</u> 1952.8). Brief annotation. Includes list
   of fragments and lost letters and emendations and correc-
   tions of letters in Noyes.

5  CORDASCO, FRANCESCO. "Smollett's German Medical Degree," <u>MLN</u>,
   65 (February), 117-19.
        Letter purportedly establishes that Smollett received
   his degree in Giessen. However, as Cordasco acknowledged
   (1952.3), the letter is a forgery.

6  CORDASCO, FRANCESCO. "An Unrecorded Medical Translation by
   Smollett," <u>N&Q</u>, 195 (November 25), 516.
        Describes translation of Roger Dibon's work as
   Smollett's, since Padua library has copy with his name on
   title page. However, <u>see</u> 1971.62.

7  DAVIS, ROBERT GORHAM. "Introduction," in <u>The Expedition of
   Humphry Clinker</u>. New York et al.: Holt, Rinehart and
   Winston, pp. v-xxiii.
        Discusses Smollett's career and his relationship to con-
   temporary and later novelists, and compares and contrasts
   <u>Humphry Clinker</u> with his earlier work. Particularly perceptive remarks on its epistolary technique and its structure.

8  GALBRAITH, LOIS HALL. "The Clerics of an Unsuccessful Physician," in <u>The Established Clergy as Depicted in English
   Prose Fiction from 1740 to 1800</u>. Philadelphia: For the
   Author, pp. 37-43. Diss., University of Pennsylvania,
   1950.

Smollett's invariably satiric treatment of the type in his novels.

9    LINSALATA, CARMINE R.  "Smollett's Indebtedness to Jarvis' Translation of Don Quijote," Symposium, 4 (May), 84-106.
     Parallel passages indicate Smollett's overwhelming indebtedness to Charles Jarvis's translation.

10   MATTHEWS, WILLIAM.  "Tarpaulin Arabick in the Days of Pepys," in Essays Critical and Historical Dedicated to Lily B. Campbell.  Berkeley and Los Angeles: University of California Press, 111-36.
     Though Smollett's nautical slang is cited in the OED, there were earlier sources.

11   NEWMAN, FRANKLIN B.  "A Consideration of the Bibliographical Problems Connected with the First Edition of Humphry Clinker," PBSA, 44 (Fourth Quarter), 340-71.
     Full account of the complex bibliographical details to be considered in attempting to determine the identity of the actual first edition of Humphry Clinker.

12   ORR, JOHN.  "Did Smollett Know Spanish?", MLR, 45 (April), 218.
     Comparison of Smollett's and Jarvis's translations of Don Quixote indicates Smollett's knowledge of Spanish.

13   [RANDALL, DAVID].  "Humphry Clinker," New Colophon, 2 (February), 379-80.
     Problems of identifying first edition of Humphry Clinker and differences between the A and B texts.

*14  RISCH, DITHMAR.  "Smollett und Deutschland.  Deutschlandbild und Aufnahme in Deutschland."  Diss., Göttingen, 1950.
     Cited in McNamee, Dissertations in English and American Literature.

15   SALE, WILLIAM M. JR.  Samuel Richardson: Master Printer. Cornell Studies in English, 37, ed. Robert C. Bald et al. Ithaca, New York: Cornell University Press, pp. 103-4, 203.
     Smollett's connection with the Universal History and Richardson's printing of his work.

16   SCHILLING, BERNARD N.  Conservative England and the Case against Voltaire.  New York: Columbia University Press, pp. 154, 201.
     Smollett's "Dying Prediction" suggests English attitude toward the shaping of events in France.

1950

*17  SHOUP, LOUISE.  "The Use of the Social Gathering as a Struc-
     tural Device in the Novels of Richardson, Fielding,
     Smollett, and Sterne."  Diss., Stanford University, 1950.
       Smollett uses social occasions in his novels primarily
     to satirize "hypocrisy and sycophancy" and rarely displays
     any enjoyment in such material.  Cited in Stanford Univer-
     sity Bulletin, 8th ser., 25 (November 30), 139–41.

 18  WELLEK, RENÉ.  "Lessing," in A History of Modern Criticism:
     1750–1950.  New Haven: Yale University Press, I, 154–55.
       Lessing's unfavorable comparison of Roderick Random to
     Gil Blas.

                              1951

  1  BOYS, RICHARD C.  "Tristram Shandy and the Conventional Nov-
     el," Papers of the Michigan Academy of Science, Arts, and
     Letters, 37 (1951), 429–30, 433.
       Compares Sterne's and Smollett's works.

  2  BRANDER, LAURENCE.  Tobias Smollett.  London, New York,
     Toronto: Longman's, Green, for British Council and the
     National Book League, 36 pp.
       Somewhat dated general account of Smollett and his work,
     particularly Roderick Random, Peregrine Pickle, Humphry
     Clinker, and the Travels.

  3  BUCKLEY, JEROME HAMILTON.  The Victorian Temper. A Study in
     Literary Culture.  Cambridge, Mass.: Harvard University
     Press, p. 33.
       Thomas Hood's particular indebtedness to Smollett.

  4  CHURCH, RICHARD.  "Four Mighty Limbs," in The Growth of the
     English Novel.  London: Methuen & Co., pp. 66–72 and
     passim.
       Sympathetic treatment emphasizes Smollett's Scottish
     background, introduction of new material to the novel, and
     his narrative ability, and compares him to contemporaries
     and describes his influence in the nineteenth century.

  5  CORDASCO, FRANCESCO.  The Bohn Libraries: A History and a
     Checklist.  New York: Burt Franklin, passim.  Indexed.
       Describes editions and reprints of Smollett's works
     published by Bohn.

  6  DAVIS, ROBERT GORHAM.  "The Sense of the Real in English Fic-
     tion," Comparative Literature, 3 (Summer), 200–217.

Includes discussion of Smollett's contributions to the development of realism in fiction (pp. 212-13).

7   DE LA TORRE, LILLIAN.  Review of Cordasco's "Smollett's German Medical Degree" (1950.5), PQ, 30 (July), 291.
      Challenges authenticity of letter Cordasco used as evidence.

8   FOSTER, JAMES R.  "Peregrine Pickle and The Memoirs of Count Grammont," MLN, 66 (November), 469-71.
      Anthony Hamilton's Memoirs of Count Grammont was likely the most immediate and important source for fortune-telling episode in Smollett's novel (Ch. 82-84).

9   GRANT, DOUGLAS.  James Thomson: Poet of "The Seasons". London: The Cresset Press, passim.  Indexed.
      Smollett and Thomson's relationships and comparison of their views on the Grand Tour, prisons, and patronage.

10  KETTLE, ARNOLD.  An Introduction to the English Novel. London: Hutchinson, I, 21, 55.
      Smollett's concern with experience and events rather than moral implications and his alteration of the picaresque.  Reprinted 1960, New York: Harper & Row.

11  KNAPP, LEWIS M. and LILLIAN DE LA TORRE.  Review of Cordasco's Letters of Tobias Smollett, 1950.4, PQ, 30 (July), 289-91.
      Challenge authenticity of new letters: 19, 26, 29, 30, 31.

12  LEYDA, JAY.  The Melville Log: A Documentary Life of Herman Melville, 1819-1891.  New York: Harcourt, Brace, pp. 367, 372, 811.
      Melville's reading of Smollett and comparisons of the two authors by nineteenth-century critics.

13  SADLEIR, MICHAEL.  XIX Century Fiction. A Bibliographical Guide.  Cambridge: Cambridge University Press; Berkeley and Los Angeles: University of California Press, II, passim. Indexed.
      Bibliographical information on Smollett's novels, including the Atom, published in the nineteenth century.

14  SPECTOR, ROBERT D.  "Language Control in the Eighteenth Century," Word Study, 27 (October), 1-2.
      Conservative attitude toward grammar, spelling, and diction in the Critical Review, 1756-63.

1951

15   SPECTOR, ROBERT D.  "Late Neo-Classical Taste," N&Q, 196
     (January 6), 11–12.
        Inadequate and biased reviews of Tristram Shandy,
     Rasselas, and Candide in the Critical Review.

16   TODD, WILLIAM B.  "Bibliography and the Editorial Problem in
     the Eighteenth Century," Studies in Bibliography, 4 (1951),
     50–51.
        Distinguishes between first and alternate editions of
     Humphry Clinker.

17   [WALPOLE, HORACE].  Horace Walpole's Correspondence with
     Thomas Chatterton etc., ed. W. S. Lewis and A. Dayle
     Wallace.  Yale Edition of Horace Walpole's Correspondence,
     ed. W. S. Lewis.  New Haven: Yale University Press, XVI,
     30.
        Walpole's 1759 attack on Smollett's political use of his
     History of England.


                              1952

1   BASTIAN, JOHN LEMUEL.  "Smollett's and Goldsmith's Histories
    and the Mid-Eighteenth Century Reaction to the Genre of
    History."  Diss., Boston University, 1952.
       Influence of new historical approaches of the Enlighten-
    ment on Smollett's histories and his use of historical
    material in Travels, the Atom, and Humphry Clinker.

2   CLINTON-BADDELEY, V. C.  "The Jolly Jack Tar Joke," in The
    Burlesque Tradition in the English Theatre after 1600.
    London: Methuen, pp. 99–100, 104, 105.
       Smollett's important contribution to the development of
    nautical characters in his novels and The Reprisal.

3   CORDASCO, FRANCESCO.  "Smollett and Fizès," MLN, 67 (May),
    360.
       Acknowledges, after a committee investigation, that let-
    ter he had offered as evidence of Smollett's German medical
    degree is a forgery.  See 1950.5 and 1952.12.

4   CORDASCO, FRANCESCO.  "Smollett and the Translation of the
    Don Quixote," MLQ, 13 (March), 23–36.
       Presents letter of 1759 to argue that Smollett's sup-
    posed translation was actually the work of Isaiah
    Pettigrew, which Smollett either supervised or lent his
    name to.  Letter is a forgery.  See 1953.7.

5  DAVIS, ROBERT GORHAM.  "A Reply," PBSA, 46 (Second Quarter),
   165.
        Acknowledges accuracy of Todd's remarks (1952.19) about
   the edition of Humphry Clinker used for the 1950 Rinehart
   edition.

6  DUDDEN, F. HOMES.  Henry Fielding: His Life, Works, and Times.
   Oxford: Clarendon Press, 2 Vols., passim.  Indexed.
        Comparison of Fielding's and Smollett's works and
   Smollett's opinions on Fielding's writing.

7  GOSSE, PHILIP.  Dr. Viper: The Querulous Life of Philip
   Thicknesse.  London: Cassell, passim.  Indexed.
        Describes Thicknesse's dislike of Smollett and attacks
   on him in three works.  Most important is Gosse's description (p. 317) of Thicknesse's annotated copy of the first
   volume of Smollett's Travels.

8  HAZEN, ALLEN T., FREDERICK B. ADAMS, JR., LOUIS A. LANDA.
   Report of Committee Investigating the Authenticity of Five
   Letters in Cordasco's Supplement, 1950.4, PQ, 31 (July),
   299-300.
        Attest to forgery of letter from Fizès on Smollett's
   German medical degree and note Cordasco's unwillingness to
   provide material for judging authenticity of the five
   spurious letters in his Supplement.  In his communication,
   however, Cordasco acknowledges that all are forgeries.

9  JOHNSON, EDGAR.  Charles Dickens: His Tragedy and Triumph.
   New York: Simon and Schuster, 2 Vols., passim.  Indexed.
        Notes on Smollett in relation to Dickens.

10 KIRBY, PAUL FRANKLIN.  The Grand Tour in Italy (1700-1800).
   New York: S. F. Vanni, passim.
        Columbia University dissertation discusses Smollett's
   views of Italy in his Travels, suggesting his acerbity, but
   admiring his style.

11 KIRCHNER, GUSTAV.  "Shaw's Pygmalion and Smollett's Peregrine
   Pickle," Die Neueren Sprachen, n.s. 1 (Part 10), 409-17.
        Comparison of Shaw's Play and episode of the young beg-
   gar woman in Smollett's novel.

12 KNAPP, LEWIS M. and LILLIAN DE LA TORRE.  "Smollett and Fizès
   (?)," MLN, 67 (January), 69-70.
        Challenges authenticity of letter Cordasco (1950.5) had
   offered as evidence of Smollett's German medical degree.
   Cordasco offers a rejoinder; Knapp and De La Torre ask for

1952

the manuscript, and Cordasco agrees to provide it (see p. 71). For Cordasco's acknowledgement of the forgery, see 1952.8.

13   KUNITZ, STANLEY J. and HOWARD HAYCRAFT. "Smollett, Tobias George," in British Authors before 1800. New York: H. W. Wilson, pp. 480-82.
       Brief, unfavorable biographical and conventional critical account.

14   LANCASTER, H. C. "The Death of William III: A Correction," MLN, 67 (June), 432.
       Rejects Cordasco's argument (1949.1) that translation of Histoire d'Angleterre was Smollett's source.

15   MENDILOW, A. A. Time and the Novel. London and New York: Peter Nevill, pp. 40-41, 126, 160.
       Relates Smollett's treatment of fictional time to early conventions of the novel and to his style.

16   NEILL, S. DIANA. "The Broad Highway," in A Short History of the English Novel. New York: Macmillan, pp. 64-69 and passim.
       Derivative, inaccurate account of Smollett's life and work.

*17  PRICKITT, HENRY B. "The Political Writings and Opinions of Tobias Smollett." Diss., Harvard University, 1952.
       Cited in Korte, 1969.15.

18   SIEBERT, FREDRICK SEATON. Freedom of the Press in England 1476-1776. Urbana, Ill.: The University of Illinois Press, pp. 330, 334, 376-80.
       Smollett's journalistic controversies on the Briton.

19   TODD, WILLIAM B. "Texts and Pretexts," PBSA, 46 (Second Quarter), 164.
       Robert G. Davis's 1950 edition of Humphry Clinker based on an inferior 1772 edition rather than on any of the 1771 editions. See 1952.5.

20   WAGENKNECHT, EDWARD. Cavalcade of the American Novel. New York et al.: Holt, Rinehart and Winston, pp. 62, 64, 350.
       Smollett's influence on Melville and James Branch Cabell's dislike of Smollett's work.

## 1953

1   ALMIRALL, CATHERINE L. "Smollett's 'Gothic': An Illustration," MLN, 68 (June), 408-10.
"Gothic" scenes in Ferdinand Count Fathom influenced by Congreve's The Mourning Bride.

2   ASTALDI, MARIA LUISA. "Uno Scozzese in Giro per L'Italia," in Letture Inglesi. Venezia: Neri Pozza Editore, pp. 61-64.
Brief sketch of Smollett, his views on Italy, and his death there.

3   BROWN, WALLACE CABLE. Charles Churchill: Poet, Rake, and Rebel. Lawrence, Kansas: University of Kansas Press, pp. 111-13, 151-52, and passim.
Literary warfare between Smollett and Churchill.

4   CROCKETT, HAROLD KELLY. "The Picaresque Tradition in English Fiction to 1770: A Study of Popular Backgrounds, with Particular Attention to Fielding and Smollett." Diss., University of Illinois, 1953.
Stresses native picaresque influences on Smollett's work, compares European picaresques, and discusses picaresque characteristics, especially in Smollett's characterization.

*5  ELISTRATOVA, A. A. "Introduction," in The Expedition of Humphry Clinker. Moscow, pp. 3-17.
Cited in Korte, 1969.15.

6   FOSTER, JAMES R. "A Forgotten Noble Savage, Tsonnonthouan," MLQ, 14 (December), 348-59.
Smollett reviewed Memoirs of the Life and Adventures of Tsonnonthouan in the Critical and later used it as one source for Lismahago's adventures in Humphry Clinker.

7   FOSTER, JAMES R. "Smollett and the Atom," PMLA, 68 (December), 1032-46.
Using internal and external evidence and comparing Smollett's political views in the Briton and attitudes toward contemporary politicians with those in the Atom, persuasively argues his authorship of the work.

8   HENDERSON, H. C. K. "Tobias Smollett as a Weather Observer," Weather, 8 (September), 275-78.
Detailed description of Smollett's account of the weather in Nice in 1764-65.

1953

9    KNAPP, LEWIS M. and LILLIAN DE LA TORRE, "Forged 'Smollett'
     Letter," MLQ, 14 (June), 228.
         Letter Cordasco (1952.4) used to claim that Smollett
     did not translate Don Quixote is a forgery.

10   LYNCH, JAMES J.  Box, Pit, and Gallery: Stage and Society in
     Johnson's London.  Berkeley and Los Angeles: University of
     California Press, passim.  Indexed.
         Brief, but worthwhile comments on Smollett's depiction
     of Garrick.

11   MOORE, CECIL A.  Backgrounds of English Literature, 1700-1760.
     Minneapolis: University of Minnesota Press, passim.  In-
     dexed.
         Describes some of the objects of Smollett's satire, in-
     cluding Shaftesbury.

12   NELSON, HOWARD L.  "Smollett's Grave," Times. London, Novem-
     ber 17, p. 9.
         Decaying conditions of the cemetery in Leghorn.  See
     13.

13   PARTRIDGE, CHARLES.  "Smollett's Grave," Times. London, Novem-
     ber 20, p. 9.
         1906 account of Smollett's burial place in Leghorn in-
     dicated deplorable conditions at that time.  See 12.

14   PRITCHETT, V. S.  "The Unhappy Traveller," in Books in Gen-
     eral.  London: Chatto & Windus, pp. 88-93.
         Reprint of 1942.7.

15   ROSSITER, CLINTON.  Seedtime of the Republic: The Origin of
     the American Tradition of Political Liberty.  New York:
     Harcourt, Brace, p. 126.
         Smollett's appeal in eighteenth-century America.

16   WARNER, OLIVER.  Captain Marryat: A Rediscovery.  London:
     Constable, passim.  Indexed.
         Comparisons of Smollett's and Marryat's works.

1954

1    ALLEN, WALTER.  "The Eighteenth Century," in The English Nov-
     el: A Short Critical Survey.  New York: E. P. Dutton, pp.
     62-72 and passim.

Relates Smollett's coarseness to moral purpose and praises narrative ability, with particular approval of Humphry Clinker. Notes influence on episodic and nautical novelists.

2    [HUME, DAVID].  New Letters of David Hume, ed. Raymond Klibansky and Ernest C. Mossner.  Oxford: Clarendon Press, pp. 173-74.
1767 letter describes unsuccessful attempt to gain a diplomatic post for Smollett because of his reputation.

3    KNAPP, LEWIS M.  "Abridgements of Smollett for Children," N&Q, n.s. 1 (November), 475.
1776 British edition reprinted in Philadelphia, 1810, of Roderick Random.  Lists other possible editions of the novel and Peregrine Pickle in America.

4    KNAPP, LEWIS M.  "Smollett," in The New Century Cyclopedia of Names, ed. Clarence L. Barnhart and W. D. Halsey.  New York: Appleton-Century-Crofts, III, 3639.
Brief, sensible account of Smollett and his work.

5    PEARSON, HESKETH.  Sir Walter Scott: His Life and Personality. New York: Harper & Brothers, passim.  Indexed.
Scott's attitude toward Smollett.

6    PRITCHETT, V. S.  "Introduction," in Humphry Clinker.  London and Glasgow: Collins; New York: W. Norton, pp. 9-14.
Despite some old-fashioned views, offers perceptive comment on Smollett's moral concerns, reactions to society, and medical and Scottish background.  Volume contains brief account of Smollett and his work by H. d. R.  Reprinted 1968.34.

7    TILLOTSON, KATHLEEN.  Novels of the Eighteen-Forties.  Oxford: Clarendon Press, pp. 30, 142, 145-47.
Smollett's relation to later novelists, particularly Dickens and Thackeray.

8    WARD, A. C.  "Tobias Smollett," in Illustrated History of English Literature.  New York: David McKay, II, 186-87.
Compares Smollett and Fielding, emphasizing his brutal realism and coarseness, but praising stylistic energy.

9    WEATHERLY, EDWARD H.  "Introduction," in The Correspondence of John Wilkes and Charles Churchill.  New York: Columbia University Press, pp. xii-xv and passim.

1955

Smollett's journalism in the Briton and his conflict
with Charles Churchill.


1955

*1   ELLISTRATOVA, A. A.  "Introduction," in Peregrine Pickle.
      Moscow, pp. 3-13.
         Cited in Korte, 1969.15.

*2   GIONO, JEAN.  "Preface," in Translation of Humphry Clinker.
      Paris: Gallimard.
         Cited in Knapp, 1966.26.

*3   GOLDBERG, MILTON A.  "The Novels of Tobias Smollett: Analysis
      in an Eighteenth-Century Mode."  Diss., Johns Hopkins Uni-
      versity, 1955.
         See Goldberg, 1959.6.  Cited in Korte, 1969.15.

4   HARDER, KELSIE B.  "Genealogical Satire in Humphry Clinker,"
      N&Q, n.s. 2 (October), 441-43.
         Smollett's subtle satire on "fantastic genealogical
      habits" of Scotsmen.

5   HUNTER, RICHARD A. and IDA MacALPINE.  "Sir Launcelot
      Greaves," TLS, December 16, p. 761.
         In first edition of his novel, Smollett borrowed pas-
      sage from William Battie's Treatise on Madness.  See
      1956.11.

6   KNAPP, LEWIS M.  "Abridgements of Smollett for Children,"
      N&Q, n.s. 2 (February), 80-81.
         Repeat of 1954.3.

7   KNOWLES, EDWIN B.  "A Note on Smollett's Don Quixote," MLQ,
      16 (March), 29-31.
         Compares Smollett's, Jarvis's, and Motteux's transla-
      tions and argues Smollett's heavy-handed use of Jarvis.
      Demolishes Cordasco's earlier article (1952.4) and lauds
      Linsalata's (1950.9).

8   McLAREN, MORAY.  The Highland Jaunt: A Study of James Boswell
      and Samuel Johnson etc.  New York: William Sloane Associ-
      ates, pp. 15, 37, 254.
         Uses Smollett's descriptions of Scotland in Humphry
      Clinker to comment on Boswell and Johnson's travels.
      Printed in Great Britain in 1954.

*9    MURAKAMI, SHIKO. Warai no Bungaku. Literature of Laughter.
         Tokyo: Kenkyusha, 216 pp.
              Includes discussion of Smollett along with Sterne.
         Cited in Annual Bibliography of Language and Literature,
         1955.

10    MYERS, SYLVIA HARCSTARK. "Ideals, Actuality, and Judgment in
         the Novels of Smollett: A Study in Development." Diss.,
         University of California, Berkeley, 1955.
              Considers Smollett's novels as evidence of his maturing
         judgment of the relationship between the ideal and real in
         human society. Stresses the importance of his non-fiction
         to final development of his balanced judgment in Humphry
         Clinker.

11    OLIVER, A. M. "The Scottish Augustans," in Scottish Poetry.
         A Critical Survey, ed. James Kinsley. London: Cassell,
         pp. 121, 122, 127, 136, 303.
              Unfavorable view of Smollett's poetry apart from "The
         Tears of Scotland," "Ode to Leven-Water," and his two
         satires.

12    QUENNELL, PETER. Hogarth's Progress. New York: Viking Press,
         pp. 268, 271, 279.
              Smollett's political journalism and his involvement in
         satiric prints.

13    RAY, GORDON N. Thackeray: The Uses of Adversity (1811-1846).
         New York et al.: McGraw-Hill, pp. 90, 344.
              Thackeray's reading of Smollett and a comparison of
         Barry Lyndon and Ferdinand Count Fathom.

*14    RUTH, FRIEDRICH. "Die Weltanschauung Tobias Smolletts."
         Diss., Heidelberg, 1955.
              Cited in Korte, 1969.15.

15    SCOTT, WILLIAM. "Smollett, Dr. John Hill, and the Failure of
         Peregrine Pickle," N&Q, n.s. 2 (September), 389-92.
              Hill's attacks on Smollett and their fiery relationship,
         centering around the publication of Peregrine Pickle.

16    SPECTOR, ROBERT D. "Attacks on the Critical Review," The
         Periodical Post Boy (June), pp. 6-7.
              Corrects errors listed in Jones, 1942.4, and adds 7
         items.

17    SPECTOR, ROBERT D. "Eighteenth Century Political Controversy
         and Linguistics," N&Q, n.s. 2 (September), 387-89.

1955

Language, usage, and grammar as tools in the political controversy engaged in by Smollett on the Briton.

18    SPECTOR, ROBERT D.  "Further Attacks on the Critical Review," N&Q, n.s. 2 (December), 535.
      Adds seven items to and corrects two errors in list in Jones, 1942.4.

19    SPECTOR, ROBERT D.  "Smollett and Admiral Byng," N&Q, n.s. 2 (February), 66-67.
      In the Continuation of the Complete History of England, Smollett uses the Byng affair to disparage the Whig ministry during the Seven Years' War.

*20   STRAUSS, ALBRECHT B.  "Design in the Novels of Tobias Smollett."  Diss., Harvard University, 1955.
      Cited in Korte, 1969.15.  Smollett's means of creating structure in his novels.

21    [WALPOLE, HORACE and WILLIAM MASON].  Horace Walpole's Correspondence with William Mason, 1, ed. W. S. Lewis et al. Yale Edition of Horace Walpole's Correspondence, ed. W. S. Lewis.  New Haven: Yale University Press, XXVIII, 41, 73.
      Walpole's 1772 letter calls Smollett "indolent," and Mason's 1773 letter attributes "Tears of Scotland" to William Hamilton.

22    WASSERMAN, EARL R.  "Smollett's Satire on the Hutchinsonians," MLN, 70 (May), 336-37.
      John Hutchinson, the original of Sir Mungo Barebones in Fathom, provides satirical portrait of the Hutchinsonians.

1956

1     ALLEN, WALTER.  "Introduction," in Peregrine Pickle.  Everyman's Library, no. 838.  London: Dent; New York: Dutton, I, v-ix.
      Perceptive introduction to Smollett's work compares it to Hogarth's and Rowlandson's and emphasizes relationships to conventions of his period, particularly in treatment of brutality.

2     BARNHART, CLARENCE L. and WILLIAM D. HALSEY.  "Smollett, Tobias George," in The New Century Handbook of English Literature.  New York: Appleton-Century-Crofts, pp. 1014-15.
      Praises his narrative power, prose style, and humor.

3  CHAMBERS, ROBERT.  Smollett: His Life and a Selection from His
   Writings.  Louisville: Lost Cause Press, vi + 221 pp.
      Reprint of 1867.3.

4  DÉDÉYAN, CHARLES.  A.-R. Lesage: Gil Blas.  Paris: Centre de
   Documentation Universitaire, pp. 13, 240, 243-45.
      Smollett's translation and use of Gil Blas.

5  DOOLEY, ROGER B.  "The Catholic in the Eighteenth-Century Novel."  Diss., Catholic University of America, 1956.  Abstract Published by Catholic University of America Press,
   Washington, D.C.
      Smollett's anti-clerical attitudes in Roderick Random
   and Peregrine Pickle.

6  HALSBAND, ROBERT.  "Last Words," in The Life of Lady Mary
   Wortley Montagu.  Oxford: Clarendon Press, pp. 288-89.
      Smollett's review of Lady Mary's letters in the Criti-
   cal.

7  HAMILTON, ARCHIBALD.  George Bernard Shaw: Man of the Century.
   New York: Appleton-Century-Crofts, pp. 614, 822.
      Denies Shaw's use in Pygmalion of Peregrine Pickle.

8  HECHT, J. JEAN.  The Domestic Servant Class in Eighteenth-
   Century England.  London: Routledge & Kegan Paul, pp. 3,
   14, 49, 202, 212.
      Smollett's perceptions as an observer of social life.

9  HUDSON, A. EDWARD A. and ARTHUR HERBERT.  "James Lind: His
   Contributions to Shipboard Sanitation," Journal of the
   History of Medicine and Allied Sciences, 11 (January), 3.
      Importance of Roderick Random in calling attention to
   abominable conditions of a seaman's life.

10 HUNTER, RICHARD A. and IDA MACALPINE.  "Smollett's Reading in
   Psychiatry," MLR, 51 (July), 409-11.
      Familiarity with William Battie's Treatise on Madness
   and two reviews on the subject by Smollett in the Critical.

11 HUNTER, RICHARD A. and IDA MACALPINE.  "Tobias Smollett, M.D.
   and William Battie, M.D.," Journal of the History of Medicine and Allied Sciences, 11 (January), 102-3.
      Passage in Launcelot Greaves copied almost directly
   from Battie's Treatise on Madness.  See 1955.5.

1956

12   JAMES, HENRY. "The Middle Years," in Henry James Autobiogra-
        phy, ed. Frederick W. Duppee. New York: Criterion Books,
        pp. 549, 567.
            Smollett's realistic descriptions.

13   JONES, CLAUDE E. "The Critical Review and Some Major Poets,"
        N&Q, n.s. 3 (March), 114-15.
            Attitudes toward Milton, Spenser, Pope, and others dur-
        ing years of Smollett's editorship.

14   JONES, CLAUDE E. "The Critical Review's First Thirty Years,"
        N&Q, n.s. 3 (February), 78-80.
            Conservative and reactionary attitudes during Smollett's
        years as editor.

15   KNAPP, LEWIS M. "Smollett Letter to Samuel Mitchelson," N&Q,
        n.s. 3 (June), 262.
            1767 letter deals with Alexander Campbell prior to
        Smollett's antagonism as expressed in character of
        Paunceford in Humphry Clinker.

16   LINSALATA, CARMINE R. Smollett's Hoax: Don Quixote in En-
        glish. Stanford: Stanford University Press, ix + 116 pp.
            Smollett did not know Spanish and plagiarized his trans-
        lation from Charles Jarvis's. Where he tried to improve on
        Jarvis, he lost the spirit of the original. Linsalata sug-
        gests that Smollett used a team of hack writers. Appen-
        dices include parallel passages from the two works, compar-
        isons with others, and a list of Smollett's use of Jarvis's
        footnotes. Reprinted 1967.29.

17   McKILLOP, ALAN D. "Tobias Smollett," in The Early Masters of
        English Fiction. Lawrence, Kansas: University of Kansas
        Press, pp. 147-81.
            Intelligent and perceptive critical survey stresses
        effective style and vitality admired by contemporaries.
        Notes his greater easiness with traditional rather than
        newer forms of fiction. A good general picture of his fic-
        tional world of oddities, and worthwhile discussion of use
        of the grotesque and development of type characterization.

18   MELCHIORI, GIORGIO. "Joyce and the Tradition of the Novel,"
        in The Tightrope Walkers: Studies of Mannerism in Modern
        English Literature. New York: Macmillan, pp. 46-49.
            Interesting comparison of word-play in Humphry Clinker
        with that in Joyce's novels.

19  MILIC, LOUIS T.  "Sterne and Smollett's Travels," N&Q, n.s. 3
(February), 80-81.
Sterne's parody and ironic treatment of Smollett's work
throughout A Sentimental Journey.

20  RIST, ÉDOUARD.  "Une Consultation Médicale au XVIIIe Siècle,"
La Revue de Paris, 63 (January), 112-25.
Full account and assessment of personalities and issues
involved in Smollett's consultation with Dr. Antoine Fizès
during his travels in France.

21  SPECTOR, ROBERT D.  "Additional Attacks on the Critical Review," N&Q, n.s. 3 (October), 425.
Adds three items from the London Chronicle in 1759,
1761, and 1762 to list in Jones, 1942.4.

22  VOISINE, J.  "Les Anglais en Provence au XVIIIe Siècle," Re-
vue de Littérature Comparée, 30 (January-March), 15-27.
Compares Smollett's views in his Travels with those of
Lord Chesterfield, Lady Mary Wortley Montagu, and Arthur
Young.


1957


1  BLOOM, EDWARD A.  "'Labors of the Learned': Neoclassic Book
Reviewing Aims and Techniques," SP, 54 (October), 537-63.
Some of the reasons for the success of the Critical Re-
view and its general characteristics.

2  BLOOM, EDWARD A.  Samuel Johnson in Grub Street.  Providence:
Brown University Press, passim.  Indexed.
Smollett's work in relation to journalistic conditions
in the eighteenth century.

3  BOND, RICHMOND P.  "Introduction," in Studies in the Early English Periodical, ed. Richmond P. Bond.  Chapel Hill: The
University of North Carolina Press, pp. 35-37.
Reviewing methods of the Critical unsatisfactory, but an
improvement over predecessors' and development toward modern reviews.

4  BUTT, JOHN and KATHLEEN TILLOTSON.  Dickens at Work.  London:
Methuen, passim.  Indexed.
Smollett's influence on Dickens's early novels.

5  DOBSON, JESSE.  "Smollett the Surgeon," Annals of the Royal
College of Surgeons of England, 20 (April), 260-64.

1957

Details of Smollett's medical career, including identi-
fication of examiners for his qualification as surgeon's
mate as described in Roderick Random.

6   FRYE, NORTHROP. Anatomy of Criticism: Four Essays. Prince-
    ton: Princeton University Press, p. 179.
        Relates plot of Humphry Clinker to myths of ritual
    death.

7   HUMPHREYS, A. R. "Fielding and Smollett," in The Pelican
    Guide to English Literature: From Dryden to Johnson, ed.
    Boris Ford, Vol. IV. Baltimore: Penguin Books, pp. 313-32.
        Intelligent comparison appraises their importance to the
    development of the novel. Fielding's qualities are more
    enduring, offering greater degree of general philosophical
    truth about man's nature. Sees lightening in Smollett's
    work, moving away from picaresque violence to the good
    humor in Humphry Clinker.

8   JONES, CLAUDE E. "Smollett Editions in Eighteenth-Century
    Britain," N&Q, n.s. 4 (June), 252.
        Includes novels, Atom, Travels, histories, several
    translations, and some miscellaneous works.

9   JONES, CLAUDE E. "Tobias Smollett (1721-1771)--the Doctor as
    Man of Letters," Journal of the History of Medicine and
    Allied Sciences, 12 (July), 337-48.
        Smollett's contributions to medical literature and the
    importance of his medical training to his development of
    fictional characters and settings.

10  KNAPP, LEWIS M. "Smollett's Translation of Don Quixote: Data
    on Its Printing and Copyright," N&Q, n.s. 4 (December),
    543-44.
        William Strahan's printing bill of February, 1755.

11  LETTIS, RICHARD LINCOLN. "A Study of Smollett's Sir Launcelot
    Greaves." Diss., Yale University, 1957.
        Summarizes novel's critical history, analyzes work in
    relation to Don Quixote and contemporary fiction, relates
    it to Smollett's other work, particularly his journalism,
    and, in an appendix, annotates the novel and collates the
    serial publication, the 1762 and Shakespeare Head editions.

12  McCORMICK, JOHN. Catastrophe and Imagination. An Interpreta-
    tion of the Recent English and American Novel. London, New
    York, Toronto: Longmans, Green, pp. 21, 120, 136, 137, 144,
    147.

Smollett's influence on later novelists and comparison
with contemporaries, particularly Fielding.

13   MOORMAN, MARY. William Wordsworth. A Biography. The Early
     Years, 1770-1803. Oxford: Clarendon Press, p. 198.
          Influence of Smollett's "Ode to Leven Water" on
     Wordsworth.

14   PROCTOR, MORTIMER R. The English University Novel. Univer-
     sity of California Publications, English Studies, 15.
     Berkeley and Los Angeles: University of California Press,
     pp. 45-46.
          Peregrine Pickle's university experiences in relation to
     later development of the university novel.

15   ROPER, DEREK. "Tobias Smollett and the Founders of His 'Re-
     view,'" Call Number (Library of the University of Oregon),
     19 (1957), 4-9.
          Describes marked copy of first two volumes of Critical
     Review in the university's library. See 1959.10.

16   SCOTT, WILLIAM. "Smollett's 'The Tears of Scotland': A Hith-
     erto Unnoticed Printing and Some Comments on the Text,"
     RES, n.s. 8 (February), 38-42.
          Discusses textual problems of the poem and describes
     poor text in 1750 periodical, Mitre and Crown, apparently
     reprinted from the Craftsman.

*17  SHEINKER, V. "Tobias Smollett's Ferdinand Count Fathom,"
     Uchenye Zapiski Leningradskogo Universiteta (Transactions
     of Leningrad University), no. 234 (1957), 3-22.
          Cited in 1969.15.

*18  SHEINKER, V. "Tobias Smollett's Roderick Random," Uchenye
     Zapiski Murmanskogo Pedinstituta (Transactions of the
     Murmansk Pedagogical College), 1 (1957), 23-62.
          Cited in 1969.15.

19   STAMM, RUDOLF. Englische Literatur. Bern: A Francke, pp.
     244-45.
          Brief account of secondary material on Smollett's life
     and work.

20   TAYLOR, ARCHER. "Proverbial Materials in Tobias Smollett, The
     Adventures of Sir Launcelot Greaves," Southern Folklore
     Quarterly, 21 (June), 85-92.
          Lists and annotates "proverbial phrases" and "proverbial
     comparisons" used in the novel.

1957

21 VARMA, DEVENDRA P. <u>The Gothic Flame</u>. London: Arthur Barker,
   pp. 38-40, 107, 178-79, 206, 214.
   Links <u>Ferdinand Count Fathom</u> to the later Gothics, particularly Radcliffe's novels.

22 WARDLE, RALPH M. <u>Oliver Goldsmith</u>. Lawrence, Kansas: Univer-
   sity of Kansas Press, passim. Indexed.
   Personal and literary relationships of Goldsmith and
   Smollett. Reprinted 1969, Hamden, Conn.: Archon Books.

23 WATT, IAN. <u>The Rise of the Novel: Studies in Defoe,</u>
   <u>Richardson and Fielding</u>. Berkeley and Los Angeles: University of California Press, passim. Indexed.
   Smollett's relationship to development of the novel, his
   use of names, his techniques, and his treatment and view of
   society.

<u>1958</u>

1 ANON. "The University Novel," <u>TLS</u>, February 21, p. 101.
   Origins of the university novel in coarse novels derived
   from Smollett.

2 ANON. "Absorbing Japan," <u>TLS</u>, August 8, p. 446.
   Smollett's use of Japan in <u>Adventures of an Atom</u>.

3 BATTENHOUSE, HENRY M. "Jane Austen," in <u>English Romantic</u>
   <u>Writers</u>. Great Neck, New York: Barron's Educational Series, pp. 248-49.
   Compares Smollett's and Austen's realistic techniques.

4 BELL, INGLIS F. and DONALD BAIRD. "Smollett, Tobias," in <u>The</u>
   <u>English Novel 1578-1956. A Checklist of Twentieth-Century</u>
   <u>Criticism</u>. Denver: Alan Swallow, pp. 113-14.
   Lists secondary works on the novels.

5 CLIFFORD, JAMES L. "The Eighteenth Century," in <u>Contemporary</u>
   <u>Literary Scholarship: A Critical Review</u>, ed. Lewis Leary.
   New York: Appleton-Century-Crofts, p. 103.
   Brief descriptions of some studies of Smollett's work.

6 CONNELY, WILLARD. "The Roaming Invalid," in <u>Laurence Sterne</u>
   <u>as Yorick</u>. London: The Bodley Head, p. 119.
   Mrs. Sterne's corroboration of Smollett's condemnatory
   report on Dr. Antoine Fizès's medical practices.

7   CORDASCO, FRANCESCO.  "Smollett in Dutch," N&Q, n.s. 5
        (April), 181.
            Records catalogue listing of a Smollett work and asks
        for further information.

8   CRUMMER, EDWARD P.  "Robert Stobo," N&Q, n.s. 5 (April), 180.
            1770 letter on suicide of Stobo, original of Lismahago
        in Humphry Clinker.

9   DOOLEY, D. J.  "Some Uses and Mutations of the Picaresque,"
        Dalhousie Review, 37 (Winter), 363-77.
            Smollett's use of picaresque tradition and influence on
        nineteenth-century writers.

10  HEMLOW, JOYCE.  The History of Fanny Burney.  Oxford: Claren-
        don Press, passim.  Indexed.
            Burney's reading and uses of Smollett's work.

11  HOWES, ALAN B.  Yorick and the Critics: Sterne's Reputation in
        England, 1760-1868.  Yale Studies in English, 139.  New
        Haven: Yale University Press, passim.  Indexed.
            Detailed account of many works in which writings of
        Sterne and Smollett have been compared.

12  JONES, CLAUDE E.  "The English Novel: A Critical View," MLQ,
        19 (June), 147-59 and (September), 213-24.
            Critical standards, attitudes toward readers, publish-
        ers, and circulating libraries of reviewers of novels in
        the Critical Review.

13  KING, LESTER S.  "The Practice of Medicine," in The Medical
        World of the Eighteenth Century.  Chicago: University of
        Chicago Press; London: Cambridge University Press, pp. 304-
        7.
            Smollett's skeptical view of medicinal benefits of min-
        eral waters in Humphry Clinker and Essay on the External
        Use of Water.

14  LEVIN, HARRY.  "Don Quixote and Moby Dick," in Contexts of
        Criticism.  Cambridge, Mass.: Harvard University Press, pp.
        98, 101.
            Influence of Smollett's translation of Don Quixote and
        that of his picaresque on Melville.

15  NOYES, ROBERT GALE.  The Neglected Muse: Restoration and Eigh-
        teenth Century Tragedy in the Novel (1740-1780).  Provi-
        dence: Brown University Press, pp. 99-101 and passim.

1958

> Smollett's dramatic and theatrical interests, particu-
> larly his treatment of Garrick and others in Peregrine
> Pickle.

16    OROWITZ, MILTON. "Smollett and the Art of Caricature," Spec-
      trum, 2 (Fall), 155-67.
>     Discusses significance, techniques, and range of
>     Smollett's caricature and distinguishes it from Fielding's,
>     Sterne's, and Dickens's. Describes Smollett's practice as
>     an unsentimental treatment of the dehumanizing forces of
>     society.

17    RATHBURN, ROBERT C. "The Makers of the British Novel," in
      From Jane Austen to Joseph Conrad. Essays Collected in Mem-
      ory of James T. Hillhouse, ed. Robert C. Rathburn and
      Martin Steinmann, Jr. Minneapolis: University of Minnesota
      Press, pp. 7, 8, 10, 13, 15, 18-19, 21, 194.
>     Relationships of Smollett's art to that of contemporar-
>     ies and nineteenth-century writers.

18    RAY, GORDON N. Thackeray: The Age of Wisdom (1847-1863). New
      York et al.: McGraw-Hill, pp. 124, 142, 410.
>     Thackeray's opinion of Smollett and some comparison of
>     their work.

*19   SHEINKER, V. "Peregrine Pickle and Some Features of
      Smollett's Satire," Uchenye Zapiski Murmanskogo Pedinsti-
      tuta (Transactions of the Murmansk Pedagogical College), 2
      (1958), 179-202.
>     Cited in Korte, 1969.15.

20    SPECTOR, ROBERT D. "Attacks on the Critical Review in the
      Court Magazine," N&Q, n.s. 5 (July), 308.
>     Adds six items to list in Jones, 1942.4.

21    WARNER, OLIVER. English Maritime Writing: Hakluyt to Cook.
      Writers and Their Work, no. 105. London: Longmans, Green,
      for the British Council and the National Book League, p.
      26.
>     Praises Smollett's contribution to nautical writing.

22    WITTIG, KURT. The Scottish Tradition in Literature. Phila-
      delphia: Dufour Editions, passim. Indexed.
>     Smollett belonged to mainstream of English rather than
>     Scottish literature.

## 1959

1   BATSON, ERIC J.   "Eliza's Prototypes?," TLS, November 13, p.
    668.
        Peregrine Pickle a subconscious source for Shaw's char-
    acter in Pygmalion.

*2   BIRCH, J. B.   "Social Satire in the Novels of Tobias
    Smollett."  M.A. Thesis, University of London, 1959.
        Cited in University of London. Theses and Dissertations.

*3   BRUCE, D. J.   "Smollett and the Animal Economy."  M.A. Thesis,
    University of London, 1959.
        Cited in University of London. Theses and Dissertations.

4   BUTT, JOHN.   "Bleak House Once More," Critical Quarterly, 1
    (Winter), 302-7.
        Traces development of Dickens's artistry away from
    Smollett's early influence.

5   GEORGE, M. DOROTHY.   "Pitt, Bute, and George III," in English
    Political Caricature to 1792. A Study of Opinion and Propa-
    ganda.  Oxford: Clarendon Press, I, 121-22 and plate 32.
        Smollett as target of political satire in a print.

6   GOLDBERG, M. A.   Smollett and the Scottish School. Studies in
    Eighteenth-Century Thought.  Albuquerque: University of New
    Mexico Press, xiii + 191 pp.
        Considering Smollett's fiction in relation to the Scot-
    tish Common Sense philosophers, discusses each novel with
    regard to a pair of antithetical philosophical concepts.
    Each reveals a structure and argument designed to present
    a middle ground between extremes.  Proposed pairings: rea-
    son and passion in Roderick Random; imagination and judg-
    ment in Peregrine Pickle; art and nature in Fathom; bene-
    volence and self-love in Launcelot Greaves; and primitivism
    and progress in Humphry Clinker.  Unconvincing in its
    thesis, the book offers a rich background in eighteenth-
    century thought.

7   GOLDEN, MORRIS.   "Two Essays Erroneously Attributed to
    Goldsmith," MLN, 74 (January), 13-16.
        Two essays in British Magazine, August, 1760, probably
    Smollett's.

8   JONES, CLAUDE E.   "Dramatic Criticism in the Critical Review,
    1756-1785," MLQ, 20 (March), 18-26, (June), 133-44.

1959

Principles of dramatic criticism in the review during
years of Smollett's editorship (1756-63).

9   OROWITZ, MILTON. "Craft and Vision in the Novels of Smollett:
The Uses of Caricature." Diss., University of California,
Berkeley, 1959.
    Concerned with the social views expressed in Smollett's
uses of caricature in Roderick Random, Peregrine Pickle,
and Humphry Clinker, and shows the changes in Smollett's
methods as caricature becomes less important and more
Dickensian in his balanced view of life in his final novel.

10  ROPER, DEREK/ "Smollett's 'Four Gentlemen': The First Contributors to the Critical Review," RES, n.s. 10 (February),
38-44.
    Expanded version of 1957.15 describes the reviewers
listed in a marked copy of the first two volumes. Lists
contributors and gives contributions of Smollett as well as
a key to all the reviewers noted in the volumes.

11  RYSKAMP, CHARLES. William Cowper of the Inner Temple, Esq. A
Study of His Life and Works to the Year 1768. Cambridge:
University Press, pp. 233-36 and passim.
    Information on aid provided for Smollett's edition of
Voltaire.

12  SPECTOR, ROBERT D. "Smollett's Use of Tsonnonthouan," N&Q,
n.s. 6 (March), 112-13.
    Excerpt printed in British Magazine suggests Smollett
reviewed novel in Critical and used it in Humphry Clinker
and the Atom.

13  STANG, RICHARD. The Theory of the Novel in England 1850-1870.
New York: Columbia University Press, pp. 4, 22, 101-2, 135,
153, 179, 205, 218.
    Various nineteenth-century responses to Smollett's nov-
els.

14  STRAUSS, ALBRECHT. "Eliza's Prototypes?," TLS, December 11,
p. 725.
    Shaw's denial is proof he was not indebted to Smollett
for character in Pygmalion.

15  STRAUSS, ALBRECHT B. "On Smollett's Language: A Paragraph in
Ferdinand Count Fathom," in Style in Prose Fiction. English Institute Essays, 1958, ed. Harold C. Martin. New
York: Columbia University Press, pp. 25-54.
    Whatever Smollett's virtues, the reader should be aware
of his inability to convey adequately the uncomical

emotional life of his characters, the failings of his figu-
rative language, and the overall conventionality and hol-
lowness of his diction.

16  WEINTRAUB, STANLEY.  "Eliza's Prototypes?," TLS, November 13,
p. 668.
Peregrine Pickle Shaw's source for character in
Pygmalion.


## 1960

1  ANON.  "The Virginia and Richard Ehrlich Collection," Boston
Public Library Quarterly, 12 (April), 103-9.
Addition of Smollett material to the collection.

2  ATHERTON, JAMES S.  The Books at the Wake: A Study of Literary
Allusions in James Joyce's Finnegans Wake.  New York: The
Viking Press, p. 280.
References and allusions to Smollett's work suggest
Joyce's admiration for his novels.

3  BOGGS, W. ARTHUR.  "Hassock of Hair," N&Q, n.s. 7 (February),
72-73.
Win Jenkins's use of phrase in Humphry Clinker predates
that in OED.  Editorial note indicates a use in 1754.

4  [COOPER, JAMES FENIMORE].  The Letters and Journals of James
Fenimore Cooper, ed. James Franklin Beard.  Cambridge,
Mass.: Belknap Press of Harvard University Press, I, 375;
IV, 266, 276.
On visit to Smollett's tomb in Leghorn and on the inade-
quacy of treating Smollett's characters as autobiographic-
al.  Volume IV published in 1964.

5  DAICHES, DAVID.  "The Novel: Richardson to Austen," in A Cri-
tical History of English Literature.  New York: Ronald
Press, II, 727-31.
Sees Smollett's novels as picaresque, except for Humphry
Clinker, and summarizes them with not very favorable com-
ments.  2nd ed. 1970.

6  DAVIS, BERTRAM H.  Johnson before Boswell: A Study of Sir John
Hawkins' Life of Samuel Johnson.  New Haven: Yale Univer-
sity Press, passim.  Indexed.
Hawkins's unfavorable treatment of Smollett.

7    [EMERSON, RALPH WALDO]. Journals and Miscellaneous Notebooks
     of Ralph Waldo Emerson, ed. William H. Gilman et al.  Cam-
     bridge, Mass.: Belknap Press of Harvard University Press,
     I, 396.
          Reads Peregrine Pickle in 1819-24 period.

8    ENGEL, MONROE.  "Foreword," in The Expedition of Humphry
     Clinker.  A Signet Classic.  New York: The New American
     Library, pp. v-ix.
          Contrasting Humphry Clinker with Smollett's earlier nov-
     els, finds its success resulting from rejection of a pica-
     resque tradition inconsistent with English social values.

9    GASSMAN, BYRON W.  "The Background of Humphry Clinker."
     Diss., University of Chicago, 1960.
          Detailed account of Smollett's novel in relation to
     autobiographical material and its cultural and social
     milieu.  Particularly strong in discussion of the political
     and religious background.

10   KNAPP, LEWIS M.  "Another Letter from Smollett to Dr. William
     Hunter," N&Q, n.s. 7 (August), 299-300.
          1763 letter from Boulogne throws light on the Travels.

11   KOBLER, JOHN.  The Reluctant Surgeon. A Biography of John
     Hunter.  Garden City, New York: Doubleday, pp. 30, 36, 38,
     77, 131-33.
          Smollett's Scottish background, relations, and friend-
     ships with William Smellie, the Hunter brothers, and
     others.

12   LAWS, SHEILA YOUNG.  "The Evolving Comic Spirit in the Novels
     of Tobias Smollett."  M.A. Thesis, University of Tennessee,
     1960.
          Smollett's use of "ludicrousness, satire, wit, and hu-
     mor" in his novels and the development of his comic tech-
     nique.

13   McCOMBIE, F.  "Count Fathom and El Buscón," N&Q, n.s. 7
     (August), 297-99.
          Influence of Quevedo's La Vida del Buscón may be seen in
     use of the picaresque, resemblances in characters' experi-
     ences and circumstances.

14   PAULSON, RONALD.  "Satire in the Early Novels of Smollett,"
     JEGP, 59 (July), 381-402.
          Relates Smollett's novels to the techniques of formal
     verse satire and concludes that he managed to break from

its conventional limitations only with his use of multiple
satirists and travel literature in Humphry Clinker.

15   ROSENBERG, EDGAR.   From Shylock to Svengali: Jewish Sterotypes
     in English Fiction.   Stanford: Stanford University Press,
     passim.  Indexed.
        Even Smollett's one favorable portrait of the Jew in
     Ferdinand Count Fathom is a stereotype.

16   SEN, SAILENDRA KUMAR.  "Sheridan's Literary Debt: The Rivals
     and Humphry Clinker," MLQ, 21 (December), 291-300.
        Borrowings from Smollett, while contributing to
     Sheridan's humor, adversely affected the plot of his come-
     dy.  Believes indebtedness has been exaggerated.

17   SPECTOR, ROBERT D.  "Attacks on the Critical Review in the
     Literary Magazine," N&Q, n.s. 7 (August), 300-301.
        Three attacks in 1757 not listed in Jones, 1942.4.

18   SPECTOR, ROBERT D.  "The Monthly and Its Rival," BNYPL, 64
     (March), 159-61.
        Competition from the Critical Review put pressure on the
     Monthly to expand to American market, increase its size,
     and adopt new features.

19   STEVENSON, LIONEL.  The English Novel: A Panorama.  Boston:
     Houghton Mifflin, The Riverside Press, Cambridge, pp. 99-
     102, 111-12, 114-15, 132-33, 143-44, and passim.
        Discusses Smollett's novels in relation to contemporary
     development of the genre; emphasizes the experiential and
     autobiographical, his vulgarity and brutality, gross exag-
     geration and episodic technique.

20   TAVE, STUART M.  The Amiable Humorist: A Study in the Comic
     Theory and Criticism of the Eighteenth and Early Nineteenth
     Centuries.  Chicago: University of Chicago Press, passim.
     Indexed.
        Various comments on Smollett's work in relation to comic
     practice and theory of his period and following generation.

21   [WALPOLE, HORACE].  Horace Walpole's Correspondence with Sir
     Horace Mann, 6, ed. W. S. Lewis et al.  Yale Edition of
     Horace Walpole's Correspondence, ed. W. S. Lewis.  New
     Haven: Yale University Press, XXII, 306.
        1765 letter on Smollett's deficient treatment of poli-
     tics in his history.

1961

1   BAKER, SHERIDAN.  "Humphry Clinker as Comic Romance," Papers
    of the Michigan Academy of Science, Arts, and Letters, 46
    (1961), 645-54.
        Sees novel as last major work in an unrecognized eigh-
    teenth-century genre of comic romance.  Smollett burlesques
    the traditional romance by inverting chivalric ideals and
    leveling man's pretensions with scatological satire.  Re-
    printed 1965.4.

2   BLOOM, EDWARD A.  "Neoclassic 'Paper Wars' for a Free Press,"
    MLR, 56 (October), 481-96.
        Smollett's Critical Review and Briton in the journalis-
    tic warfare of their period.

3   BOGGS, W. ARTHUR.  "Win Jenkins' Malapropisms," Jammu &
    Kashmir University Review, 4 (December), 130-40.
        Discusses various elements Smollett employs in creating
    Win's vocabulary in Humphry Clinker and notes lack of con-
    sistency as he emphasizes comic purposes.

4   BURNS, WAYNE.  Charles Reade: A Study in Victorian Authorship.
    New York: Bookman Associates, pp. 76-78, 157.
        Reade's favorable opinion of Smollett and indebtedness
    to his work.

5   CRAIG, DAVID.  "Fiction and the Scottish Reading Public," in
    Scottish Literature and the Scottish People 1680-1830.
    London: Chatto & Windus, pp. 208-11.
        On the reading of Smollett in Scotland.

*6  FARRELL, WILLIAM JOSEPH.  "Rhetorical Elements in the Eigh-
    teenth-Century English Novel."  Diss., University of
    Wisconsin, 1961.
        Relationship between character and situation changes and
    the style of Ferdinand Count Fathom and Sir Launcelot
    Greaves.  Cited in Dissertation Abstracts, Vol. 22, 1976.

7   GRIFFITH, PHILIP MAHONE.  "Fire Scenes in Richardson's
    Clarissa and Smollett's Humphry Clinker: A Study of a Lit-
    erary Relationship in the Structure of the Novel," Tulane
    Studies in English, 11 (1961), 39-51.
        Sees farcical fire scenes in Smollett's novels as satir-
    ic parody on Richardson's scene and relates Smollett's use
    of two such episodes to the rhythmic structure of his nov-
    el.

*8   KNAPP, LEWIS M.  "A Rare Set of Smollett's Novels," Notes from
     the Rare Books Room. University of Colorado, no. 10.
          Cited in 1971.61.

 9   KNAPP, MARY E.  Prologues and Epilogues of the Eighteenth Cen-
     tury. Yale Studies in English, 149.  New Haven: Yale Uni-
     versity Press, p. 153.
          Epilogue to The Reprisal indicates raucous conduct of
     audiences.

10   LLOYD, CHRISTOPHER and JACK L. S. COULTER.  "Tobias Smollett,"
     in Medicine and the Navy, 1200-1900.  Edinburgh and London:
     E. & S. Livingstone, III, 25-28.
          Smollett's nautical material in Roderick Random effec-
     tive propaganda.

11   McLAREN, MORAY.  "Tobias Smollett or the Disputatious Scot,"
     in The Wisdom of the Scots.  New York: St. Martin's Press,
     pp. 240-43.
          Relates Humphry Clinker to Smollett's Scottishness and
     notes his contribution to scatological writing.

12   PECK, LOUIS F.  A Life of Matthew G. Lewis.  Cambridge, Mass.:
     Harvard University Press, p. 28.
          1798 defense of The Monk argued it less harmful to mo-
     rality than Peregrine Pickle or Ferdinand Count Fathom.

13   ROPER, DEREK.  "The Politics of the Critical Review, 1756-
     1817," Durham University Journal, 53 (June), 117-22.
          Under Smollett moved from impartial position to Tory
     support for Lord Bute in the early 1760s.

14   SHERWIN, OSCAR.  Goldy: The Life and Times of Oliver
     Goldsmith.  New York: Twayne Publishers, passim.  Indexed.
          Smollett in Grub St. milieu and his relations with
     Goldsmith.

15   SHERWIN, OSCAR.  John Wesley: Friend of the People.  New York:
     Twayne Publishers, pp. 52-53, 156-57.
          Smollett's portrait of Methodism in Humphry Clinker not
     altogether unfriendly, and Wesley used his history in his
     own work.

16   WAGONER, MARY HERMIONE SPARKS.  "The Changing Patterns of
     Humor in the Novels of Tobias Smollett."  Diss., University
     of Texas, 1961.

1961

       Analyzes Smollett's development in his five novels from a picaresque to a comic writer and discusses changes in his social attitudes and literary techniques as a part of his expanded and more mature comic vision.

17    WEBSTER, GRANT.  "Smollett and Shaw: A Note on a Source for Heartbreak House," Shaw Review, 4 (September), 16-17.
       Shaw's nautical setting parallels Smollett's nautical house in Peregrine Pickle.

## 1962

1    ADAMS, PERCY G.  "Fireside Travelers, before Defoe," in Travelers and Travel Liars, 1660-1800.  Berkeley and Los Angeles: University of California Press; London: Cambridge University Press, pp. 89-90 and passim.
       Relates Smollett's plagiarism in Compendium of Authentic and Entertaining Voyages and his Travels to contemporary practices.

2    AUBRUN, C.  "Smollett and Cervantes," EA, 15 (April-June), 122-29.
       Smollett did not translate Don Quixote, but supervised team of hacks.

3    BREDVOLD, LOUIS I.  "The Mid-Century: Johnson and His Circle," in The Literature of the Restoration and the Eighteenth Century, 1660-1798. A History of English Literature, ed. Hardin Craig.  New York: Collier Books, III, 152-54.
       Unfavorable account of work of Smollett, an irritable genius, but ends with favorable comments on Humphry Clinker.  Originally published in 1950, London: Oxford University Press.

4    [COVENTRY, FRANCIS].  An Essay on the New Species of Writing Founded by Mr. Fielding, ed. Alan D. McKillop.  Augustan Reprint Society, No. 95.  Los Angeles: William Andrews Clark Memorial Library, University of California.
       Reprint of 1751.15.  McKillop's notes and introduction provide context of the attack on Smollett.

5    DAVIS, WENDELL EUGENE.  "The World of Smollett's Novels."  Diss., Western Reserve University, 1962.
       Studies effect of travels and setting on Smollett's novels and shows an irregular but gradual development in his appreciation of such matters for his fiction as a result of

his work as playwright, translator, and editor. Concentrates on the experimental character of Smollett's novels.

6   EVANS, BERGEN. "Introduction," in Roderick Random. A Premier
    World Classic. Greenwich, Conn.: Fawcett Publications,
    pp. v–viii.
        Brief appreciative essay on Smollett's energetic style
    discounts arguments that give moral significance to his
    episodic narrative.

7   GUILLÉN, CLAUDIO. "Toward a Definition of the Picaresque," in
    Proceedings of the IIId Congress of the International Comparative Literature Association, ed. W. A. P. Smit. The
    Hague: Mouton & Co., passim. Indexed.
        Picaresque characteristics of Smollett's style in novels. Essay is reprinted in Literature as System, 1971,
    Princeton: Princeton University Press.

8   HODGART, M. J. C. Samuel Johnson and His Times. New York:
    Arco Publishing Company; London: Batsford, pp. 39, 57.
        Smollett foremost journalist of his period, but less
    important novelist than his major contemporaries.

9   HORN, ANDRÁS. "Some Picaresque Features: Smollett," in
    Byron's "Don Juan" and the Eighteenth-Century English Novel. Schweizer Anglistische Arbeiten, Swiss Studies in
    English, 51. Bern: Francke Verlag, pp. 49–60.
        Discusses Byron's indebtedness to picaresque tradition
    through Smollett as its most important English practitioner. Considers relationships in structure, characterization, and attitudes.

10  LOTT, JOHN RAYMOND. "The Vogue of the Betrayed-Woman Theme in
    English Fiction, 1740–1775." Diss., Duke University, 1962.
        Relates Smollett's treatment of the subject in his novels––particularly Roderick Random and Peregrine Pickle––to
    that of his contemporaries.

*11 McCOMBIE, F. "The Novels of Tobias Smollett," M. Litt.
    Thesis, University of Durham, 1962.
        Cited in Index to Theses Accepted for Higher Degrees in
    the Universities of Great Britain and Ireland.

12  McCULLOUGH, NORMAN V. "The Novel and the Man of Colour," in
    The Negro in English Literature: A Critical Introduction.
    Ilfracombe, Devon: Arthur H. Stockwell, pp. 127–29.
        Unfavorable treatment of the Negro in Humphry Clinker.

1962

13  MARSHALL, PERCY. "Tobias Smollett," in <u>Masters of the English
    Novel</u>. London: Dennis Dobson, pp. 60-75.
        Comparison with Fielding and Richardson emphasizes the
    importance of his Scottish background, medical and nautical
    experiences, autobiographical material, and influence of
    the picaresque.

14  MAXWELL, J. C. "French Borrowings in <u>Ferdinand Count Fathom</u>,"
    <u>N&Q</u>, n.s. 9 (January), 18-19.
        Three items antedate any listed use in English.

15  MAYO, ROBERT D. "Original Fiction in the Miscellanies," in
    <u>The English Novel in the Magazines</u>. Evanston, Illinois:
    Northwestern University Press; London: Oxford University
    Press, pp. 273-88 and passim.
        Describes Smollett's connection with <u>British Magazine</u>
    and its publication of <u>Sir Launcelot Greaves</u>, the first
    original work of its length written particularly for serial
    publication by a major author. Considers relationship of
    the form of the novel to serial publication. References to
    Smollett's other works are scattered throughout; <u>see</u>, par-
    ticularly, pp. 194-96 for <u>Peregrine Pickle</u>.

16  PARK, WILLIAM JOHN III. "The Mid-Eighteenth Century English
    Novel." Diss., Columbia University, 1962.
        Considers the aesthetic, social, and moral conventions
    underlying the novels of Smollett in relation to the works
    of his contemporaries.

17  PRYDE, GEORGE S. <u>Scotland from 1603 to the Present Day</u>.
    London et al.: Thomas Nelson and Sons, pp. 111, 112, 171.
        Smollett belongs more to the English than Scottish tra-
    dition.

18  ROMBERG, BERTIL. <u>Studies in the Narrative Technique of the
    First-Person Novel</u>. Stockholm: Almqvist & Wiksell, pp. 51,
    52, 71-72, 77, 89, 313, 314, 338.
        Narrative devices in <u>Roderick Random</u>, <u>Humphry Clinker</u>,
    and the <u>History and Adventures of an Atom</u>.

19  RUDÉ, GEORGE. "'Wilkes and Liberty!'" in <u>Wilkes and Liberty</u>,
    <u>A Social Study of 1763 to 1774</u>. Oxford: Clarendon Press,
    pp. 20-21.
        The <u>Briton</u>'s role in political controversy.

20  STONE, GEORGE WINCHESTER JR., ed. <u>The London Stage 1660-1800
    (1747-1776)</u>. Carbondale, Ill.: Southern Illinois Press,
    Part 4, Vols. 1-3, passim. Indexed.

Information about <u>Alceste</u> and the stage productions of
<u>The Reprisal</u>.

21  WILSON, J. STUART.  "Novel into Play: The Influence of
Richardson, Fielding, Smollett, and Sterne upon the Later
English Drama."  Diss., Rice University, 1962.
    Concerned with the relationship of Smollett's novels to
the development of English comic drama after 1760 in the
plays of Arthur Murphy, George Colman, Samuel Foote, later
dramatists, and particularly Richard Brinsley Sheridan.

## 1963

1  ALBERTS, ROBERT C.  "The Fantastic Adventures of Captain
Stobo," <u>American Heritage</u>, 14 (August), 65-77.
    Biographical account, particularly the military adven-
tures, of Stobo, purportedly the original of Lismahago in
<u>Humphry Clinker</u>.

2  ALTICK, RICHARD D.  <u>The Art of Literary Research</u>.  New York:
W. W. Norton, passim.  Indexed.
    Smollett's work in relation to modern research and the
particular problems created by the forged letters published
by Francesco Cordasco.  Revised edition in 1975.

*3  AL-USAILY, MOHAMMED AWAD.  "Satire in the Novels of Smollett."
Diss., Edinburgh University, 1963.
    Detailed description of the examples of satire in
Smollett's work.  Cited in Boucé, 1976.9.

4  BAKER, SHERIDAN.  "The Idea of Romance in the Eighteenth-Century Novel," <u>Papers of the Michigan Academy of Science,
Arts, and Letters</u>, 49 (1963), 507-22.
    Uses Smollett's work to argue for a special influence of
the romance tradition on the eighteenth-century English
novel.

5  BAKER, SHERIDAN.  "The Idea of Romance in the Eighteenth-Century Novel," <u>Studies in English Literature (English Number.
English Literary Society of Japan)</u>, 39 (1963), 57-59.
    Reprints comments on <u>Humphry Clinker</u> as comic romance
from 1961.1.

6  BATE, WALTER JACKSON.  <u>John Keats</u>.  Cambridge, Mass.: Harvard
University Press, pp. 276-77, 610.
    Keats's reading, opinions, and imitations of Smollett.

1963

7    BOGGS, W. A.  "Smollett's Coinages in the Win Jenkins Let-
        ters," Language Quarterly, 2 (Fall), 2-4.
            Eight words used either initially or in a new sense in
        Humphry Clinker and Smollett's extensive knowledge of lin-
        guistics.

8    CLIFFORD, JAMES L.  "Pallet in Peregrine Pickle," N&Q, n.s.
        10 (December), 465.
            Evidence that Smollett had real model for his character
        and request for help in identification.

9    DAVIS, EARLE.  "Humor in Motion: The Face-Caricature Tech-
        nique," in The Flint and the Flame: The Artistry of Charles
        Dickens.  Columbia, Mo.: University of Missouri Press, pp.
        18-30 and passim.
            Intelligent and detailed discussion of Dickens's use of
        Smollett's descriptive, expository, and narrative tech-
        niques.

10   FREEMAN, JOHN.  Literature and Locality. The Literary Topogra-
        phy of Britain and Ireland.  London: Cassell, passim.  In-
        dexed.
            Smollett's associations with places in Scotland and
        England.

11   GASSMAN, BYRON.  "The Briton and Humphry Clinker," SEL, 3
        (Summer), 397-414.
            Discusses Smollett's attitude toward government, politi-
        cians, and the role of the press in Britain, and, although
        denying a coherent political system in Humphry Clinker, ar-
        gues reasonably that later works offer fairly consistent
        conservative point of view.

12   HANNUM, HOWARD LEON.  "Tobias Smollett: Fiction and Carica-
        ture."  Diss., University of Pennsylvania, 1963.
            Detailed analysis of relationships between Smollett's
        novels and printing and engraving techniques.  Shows
        Smollett's broad knowledge and use of graphic art particu-
        larly for purposes of caricature.

13   HOLLINGSWORTH, KEITH.  The Newgate Novel, 1830-1847: Bulwer,
        Ainsworth, Dickens, & Thackeray.  Detroit: Wayne State Uni-
        versity Press, pp. 68, 84, 126.
            Smollett's influence in the nineteenth century.

14   HUNTING, ROBERT.  "Footnote to a Comparative Study: Smollett
        and Ibsen," N&Q, n.s. 10 (June), 228-29.

Parallel situations in Smollett's <u>Essay on the External Use of Water</u> and Ibsen's <u>An Enemy of the People</u>.

15  JACK, IAN.  <u>English Literature, 1815-1832</u>.  Oxford History of English Literature, 10, ed. Bonamy Dobrée et al.  New York and Oxford: Oxford University Press, pp. 152, 202, 225, 266, 434.
    Opinions of Smollett's work by Scott, Hazlitt, and T. H. Lister, and Smollett's influence on Thomas Hood.

16  JAMES, LOUIS.  <u>Fiction for the Working Man, 1830-1850</u>.
    London, New York, Toronto: Oxford University Press, p. 152.
    Smollett's influence on Victorian novelists dealing with naval romances.

17  KNAPP, LEWIS M.  <u>Tobias Smollett: Doctor of Men and Manners</u>.
    New York: Octagon Books, xiii + 362 pp.
    Reprint of 1949.12.

18  KNAPP, LEWIS M.  <u>The Works of Tobias Smollett and Related Material. Collected by Lewis M. Knapp</u>.  Colorado Springs: Printed by the Author, 16 pp.
    Experiences in collecting Smollett material and his collection of Smollett's works and Smollettiana.

19  KNAPP, LEWIS M. and LILLIAN DE LA TORRE.  "Smollett, Mackercher and the Annesley Claimant," <u>ELN</u>, 1 (September), 28-33.
    Smollett's material for the case in <u>Peregrine Pickle</u> came from Mackercher, Annesley's supporter.

20  LUKÁCS, GEORG.  <u>The Historical Novel</u>, trans. Hannah and Stanley Mitchell.  Boston: Beacon Press, pp. 20, 66, 201.
    Correctness, specificity, and use of history in Smollett's novels and comparisons with Goethe's.  First published in Moscow in 1937.

21  McBURNEY, WILLIAM.  "Introduction," in <u>Four Before Richardson. Selected English Novels, 1720-1727</u>.  Lincoln: University of Nebraska Press, pp. xi-xii, xx-xxii.
    Smollett's attitude toward earlier English fiction and resemblances between his work and <u>The Jamaica Lady</u> (1720).

22  PIPER, WILLIAM BOWMAN.  "The Large Diffused Picture of Life in Smollett's Early Novels," <u>SP</u>, 60 (January), 45-56.
    Carefully analyzing methods of characterization in first three novels, demonstrates their relationship to Smollett's

1963

personality and desire to create a "large diffused picture
of life" as expressed in preface to Ferdinand Count Fathom.

23  REA, ROBERT R.  The English Press in Politics, 1760-1774.
Lincoln: University of Nebraska Press, pp. 29-33 and passim.
Smollett's political attitudes and his attempt at political propaganda in the Briton, unsuccessful because of his
temperament.

24  REID, J. C.  Thomas Hood.  London: Routledge & Kegan Paul, pp.
124, 171, 203-4.
Smollett's considerable influence on Hood's work.

25  RENWICK, W. L.  "Views of Men, Manners, and Society," in
English Literature: 1789-1815.  Oxford History of English
Literature, 9, ed. F. P. Wilson and Bonamy Dobrée.  Oxford:
Clarendon Press, pp. 60-61, 68.
Describes unwillingness to properly acknowledge
Smollett's narrative strength and notes influence on John
Moore and Charlotte Smith.

26  SHERBO, ARTHUR.  New Essays by Arthur Murphy.  East Lansing,
Michigan: Michigan State University Press, passim.  Indexed.
Discusses Smollett's relationships with Murphy in their
periodical criticism and reprints reviews in which Smollett
and the Critical Review are attacked.

27  SHERWIN, OSCAR.  "Paris Fashion," in A Gentleman of Wit and
Fashion: The Extraordinary Life and Times of George Selwyn.
New York: Twayne Publishers, p. 218.
Contrasts provincial attitudes in Smollett's Travels
with more cosmopolitan views of contemporaries.

28  SPECTOR, ROBERT D.  "Introduction," in Seven Masterpieces of
Gothic Horror.  New York: Bantam Books, p. 6.
Gothic scenes in Fathom originate in earlier drama.

29  WEBSTER, GRANT.  "The Novels of Tobias Smollett: A Study in
Structures."  Diss., Ohio State University, 1963.
Using the principles of mythological criticism concerned
with romances, examines the structures of Smollett's five
novels.  Discusses Smollett's mixture of various types of
satire, his methods of undercutting sentiment, and yet his
sympathies for sentimental ideals.

## 1964

1    ALTER, ROBERT.  "The Picaroon as Fortune's Plaything," in
     Rogue's Progress: Studies in the Picaresque Novel.  Cam-
     bridge, Mass.: Harvard University Press, pp. 58-79.
         Roderick Random consciously follows continental pica-
     resque despite modifications in the tradition, and Roderick
     is a picaresque hero.  As a natural outsider to English
     society, Smollett makes even his satire conform to the
     genre, but the infusion of sentiment in the novel fore-
     shadows the general decline of the picaresque in European
     literature.  Reprinted 1965.1.

2    BACHE, KAYE ELIZABETH.  "The Narrative Posture of Four Novels
     of Tobias Smollett."  Diss., University of Wisconsin, 1964.
         Analyzes the narrative prose in Smollett's novels, ex-
     cluding Launcelot Greaves, as a means of comprehending his
     intentions and the forces stimulating them.  Concentrates
     primarily on fundamental structure, point of view, and dic-
     tion in each of the novels.

3    BARTH, JOHN.  "Afterword," in The Adventures of Roderick
     Random.  A Signet classic.  New York: New American Library,
     pp. 469-79.
         Limited in its understanding of the eighteenth century
     and of Smollett's work generally, sees Smollett as an un-
     subtle, though energetic, novelist, good for a single
     reading, and finds Roderick Random an extension of his
     irascible personality.

4    BOGGS, W. ARTHUR.  "A Win Jenkins' Lexicon," BNYPL, 68 (May),
     323-30.
         Excluding obvious malapropisms in Humphry Clinker, pre-
     sents a helpful lexicon of other difficult words in Win's
     vocabulary.

5    [BOSWELL, JAMES].  Boswell's Life of Johnson together with
     Boswell's Journal of a Tour to the Hebrides and Johnson's
     Diary of a Journey into North Wales, ed. G. B. Hill and L.
     F. Powell.  2nd ed., 6 Vols.  Oxford: Clarendon Press,
     passim.  Indexed.
         Modern edition contains detailed notes referring to
     Smollett and his work.  1st ed. in 1934.

6    BRISSENDEN, R. F.  "Sterne and Painting," in Of Books and
     Humankind: Essays and Poems Presented to Bonamy Dobrée, ed.
     John Butt et al.  London: Routledge and Kegan Paul, pp.
     103, 107.

1964

Comparison of Sterne's and Smollett's descriptions of art connoisseurs and relation of Smollett's "Dedication" in *Fathom* to the traditional parallel of painting and literature.

7   BRUCE, DONALD. *Radical Doctor Smollett*. London: Gollancz, 240 pp.
      Although enthusiastic about Smollett and his work, erratic in interpretations and unreliable in facts and details. Considers the intellectual, scientific, social, political, and aesthetic background against which he wrote and discusses his treatment of such subjects as philosophy, medicine, poverty, and government, invariably depicting him as a radical. Also considers structure, imagery, style, and satiric and ironic techniques of the novels. American edition in 1965, Boston: Houghton Mifflin, the Riverside Press, Cambridge.

8   CARROLL, JOHN. *Selected Letters of Samuel Richardson*. Oxford: Clarendon Press, pp. 14, 173, 328-29.
      Carroll describes their relationship and includes 1756 letter from Richardson on unfavorable comment on his work in *Critical*.

9   CLIFFORD, JAMES L. "Introduction," in *The Adventures of Peregrine Pickle in which Are Included Memoirs of a Lady of Quality*. Oxford English Novels. London, New York, Toronto: Oxford University Press, pp. xv-xxix.
      Gives available facts about composition, reception, and reputation, and summarizes differences between first and revised editions. Discusses influences on mixture of techniques and stresses narrative abilities and characterization.

10  COCHRANE, J. A. *Dr. Johnson's Printer: The Life of William Strahan*. London: Routledge & Kegan Paul, passim. Indexed.
      Useful information about publication, editions, and profits of *Roderick Random*, *Humphry Clinker*, *History of England*.

11  EDITORS. "Pallet in *Peregrine Pickle*," *N&Q*, n.s. 11 (December), 478.
      Calls attention to Paulson's essay in *SEL* identifying Smollett in reference to Clifford's query, 1963.8.

12  FOLTINEK, HERBERT. "Über die Methode des Motivvergleichs: Dargestellt an Englischen Literaturwerken," *English Miscellany*, 15 (1964), 103-33.

Relationship of structural patterns in Humphry Clinker and other English works, particularly Nicholas Nickleby.

13    FRIEDSON, ANTHONY M.  Literature through the Ages.  New York: Sterling, pp. 61, 64, 73.
      Smollett and the picaresque and epistolary novel forms.

14    FRYER, PETER.  Mrs. Grundy: Studies in English Prudery.  New York: London House & Maxwell, British Book Centre, pp. 43, 80, 306.
      Smollett's diction in relation to obscenity and offensiveness.

15    HAMMOND, REGINALD J. W.  "Dumbarton," in The Complete Scotland.  8th ed.  London and Melbourne: Ward, Lock, p. 151.
      On a Smollett statue in suburbs of Dumbarton.

16    JEFFERSON, D. W.  "Speculations on Three Eighteenth-Century Prose Writers," in 1964.6, pp. 81-83.
      Examines the elements of the conventions of Augustan prose style in Ferdinand Count Fathom.

17    JOHNSTON, ARTHUR.  Enchanted Ground: The Study of Medieval Romance in the Eighteenth Century.  London: University of London, Athlone Press, pp. 72-73, 237.
      Smollett's attitude toward the romance and his failure with it in Launcelot Greaves.

18    KARL, FREDERICK R.  An Age of Fiction: The Nineteenth Century British Novel.  New York: Farrar, Straus and Giroux, passim.  Indexed.
      Smollett's role in development of the genre and his influence in the nineteenth century.

19    KIELY, ROBERT.  Robert Louis Stevenson and the Fiction of Adventure.  Cambridge, Mass.: Harvard University Press, pp. 91, 93.
      Comparisons of Stevenson's and Smollett's fictional techniques.

20    KNAPP, LEWIS M.  "The Keys to Smollett's Atom," ELN, 2 (December), 100-102.
      Discusses various keys and prints one from 1769 copy.

21    LOOFBOUROW, JOHN.  Thackeray and the Form of Fiction.  Princeton: Princeton University Press, passim.  Indexed.
      General comparisons of Thackeray's and Smollett's techniques.

1964

22  PAULSON, RONALD. "Smollett and Hogarth: The Identity of
    Pallet," SEL, 4 (Summer), 351-59.
       Argues persuasively that Hogarth was model for
    Smollett's character in Peregrine Pickle and suggests his
    friendship with Garrick and Fielding led to the caricature.

23  PRESTON, THOMAS R. "Smollett and the Benevolent Misanthrope
    Type," PMLA, 79 (March), 51-57.
       Argues convincingly that Bramble in Humphry Clinker,
    while related to Smollett's personality, belongs to a tra-
    dition of "benevolent misanthropic satirists" used by other
    eighteenth-century writers.

24  SAUNDERS, J. W. "The Romantic Dilemma," in The Profession of
    English Letters. London: Routledge and Kegan Paul;
    Toronto: University of Toronto Press, pp. 151-54 and pas-
    sim.
       Interesting on commercial side of Smollett's career, but
    unsympathetic to work, described in terms of autobiography.

*25 WARNER, JOHN MAYNARD. "Smollett and the Minor Comic Novel,
    1750-1770." Diss., Harvard University, 1964.
       Cited in Korte, 1969.15.

26  WARNER, OLIVER. "Tobias Smollett," in English Literature: A
    Portrait Gallery. London: Chatto & Windus, pp. 68-69.
       Emphasizes autobiographical and nautical material and
    prints portrait by unknown artist.

27  WATSON, GEORGE. "Introduction," in Maria Edgeworth's Castle
    Rackrent. Oxford English Novels. London, New York,
    Toronto: Oxford University Press, p. vii.
       Contrasts Edgeworth's regionalism with Smollett's exag-
    geration of provincial characters.

28  WOLFF, ERWIN. "Welt als Panorama: Tobias Smollett," in Der
    Englische Roman im 18. Jahrhundert. Wesen und Formen.
    Göttingen: Vandenhoeck & Ruprecht, pp. 104-22.
       General account emphasizes relationship of the form of
    his novels to concern for a realistic portrayal of his
    society.

1965

1   ALTER, ROBERT. "The Picaroon as Fortune's Plaything," in
    1965.30, pp. 131-53.
       Reprint of 1964.1.

2   ALTICK, RICHARD D.  Lives and Letters: A History of Literary
    Biography in England and America.  New York: Alfred A.
    Knopf, pp. 37, 72, 93, 287, 365.
        Relationship of Smollett's realism to literary biogra-
    phy.

3   BAINE, RODNEY M.  Thomas Holcroft and the Revolutionary Novel.
    University of Georgia Monographs, No. 13.  Athens, Ga.:
    University of Georgia Press, passim.  Indexed.
        Smollett's influence on Holcroft's work.

4   BAKER, SHERIDAN.  "Humphry Clinker as Comic Romance," in
    1965.30, pp. 154-64.
        Reprint of 1961.1.

5   BOGGS, W. ARTHUR.  "Dialectical Ingenuity in Humphry Clinker,"
    PLL, 1 (Autumn), 327-37.
        Smollett created Win Jenkins's language from a variety
    of incompatible linguistic and dialectal sources and hood-
    winked his uninformed English readers.

6   BOGGS, W. ARTHUR.  "Shakespeare and Win," ANQ, 3 (June), 149-
    50.
        Win's malapropisms in Humphry Clinker from Shakespeare.

7   BOGGS, W. ARTHUR.  "Some Standard Eighteenth-Century English
    Usages," Quarterly Journal of Speech, 51 (October), 304-6.
        Some legitimate words Win uses may seem substandard to
    modern readers; Smollett's use for creating comic charac-
    ter.

8   BOGGS, W. ARTHUR.  "Win Jenkins' Archaisms and Proverbial
    Phrases," Language Quarterly, 4 (Fall-Winter), 33-36.
        Attributes her limited use of archaisms in Humphry
    Clinker to Smollett's other linguistic interests, and finds
    her proverbial phrases and expressions lack creativity.

9   BOGGS, W. ARTHUR.  "Win Jenkins' First Citations in the
    O.E.D.," Word Study, 41 (October), 5.
        Notes citations from Smollett in OED and that four of
    the first for a word or phrase are from Win in Humphry
    Clinker.

10  BOUCÉ, PAUL-GABRIEL.  "Smollett's Libel," TLS, December 30,
    p. 1218.
        Libelous paragraph on Knowles's pamphlet did not appear
    in later printings of the Critical Review.

1965

11    BRUCE, DONALD, W. M. PARKER, and <u>TLS</u> REVIEWER.  "Bawling about
         Smollett," <u>TLS</u>, January 21, p. 54.
            Exchange about Bruce's <u>Radical Dr. Smollett</u> and about
         Smollett's having been a Scot rather than an Englishman.

12    ELMER, ROBERT WATSON.  "Structure in the Early Novels of
         Smollett."  Diss., Columbia University, 1965.
            Argues against a satirical structure in <u>Roderick Random</u>,
         <u>Peregrine Pickle</u>, and <u>Fathom</u> and examines what he regards
         as their varied principles of organization derived from
         comic, melodramatic, and other sources.

13    [EMERSON, RALPH WALDO].  <u>Journals and Miscellaneous Notebooks</u>
         <u>of Ralph Waldo Emerson</u>, ed. Merton M. Sealts, Jr.  Cambridge,
         Mass.: Belknap Press of Harvard University Press, V, 202.
            Smollett as a writer concerned only with the real.

14    FORD, GEORGE H.  <u>Dickens and His Readers: Aspects of Novel-</u>
         <u>Criticism since 1836</u>.  Princeton: Princeton University
         Press, passim.  Indexed.
            Dickens's appreciation and indebtedness and some nine-
         teenth-century views of Smollett.

15    GASSMAN, BYRON.  "Religious Attitudes in the World of <u>Humphry</u>
         <u>Clinker</u>," <u>Brigham Young University Studies</u>, 6 (Winter), 65-
         72.
            Smollett's treatment of Methodism emanates from concern
         for reason and order and an extension of general rejection
         of fanaticism, enthusiasm, and superstition.

16    HANDOVER, P. M.  <u>A History of the London Gazette 1665-1965</u>.
         London: Her Majesty's Stationery Office, pp. 55-56.
            Uninformed comment on the <u>Briton</u> and <u>Critical Review</u>.

*17   JENNINGS, EDWARD MORTON III.  "Reader-Narrative Relationships
         in <u>Tom Jones</u>, <u>Tristram Shandy</u>, and <u>Humphry Clinker</u>."
         Diss., University of Wisconsin, 1965.
            Ways in which epistolary method involves the reader and
         how Smollett emphasizes Bramble's views over those of
         others.  Cited in <u>Dissertation Abstracts</u>, 26, 3303-4.

18    KLUKOFF, PHILIP J.  "A Smollett Attribution in the <u>Critical</u>
         <u>Review</u>," <u>N&Q</u>, n.s. 12 (June), 221.
            Argues Smollett's authorship of editorial preface in
         1761.

*19   KLUKOFF, PHILIP J.  "Smollett and the <u>Critical Review</u>: Criti-
         cism of the Novel."  Diss., Michigan State University, 1965.

Examines Smollett's possible influence and attempts to
determine the principles at work in the periodical itself.
Cited in Dissertation Abstracts, 27, 748-A.

20   KNAPP, LEWIS M.   "Comments on Smollett by the Rev. Dr. Thomas
     Birch," N&Q, n.s. 12 (June), 218-21.
     MS. letters (1746-62) concern Smollett's translations,
     Alceste, novels, history, and journalism, and express an-
     tagonism toward Smollett himself.

21   KNAPP, LEWIS M.   "The 'Prophecy' Attributed to Smollett," RES,
     n.s. 16 (May), 177-82.
     History of work attributed to Smollett traces it to
     1794, shows its enormous popularity and various publica-
     tions, and concludes with Knapp's being disposed to accept
     it as Smollett's.

22   KNAPP, LEWIS M.   "Smollett's Translation of Fénelon's
     Telemaque," PQ, 44 (July), 405-7.
     Convincing evidence that Smollett translated the work
     and argument for its being a superior job.

23   McKILLOP, ALAN D.   "Local Attachment and Cosmopolitanism--the
     Eighteenth-Century Pattern," in From Sensibility to Roman-
     ticism: Essays Presented to Frederick A. Pottle, ed.
     Frederick W. Hilles and Harold Bloom.  New York: Oxford
     University Press, p. 200.
     Basis for Smollett's chauvinism in his Travels.

24   MARCUS, STEVEN.   "The Blest Dawn," in Dickens; from Pickwick
     to Dombey.  New York: Basic Books, passim.  Indexed.
     Minimizes importance of Dickens's indebtedness to
     Smollett.

25   [MONTAGU, LADY MARY WORTLEY].   The Complete Letters of Lady
     Mary Wortley Montagu, ed. Robert Halsband.  Oxford:
     Clarendon Press, I, 5; II, 78; III, 2-3, 9, 66, 78, 88,
     180, 219.
     Smollett's opinion of her letters and her responses to
     his novels.

26   PARREAUX, ANDRÉ.   Smollett's London: A Course of Lectures De-
     livered at the University of Paris, 1963-64.  Paris: A. G.
     Nizet, 189 pp.
     Entertaining and illuminating description of London in
     Smollett's time makes good use of his work for illustrative
     material.

1965

27   PAULSON, RONALD. Hogarth's Graphic Works. New Haven and
        London: Yale University Press, I, passim. Indexed.
             Relationship of Smollett's technique to Hogarth's art;
        his caricature of Hogarth; and Hogarth's illustration of
        Smollett's work. Revised in 1970.

28   REID, B. L. "Smollett's Healing Journey," Virginia Quarterly
        Review, 41 (Autumn), 549-70.
             Despite circular journey in Humphry Clinker, character
        development provides a theme of the quest for spiritual
        health which does not end where the action had begun. Re-
        printed 1969.23.

29   RENWICK, W. L. "Introduction," in John Moore's Mordaunt.
        Oxford English Novels. London, New York, Toronto: Oxford
        University Press, pp. x-xi, xvii.
             Moore's relations with Smollett, appearance in Humphry
        Clinker, his edition of Smollett's work, and a comparison
        of their art.

30   SPECTOR, ROBERT D. "Introduction," in Essays on the Eigh-
        teenth-Century Novel, ed. Robert D. Spector. Bloomington
        and London: Indiana University Press, pp. vii-xii.
             Smollett's role in development of the novel and critical
        approaches to his work. Volume reprints two essays (1965.1
        and 4) and includes a selected secondary bibliography.

31   STEEVES, HARRISON R. "Sad Dogs and Saints: Tobias Smollett,"
        in Before Jane Austen: The Shaping of the English Novel in
        the Eighteenth Century. New York et al.: Holt, Rinehart
        and Winston, pp. 131-59.
             Weak account sees Roderick Random and Peregrine Pickle
        as mixture of picaresque and sentimental, but infused with
        vitality of style and lively episodes. Dismisses other
        work, except Humphry Clinker, in a sentence. Finds Humphry
        Clinker, although questionably a novel, his best work, less
        exaggerated and almost realistic.

32   WAGENKNECHT, EDWARD. Dickens and the Scandalmongers: Essays
        in Criticism. Norman: University of Oklahoma Press, p.
        135.
             Wemmick's house in Great Expectations borrowed from
        Commodore Trunnion's in Peregrine Pickle.

33   WILES, R. M. Freshest Advices: Early Provincial Newspapers in
        England. Columbus: Ohio State University Press, p. 334.
             Roderick Random serialized in Sussex Weekly Advertiser.

228

34 YOUNG, DOUGLAS. Edinburgh in the Age of Walter Scott.
   Norman: University of Oklahoma Press, pp. 112-13 and passim.
      General account of Smollett's work.


                              1966

1 BEKER, MIROSLAV. "The Theme of Plain Honesty in English Literature," Studia Romanica et Anglica, 21-22 (July-Decem-
   ber), pp. 277-88,
      Bramble in Humphry Clinker type character since
   Shakespeare.

2 BENJAMIN, LEWIS S. The Life and Letters of Tobias Smollett
   (1721-1771). New York: Kennikat Press, 319 pp.
      Reprint of 1926.2. See Melville, Lewis.

3 BEVIS, RICHARD W. "Smollett and The Israelites," PQ, 45
   (April), 387-94.
      Sufficient circumstantial evidence for Smollett attribu-
   tion.

4 BOGGS, W. ARTHUR. "Bid in the Sense of Command as a Preter-
   ite," Language Quarterly, 4 (Spring-Summer), 34.
      Quotation from Humphry Clinker as an illustration.

5 BOGGS, W. ARTHUR. "'Birthday Suit' and 'Cheese-Toaster,'"
   N&Q, n.s. 13 (December), 465.
      Smollett's use earlier than listings in OED.

6 BOGGS, W. ARTHUR. "Win Jenkins' Addenda to Mr. Murray's Dictionary," Discourse, 9 (Winter), 83-91.
      Thirty-five of her words and phrases in Humphry Clinker
   offer new information to be added to the OED.

7 BOUCÉ, PAUL-GABRIEL. "Les Procédes du Comique dans Humphry
   Clinker," Études Anglaises: Actes du Congrès de Lille, 25
   (1966), 53-75.
      Careful analysis of characterization, structure, lan-
   guage, and symbolism in comic technique of Humphry Clinker.
   Without dismissing development from earlier novels, emphasizes its distinctiveness.

8 BRADBROOK, FRANK W. Jane Austen and Her Predecessors. Cambridge: University Press, pp. 52, 120.
      Compares Hogarth's and Smollett's art and suggests
   Smollett's coarseness prevented influence on Jane Austen.

1966

9   CASH, ARTHUR H.  "Sentimental Commerce," in Sterne's Comedy of
    Moral Sentiments: The Ethical Dimension of the "Journey".
    Duquesne Studies Philological Series, 6.  Pittsburgh:
    Duquesne University Press, pp. 31-34, 52.
        Sterne's Sentimental Journey deliberately responds to
    Smollett's Travels.  See, too, pp. 95-96.

10  CROSSLAND, MARGARET.  A Traveller's Guide to Literary Europe.
    London: Hugh Evelyn, II, passim.  Indexed.
        Sensationalized account of Smollett and places associ-
    ated with him.

11  DAY, ROBERT ADAMS.  Told in Letters: Epistolary Fiction before
    Richardson.  Ann Arbor: University of Michigan Press, pas-
    sim.  Indexed.
        Compares Smollett's and pre-Richardsonians' techniques.

12  DONOVAN, ROBERT ALAN.  "Humphry Clinker and the Novelist's
    Imagination," in The Shaping Vision: Imagination in the
    English Novel from Defoe to Dickens.  Ithaca, New York:
    Cornell University Press, pp. 118-39.
        Imaginative development in Humphry Clinker transforms
    raw materials, through characters and their relationships,
    into an effective fictional structure, although the novel
    has too often been praised only for non-fictional charac-
    teristics.

*13 ELISTRATOVA, A. A.  Anglyisky Roman Epochy Prosvestehenia
    (English Novel of the Enlightenment).  Moscow: Nauka, 472
    pp.
        "Smollett's early novels . . . closely related to the
    ideas and vision of Richardson and Fielding's period, but
    Humphry Clinker [is related] to the post-Sternian period."
    L. Arinshtein, review in PQ, 47 (July, 1968), 330.

14  FISHER, FRANKLIN FREDERICK.  "Smollett and the Premises of
    Fiction in the Eighteenth Century."  Diss., University of
    California, Santa Barbara, 1966.
        Examines novels according to conventions created by
    Fielding, and argues that Smollett's inability to reconcile
    them with his attempts at psychological realism in his
    characterization or to find a compromise between reality
    and fictional form is destructive of his art.

15  GARROW, SCOTT.  "A Study of the Organization of Smollett's The
    Expedition of Humphry Clinker," Southern Quarterly, 4
    (July), 349-63; 5 (October), 22-46.

Describes the work as a hybrid "epistolary travel book"
and argues the advantages that Smollett gained by his multiple epistolary point of view as well as his mixture of
genres.  Includes worthwhile comment on plot, language,
theme, and autobiographical elements in the novel.

16   GOLDEN, MORRIS.  Fielding's Moral Psychology.  Amherst: The
        University of Massachusetts Press, pp. 39, 125, 146.
           Comments on Smollett's comic principles and dread of
        political and social chaos.

17   [GOLDSMITH, OLIVER].  Collected Works of Oliver Goldsmith, ed.
        Arthur Friedman.  Oxford: Clarendon Press, 5 Vols., passim.
        Indexed.
           Goldsmith's writings and opinions on Smollett's work.

18   GORDON, IAN A.  The Movement of English Prose.  English Lan-
        guage Series, ed. Randolph Quirk.  London: Longmans, Green,
        pp. 140-41, 163.
           Relationship of diction and style to Smollett's comic
        purposes.

*19   GRANT, DAMIAN.  "'Form' and 'Essence' in Smollett: A Study of
        His Work in Relation to Eighteenth-Century Criticism and
        Aesthetics."  M.A. Thesis, University of London, 1966.
           Cited in Index to Theses Accepted for Higher Degrees in
        the Universities of Great Britain and Ireland.  See
        1977.13.

20   HARTLEY, LODWICK.  Laurence Sterne in the Twentieth Century:
        An Essay and a Bibliography of Sternean Studies, 1900-1965.
        Chapel Hill: University of North Carolina Press, passim.
        Indexed.
           Secondary works comparing Smollett and Sterne or dealing
        with their relationship.

*21   KLUGE, WALTER.  Die Szene als Bauelement des Erzählers im
        Englischen Roman des Achtzehnten Jahrhunderts.  Munich:
        n.p., 222 pp.
           Smollett's novels in relation to "the typology and func-
        tioning of scene in prose fiction."  Cited in PQ, 46 (July,
        1967), 319.

22   KLUKOFF, PHILIP J.  "Smollett and the Critical Review: Criti-
        cism of the Novel, 1756-1763," Studies in Scottish Litera-
        ture, 4 (October), 89-100.
           Relates Smollett's conception of a novel and his aes-
        thetic principles to views expressed in the Critical.

1966

23    KLUKOFF, PHILIP J.   "Smollett as the Reviewer of Jeremiah
          Grant," N&Q, n.s. 13 (December), 466.
               Suggests Smollett's review in Critical in 1763 and his
          general influence on reviews of novels in the periodical.

24    KLUKOFF, PHILIP J.   "Two Smollett Attributions in the Critical
          Review: The Reverie and Tristram Shandy," N&Q, n.s. 13
          (December), 465-66.
               Smollett wrote three reviews (two on Tristram Shandy) in
          1761 and 1762.

25    KNAPP, LEWIS M.   "Early Scottish Attitudes toward Tobias
          Smollett," PQ, 45 (January), 262-69.
               Valuable details about Smollett's associations with
          Scotsmen and their attitudes toward him.

26    KNAPP, LEWIS M.   "Introduction," in The Expedition of Humphry
          Clinker.  Oxford English Novels.  London, New York,
          Toronto: Oxford University Press, pp. ix-xvii.
               Covers background, composition, reception, and reputa-
          tion.  Relates novel to Smollett's interests, personality,
          and experiences and offers brief comment on its techniques.

27    KRONENBERGER, LOUIS, W. C. ROGERS, GEORGE D. CROTHERS.
          "Tobias George Smollett: Humphry Clinker," in Invitation to
          Learning: English & American Novels, ed. George D.
          Crothers.  New York and London: Basic Books, pp. 44-52.
               Discursive, ill-informed popular commentary on the nov-
          el.

28    LANG, PAUL HENRY.  George Frederic Handel.  New York: W. W.
          Norton, pp. 484, 501-2.
               Discusses Smollett's Alceste and suggests financial
          reasons for its failure to be produced.

29    LAUBER, JOHN.  Sir Walter Scott.  Twayne's English Authors
          Series, ed. Sylvia Bowman.  New York: Twayne Publishers,
          pp. 42, 105, 125.
               Smollett's influence on Scott and relationship of their
          work.

30    MELVILLE, LEWIS.  See Benjamin, Lewis S.

31    PARK, WILLIAM.  "Fathers and Sons--Humphry Clinker," Litera-
          ture and Psychology, 16 (Nos. 3 and 4), 166-74.
               Discusses archetypal characteristics in its mythic
          structure of father-and-son discovery and the psychological
          consequences that provide its "pattern of images and mo-
          tifs."

32    POTTLE, FREDERICK A.  James Boswell: The Earlier Years, 1740–
      1769.  New York et al.: McGraw-Hill, passim.  Indexed.
          Describes Boswell's correspondence with Smollett and
      coaxing him to review early work and suggests Boswell imi-
      tated him in apprentice work.

33    ROGERS, KATHERINE M.  "The Nineteenth Century," in The Trou-
      blesome Helpmate. A History of Misogyny in Literature.
      Seattle and London: University of Washington Press, pp.
      202–3.
          Treatment of Grizzle Pickle in Peregrine Pickle and
      Tabitha in Humphry Clinker.

34    ROUSSEAU, GEORGE.  "Doctors and Medicine in the Novels of
      Tobias Smollett."  Diss., Princeton University, 1966.
          Ways in which medicine and science enter Smollett's fic-
      tion, significance of his satiric use of the subject to
      comment on more general social disorders, and the means by
      which the material is assimilated into art.  Offers rich
      detail of the medical controversies and various personali-
      ties that Smollett draws upon for his work.

35    SACKS, SHELDON.  "The Great, Useful, and Uncommon Doctrine,"
      in Fiction and the Shape of Belief: A Study of Henry
      Fielding with Glances at Swift, Johnson, and Richardson.
      Berkeley and Los Angeles: University of California Press,
      pp. 270–71.
          Humphry Clinker more pleasing in its parts than in its
      overall artistic effect.

36    SCHOLES, ROBERT and ROBERT KELLOGG.  The Nature of Narrative.
      New York: Oxford University Press, passim.  Indexed.
          Narrative techniques in Roderick Random related to pica-
      resque and realism and those in Fathom to point of view.

*37   SHAW, JAMES WEST.  "Caricature in the Novels of Tobias
      Smollett: Its Form and Function."  Diss., University of
      Michigan, 1966.
          Smollett's use and development of caricature for serious
      thematic purposes is brought to its highest efficiency in
      Humphry Clinker.  Cited in Dissertation Abstracts, 28, 242–
      A.

38    [SHERIDAN RICHARD BRINSLEY].  The Letters of Richard Brinsley
      Sheridan, ed. Cecil Price.  Oxford: Clarendon Press, I, 61–
      62.
          1772 letter objects to "natural" characterization in
      Smollett's novels.

1966

39    SPEARMAN, DIANA. The Novel and Society. New York: Barnes &
      Noble, passim. Indexed.
         Critical of Smollett's use of picaresque, Don Quixote,
      and exaggeration as reflecting society in his novels.

40    SPECTOR, ROBERT D. English Literary Periodicals and the Cli-
      mate of Opinion during the Seven Years' War. The Hague and
      Paris: Mouton, passim. Indexed.
         Treatment of politics, religion, science, literature,
      and language in the Briton, British Magazine, and Critical
      Review.

41    STARKIE, WALTER F. "Miguel de Cervantes and the English Nov-
      el," Essays by Divers Hands being the Transactions of the
      Royal Society of Literature, 34 (1966), 159-79.
         Cervantes's influence on Smollett.

42    TEMPLE, RUTH and MARTIN TUCKER. "Tobias George Smollett," in
      Moulton's Library of Literary Criticism of English and
      American Authors through the Beginning of the Twentieth
      Century. Abridged, Revised and with Additions. New York:
      Frederick Ungar, II, 281-95.
         Brief account, secondary bibliography, and excerpts from
      critical and biographical works.

43    WAGONER, MARY. "On the Satire in Humphry Clinker," PLL, 2
      (Spring), 109-16.
         Although structure of his novels is generally pica-
      resque, satire and its values derive from Swift and Pope.


                              1967

1     BLOCH, TUVIA. "Smollett's Quest for Form," MP, 65 (November),
      103-13.
         Smollett arrived at the form of Humphry Clinker as a re-
      sult of his failure to adapt effectively Fielding's tech-
      niques in the earlier novels.

2     BOUCÉ, PAUL-GABRIEL. "The 'Chinese Pilot' and 'Sa-Rouf' in
      Smollett's Atom," ELN, 4 (June), 273-75.
         Two identifications given in key to the Atom published
      in 1926 edition of Smollett's Works are inaccurate.

3     BOUCÉ, PAUL-GABRIEL. "Smollett Criticism, 1770-1924: Correc-
      tions and Additions," N&Q, n.s. 14 (May), 184-87.
         Lists errors and omissions and offers comment on 33
      items in Cordasco's bibliography, 1948.7.

4   BOUCÉ, PAUL-GABRIEL. "Smollett and the Expedition against
     Rochefort (1757)," MP, 65 (August), 33-38.
         Gives background of Knowles's libel case against
     Smollett and attributes Smollett's motives to psychological
     effect of personal experiences in the expedition at Cartha-
     gena in 1741 and to his rational appraisal of Knowles's
     failure at Rochefort.

5   BOYCE, BENJAMIN. The Benevolent Man: A Life of Ralph Allen of
     Bath. Cambridge, Mass.: Harvard University Press, passim.
     Indexed.
         Some notes on Smollett in relation to the city of Bath.

6   BRACK, O. M. JR. "The Bicentennial Edition of the Works of
     Tobias Smollett," Books at Iowa, No. 7 (November), pp. 41-
     42.
         Discoveries and problems in preparation of the edition.

7   BURTON, ELIZABETH. "Of Diversions and Amusements," in The
     Pageant of Georgian England. New York: Charles Scribner's
     Sons, pp. 291, 293.
         Smollett's novels in relation to their social function.

8   CARVER, P. L. The Life of a Poet. A Biography of William
     Collins. New York: Horizon Press, passim. Indexed.
         Smollett's opinion of Collins's work and a comparison of
     Collins's "To Peace" and Smollett's "Tears of Scotland."

*9  CLEMENTS, FRANCES MARION. "Social Criticism in the English
     Novel, 1740-1754." Diss., Ohio State University, 1967.
         Social criticism in Roderick Random and Peregrine Pickle
     in context of contemporary novelists' responses to condi-
     tions of their time. Cited in Dissertation Abstracts, 28,
     5010-A.

10  DRISKELL, LEON V. "Looking for Dustwich," Texas Studies in
     Literature and Language, 9 (Spring), 85-90.
         Theme of Humphry Clinker is the disparity between ap-
     pearance and reality as Smollett indicates in the ironic
     discrepancy between the prefatory letters of Dustwich and
     Davis and what follows in the novel.

11  EVANS, DAVID L. "The Developing Satire of Smollett's Novels."
     Diss., University of Washington, 1967.
         With some exception for Ferdinand Count Fathom,
     Smollett's novels are most effective in their essentially
     Augustan satiric intentions and they represent a variety of
     experiments with the devices of satire.

1967

12    EVANS, DAVID L.   "Humphry Clinker: Smollett's Tempered Augus-
      tanism," Criticism, 9 (Summer), 257-74.
            The novel, whose hero presents the values of the country
      gentry, is an attempt to retain the "myth of rural simpli-
      city, refinement and order" in which the Dennison material
      offers a model for imitation.

*13   FISHER, FRANKLIN F.   "Smollett and the Premises of Fiction in
      the Eighteenth Century."  Diss., University of California,
      Santa Barbara, 1967.
            Cited in McNamee, Dissertations in English and American
      Literature, Supplement 1.

14    FROHOCK, W. M.   "The Idea of the Picaresque," Yearbook of Com-
      parative and General Literature, 16 (1967), 51.
            Smollett's difficulties in adapting the picaresque in
      Roderick Random.

15    GEORGE, M. DOROTHY.   Hogarth to Cruikshank: Social Change in
      Graphic Satire.  New York: Walker, passim.  Indexed.
            Relates Smollett's work to social climate and satiric
      art, particularly Hogarth's and Rowlandson's.

*16   GIDDINGS, ROBERT.   "A Study of Smollett and the Tradition in
      Which He Wrote."  M. Litt. Thesis, University of Bristol,
      1967.
            Cited in Index to Theses Accepted for Higher Degrees in
      the Universities of Great Britain and Ireland.  See
      1968.17.

17    GIDDINGS, ROBERT.   The Tradition of Smollett.  London:
      Methuen, 215 pp.
            Smollett's major achievement was in bringing to a culmi-
      nation the picaresque tradition in English, and his special
      ability was to use it for sharply effective social and sa-
      tiric comment.  Failure to appreciate the particular quali-
      ties of the picaresque has obscured his mastery in
      Peregrine Pickle, a novel vastly superior to Humphry
      Clinker, despite the latter's splended use of epistolary
      form for comic purposes.  For Giddings, Smollett's interest
      in the picaresque terminated with Ferdinand Count Fathom.

18    GRANT, DAMIAN J.   "Unpublished Additions to Smollett's
      Travels," N&Q, n.s. 14 (May), 187-89.
            Corrections and additions in Smollett's printed copy,
      but omitted from Seccombe's 1907 edition.

19  HOWELL, ELMO. "Inversion and the 'Female' Principle: William
    Faulkner's 'A Courtship,'" Studies in Short Fiction, 4
    (Summer), 314.
       Compares Faulkner's and Smollett's romantic scenes.

20  ISER, WOLFGANG. "Wirklichkeit und Form in Smolletts Humphry
    Clinker," in Europäische Aufklärung: H. Dieckmann zum 60
    Geburtstag, ed. Hugo Friedrich and Fritz Schalk. Munich:
    Fink, pp. 87-115.
       Relating epistolary technique and structure to reader's
    expectations suggests means of achieving verisimilitude in
    the novel. See 1969.14 and 1974.22.

21  JUMP, JOHN D. "Literary Echoes in Byron's Don Juan," N&Q,
    n.s. 14 (August), 302.
       Apparent indebtedness (II, 105) to Humphry Clinker.

22  KENT, JOHN P. "Smollett's Translation of the Gil Blas: A
    Question of Text," ELN, 5 (September), 21-26.
       Smollett used 1732-37 text for his translation.

23  KIRK, CLARE M. "'A Whimsically Dismal Figure,'" in Oliver
    Goldsmith. Twayne's English Authors Series, 47, ed. Sylvia
    Bowman. New York: Twayne Publishers, pp. 26, 31-33.
       Smollett and Goldsmith's relationship, particularly in
    regard to the British Magazine.

24  KLUKOFF, PHILIP J. "New Smollett Attributions in the Critical
    Review," N&Q, n.s. 14 (November), 418-19.
       Argues unconvincingly that Smollett reviewed Johnson's
    Rasselas, Adam Smith's Theory of Moral Sentiments, and
    Alexander Gerard's Essay on Taste.

25  KNAPP, LEWIS M. "Smollett, Tobias George," in Collier's En-
    cyclopedia, ed. W. D. Halsey et al. New York: Crowell,
    Collier and Macmillan, XXI, 98-100.
       Good brief account of his personality and three major
    novels.

26  KORTE, DONALD M. "Satire in Verse and Prose--A Study of
    Smollett." Diss., Syracuse University, 1967.
       Close examination of Advice and Reproof themselves and
    in relation to Pope's satires, Roderick Random, Launcelot
    Greaves, and Humphry Clinker.

27  KORTE, DONALD M. "Tobias Smollett's Advice and Reproof,"
    Thoth, 8 (Spring), 45-65.

1967

Argues use of Pope as a model; annotations suggest various indebtedness and the objects of Smollett's satire.

*28 LE-THANH, CHAU M. "Tobias Smollett and the Works of Mr. De Voltaire." Diss., University of Chicago, 1967.
Cited in McNamee, <u>Dissertations in English and American Literature</u>, Supplement 1.

29 LINSALATA, CARMINE R. <u>Smollett's Hoax: Don Quixote in English</u>. New York: AMS Press, ix + 116 pp.
Reprint of 1956.16.

30 [MACKENZIE, HENRY]. <u>Henry Mackenzie's Letters to Elizabeth Rose</u> etc., ed. Horst W. Drescher. Edinburgh and London: Oliver and Boyd, pp. 18, 95-96.
In 1769 and 1771 praises <u>Humphry Clinker</u> and Smollett's character and notes his ill-treatment.

31 MILLER, STUART. <u>The Picaresque Novel</u>. Cleveland: The Press of Case Western Reserve University, passim. Indexed.
Uses <u>Roderick Random</u> to discuss eighteenth-century example of the classic picaresque.

32 MUSHER, DANIEL M. "The Medical Views of Dr. Tobias Smollett (1721-1771)," <u>Bulletin of the History of Medicine</u>, 41 (September-October), 455-62.
Reviews Smollett's medical ideas in <u>Essay on the External Use of Water</u>, novels, and <u>Travels</u> and concludes that he was a brilliant observer and writer on physical and emotional health.

33 OSMAN, C. A. "Smollett's Visits to Spas," <u>N&Q</u>, n.s. 14 (November), 422.
Details his several visits from 1757 on.

34 PARK, WILLIAM. "Change in the Criticism of the Novel after 1760," <u>PQ</u>, 46 (January), 34-41.
Includes discussion of criticism of <u>Roderick Random</u>, <u>Peregrine Pickle</u>, and the aesthetic principles of the <u>Critical Review</u>.

35 PARKER, ALEXANDER A. "The Picaresque Tradition in England and France," in <u>Literature and the Delinquent: the Picaresque Novel in Spain and Europe, 1599-1753</u>. Edinburgh: Edinburgh University Press, pp. 126-31.
<u>Roderick Random</u> and more completely <u>Fathom</u> are the last significant use of the picaresque by an important European novelist.

36  PAULSON, RONALD.  "Smollett: The Satirist as a Character
    Type," in Satire and the Novel in Eighteenth-Century
    England.  New Haven and London: Yale University Press, pp.
    165-208 and passim.
        Traces particular way satire develops from Smollett's
    first novel through Humphry Clinker.  Describes initial
    adaptation of the picaresque for satiric purposes and sub-
    sequent attempts to study satire through characters who
    themselves function as various kinds of satirists.

37  PIOZZI, HESTER LYNCH [THRALE].  Observations and Reflections
    Made in the Course of a Journey through France, Italy, and
    Germany, ed. Herbert Barrows.  Ann Arbor: University of
    Michigan Press, pp. xv, 174-75.
        Brief comments on Smollett's Travels.

38  POTTLE, FREDERICK A.  "The Part Played by Horace Walpole and
    James Boswell in the Quarrel between Rousseau and Hume: A
    Reconsideration," in Horace Walpole: Writer, Politician,
    and Connoisseur, ed. Warren Hunting Smith.  New Haven and
    London: Yale University Press, pp. 272, 283.
        Denies Boswell wrote letter in 1766 newspaper praising
    Smollett.  See 1766.12.

39  QUINTANA, RICARDO.  Oliver Goldsmith: A Georgian Study.  Mas-
    ters of World Literature, ed. Louis Kronenberger.  New York
    and London: Macmillan, passim.  Indexed.
        Goldsmith's work on Critical Review and British Magazine
    and his use of Smollett's History of England.

40  ROSS, ANGUS.  "Introduction," in The Expedition of Humphry
    Clinker.  Penguin English Library.  Harmondsworth, Middle-
    sex: Penguin Books, pp. 7-19.
        Judicious analysis properly balances novel's autobio-
    graphical features with an understanding of Smollett's cre-
    ative talent rooted in his strong sensitivities and aware-
    ness of the values of grotesque eccentricities.

41  ROUSSEAU, GEORGE S.  "Matt Bramble and the Sulphur Controversy
    in the XVIIIth Century: Medical Background of Humphry
    Clinker," JHI, 28 (October-December), 577-89.
        Bramble expresses Smollett's attitudes toward medicine
    and displays his extensive knowledge.  Rousseau examines
    these in detail and provides background for Smollett's
    novel, particularly the controversy over medicinal values
    of sulphur.

1967

42   ROUSSEAU, GEORGE S.  "Smollett's Acidum Vagum," Isis, 58 (Sum-
     mer), 244-45.
          Annotates the term--vague acid--which appears in Sir
     Launcelot Greaves.

43   SHERBO, ARTHUR.  Christopher Smart: Scholar of the University.
     East Lansing: Michigan State University Press, passim.  In-
     dexed.
          Discusses Smollett's personal and literary relations
     with Smart and Smollett's imprisonment.

44   SHERBURN, GEORGE.  "The Restoration and Eighteenth Century
     (1660-1789)," in A Literary History of England, ed. Albert
     C. Baugh.  2nd ed.  New York: Appleton-Century-Crofts, III,
     961-64 and passim.
          Reprint of 1948.23, with additional bibliography.

*45  SHOUMATOFF, A.  "Matthew Bramble's Rural Ideal."  B.A. Honors
     Thesis, Harvard University, 1967.
          Cited in 1977.25.

46   STEVICK, PHILIP.  "Stylistic Energy in the Early Smollett,"
     PQ, 64 (October), 712-19.
          Smollett's first three novels engage the reader's inter-
     est through their hyperbolic style rather than through
     their characters and episodes.

47   STEVICK, PHILIP.  The Theory of the Novel.  New York: The Free
     Press; London: Collier-Macmillan, p. 11.
          Briefly discusses Smollett's definition of a novel.

48   STOUT, GARDNER D. JR.  "Introduction," in Sterne's A Senti-
     mental Journey through France and Italy by Mr. Yorick.
     Berkeley and Los Angeles: University of California Press,
     passim.  Indexed.
          Discusses composition, publication, sales, reputation,
     and characteristics of Smollett's Travels and Sterne's
     attitude toward and use of the work.  Notes offer worth-
     while detail about relationship of the two travel books.

49   TREASE, GOEFFREY.  The Grand Tour.  New York et al.: Holt,
     Rinehart and Winston, pp. 11, 179.
          Relates Smollett's Travels to experiences on the Grand
     Tour.

50   [WALPOLE, HORACE].  Horace Walpole's Correspondence with Sir
     Horace Mann, 7, ed. W. S. Lewis et al.  Yale Edition of
     Horace Walpole's Correspondence, ed. W. S. Lewis.  New

Haven: Yale University Press; London: Oxford University
Press, XXIII, 198.
    Walpole's low opinion in 1770 of Smollett the man.

51  WEBSTER, GRANT T.  "Smollett's Microcosms: A Satiric Device
    in the Novel," Satire News Letter, 5 (Fall), 34-37.
        Smollett's use of a minor episode with humours charac-
    ters to provide a microcosm of the larger satiric world in
    his novels.


<u>1968</u>


1   ADELSTEIN, MICHAEL E.  Fanny Burney.  Twayne's English Authors
    Series, 67, ed. Sylvia E. Bowman.  New York: Twayne Pub-
    lishers, pp. 34, 126, 150.
        Brief comparisons of Burney's and Smollett's novels.

2   ALTER, ROBERT.  Fielding and the Nature of the Novel.  Cam-
    bridge, Mass.: Harvard University Press, passim.  Indexed.
        Contrasts Fielding's and Smollett's narrative methods,
    characterization, plots, and settings.

3   BARNETT, GEORGE L.  "Tobias George Smollett," in Eighteenth-
    Century British Novelists on the Novel.  New York: Appleton
    -Century-Crofts, pp. 59-66.
        Introduces prefatory material to Smollett's novels with
    comments on his work, emphasizing autobiographical and
    picaresque.

4   BATTESTIN, MARTIN C.  "On the Contemporary Reputations of
    Pamela, Joseph Andrews, and Roderick Random: Remarks by an
    'Oxford Scholar,' 1748," N&Q, n.s. 15 (December), 450-52.
        Contemporary pamphlet praises honesty of Smollett's
    realism.

5   BLOCH, TUVIA.  "Smollett and the Jewish Naturalization Bill of
    1753," ANQ, 6 (April), 116-17.
        Friendly treatment of Jews in Fathom contrasts with that
    in rest of Smollett's work.

6   BORINSKI, LUDWIG.  "Smollett," in Der Englische Roman des 18.
    Jahrhunderts.  Frankfurt am Main and Bonn: Athenäum Verlag,
    pp. 233-48.
        Broad account of novels concerned with techniques, rela-
    tionship to contemporary influences, and comparisons with
    works of other novelists.

1968

7　BRACK, O. M. JR.　"The Ledgers of William Strahan," in <u>Editing Eighteenth-Century Texts</u>, ed. D. I. B. Smith.　Toronto: University of Toronto Press, pp. 62, 64, 70-71.
Discusses printing of Smollett's work and problems for an editor of Smollett.

8　BRONSON, BERTRAND H.　"The Writer," in <u>Man versus Society in Eighteenth-Century Britain: Six Points of View</u>, ed. James L. Clifford.　Cambridge: University Press, p. 127.
Successful epistolary method of <u>Humphry Clinker</u> added nothing to the technique of uniting fiction to its audience.

9　BURKE, JOSEPH.　"The Grand Tour and the Rule of Taste," in <u>Studies in the Eighteenth Century</u>, 1, ed. R. F. Brissenden.　Toronto: University of Toronto Press, pp. 243-44.
Description of the Circus at Bath in <u>Humphry Clinker</u>.

10　CAMERON, W. J.　"The Development of Eighteenth-Century Studies in the British Commonwealth," in 1968.9, p. 33.
"Fairly strong Smollett collection" at McMaster's.

11　CLUBBE, JOHN.　<u>Victorian Forerunner: The Later Career of Thomas Hood</u>.　Durham, N.C.: Duke University Press, pp. 19, 91-92.
Hood's indebtedness to Smollett's work, particularly <u>Humphry Clinker</u>.

*12　COHEN, MURRAY ALAN.　"Forms of True Judgment in the Eighteenth Century English Novel."　Diss., Johns Hopkins University, 1968.
Examines Smollett's satire of aesthetic and social values and concludes that his characters effect a compromise between their moral judgments and society's demands upon the individual.　Cited in <u>Dissertation Abstracts</u>, 29, 1533-A-1534-A.

*13　COZZA, ANDREA.　"Introduction," in Italian translation of <u>Roderick Random</u>.　Milan.
Cited in 1970.12.

14　DUNCAN, JEFFREY L.　"The Rural Ideal in Eighteenth-Century Fiction," <u>SEL</u>, 8 (Summer), 517-35.
Dennison episode in <u>Humphry Clinker</u> uses rural ideal to express concept of moral order as man's obligation to control his environment since physical decay reflects moral decay.

15    FELSENSTEIN, F.  "A Note on Smollett's Travels," N&Q, n.s. 15
      (December), 452-53.
          Corrections on Grant's note, 1967.18, on Seccombe's
      textual treatment of Smollett's Travels.

16    FERGUSON, WILLIAM.  "Education, Culture in Eighteenth Cen-
      tury," in Scotland 1689 to the Present.  The Edinburgh His-
      tory of Scotland, 14.  New York and Washington: Frederick
      A. Praeger, pp. 216, 223.
          Denigrates Smollett's history, but praises his Scottish-
      ness and Humphry Clinker.

*17   GOLDKNOPF, IRMA.  "Crime and Prison-Experience in the Early
      English Novel: Defoe, Fielding, Smollett."  Diss., Syracuse
      University, 1968.
          Smollett uses crime and prison material as a microcosm
      of society.  Cited in Dissertation Abstracts, 29, 1207-A.

18    GROSSVOGEL, DAVID I.  "Sterne: Tristram Shandy," in Limits of
      the Novel: Evolution of a Form from Chaucer to Robbe-
      Grillet.  Ithaca, New York: Cornell University Press, p.
      140.
          Contrasts Sterne's rounded and Smollett's flat charac-
      ters.

19    GRUNDER, HENRY.  "Smollett's Continuation of the Complete His-
      tory of England," N&Q, n.s. 15 (October), 383.
          Query gives details of an acquisition, including rare
      fifth volume dated 1765, by College of William and Mary.

20    HOGAN, CHARLES BEECHER.  The London Stage 1660-1800 (1776-
      1800).  Carbondale, Ill.: Southern Illinois University
      Press, Part 5, Vols. 1-3, passim.  Indexed.
          Information on productions of The Reprisal and The
      Israelites (attributed to Smollett).

21    JACK, IAN.  "Introduction," in Sterne's A Sentimental Journey
      through France and Italy by Mr. Yorick.  Oxford English
      Novels.  London, New York, Toronto: Oxford University
      Press, pp. xii-xiii, xvii.
          Relationship of Smollett's Travels to Sterne's works and
      Sterne's attitude toward and use of Smollett's.

22    KAHRL, GEORGE M.  Tobias Smollett Traveler-Novelist.  New
      York: Octagon Books, xxiv + 165 pp.
          Reprint of 1945.2.

1968

23   KLUKOFF, PHILIP J.  "Smollett and the Sackville Controversy,"
     Neuphilologische Mitteilungen, 69 (December 15), 617-28.
          Smollett wrote at least three reviews in Critical Review
     on George Sackville's conduct at battle of Minden.

24   KNAPP, LEWIS M.  "Smollett and Johnson, Never Cater-Cousins?,"
     MP, 66 (November), 151-54.
          Reviews evidence of their relationship and finds some
     cordiality and respect between them.

*25  LIGHTNER, CLAUDE MICHAEL.  "Calvinism and Characterization in
     the Novels of Tobias Smollett."  Diss., University of
     Illinois, 1968.
          Analyzes novels in terms of background in Calvinistic
     theology and finds variety of influences of his religious
     beliefs on characters and themes.  Cited in Dissertation
     Abstracts, 30, 329-A-330-A.

26   LINDQUIST, WAYNE PAUL.  "Smollett and the Structure of the
     Novel."  Diss., University of Iowa, 1968.
          Compares Smollett's techniques for unifying characteri-
     zation and plot with those in earlier continental pica-
     resque novels and argues for greater complexity that he
     progressively brought to the form in each of his novels,
     making a decided contribution to the genre in English.

27   McNAMEE, LAWRENCE F.  Dissertations in English and American
     Literature.  Theses Accepted by American, British and Ger-
     man Universities, 1865-1964.  New York and London: R. R.
     Bowker, passim.  Indexed.
          Supplement 1 (1969) covers 1964-68; Supplement 2 (1974)
     covers 1969-73.

28   MARTZ, LOUIS L.  The Later Career of Tobias Smollett.  Hamden,
     Conn.: Archon Books, xi + 213 pp.
          Reprint of 1942.5.

29   MAXWELL, J. C.  "Hazlitt and the European Magazine for the
     Year 1761," N&Q, n.s. 15 (January), 25.
          Hazlitt confused European Magazine with Smollett's
     British Magazine.

30   MONAD, SYLVÈRE.  Dickens the Novelist.  Norman: University of
     Oklahoma Press, passim.  Indexed.
          Good discussion of Smollett's actual influence on
     Dickens.

31  NICOLSON, MARJORIE and GEORGE S. ROUSSEAU. "This Long Dis-
    ease, My Life": Alexander Pope and the Sciences. Prince-
    ton: Princeton University Press, passim. Indexed.
        Pope's influence on Smollett's early poetry and
    Smollett's attitudes toward contemporary doctors and sci-
    entists.

32  ORWELL, GEORGE. The Collected Essays, Journalism, and Letters
    of George Orwell, ed. Sonia Orwell and Ian Angus. New
    York: Harcourt, Brace & World, I, 33, 119, 440, 455; III,
    91, 179, 244-48, 285, 338.
        Comments on Smollett's style and his relation to Shaw
    and Dickens. "Tobias Smollett: Scotland's Best Novelist"
    (pp. 244-48), reprinted from the Tribune, September 22,
    1944, describes his best works as the harmless pornography
    of Roderick Random and Peregrine Pickle, emphasizes his
    use of picaresque, and minimizes his importance.

33  PARREAUX, ANDRÉ. "Introduction," in The Expedition of Humphry
    Clinker. Boston: Houghton Mifflin, pp. xi-xxxi.
        General account of life, personality, and career. Dis-
    cusses mixture of fictional and non-fictional material,
    literary techniques, caricature, picture of society, and
    combination of bawdiness and wit.

34  PRITCHETT, V. S. "Introduction," in Humphry Clinker. London:
    Heron Books, pp. 9-14.
        Reprint of 1954.6.

*35 RICE, SCOTT BRADLEY. "Smollett's Travels through France and
    Italy and the Genre of Grand Tour Literature." Diss.,
    University of Arizona, 1968.
        The great artistic merit in the Travels is in its devel-
    opment of a literary kind rather than a rendition of
    Smollett's personal experience. Cited in Dissertation
    Abstracts, 29, 2682-A.

36  ROSENMEIER, HENRIK. "Tobias Smollett: A Study in Popular
    Taste at Mid-Century." Diss., University of Minnesota,
    1968.
        Arguing that Smollett's histories provide a guide to
    the social attitudes in his novels, describes him as a
    didactic advocate of middle-class values, modelling his
    arguments on Hume's Treatise of Human Nature and old-
    fashioned Shaftesburian ideas.

1968

*37    ROTH, BARRY.  "Smollett's Grub Street: A Study of the Develop-
       ment of an Artist."  Diss., Stanford University, 1968.
            Emphasizing the autobiographical character of Smollett's
       work, argues that his treatment of Grub Street develops
       from an immature personal response to a mature and more ob-
       jective moral assessment and his satire shifts from Juve-
       nalian to Horatian.  Cited in Dissertation Abstracts, 29,
       3981-A.

38     SAAGPAKK, PAUL F.  "A Survey of Psychopathology in British
       Literature from Shakespeare to Hardy," Literature and Psy-
       chology, 18 (Number 2-3), 147-48.
            Discusses types of psychopathological characters in
       Smollett's five novels.

39     SCOTT, WILLIAM.  "George Colman's Polly Honeycombe and Circu-
       lating Library Fiction in 1760," N&Q, n.s. 15 (December),
       465-67.
            Smollett's novels included in Colman's attack.

40     SENA, JOHN F.  "Smollett's Persona and the Melancholic Trav-
       eler: An Hypothesis," ECS, 1 (Summer), 353-69.
            Smollett's persona in the Travels is an eighteenth-
       century type of melancholy personality and Smollett uses
       contemporary medical sources as the basis for his charac-
       terization.

41     SHORT, JOHN D.  "Smollett V. Armstrong: An Ascription of 'The
       Tears of Scotland' by Dr. Charles Burney," N&Q, n.s. 15
       (December), 453-56.
            Considers claims for Armstrong's authorship, but con-
       siders it unlikely.

*42    SKINNER, MARY LYNN.  "The Interpolated Story in Selected Nov-
       els of Fielding and Smollett."  Diss., University of Ten-
       nessee, 1968.
            Interpolated narratives in Roderick Random, Peregrine
       Pickle, and Humphry Clinker considered in their organic
       relationship to the overall purposes in the novels.  Cited
       in Dissertation Abstracts, 29, 4020-A-4021-A.

43     SPECTOR, ROBERT D.  "Introduction," in Political Controversy:
       or Weekly Magazine of Ministerial and Anti-ministerial
       Essays.  New York and London: Johnson Reprint Co., I, v-x.
            Smollett's Briton and the journalistic controversy
       during the Seven Years' War.  Edition reprints 1762.21.

44    SPECTOR, ROBERT D.  Tobias George Smollett.  Twayne's English
      Authors Series, 75, ed. Sylvia E. Bowman.  New York: Twayne
      Publishers, 175 pp.
          After an introductory chapter examining Smollett's per-
      sonality and evaluating all of his writing outside the
      novels, devotes an individual chapter to each of the five
      novels.  Presents full publishing details and sources,
      assesses previous scholarship, and analyzes plot, struc-
      ture, characterization, and general techniques for each
      novel.  Argues that Smollett's novels offer various modifi-
      cations of the traditional picaresque romances.

45    TRICKETT, RACHEL.  "Jane Austen's Comedy and the Nineteenth
      Century," in Critical Essays on Jane Austen, ed. B. C.
      Southam.  London: Routledge & Kegan Paul, p. 174.
          Smollett's influence on the nineteenth-century comic
      novel.  American ed., 1969, New York: Barnes & Noble.

46    WATT, IAN.  "Serious Reflections on The Rise of the Novel,"
      Novel, 1 (Spring), 207, 218.
          Smollett's attitudes in relation to the norms of eigh-
      teenth-century fiction.

47    WHITRIDGE, ARNOLD.  Tobias Smollett: A Study of His Miscel-
      laneous Works.  Darby, Pa.: Darby Books, x + 129 pp.
          Reprint of 1925.11.

48    WILES, R. M.  "Middle-Class Literacy in Eighteenth-Century
      England: Fresh Evidence," in 1968.9, pp. 57-58.
          Information on sales and production costs of History of
      England.

49    WILLIAMS, IOAN.  "Introduction," in Sir Walter Scott on Novel-
      ists and Fiction.  New York: Barnes & Noble, pp. 3, 9, 15,
      and passim.
          Comments on Smollett's work and Scott's judgment of it.
      Text includes large segment of Scott's essay on Smollett
      and many of his other remarks.

50    WOLF, J. HARRY.  "Tobias Smollett and The Orientalist," N&Q,
      n.s. 15 (December), 456-63.
          From parallels with Smollett's work and some internal
      evidence, raises questions about his possible connection
      with The Orientalist: A Volume of Tales after the Eastern
      Taste.

### 1969

1     BERTRAND, CLAUDE-JEAN. "Humphry Clinker a 'So-called Metho-
dist,'" <u>Bulletin de la Faculté des Lettres de Strasbourg</u>,
47 (January), 189-202.
    Sketchy description of the problem of evaluating
Smollett's attitude toward Methodism in the novel.

2     BOEGE, FRED W. <u>Smollett's Reputation as a Novelist</u>. New
York: Octagon Books, Farrar, Straus & Giroux, 175 pp.
Reprint of 1947.1.

3     BOUCÉ, PAUL-GABRIEL. "A Note on Smollett's <u>Continuation of
Complete History of England</u>," <u>RES</u>, n.s. 20 (February), 57-
61.
    Smollett's account of British defeat at St. Cast in
1758 taken from a 1758 pamphlet probably by Smollett himself.

4     BUTT, JOHN. "Dickens's Christmas Books," in <u>Pope, Dickens,
and Others: Essays and Addresses</u>. Edinburgh: University
Press, pp. 128-29.
    Dickens's indebtedness but superiority to Smollett.

5     DAVIS, JAMES BOYD. "<u>The Adventures of Roderick Random</u> by
Tobias George Smollett. A Critical Edition: Edited and with
an Introduction." Diss., University of Virginia, 1969.
    Uses two texts of 1748, the 1750 revision, and the 1755
revision. Includes textual introduction as well as critical evaluation which concentrates on Smollett's intentions,
the structure of the novel, and Roderick's character.

*6     EICKELBERG, FREDERICK CHARLES. "Sensibility in the Novels of
Tobias Smollett." Diss., Kansas State University, 1969.
    Argues for Smollett's sympathetic response to sensibili-
ty and identifies thematic, stylistic, and other elements
in his work affected by Shaftesburian and other qualities
of sensibility. Cited in <u>Dissertation Abstracts</u>, 30, 1166-
A.

7     GOLDBERG, HOMER. <u>The Art of Joseph Andrews</u>. Chicago and
London: University of Chicago Press, pp. 69, 80, 284.
    Smollett's disregard of reader's response, his didactic
concern in the picaresque, and weak use of Cervantes in
<u>Launcelot Greaves</u>.

8   GORDON, ROBERT C.  Under Which King?  A Study of the Scottish
    Waverley Novels.  New York: Barnes & Noble, pp. 32, 35,
    129, 144.
        Examples of Smollett's influence on Walter Scott.

9   GREINER, WALTER F.  "Tobias Smollett, Vorwort zu Roderick
    Random (1748)," in Studien zur Entstehung der Englischen
    Romantheorie an der Wende zum 18. Jahrhundert.  Tübingen:
    Max Niemeyer Verlag, pp. 224-30.
        Relates preface to development of theory of the novel
    and emphasizes its relationship to the picaresque.

10  HELMICK, E. T.  "Voltaire and Humphry Clinker," Studies on
    Voltaire and the Eighteenth Century, 67 (1969), 59-64.
        Unconvincing argument that work on Voltaire influenced
    Smollett's attitude and technique and notes parallels be-
    tween Candide and Humphry Clinker.

11  HOPKINS, ROBERT.  "The Function of Grotesque in Humphry
    Clinker," HLQ, 32 (February), 163-77.
        Smollett's understanding of the grotesque and ability to
    use it effectively as means of his satire make Humphry
    Clinker his most successful unified work of art.

12  HOPKINS, ROBERT.  The True Genius of Oliver Goldsmith.
    Baltimore: The Johns Hopkins Press, pp. 4-5, 154-55, 206.
        Smollett's ironic methods and concern for corruption of
    fiction.

13  HOWARD-HILL, T. H.  "Smollett, Tobias George, 1721-1771," in
    Bibliography of British Literary Bibliographies.  Oxford:
    Clarendon Press, pp. 456-57.
        Bibliographies concerned with Smollett's work.

14  ISER, WOLFGANG.  "The Generic Control of the Aesthetic Re-
    sponse: An Examination of Smollett's Humphry Clinker,"
    Southern Humanities Review, 3 (Summer), 243-47.
        Abridgement of German article, 1967.20, makes some new
    points.  Reprinted with additions 1974.22.

15  KORTE, DONALD M.  An Annotated Bibliography of Smollett
    Scholarship, 1946-68.  Toronto: University of Toronto
    Press, 54 pp.
        Two hundred and forty-one items, including disserta-
    tions, arranged chronologically, with brief annotations.

1969

16    KORTE, DONALD M.  "Smollett Bibliography," N&Q, n.s. 16 (January), 34.
      Requests information for Smollett bibliography.

17    MACALPINE, IDA and RICHARD HUNTER.  George III and the Mad-Business.  New York: Pantheon Books, Random House, pp. 184-86, 323-25.
      Effect of depiction of mad-houses in Launcelot Greaves and of his description of George III's illness of 1765 in the Continuation of the Complete History, V.

18    MOORE, ROBERT ETHERIDGE.  "Hogarth and Smollett," in Hogarth's Literary Relationships.  New York: Octagon Books, Farrar, Straus, and Giroux, pp. 162-95.
      Reprint of 1948.21.

19    MORRIS, JAMES.  "Introduction," in Travels through France and Italy.  Fontwell, Sussex: Centaur Press, pp. v-xiv.
      Praises style, honesty, and perception of the work, which because of Smollett's splenetic character remains entertaining in its "twisted charm."  Edition is not new.

20    NOYES, EDWARD S.  The Letters of Tobias Smollett, M.D.  Freeport, New York: Books for Libraries, xix + 260 pp.
      Reprint of 1926.12.

21    OLSHIN, TOBY A.  "Form and Theme in Novels about Non-Human Characters, a Neglected Sub-Genre," Genre, 2 (March), 52-54.
      Major theme of Smollett's Atom spiritual rather than political.

22    PAULSON, RONALD and THOMAS LOCKWOOD.  Henry Fielding: The Critical Heritage.  The Critical Heritage Series, ed. B. C. Southam.  London: Routledge & Kegan Paul; New York: Barnes & Noble, passim.  Indexed.
      Includes many comments and criticism comparing works of Smollett and Fielding and Smollett's opinions of Fielding.

23    REID, B. L.  "Smollett's Healing Journey," in The Long Boy and Others.  Athens, Ga.: University of Georgia Press, pp. 78-99.
      Reprint of 1965.28.

24    ROUSSEAU, GEORGE S.  "Introduction," in John Hill's Hypochondriasis. A Practical Treatise (1766), ed. G. S. Rousseau.  Augustan Reprint Society, No. 135.  Los Angeles: William

Andrews Clark Memorial Library, University of California,
Los Angeles, p. vii.
    Smollett's satire of Hill's work in Humphry Clinker.

25    SCHLÜTER, KURT. "Smollett--The Expedition of Humphry Clinker,"
in Der Englische Roman. Vom Mittelalter zur Moderne, ed.
Franz K. Stanzel. Düsseldorf: August Bagel Verlag, I, 270-
311.
    Relates the novel to traditional travel literature and
contemporary examples, discusses ties to Smollett's work,
particularly the Present State, and analyzes particular
epistolary and comic techniques.

26    SCHOLES, ROBERT. "On Realism and Genre," Novel, 2 (Spring),
271.
    Smollett's relationship to the picaresque tradition.

27    SCHOLES, ROBERT. "Towards a Poetics of Fiction: 4) An Approach through Genre," Novel, 2 (Winter), 106, 108.
    Praises Smollett's work in relation to the picaresque.

28    SHAWCROSS, JOHN T. "Tobias Smollett, 1721-1771," in The Critical Temper: A Survey of Modern Criticism etc., ed. Martin
Tucker. New York: Frederick Ungar, II, 193-99.
    Brief account of life and work and excerpts from eleven
modern critical commentaries on his writing.

29    SHERBO, ARTHUR. "Character Description in the Novel," in
Studies in the Eighteenth Century English Novel. n.p.:
Michigan State University Press, pp. 177-207 and passim.
    More concerned about plot than characterization,
Smollett uses physical description chiefly for grotesque
minor figures, relies on animal imagery, and presents
stereotyped women.

30    SHERBO, ARTHUR. "Win Jenkins' Language," PLL, 5 (Spring),
199-204.
    Finds Win Jenkins's language in Humphry Clinker less in-
genious than W. Arthur Boggs suggests in articles on the
subject. See 1963.7, 1964.4, 1965.5.

31    SMOUT, T. C. A History of the Scottish People, 1560-1830.
London: Collins, pp. 489, 496, 503.
    Despite some Scottish material in his novels, Smollett
essentially an English writer.

1969

32   T., J. H. "Tobias Smollett (1721-1771) Scottish Novelist,"
     Journal of the American Medical Association, 208 (April 7),
     141-42.
       Ill-informed account of Smollett's life and work.

33   TODD, WILLIAM B. "Bibliography and the Editorial Problem in
     the Eighteenth Century," in Bibliography and Textual Criti-
     cism: English and American Literature 1700 to the Present,
     ed. O. M. Brack, Jr. and Warner Barnes. Chicago and
     London: University of Chicago Press, pp. 139-53.
     Reprint of 1951.16.

34   TREASURE, GEOFFREY. "Tobias Smollett," in Who's Who in His-
     tory, ed. C. R. N. Routh. New York: Barnes & Noble, IV,
     154-57 and passim.
       General account emphasizes his "truculent life."

35   WAINGROW, MARSHALL. The Correspondence and Other Papers of
     James Boswell Relating to the Making of the Life of
     Johnson. Yale Editions of the Private Papers of James
     Boswell (Research Edition). Boswell's Correspondence, 2.
     New York and Toronto: McGraw Hill, passim. Indexed.
       Boswell's attempt to check material on Smollett for Life
     of Johnson and quarrel between Boswell and Smollett about
     Boswell's book on Corsica.

36   WEST, WILLIAM A. "Matt Bramble's Journey to Health," Texas
     Studies in Literature and Language, 11 (Fall), 1197-1208.
       Examines psychology and humoral pathology in presenta-
     tion of Matt's ailments in Humphry Clinker and concludes
     that Matt's return to health is the novel's central con-
     cern.

1970

1   ALLEN, WALTER. "The Comedy of Dickens," in Dickens 1970, ed.
     Michael Slater. New York: Stein and Day, pp. 6-8, 14-15.
       Compares grotesque in Smollett, Dickens, and Wyndham
     Lewis.

2   ANDERSON, JOHN P. "Bibliography of Tobias George Smollett,"
     in Francesco Cordasco, Eighteenth Century Bibliographies.
     Metuchen, New Jersey: The Scarecrow Press, pp. 207-30.
     Reprint of 1887.1.

3   BARLOW, SHERYL. "The Deception of Bath: Malapropisms in
     Smollett's Humphrey [sic] Clinker," Michigan Academician,

2 (Spring), 13-24.
Win's and Tabitha's malapropisms contribute to the satire in the novel and its theme is the clash between appearance and reality. Poorly researched, but offers two useful tables on the characters' vocabulary.

4   BATTESTIN, MARTIN C. "Tom Jones: The Argument of Design," in The Augustan Milieu: Essays Presented to Louis A. Landa, ed. Henry Knight Miller et al. Oxford: Clarendon Press, pp. 304, 318-19.
Comments on the improbable plot of Roderick Random.

5   BLOCH, TUVIA. "A Source for Smollett's Sir Mungo Barebones," N&Q, n.s. 17 (March), 95-96.
Theologian John Hutchinson model for character in Fathom.

6   BOUCÉ, PAUL-GABRIEL. "Humphry Clinker: Esquisse de Panorama Critique," EA, 23 (October-December), 425-35.
Evaluative bibliographical account of modern editions and diversified criticism of the novel.

7   BRACK, O. M., JR. "The History and Adventures of an Atom, 1769," PBSA, 64 (Third Quarter), 336-38.
Details of the probable first printing and reasons for mystery surrounding its publisher.

8   BRACK, O. M., JR. and JAMES B. DAVIS. "Smollett's Revisions of Roderick Random," PBSA, 64 (Third Quarter), 295-311.
Discusses changes in second through fourth editions and argues most important were in second.

9   CLIFFORD, JAMES L. "Testing Authenticity," in From Puzzles to Portraits: Problems of a Literary Biographer. Chapel Hill: University of North Carolina Press, p. 70.
Problems posed by Cordasco's publication of forged Smollett letters.

10  CLUBBE, JOHN. "Introduction," in Selected Poems of Thomas Hood. Cambridge, Mass.: Harvard University Press, pp. 15, 20.
Smollett's influence, particularly on Up the Rhine.

11  CORDASCO, FRANCESCO. "Smollett Criticism, 1770-1924. A Bibliography Enumerative and Annotative" and "Smollett Criticism, 1925-1945: A Compilation," in Francesco Cordasco, Eighteenth Century Bibliographies. Metuchen, N.J.: The Scarecrow Press, pp. 7-53.

1970

        Reprints of 1947.2 and 1948.7. Introduction lists some works that have corrected Cordasco's errors.

12    COZZA, ANDREA. Tobias Smollett. Biblioteca di Studi Inglesi, 19, ed. Agostino Lombardo. Bari: Adriatica Editrice, 329 pp.
        Although hardly original, this book makes available in Italy a thorough discussion of all Smollett's work, an adequate biographical sketch, and an up-to-date selected bibliography. An appendix provides a good account of Smollett's reputation and influence.

13    DILLINGHAM, WILLIAM B. "Melville's Long Ghost and Smollett's Count Fathom," AL, 42 (May), 232-35.
        Detailed comparison of Melville's rogue in Omoo and Smollett's character demonstrates great indebtedness.

*14    DUKE, LORAINE JOANNA. "Crime, Law, and Prison Experience in the Novels of Tobias Smollett." Diss., University of Tennessee, 1970.
        Smollett wrote more extensively and intensively on the subject than any previous writer and led the way to the "Newgate Novels" of the next century. Cited in Dissertation Abstracts, 31, 4709-A - 4710-A.

15    FORD, GEORGE H. "Dickens and the Voices of Time," NCF, 24 (March), 438.
        Dickens's development beyond Smollett's influence.

16    FORSYTH, WILLIAM. "Chapter IX," in The Novels and Novelists of the Eighteenth Century. Port Washington, N.Y.: Kennikat Press, pp. 278-303.
        Reprint of 1871.4.

17    GEORGE, M. D. "George III and the Mad Business," TLS, January 29, p. 110.
        Smollett had to revise last volume of his History (1765) after printing because of references to the king's madness.

18    GERBER, PHILIP L. and ROBERT J. GEMMETT. "Picaresque and Modern Literature: A Conversation with W. M. Frohock," Genre, 3 (June), 194.
        How Roderick Random diverges from the picaresque.

19    GRAVES, WILLIAM THOMAS. "National Characters in the Novels of Henry Fielding, Samuel Richardson, and Tobias Smollett." Diss., New York University, 1970.

Discusses Smollett's use of national stereotypes and
attributes his approach to his sense of Scottish aliena-
tion, leading him to attempt reconciliation of heroes' in-
dividualism with the political and social values of the
larger culture.

20    GREENE, DONALD.  "The Country and Its People," in The Age of
        Exuberance: Backgrounds to Eighteenth-Century English Lit-
        erature.  New York: Random House, pp. 49-50.
            Pygmalion-like story in Peregrine Pickle suggests lan-
        guage barriers to social change were easier to overcome in
        the period.

21    HARVEY, JOHN.  Victorian Novelists and Their Illustrators.
        London: Sidgwick & Jackson, passim.  Indexed.
            Dickens indebted to Smollett, but techniques differed.

22    HOLTZ, WILLIAM V.  "The Art of Painting the Passions," in
        Image and Immortality: A Study of Tristram Shandy.  Provi-
        dence: Brown University Press, pp. 40-46, 53 and passim.
            Compares Sterne's and Smollett's narrative and stylistic
        techniques and their use of pictorial art, particularly
        Hogarth's.

23    JONES, CLAUDE E.  Smollett Studies.  New York: Phaeton Press,
        xi + 133 pp.
            Reprint of 1942.4.

24    KENT, WILLIAM.  An Encyclopaedia of London, rev. Godfrey
        Thompson.  London: J. M. Dent & Sons, passim.  Indexed.
            Places associated with Smollett and his work.

25    KLUKOFF, PHILIP J.  "Smollett's Defense of Dr. Smellie in the
        Critical Review," Medical History, 14 (January), 31-41.
            Smollett reviewed Elizabeth Nihell's A Treatise on the
        Art of Midwifery in the Critical (1760) and her attack on
        Critical.

26    KNAPP, LEWIS M.  The Letters of Tobias Smollett.  Oxford:
        Clarendon Press, xxiv + 161 pp.
            Publishes 108 letters to 32 identified and two unidenti-
        fied correspondents.  Three letters previously unpublished,
        but Knapp offers corrections and additions for many others.
        Gives list of letters unlocated or destroyed, forged let-
        ters, and documents with Smollett's signature.  Introduc-
        tion evaluates significance of the letters.

1970

27 KORTE, DONALD M. "Verse Satire and Smollett's Humphry
Clinker," Studies in Scottish Literature, 7 (January), 188-
92.
Parallels of Pope's fourth Moral Essay and Baynard material in the novel suggests work was influenced by formal
verse satire.

28 KUHN, ALBERT J. "Introduction," in Three Sentimental Novels.
New York et al.: Holt, Rinehart and Winston, p. xv.
Contrasts Sterne's and Smollett's temperaments in their
travels.

29 LEAVIS, Q. D. "Dickens and Smollett," in F. R. Leavis and Q.
D. Leavis, Dickens the Novelist. New York: Pantheon Books,
Random House, pp. 30-33.
Dickens's use of Smollett's work became increasingly
subtle and complex until subsumed and transformed by his
genius.

30 MARPLES, MORRIS. Poor Fred and the Butcher. Sons of George
II. London: Michael Joseph, pp. 14, 117-18, 193.
Praises Smollett's descriptive talents and poetry.

31 [MEREDITH, GEORGE]. The Letters of George Meredith, ed. C. L.
Cline. Oxford: Clarendon Press, I, 57.
1860 letter contrasts his and Smollett's art.

*32 MILLER, DANIEL JONATHAN. "Estrangement and Integration,
Stasis and Motion in the Novels of Tobias Smollett."
Diss., University of Massachusetts, 1970.
Concerns "recurrent impulses, or impulse-motifs" as
they appear in Smollett's novels and represent those oppos-
ing tensions Smollett himself expressed and attempted to
reconcile through his work, succeeding finally through Matt
in Humphry Clinker. Cited in Dissertation Abstracts, 31,
4727-A-4728-A.

33 PARK, WILLIAM. "What Was New about the 'New Species of Writing,'" Studies in the Novel, 2 (Summer), 112-30.
Includes relationship of Smollett's novels to works of
predecessors and contemporaries.

34 POWELL, L. F. "Tobias Smollett and William Huggins," in Eighteenth-Century Studies in Honor of Donald F. Hyde, ed. W.
H. Bond. New York: The Grolier Club, pp. 311-22.
Nine new letters from Smollett to Huggins between 1751
and 1760 and one further letter undated.

35  RICE, SCOTT B. "The Significance of Smollett's Weather Register," N&Q, n.s. 17 (March), 94-95.
      Device in Travels complies with conventions of the
genre.

36  SMITH, JANET ADAM. "Some Eighteenth-Century Ideas of Scotland," in Scotland in the Age of Improvement etc., ed. N.
T. Phillipson and Rosalind Mitchison. Edinburgh: University Press, p. 109.
      Smollett's response to Colloden stirred by resentment of
English conduct rather than Jacobite sympathies.

37  SPEER, DIANE PARKIN. "Heinlein's The Door into Summer and
Roderick Random," Extrapolation, 12 (December), 30-34.
      Unconvincing parallels between their characterization,
plot, and satire.

38  STEVICK, PHILIP. The Chapter in Fiction: Theories of Narrative Division. Syracuse: Syracuse University Press, pp.
116-19, 132-37.
      Relates discontinuity of narrative techniques in Humphry
Clinker to thematic concerns and discusses use of chapters
in Peregrine Pickle to accommodate picaresque needs.

39  UNDERWOOD, GARY N. "Linguistic Realism in Roderick Random,"
JEGP, 69 (January), 32-40.
      Particular characteristics of Smollett's creditable, if
limited, use of dialect to achieve realism in the novel.

40  WALSH, P. G. The Roman Novel: The "Satyricon" of Petronius
and the "Metamorphoses" of Apuleius. Cambridge: University
Press, pp. 241-43.
      Smollett's picaresque not influenced by Petronius or
Apuleius, but by Cervantes and Le Sage.

41  WILLIAMS, IOAN. Novel and Romance, 1700-1800: A Documentary
Record. New York: Barnes & Noble, passim. Indexed.
      Introduction, notes, selections present Smollett's role
in developing attitudes toward and theory of the novel.

42  WILSON, ANGUS. The World of Charles Dickens. London: Martin
Secker & Warburg, pp. 35, 37, 105, 132.
      Smollett's one of many influences on Dickens and never a
matter of simple borrowing.

1971

*1    ALCOKE, DONALD MILO. "The World as Spectacle: The Pictorial
Novels of Smollett." Diss., Northwestern University, 1971.
    Considers influences on and development of Smollett's
pictorial techniques, and argues his failure to reconcile
his caricature with moral and ethical intentions until
Humphry Clinker. Cited in Dissertation Abstracts, 32,
3239-A.

*2    AUTY, SUSAN G. "Anti-Splenetic Mirth in the Novels of the
Mid-Eighteenth Century." Diss., University of Toronto,
1971.
    Cited in University of Toronto Doctoral Theses 1968-
1975. See 1975.2.

3    BÄCKMAN, SVEN. This Singular Tale: A Study of "The Vicar of
Wakefield" and Its Literary Background. Lund Studies in
English, 40, ed. Claes Schaar and Jan Svartvik. Lund:
C. W. K. Gleerup, passim. Indexed.
    Smollett's theory of the novel and his techniques and
Goldsmith's use of his work for the Vicar of Wakefield.

4    BARASCH, FRANCES K. The Grotesque: A Study in Meanings. The
Hague and Paris: Mouton, passim. Indexed.
    Smollett's use of the grotesque and later responses to
it.

*5    BEASLEY, JERRY C. "The Minor Fiction of the 1740's: A Back-
ground Study of the Novels of Richardson, Fielding, and
Smollett." Diss., Northwestern University, 1971.
    Cited in McNamee, Dissertations in English and American
Literature, Supplement 2.

6    BOUCÉ, PAUL-GABRIEL. "Eighteenth- and Nineteenth-Century
Biographies of Smollett," in 1971.61, pp. 201-30.
    Pre-twentieth-century biographers used Smollett's fic-
tional works to create "inverted biography." From 1796 to
1821 treatment was favorable, but declined until 1860, when
interest again awakened in his work and biography became
more discriminating.

7    BOUCÉ, PAUL-GABRIEL. Les Romans de Smollett: Étude Critique.
Publications de la Sorbonne, Littératures 1. Paris: Librairie Marcel Didier, 470 pp.
    Most thoroughly detailed study discusses life and char-
acter as they relate to Smollett's work and examines influences, particularly of Don Quixote and Gil Blas. Focuses

mainly on the structure of the five novels, comparing
Roderick Random and Peregrine Pickle, Fathom and Greaves,
and dealing separately with Humphry Clinker. In a more
general treatment, considers Smollett's realism, comedy,
and style. Work includes careful evaluation of Smollett
scholarship and presents two appendices: work posthumously
attributed to Smollett; chronological table on life and
work. Trans. and abridged 1976.9.

8    BUTT, JOHN. "Smollett's Achievement as a Novelist," in
     1971.61, pp. 9-23.
         Not very sympathetic general survey emphasizes the nov-
     els, particularly in their attempt to reject romance for
     "familiar scenes in an uncommon and amusing point of view."
     Sees Smollett in Humphry Clinker overcoming to some extent
     limitations imposed by his conception of the novel. Some
     interesting comment on the effect of caricature on
     Smollett's journalistic technique.

9    CANEPA, ANDREW M. "From Degenerate to Scoundrel to Noble Sav-
     age: The Italian Stereotype in 18th-Century British Travel
     Literature," English Miscellany, 22 (1971), 107-46.
         Smollett the most antipathetic of the travel writers in
     his stereotypical portrayal of Italians in his Travels.

10   [CHATTERTON, THOMAS]. The Complete Works of Thomas Chatterton:
     A Bicentenary Edition, ed. Donald S. Taylor with Benjamin
     B. Hoover. Oxford: Clarendon Press, II, 1051, 1120, 1145.
         Smollett's literary warfare with Wilkes and Chatterton's
     use of Ferdinand Count Fathom.

*11  CHEEVER, LEONARD ALFRED. "The Good Life: The Development of
     a Concept in Smollett's Novels." Diss., University of
     Southern California, 1971.
         Smollett's moral and didactic concern with the "good
     life" is imperfectly conveyed in Roderick Random, but suc-
     cessfully in the active examples of Launcelot Greaves and
     Humphry Clinker. Cited in Dissertation Abstracts, 32,
     4557-A.

12   CLIFFORD, JAMES L. "Tobias Smollett," in Atlantic Brief
     Lives: A Biographical Companion to the Arts, ed. Louis
     Kronenberger and Emily Morison Beck. Boston and Toronto:
     An Atlantic Monthly Press Book, Little, Brown, pp. 720-23.
         Informed brief description of his personality and work.

13   COLLINS, PHILIP. Dickens: The Critical Heritage. The Criti-
      cal Heritage Series. New York: Barnes & Noble, passim.
      Indexed.
           Comments from nineteenth-century criticism comparing
      Dickens and Smollett.

14   DE LA TORRE, LILLIAN. "New Light on Smollett and the Annesley
      Cause," RES, n.s. 22 (August), 274-81.
           Supports earlier argument about accuracy of Smollett's
      treatment of the Annesley cause in Peregrine Pickle.

15   DENIZOT, PAUL. "Un Mal Aimée: La Lady de Quality de
      Smollett," Les Langues Modernes, 65 (March-April), 129-32.
           Perceptive discussion of Lady Vane's memoirs in
      Peregrine Pickle makes interesting points about its style
      and intentions and compares it with Defoe's Moll Flanders
      and Roxanna.

16   DENNE, CLARENCE JOHN, JR. "The Prideful Self: Satiric Object
      in the Major Novels of Tobias Smollett." Diss., University
      of Pittsburgh, 1971.
           Considers primary concern in the satire of Roderick
      Random, Peregrine Pickle, and Humphry Clinker to be the
      social effects of egotism and argues that Smollett presents
      his views negatively in the first two novels and by affir-
      mative example in Humphry Clinker.

17   EAVES, T. C. DUNCAN and BEN D. KIMPEL. Samuel Richardson: A
      Biography. Oxford: Clarendon Press, pp. 510-13 and passim.
           Personal and professional relationships of Smollett and
      Richardson, their opinions of each other's work, and com-
      parison of their novels.

18   EVANS, DAVID L. "Peregrine Pickle: The Complete Satirist,"
      Studies in the Novel, 3 (Fall), 258-74.
           Smollett uses hero as a satirist to explore devices and
      significance of the form, but has difficulty combining
      hero's satiric role with part he plays in a melodramatic
      bildungsroman.

19   FELSENSTEIN, F. "An Unrecorded Smollett Letter," Ariel: A
      Review of International English Literature, 2 (October),
      87-89.
           1771 Leghorn letter concerns a Mr. Cochrane and de-
      scribes Smollett's health.

20   FIELDING, ROGER. "Unlucky Doctor Smollett," History of Medi-
      cine, 3 (Autumn), 11-12.

Despite considerable talents, events and his own personality contributed to make Smollett unfortunate.

21   FREDMAN, ALICE GREEN. "The Picaresque in Decline: Smollett's
First Novel," in English Writers of the Eighteenth Century,
ed. John H. Middendorf. New York and London: Columbia
University Press, pp. 189-207.
     The abatement of humor, change in tone, alteration in
the hero's character, and infusion of romance and emotion-
alism, all distinguish Roderick Random from its picaresque
predecessors, indicating the decline of the genre.

22   FUSSELL, PAUL. Samuel Johnson and the Life of Writing. New
York: Harcourt, Brace, Jovanovich, passim. Indexed.
     Smollett's work in its literary milieu and the effect of
his kind of fiction on Johnson's concern for the writer's
responsibility to his audience.

23   GASSMAN, BYRON. "The Economy of Humphry Clinker," in 1971.61,
pp. 155-68.
     Smollett fuses three strands of his novel to achieve an
effect close to unity. Through the relationship of "re-
porting, characterizing, and moralizing" elements, he creates an effective didactic account of the milieu during the
1760s.

24   GRANT, DAMIAN. "Introduction," in The Adventures of Ferdinand
Count Fathom. Oxford English Novels. London, New York,
Toronto: Oxford University Press, pp. xi-xxi.
     Details weaknesses due to derivativeness and unsuccess-
ful attempts at experimentation, but praises style and particular episodes. Discounts claims in preface for moral
intentions.

25   GREENE, DONALD. "Smollett the Historian," in 1971.61, pp. 25-
56.
     Rejects judgment that History of England is dull and a
simple expression of eighteenth-century Toryism and argues
the readability of the work and the complexity of its
political views.

26   GUILLÉN, CLAUDIO. "Toward a Definition of the Picaresque," in
Literature as System. Essays toward the Theory of Literary
History. Princeton: Princeton University Press, pp. 84,
86, 98, 102.
     Picaresque characteristics of Smollett's work.

1971

*27   GULIEV, G.  "Puteshestviya Cherez Veka: K. 250-Letiya so dnya
        Rozhdeniya T. G. Smoletta" (Journeys through the Centuries.
        The 250th Anniversary of the Birth of T. G. Smollett),
        Literaturnyi Azerbaidzhan, Baku, 3 (1971), 141-43.
            Cited in Annual Bibliography of English Language and
        Literature for 1971.

 28   HANNAY, DAVID.  Life and Writings of Tobias George Smollett.
        Freeport, New York: Books for Libraries, 163 + x pp.
            Reprint of 1887.4 includes the bibliography by John P.
        Anderson.

 29   HART, FRANCIS R.  Lockhart as Romantic Biographer.  Edinburgh:
        Edinburgh University Press, pp. 60, 96.
            John Lockhart's opinions of Smollett's work.

 30   HAYMAN, JOHN G.  "Notions on National Characters in the Eigh-
        teenth Century," HLQ, 35 (November), 7.
            Smollett's view of the French in context of conventional
        attitudes.

 31   HIBBERT, CHRISTOPHER.  The Personal History of Samuel Johnson.
        New York et al.: Harper & Row, pp. 111-12.
            Smollett's help in having Johnson's servant released
        from navy.

 32   HIRSCH, DAVID H.  Reality and Idea in the Early American Nov-
        el.  The Hague and Paris: Mouton, passim.  Indexed.
            Smollett's influence on Hugh Henry Brackenridge.

*33   JENKINS, MARITA JENNIFER ANNE.  "The Influence of the Drama
        on the Novels of Defoe and Smollett."  Diss., University of
        Texas at Austin, 1971.
            Smollett's indebtedness to English playwrights, his use
        of stage conventions and dramatic structure, and his
        achievement of dramatic quality in Humphry Clinker through
        his multiple points of view.  Cited in Dissertation Ab-
        stracts, 32, 5741-A.

 34   KAHRL, GEORGE M.  "Smollett as a Caricaturist," in 1971.61,
        pp. 169-200.
            Relates Smollett's techniques to methods and ideas of
        Thomas Patch and William Hogarth and demonstrates his
        progress in caricature so that his initial journalistic
        realism is transformed into imaginative expressionistic
        caricature in Matt Bramble in Humphry Clinker.

35   KEARFUL, FRANK J.   "Spanish Rogues and English Foundlings: On
     the Disintegration of Picaresque," Genre, 4 (December),
     388-89.
          Despite using picaresque conventions, Smollett's novels
     do not belong to the genre.

36   KNAPP, LEWIS M.   "Rare and Unrecorded Publications of
     Smollett's Works," N&Q, n.s. 18 (September), 338-39.
          A six-volume Dublin edition of his Works, a pirated
     printing of The Reprisal, an 1840 edition of Peregrine
     Pickle, and an Italian translation of "Ode to Mirth."

37   KNAPP, LEWIS M.   "Tobias George Smollett, 1721-1771," in New
     Cambridge Bibliography of English Literature, ed. George
     Watson.   Cambridge: Cambridge University Press, II, 962-70.
          Bibliographies, collected editions, individual publica-
     tions, questionable attributions, and biographical and cri-
     tical secondary works.

38   KNOEPFLMACHER, U. C.   Laughter & Despair. Readings in Ten
     Novels of the Victorian Era.   Berkeley, Los Angeles, and
     London: University of California Press, passim.   Indexed.
          Relationships of Smollett's novels to Trollope's and
     Eliot's.

39   KORTE, DONALD M.   "Smollett's Advice and Reproof: Apprentice-
     ship in Satire," Studies in Scottish Literature, 8 (April),
     239-53.
          Sees the two poems as best evidence of the influence of
     formal verse satire on Smollett's novels and argues their
     continuing influence throughout his work.

40   LANE, LAURIAT JR.   "Dickens and Melville, Our Mutual Friends,"
     Dalhousie Review, 51 (Autumn), 318-19.
          Smollett's influence on both Melville and Dickens.

41   McCOMBIE, FRANK.   "The Strange Distemper of Narcissa's Aunt,"
     N&Q, n.s. 18 (February), 55-56.
          Source of the "splenetic" ailment of the character in
     Roderick Random was Du Laurens's Discourse upon the Dis-
     eases of Melancholie, translated in 1599.

42   MANNING, SYLVIA BANK.   Dickens as Satirist.   Yale Studies in
     English, 176.   New Haven and London: Yale University Press,
     pp. 243-44 and passim.
          Smollett's influence virtually disappears in Dickens's
     mature work.

1971

43  MILIC, LOUIS T.  "Information Theory and the Style of <u>Tristram</u>
    <u>Shandy</u>," in <u>The Winged Skull. Papers from the Laurence</u>
    <u>Sterne Bicentenary Conference</u>, ed. Arthur H. Cash and John
    M. Stedmond.  Kent, Ohio: Kent State University Press, pp.
    242-43.
        Considers <u>Tristram Shandy</u>'s bawdiness in the context of
    Smollett's early novels.

44  MITCHELL, P. M.  <u>A History of Danish Literature</u>.  2nd ed.  New
    York: Kraus-Thomson for the American Scandinavian Founda-
    tion, pp. 91, 130, 151.
        Publication and reputation of Smollett's work in nine-
    teenth-century Denmark.

45  PAULSON, RONALD.  <u>Hogarth: His Life, Art, and Times</u>.  New
    Haven and London: Yale University Press for the Paul Mellon
    Centre for Studies in British Art (London), II, passim.
    Indexed.
        Smollett's relations with contemporaries, his views on
    art, and his work on the <u>Critical Review</u>.

46  PAULSON, RONALD.  "The Pictorial Circuit & Related Structures
    in 18th-Century England," in <u>The Varied Pattern: Studies</u>
    <u>in the 18th Century</u>, ed. Peter Hughes and David Williams.
    Publications of the McMaster University Association for
    18th-Century Studies, 1.  Toronto: A. M. Hakkert, pp. 168,
    179-80.
        Relates group-narrative method of <u>Humphry Clinker</u> to
    devices in English painting in the century.

47  PAULSON, RONALD.  "The Pilgrimage and the Family: Structures
    in the Novels of Fielding and Smollett," in 1971.61, pp.
    57-78.
        The motifs of the family and the pilgrimage provide the
    structural principles of <u>Roderick Random</u>, <u>Humphry Clinker</u>,
    but more particularly <u>Peregrine Pickle</u>, and the play be-
    tween them--the family representing the norm and the pil-
    grimage a rebellious deviation--offers a unifying principle
    within the loose picaresque framework.

48  PETTER, HENRI.  <u>The Early American Novel</u>.  Columbus: Ohio
    State University Press, pp. 53-54, 58, 104.
        Smollett's immorality according to nineteenth-century
    views and his influence on Tabitha Tenney.

*49  PINTEA, GABRIELA-MARIA.  "Secolul Fericit" (The Happy Cen-
    tury), <u>Ramuri</u>, 8 (May), 17.

Cited in <u>Annual Bibliography of English Language and Literature for 1971</u>.

*50    RASMUSSEN, KIRK GLENN. "The Hero: Motifs of Initiation in Eighteenth-Century British Fiction." Diss., University of Utah, 1971.
        Roderick Random's assimilation of English cultural values is a means of gaining access into a society that places a premium on reason rather than passion. Cited in <u>Dissertation Abstracts</u>, 32, 1484-A.

51    RAWSON, C. J. "Fielding and Smollett," in <u>Dryden to Johnson. Sphere History of Literature in the English Language</u>, ed. Roger Lonsdale. London: Barrie & Jenkins, IV, 259-301.
        Although offering valuable insights into Smollett's work, emphasizes his inferiority to Fielding as a novelist.

52    REID, J. C. <u>Bucks and Bruisers. Pierce Egan and Regency England</u>. London: Routledge & Kegan Paul, pp. 56, 115, 183, 197, 203, 210.
        Egan's admiration for and use of Smollett's work.

53    ROSENBERG, SONDRA. "Travel Literature and the Picaresque Novel," <u>Enlightenment Essays</u>, 2 (Spring), 40-47.
        Smollett's uncompelling, loosely structured <u>Travels</u> adheres to the conventions of the genre.

*54    ROSENBLUM, MICHAEL. "Smollett and the Art of Satire." Diss., University of Chicago, 1971.
        Cited in McNamee, <u>Dissertations in English and American Literature</u>, Supplement 2.

55    ROSS, ANGUS. "Smollett, Tobias George," in <u>The Penguin Companion to English Literature</u>, ed. David Daiches. New York: McGraw-Hill, pp. 486-87.
        Brief, perceptive assessment of Smollett and his work.

*56    ROTELLA, PILAR. "From Picaresque to Cervantean: A Study of Smollett's Novels." Diss., University of Chicago, 1971.
        Cited in 1978.9.

57    ROUSSEAU, GEORGE S. "Pineapples, Pregnancy, Pica, and <u>Peregrine Pickle</u>," in 1971.61, pp. 79-109.
        Discusses theories of obstetrics alluded to in Chapters 5 and 6 of the novel and relates the pineapple episode to eighteenth-century attempts to explain the role of imagination in childbirth. Demonstrates Smollett's use of

contemporary sources to convert his medical and scientific
interests to comic purposes in his novel.

58  ROUSSEAU, GEORGE S.  Review Article, ECS, 4 (Spring), 336-42.
    Rejects picaresque label and argues that the forms of
    Smollett's novels cannot be categorized and differ radic-
    ally from those of his contemporaries.

59  ROUSSEAU, GEORGE S.  "Smollett and the Picaresque: Some Ques-
    tions about a Label," SBHT, 12 (Spring), 1886-1904.
    Picaresque label inappropriate to Smollett's novels, and
    only Roderick Random meets some of the requirements of the
    type.  See 1972.8.

60  ROUSSEAU, GEORGE S.  "Tobias Smollett: Doctor by Design, Writ-
    er by Choice," Journal of the American Medical Association,
    216 (April 5), 85-89.
    Analyzes Smollett's career in medicine, speculates on
    reasons for his choice of a literary life, and attempts a
    psychological assessment of his personality.

61  ROUSSEAU, GEORGE S. and PAUL-GABRIEL BOUCÉ.  Tobias Smollett:
    Bicentennial Essays Presented to Lewis M. Knapp.  New York:
    Oxford University Press, 260 pp.
    Ten essays listed independently here.  Includes list of
    Knapp's works on Smollett.

62  ROUSSEAU, GEORGE S. and PAUL-GABRIEL BOUCÉ.  "Tobias Smollett
    and Roger Dibon: The Case of the Elusive Translation," N&Q,
    n.s. 18 (February), 55.
    Conclude that work described by Cordasco (1950.6) does
    not exist.

63  RUDÉ, GEORGE.  Hanoverian London, 1714-1808.  Berkeley and Los
    Angeles: University of California Press, passim.  Indexed.
    Smollett's realism in terms of his middle-class values
    and urban concerns.

64  SEKORA, JOHN.  "Two Corrections to Spector's English Literary
    Periodicals," N&Q, n.s. 18 (September), 338.
    One misattribution and one misquotation from the Briton
    in Spector, 1966.40.

65  SMITH, ALBERT.  "The Printing and Publication of Smollett's
    Peregrine Pickle," Library, 5th ser., 26 (March), 39-52.
    Strong case for William Strahan's having been the
    printer, a distributor, and a primary copyright owner of
    the first edition.

66    SPECTOR, ROBERT D.   "Smollett's Traveler," in 1971.61, pp.
      231-46.
          While using material from his own journey, Smollett's
      Travels, through its design, persona, and selection, cre-
      ates a didactic fiction to display English superiority over
      the French and Italians.

67    STANZEL, FRANZ.  Narrative Situations in the Novel: Tom Jones,
      Moby-Dick, The Ambassadors, Ulysses, trans. James P.
      Pusack.  Bloomington and London: Indiana University Press,
      pp. 44, 46-47, 65, 67.
          Smollett's use of point of view in Peregrine Pickle and
      Roderick Random.

68    STEVICK, PHILIP.  "Smollett's Picaresque Games," in 1971.61,
      pp. 111-30.
          Applies modern game theories to Roderick Random and
      Peregrine Pickle and considers the role-playing of
      Smollett's heroes, citing examples of their mimicry to sug-
      gest their values and personalities and to explain the am-
      biguity of their characters.  Their ambivalence leads to
      the unresolved, episodic structure of the novels.

69    STRATMAN, CARL J., D. G. SPENCER, and M. E. DEVINE.
      "Smollett, Tobias," in Restoration and Eighteenth Century
      Theatre Research: A Bibliographical Guide, 1900-1968.
      Carbondale and Edwardsville: Southern Illinois University
      Press; London and Amsterdam: Feffer & Simons, pp. 693-94.
          Lists and describes seven secondary sources on Smollett
      in relation to the theater.

70    TREADWELL, T. O.  "The Two Worlds of Ferdinand Count Fathom,"
      in 1971.61, pp. 131-53.
          Attacked for adopting the Fielding tradition of the nov-
      el as a picture of man as he is, in Fathom Smollett seeks
      to unite it with moralistic demands for a portrayal of man
      as he should be and tries to reconcile realism and romance
      by balancing his villain with a hero, thus creating two
      separate worlds within the novel.

71    UPHAUS, ROBERT W.  "Sentiment and Spleen: Travels with Sterne
      and Smollett," Centennial Review, 15 (Fall), 406-21.
          More at issue between Smollett and Sterne than the
      simple differences between their personalities.  Their
      quarrel, which carried into Humphry Clinker, concerns the
      definitions and characteristics of spleen and sentiment.

### 1972

1    ADBURGHAM, ALISON. Women in Print: Writing Women and Women's
     Magazines from the Restoration to the Accession of
     Victoria. London: George Allen and Unwin, passim. In-
     dexed.
          Smollett's works related to circulating libraries, peri-
     odicals, and serialization.

2    ANON. "The Scottish Society of the History of Medicine. Re-
     port of Proceedings," Medical History, 16 (April), 158.
          Smollett's obituary notice in the Scots Magazine and
     Armstrong's inscription for his Leghorn monument.

*3   BARTZ, FREDRICA KATHRYN. "Half-Beast: Image, Theme, and Sa-
     tirical Purpose in the Novels of Tobias Smollett." Diss.,
     Michigan State University, 1972.
          Careful study of relationships of imagery, themes, and
     satire indicates more effectiveness and importance of
     Smollett's novels than have been attributed to them.
     Smollett seeks to present man's capacity for kindness and
     generosity which separates him from the animals. Cited in
     Dissertation Abstracts, 33, 6300-A.

4    BEASLEY, JERRY C. A Check List of Prose Fiction Published in
     England 1740-1749. Charlottesville: University Press of
     Virginia for Bibliographical Society of the University of
     Virginia, passim. Indexed.
          Information on Roderick Random, Peregrine Pickle, and
     Smollett's translation of Gil Blas.

5    BJORNSON, RICHARD. "The Picaresque Identity Crisis," in The
     Novel and Its Changing Form, ed. R. G. Collins. Mosaic
     Essay Series. Winnipeg: University of Manitoba Press, p.
     24.
          Difference between Roderick Random and traditional
     picaresque hero.

6    BLYTHE, HAROLD RUSSELL, JR. "The Half-Perceived, Half-Created
     World of Tobias Smollett: The History of the Novel in Mini-
     ature." Diss., University of Louisville, 1972.
          Argues that Smollett develops from a traditional pica-
     resque writer to a sophisticated, self-conscious craftsman.
     Despite continued use of realism, his novels experiment
     with various techniques to involve his readers in the co-
     operative creation of their fictional worlds.

7   BOUCÉ, PAUL-GABRIEL. "Archibald Campbell on Smollett's
        Style," Studies in Scottish Literature, 9 (April), 211-17.
            Campbell's praise of Smollett's style in his History in
        keeping with general estimate of the work in his century.

8   BOUCÉ, PAUL-GABRIEL. "Smollett's Pseudo-picaresque: A Re-
        sponse to Rousseau's Smollett and the Picaresque," SBHT,
        14 (Fall), 73-79.
            Refines Rousseau's (1971.59) definition and disputes
        particular points. More picaresque characteristics in
        Fathom than in Roderick Random, but neither is picaresque.

9   BRUCE, DONALD. "Smollett and the Sordid Knaves," Contemporary
        Review, 220 (February), 133-38.
            More disposed to Tories than Whigs, but attached to
        neither, Smollett favored social reform rather than social
        reconstruction.

10  DE LA TORRE, LILLIAN. "The Melting Scot: A Postscript to
        Peregrine Pickle (1751-1772)," ELN, 10 (September), 20-27.
            Subsequent history of the two principals whose cause
        Smollett had supported in his novel: James Annesley and
        Daniel Mackercher.

11  DENIZOT, PAUL. "Féminisme et Immoralité chez Trois Person-
        nages de Defoe et Smollett," in Aspects du Feminisme en
        Angleterre, ed. Michèle Plaisant et al. Lille: Publica-
        tions de l'Universite de Lille, pp. 51-67.
            Analysis of character of Lady Vane in Peregrine Pickle
        and the condition of women in eighteenth-century England.

12  DEWHURST, KENNETH. "Some Letters of Dr. Thomas Willis (1621-
        1675)," Medical History, 16 (January), 63.
            Relationship of Smollett's Essay on the External Use of
        Water and his medical career.

13  FAUCHERY, PIERRE. La Destinée Féminine dans le Roman Européen
        du Dix-Huitième Siècle 1713-1807. Essai de Gynécomythie
        Romanesque. Paris: Librairie Armand Colin, passim. In-
        dexed.
            Extensive discussion of Smollett's treatment of women in
        all his novels as it relates to the myths about women in
        the eighteenth century.

*14 FELSENSTIEN, F. E. "A Critical Edition of Smollett's Travels
        through France and Italy (1766)." Diss., University of
        Leeds, 1972.

1972

Cited in <u>Index to Theses Accepted for Higher Degrees by</u>
<u>the Universities of Great Britain and Ireland</u>.

15  FRANKE, WOLFGANG. "Smollett's <u>Humphry Clinker</u> as a 'Party-
Novel,'" <u>Studies in Scottish Literature</u>, 9 (October-Janu-
ary, 1971-72), 97-106.
Structure and other fictional elements designed to convey Smollett's propagandistic message and create a sympathetic response from English readers to Scotland.

16  GOLDEN, MORRIS. <u>The Self Observed: Swift, Johnson, Wordsworth</u>.
Baltimore and London: The Johns Hopkins Press, passim. Indexed.
Smollett's fiction in relation to tradition and in its
perception of reality.

17  GÖLLER, KARL HEINZ. <u>Romance und Novel. Die Aufänge des En-</u>
<u>glischen Romans</u>. Nürnberg und Regensburg: Verlag Hans
Carl, passim. Indexed.
Picaresque characteristics of Smollett's work.

18  GRABAND, GERHARD, VIKTOR LINK, and PETER NÜBOLD. "Quantita-
tive Methoden zur Stilanalyse von Texten: T. G. Smollett,
<u>Roderick Random</u> (1748) and <u>Humphry Clinker</u> (1771)," <u>Mit-</u>
<u>tellungen der Technischen Universität Carolo-Wilhelmina</u>
<u>zu Braunschweig</u>, 7, No. 4 (1972), 6 pp.
Computer analysis of style in the two novels.

19  HIGHSMITH, JAMES MILTON. "Smollett's Nancy Williams: A Mirror
for Maggie," <u>English Miscellany</u>, 23 (1972), 113-23.
Unconvincing argument that episode in <u>Roderick Random</u>
derives from tradition of mirror literature--cautionary
tales for magistrates--and is used to provide some form to
the loose narrative and to separate it from journalism.

*20  INGER, A.  Introductory Article to Russian Translation of
<u>Humphry Clinker</u>. Moscow: Khudozhestvennaya Literatura.
Cited in <u>Annual Bibliography of English Language and</u>
<u>Literature for 1972</u>.

21  ISER, WOLFGANG. <u>Der Implizite Leser: Kommunikationsformen des</u>
<u>Romans von Bunyan bis Beckett</u>. Munich: Wilhelm Fink.
<u>See</u> trans., 1974.22.

22  JACK, R. D. S. "The Novel and Scott," in <u>The Italian Influ-</u>
<u>ence on Scottish Literature</u>. Edinburgh: University Press,
pp. 197-213.

Discusses Smollett's treatment of Italy and Italians and his sources in Italian literature and argues his importance in developing Italian influence in the Scottish novel. Reprinted generally 1973.23.

*23 JEFFREY, DAVID K. "Image Structures in Smollett's Novels." Diss., University of North Carolina, 1972.

Examines ways in which concepts of order provide structure in Smollett's novels and argues for a greater effectiveness of his increasingly complex narrative techniques, particularly in their use of image-clusters, as he progresses to his major achievement in Humphry Clinker. Cited in Dissertation Abstracts, 33, 4418-A.

24 KIELY, ROBERT. The Romantic Novel in England. Cambridge, Mass.: Harvard University Press, passim. Indexed.

Contrasts Smollett's rationalistic ideas and practices in the novel with those in later romantic novels.

25 MALLEY, TERENCE. Richard Brautigan. Writers for the Seventies. New York: Warner Paperback Library, p. 19.

Brautigan's use of Smollett's technique of self-dramatization of character.

*26 MILES, P. R. "An Anatomy of Judgement: The Novels of Tobias Smollett." M.A. Thesis, University of Birmingham, 1972.

Cited in Index to Theses Accepted for Higher Degrees by the Universities of Great Britain and Ireland.

27 NOVAK, MAXIMILLIAN E. "Fiction and Society in the Early Eighteenth Century," in England in the Restoration and Early Eighteenth Century: Essays on Culture and Society, ed. H. T. Swedenberg, Jr. Publications of the 17th and 18th Centuries Studies Group, U.C.L.A. Berkeley, Los Angeles, London: University of California Press, pp. 69-70.

Relates Smollett's fiction to social and moral climate of his period and to works of minor writers.

28 PAGE, NORMAN. The Language of Jane Austen. New York: Barnes & Noble; London: Basil Blackwell & Mott, pp. 140, 186.

Contrasts Austen's and Smollett's nautical dialogue and relates epistolary methods in Pride and Prejudice and Humphry Clinker.

29 PAULSON, RONALD. Rowlandson: A New Interpretation. New York: Oxford University Press, pp. 8, 38-39, 77-78.

Smollett's view of the picturesque and relationship of his novels to Rowlandson's art.

1972

30   PAWLYK, JOHN EDWARD.  "The Expedition of Humphry Clinker:
     Method and Consequences of a Multiple First-Person Focus of
     Narration."  Diss., Syracuse University, 1972.
         Analyzes ways Smollett controls multiple point of view
     in the novel to express his sympathies for traditional and
     communal rather than individualistic values.  Also discus-
     ses relationship between David Hume's epistemological views
     and some of Smollett's themes in Humphry Clinker.

31   PRATT, T. K.  "Linguistics, Criticism, and Smollett's Roderick
     Random," UTQ, 42 (Fall), 26-39.
         An illuminating analysis of the style of Roderick Random
     and demonstrates the value of a linguistic approach to
     criticism.

32   QUENNELL, PETER.  Samuel Johnson: His Friends and Enemies.
     New York et al.: American Heritage Press, McGraw-Hill, pp.
     158, 166, 174.
         Relationship of Fanny Burney's Evelina to Smollett's
     novels.

33   RAWSON, C. J.  Henry Fielding and the Augustan Ideal under
     Stress: "Nature's Dance of Death" and Other Studies.
     London and Boston: Routledge & Kegan Paul, pp. 54-55, 81-
     83, 114, 139, 259.
         Comparisons with Fielding's techniques suggest
     Smollett's Gothic mode of characterization and description,
     which delights in violations of orderliness.

34   RICE, SCOTT.  "The Satiric Persona of Smollett's Travels,"
     Studies in Scottish Literature, 10 (July), 33-47.
         Travels is a satire and its unity is achieved through
     the complex character of its persona.

35   RICE, SCOTT.  "Smollett's Travels and the Genre of Grand Tour
     Literature," Costerus, 1 (1972), 207-20.
         Considers content, form, and purpose in Travels in terms
     of genre of grand tour literature and sees its unity coming
     from conventions of the form.

36   ROSS, ANGUS.  "The 'Show of Violence' in Smollett's Novels,"
     YES, 2 (1972), 118-29.
         Discusses contribution of rhetorical and tactical uses
     of violence to Smollett's particular fictive world.

37   ROSS, JOHN A.  "History of the Liverpool Teaching Hospitals
     until 1907," Medical History, 16 (October), 370-71.

Praises description of naval examining board in <u>Roderick Random</u>.

38  ROUSSEAU, GEORGE S.  "Controversy or Collusion?  The 'Lady Vane' Tracts," <u>N&Q</u>, n.s. 19 (October), 375-78.
Relationship of John Hill's <u>History of a Woman of Quality</u> and some pamphlets to memoirs in <u>Peregrine Pickle</u>.

39  ROUSSEAU, GEORGE S.  "Smollett and Sterne: A Revaluation," <u>Archiv für das Studium der Neueren Sprachen und Literaturen</u>, 208 (April), 286-97.
Contrasts their art and presents an unfavorable portrait of Smollett and his work and the biographical and critical treatment the novelist has received.

40  SCAFIDEL, BEVERLY.  "Smollett's <u>Humphry Clinker</u>," <u>Explicator</u>, 30 (March), no. 54.
Chowder, the dog, reflects various elements of the Bramble entourage.

41  [SCOTT, WALTER].  <u>The Journal of Sir Walter Scott</u>, ed. W. E. K. Anderson.  Oxford: Clarendon Press, pp. 279, 627, 676.
Scott's close familiarity with Smollett's work.

42  SEKORA, JOHN.  "Smollett and Social Controversy: Luxury, Politics, and <u>Humphry Clinker</u>."  Diss., Princeton University, 1972.
Examines <u>Humphry Clinker</u> in the light of Smollett's writings on history, politics, and a variety of other subjects and attempts to provide the social and historical context of the novel.

43  SHINAGEL, MICHAEL.  "<u>Memoirs of a Woman of Pleasure</u>: Pornography and the Mid-Eighteenth-Century English Novel," in <u>Studies in Change and Revolution: Aspects of English Intellectual History, 1640-1800</u>, ed. Paul J. Korshin.  Menston, Yorkshire: The Scolar Press, pp. 211, 215-17, 231-32, 234.
Compares Smollett's and John Cleland's attitudes toward the function of the novel and discusses their views of each other's work.

44  STARR, NATHAN.  "Smollett's Sailors," <u>American Neptune</u>, 32 (April), 81-99.
Discusses sources for nautical characters and scenes, Smollett's contribution to the tradition, and relation of his fiction to actualities of seafaring life.

1972

45    THOMSON, DAVID. "Partie de Campagne," in Wild Excursions: The
      Life and Fiction of Laurence Sterne. New York et al.:
      McGraw-Hill, pp. 214, 215, 224, and passim.
            Compares Smollett's and Sterne's travel accounts and
      comments favorably on Smollett's honesty and detail.

46    TUCKER, SUSIE I. "Extension," in Enthusiasm: A Study in
      Semantic Change. Cambridge: University Press, pp. 76-77.
            Pallet in Peregrine Pickle links enthusiasm and madness.

*47   VINCENT, THOMAS B. "The Influence of Ontological and Epis-
      temological Assumption on Form and Structure in the Eigh-
      teenth Century Novel: A Study of the Major Works of
      Richardson, Smollett, and Sterne." Diss., Queens (Canada),
      1972.
            Cited in McNamee, Dissertations in English and American
      Literature, Supplement 2.

48    WARNER, JOHN M. "Smollett's Development as a Novelist,"
      Novel, 5 (Winter), 148-61.
            Influenced by Locke's epistemology, Smollett sought an
      adequate form to express his views, and his probing turned
      him from the episodic picaresque to creation of a more co-
      herent fictional world.

49    WICKS, ULRICH. "Picaro, Picaresque: the Picaresque in Liter-
      ary Scholarship," Genre, 5 (June), 153-92.
            Includes discussion of many works in which picaresque
      characteristics of Smollett are considered.

50    WILLIAMSON, GEOFFREY. The Ingenious Mr. Gainsborough. Thomas
      Gainsborough: A Biographical Study. New York: St. Martin's
      Press, passim. Indexed.
            Smollett's experiences at Bath; the accuracy of his
      depiction of persons and events; and Gainsborough's reading
      of his works.

1973

1     ALLEN, WALTER. "The Virtues of the Epistolary Novel," TLS,
      January 26, pp. 97-98.
            Use of epistolary techniques for characterization in
      Humphry Clinker.

2     ANON. "Smollett," in Brockhaus Enzyklopädie. Wiesbaden: F.
      A. Brockhaus, XVII, 517-18.
            Brief account of work and a bibliography.

1973

*3    BATESEL, BILLY PAUL.  "Comic Pattern in the Novels of
      Smollett."  Diss., University of Missouri, Columbia, 1973.
          Contrasts idyllic rural conclusions to main body of
      urban realism in the novels and analyzes relationship by
      applying Northrop Frye's definition of comedy.  Comic pat-
      tern functions more effectively in earlier novels than in
      Humphry Clinker, which moves away from comedy.  Cited in
      Dissertation Abstracts, 35, 1037-A.

4     BEASLEY, JERRY C.  "English Fiction in the 1740s: Some Glan-
      ces at the Major and Minor Novels," Studies in the Novel,
      5 (Summer), 155-75.
          Relationship of Smollett's novels--particularly Roderick
      Random--to characteristics of minor fiction of the period.

*5    BEDINGFIELD, MARY DOLOROSA.  "Farce, Tobias Smollett and the
      Comic Novel."  Diss., University of California, Los
      Angeles, 1973.
          Discusses function of farce in structure and style of
      novels and relates Smollett's farcical techniques to effec-
      tiveness of his comic intentions.  Cited in Dissertation
      Abstracts, 34, 7180-A.

6     BENTLEY, CHRISTOPHER.  "Introduction," in Robert Paltock's
      Life and Adventures of Peter Wilkins.  Oxford English Nov-
      els.  London, New York, Toronto: Oxford University Press,
      pp. xii-xiii.
          Compares early portions of Paltock's novel with Roderick
      Random.

7     BREWER, JOHN.  "The Misfortunes of Lord Bute: A Case-Study in
      Eighteenth-Century Political Argument and Public Opinion,"
      Historical Journal, 16 (March), 3-43.
          Scattered references to Smollett's work for Bute.

8     BROWN, LLOYD W.  Bits of Ivory: Narrative Techniques in Jane
      Austen's Fiction.  Baton Rouge: Louisiana State University
      Press, pp. 18, 33, 156.
          Compares Smollett's diction and epistolary technique to
      Austen's.

9     BUCK, HOWARD SWAZEY.  A Study in Smollett: Chiefly "Peregrine
      Pickle," with a Complete Collation of the First and Second
      Editions.  Mamaroneck, New York: Paul R. Appel, xii + 216
      pp.
          Reprint of 1925.4.

1973

10   BURGESS, RENATE. <u>Portraits of Doctors and Scientists in the</u>
     <u>Wellcome Institute of the History of Medicine</u>. London:
     Wellcome Institute of the History of Medicine, passim. In-
     dexed.
          Lists Smollett portraits in the collection.

11   CARLYLE, ALEXANDER. <u>Anecdotes and Characters of the Times</u>,
     ed. James Kinsley. Oxford English Memoirs and Travels.
     London, New York, Toronto: Oxford University Press, passim.
     Indexed.
          Reprint of 1860.1, but newly edited from the MS. with
     title intended by Carlyle.

12   CAZAMIAN, LOUIS. <u>The Social Novel in England 1830-1850</u> etc.,
     trans. Martin Fido. London and Boston: Routledge & Kegan
     Paul, pp. 38, 39, 124.
          Smollett's bitter realism. Originally <u>Le Roman Social</u>
     <u>en Angleterre</u> (1903).

13   CLEMENTS, FRANCES M. "The Rights of Women in the Eighteenth-
     Century Novel," <u>Enlightenment Essays</u>, 4 (Fall-Winter), 67,
     68, 69.
          Treatment of "fallen women" in <u>Roderick Random</u> and
     <u>Peregrine Pickle</u>.

14   EVANS, DAVID. "Introduction," in <u>The Life and Adventures of</u>
     <u>Sir Launcelot Greaves</u>. Oxford English Novels. London, New
     York, Toronto: Oxford University Press, pp. ix-xx.
          Available evidence of uncertain circumstances of compo-
     sition; unfavorable reception, poor reputation, but more
     favorable recent criticism. Relates novel to Smollett's
     experiences and use of <u>Quixote</u> and focuses on its comedy
     and satire and some of its characterization.

15   EVANS, JAMES E. "Smollett's Verbal Performances in <u>Peregrine</u>
     <u>Pickle</u>," <u>Notre Dame English Journal</u>, 8 (Spring), 87-97.
          Considers stylistic variety in <u>Peregrine Pickle</u> equal to
     anything in <u>Roderick Random</u> and <u>Humphry Clinker</u>.

16   FELSENSTEIN, FRANK. "'None of Your Knockers-Down': John
     Fielding and Smollett's Watch," <u>EA</u>, 26 (July-September),
     269-77.
          Details of a robbery and its outcome in 1754 in which
     Smollett was a victim.

17   FOLTINEK, HERBERT. "Epithalemiums-Stellen in den Romanen
     Tobias Smolletts," in <u>Festschrift Prof. Dr. Herbert Koziol</u>
     <u>sum Siebzigsten Geburtstag</u>, eds. Gero Bauer et al. Wiener

Beiträge zur Englischen Philologie, 75. Vienna: Wilhelm
Braumüller, pp. 63-73.
Smollett's treatment of marriage scenes in his novels
indebted to common type of literary epithalamium.

18    FORD, R. M.   "A Verbal Echo: Humphry Clinker and Johnson's
Journey," N&Q, n.s. 20 (June), 221.
Johnson unconsciously used a phrase from Smollett in his
Journey to the Western Islands of Scotland.

19    GILLESPIE, NAN,   "All That the Riviera Is, It Owes to Tobias
Smollett," New York Times, May 10, Section 10 ("Travel"),
p. 9.
Ascribes later interest in Nice to Smollett's description in his Travels.

*20    HABIB, MOHAMMAD.   "Sterne's Realism: A Critical Study."
Diss., University of Utah, 1973.
Compares Smollett's and Sterne's realism and argues that
Smollett's travel book is more conventional and more
limited in imaginative qualities. See, particularly, Ch.
4. Cited in Dissertation Abstracts, 34, 4203-A.

21    HART, FRANCIS R.   "Limits of the Gothic: The Scottish Example," in Studies in Eighteenth-Century Culture: Racism in
the Eighteenth Century, 3, ed, Harold E. Pagliaro.
Cleveland and London: The Press of Case Western Reserve
University, pp. 139-45.
Relationship of Gothic to other fictional elements in
Fathom and significance of use of the grotesque to create
a related Gothic emotional horror in Smollett's major
works.   Reprinted 1978.11.

22    HOWARD, PATSY C.   "Tobias Smollett," in Theses in English
Literature 1894-1970.   Ann Arbor, Michigan: Pierian Press,
pp. 269-70.
Lists eighteen M.A. theses on Smollett and seven cross-
references.

23    JACK, R. D. S.   "Scott and Italy," in Scott Bicentenary Essays.   Slected Papers Read at the Sir Walter Scott Bicentenary Conference, ed. Alan Bell.   Edinburgh and London:
Scottish Academic Press, pp. 283-99.
Generally a reprint of 1972.22.

24    JACKEL, DAVID.   "Jane Austen and 'Thorough Novel Slang,'" N&Q,
n.s. 20 (February), 46-47.
Smollett's earlier use of a phrase than OED listing.

1973

25 KEENER, FREDERICK M. "Lord Lyttelton and Mrs. Montagu," in
English Dialogues of the Dead: A Critical History. New
York and London: Columbia University Press, pp. 85-86.
Smollett's unfavorable relations with Lyttelton.

26 McINTOSH, CAREY. The Choice of Life: Samuel Johnson and the
World of Fiction. New Haven and London: Yale University
Press, passim. Indexed.
Johnson's response to Smollett's fiction.

*27 MARTIN, PAMELA ANN MILLER. "Situational Comedy in the Novels
of Tobias Smollett." Diss., University of Texas at Austin,
1973.
Ways in which Smollett's use of dramatic techniques and
his manipulation of situational comedy reinforce the social
attitudes in his novels. Cited in Dissertation Abstracts,
34, 5190-A.

28 MAUROCORDATO, A. "Smollett," in Encyclopaedia Universalis.
Paris: Encyclopaedia Universalis France, XV, 1-2.
Stresses picaresque characteristics and compares him
favorably with Fielding.

29 NOVAK, MAXIMILLIAN E. "Freedom, Libertinism and the Picaresque," in 1973.21, pp. 35-48.
Smollett's novels are modified forms of the picaresque.

30 PAGE, NORMAN. Speech in the English Novel. English Language
Series, 8, ed. Randolph Quirk. London: Longman, pp. 47,
49, 54, 55-56, 72, 92, 93, 106, 144-45.
Smollett's techniques for rendering the spoken language,
particularly in Humphry Clinker, and his influence on
Dickens.

31 PALMER, HELEN H. and ANNE JANE DYSON. "Tobias Smollett," in
English Novel Explication. Hamden, Conn.: The Shoe String
Press, pp. 237-39.
Secondary works on Smollett's novels.

32 PANNILL, LINDA. "Some Patterns of Imagery in Humphry
Clinker," Thoth, 13 (Fall), 37-43.
Relates patterns of imagery that reveal a concern for
order and disorder, rationality and irrationality in society to the various and changing perceptions of the characters.

33 PITTOCK, JOAN. The Ascendancy of Taste: The Achievement of
Joseph and Thomas Warton. Ideas and Forms in English

Literature, ed. John Lawlor.  London: Routledge & Kegan
Paul, p. 104.
    Relates Smollett's novels to developing forms in the
genre.

34    PRICE, JOHN VALDIMIR.  <u>Tobias Smollett: The Expedition of
Humphry Clinker</u>.  Studies in English Literature, 51, ed.
David Daiches.  London: Edward Arnold, 63 pp.
    Excellent and detailed examination emphasizes relation-
ship between form and content, assesses epistolary technique, provides insights into characterization, point of
view, and emphasizes quest for a healthier understanding
of society as theme of the novel.  Valuable selected bibliography.

35    QUENNELL, PETER.  "Tobias Smollett," in <u>A History of English
Literature</u>.  Springfield, Mass.: G&C Merriam Co., pp. 259-
62.
    Generally unfavorable and unenlightening brief account.

36    ROGAL, SAMUEL J.  "A Checklist of Eighteenth-Century British
Literary Publications in Eighteenth-Century America," <u>Colby
Library Quarterly</u>, 10th ser. (December), pp. 231, 252.
    Eighteenth-century publications of Smollett's novels and
histories in America.

37    ROUSSEAU, GEORGE S.  "'No Boasted Academy of Christendom':
Smollett and the Society of Arts," <u>Journal of the Royal
Society of Arts</u>, 121 (June), 468-75; (July), 532-35;
(August), 623-28.
    Treatment of the society in Smollett's histories,
<u>Present State of All Nations</u>, and <u>Humphry Clinker</u>.  Only
the novel offers some skepticism about the organization.

38    SCHULZ, DIETER.  "'Novel,' 'Romance,' and Popular Fiction in
the First Half of the Eighteenth Century," <u>SP</u>, 70 (January), 78, 83, 90.
    Smollett's use of the term <u>novel</u> indicates growing ac-
ceptance of the form as distinct from <u>romance</u>.

39    SHUGRUE, MICHAEL.  "Smollett," in <u>The McGraw-Hill Encyclopedia
of World Biography</u>.  New York et al.: McGraw-Hill, X, 109-
11.
    Brief, forceful account emphasizes picaresque character-
istics and contrasts Smollett with his contemporaries.

40    SMITH, ALBERT H.  "<u>The Adventures of Peregrine Pickle</u>, 1758
and 1765," <u>Library</u>, 5th ser., 28 (March), 62-64.

1973


William Strahan's role as printer of and his copyright
interest in the second and third editions.

41   SMITH, ALBERT H.   "A Duplicate Setting in the Second Edition
of Smollett's Roderick Random," Library, 5th ser., 28 (December), 309-18.
Notes two settings of Sheet B in Volume 1, compares
them, and relates to an expanded printing to meet an in-
creased demand.

42   STEEVES, EDNA L.   "Pre-Feminism in Some Eighteenth-Century
Novels," Texas Quarterly, 16 (Autumn), 50-51.
Describes Smollett's male-dominated society and the
ideal of the submissive woman in his novels.

43   STONE, ELIZABETH E.   "The Transformation of Anger to Art: A
Study of Tobias Smollett's Novels." Diss., New York University, 1973.
Progression in Smollett's attitude toward and treatment
of anger in the heroes of his novels develops from his
shared responses to an ironic, more detached comment, until
in Humphry Clinker his handling of the subject subtly
transforms the passion into art.

*44   TAYLOR, SHEILA LEA.   "Form and Function in the Picaresque
Novel." Diss., University of California, Los Angeles,
1973.
Includes discussion of the hermetic form of the picaresque as it functions in the structure and theme of
Roderick Random.  Cited in Dissertation Abstracts, 34,
3359-A.

45   WADDINGTON, IVAN.   "The Struggle to Reform the Royal College
of Physicians, 1767-1771: A Sociological Analysis," Medical
History, 17 (April), 118.
Nature of Smollett's medical education.

46   WARDROPER, JOHN.   "An Incomparable Subject for a Print," in
Kings, Lords and Wicked Libellers. Satire and Protest
1760-1837.  London: John Murray, pp. 36-38.
Wilkes demolished Smollett as a polemical journalist in
the Briton-North Briton controversy.

47   WARNER, JOHN M.   "The Interpolated Narratives in the Fiction
of Fielding and Smollett: An Epistemological View," Studies
in the Novel, 5 (Fall), 271-83.
Smollett's ability in Humphry Clinker to balance the
interpolations with his main narrative constitutes the

superiority of his final work. Smollett's achievement of
unity comes from his recognition of the proper relationship
between external reality and his perception of it.

48  WILLIAMS, GEORGE G. and MARIAN and GEOFFREY WILLIAMS. <u>Guide
to Literary London</u>. New York: Hastings House, passim. Indexed.
Places associated with Smollett and his work.


## 1974

1  BATTEN, CHARLES L. JR. "<u>Humphry Clinker</u> and Eighteenth-Century Travel Literature," <u>Genre</u>, 7 (December), 392-408.
Examined against the background of the genre, Smollett's
work should not be read as a novel, with expectations of
appropriate unity, but rather as a brilliant fictional
adaptation of the travel book.

2  BATTESTIN, MARTIN C. <u>The Providence of Wit. Aspects of Form
in Augustan Literature and the Arts</u>. Oxford: Clarendon
Press, pp. 135, 150, 162-63.
Smollett relies unsatisfactorily on Providence to re-
solve his plots.

3  BLAMIRES, HARRY. "The Eighteenth-Century Novel," in <u>A Short
History of English Literature</u>. London: Methuen & Co., pp.
246-49.
Smollett's work entertaining and lively in its caricatures, but undisciplined, arising from his experiences and
emotions.

4  BRACK, O. M. JR. and ROBERT E. KELLEY. <u>The Early Biographies
of Samuel Johnson</u>. Iowa City: University of Iowa Press,
passim. Indexed.
Reprints four early lives of Johnson which include material on Smollett.

5  BRISSENDEN, R. F. <u>Virtue in Distress: Studies in the Novel of
Sentiment from Richardson to Sade</u>. London: The Macmillan
Press; New York: Harper & Row, Barnes & Noble Import Divi-
sion, passim. Indexed.
Complex relation of sentiment and reason in Smollett's
novels.

*6  BUTLER, SYDNEY JAMES. "Masks of Reality: The Rhetoric of Nar-
ration in the Eighteenth-Century English Novel." Diss.,
University of British Columbia, 1974.

1974

> Smollett's use of his quixotic material in <u>Launcelot
> Greaves</u> to examine the realities of eighteenth-century
> life. Cited in <u>Dissertation Abstracts</u>, 35, 7249-A-7250-A.

7    BYRD, MAX. <u>Visits to Bedlam: Madness and Literature in the
Eighteenth Century</u>. Columbia, S.C.: University of South
Carolina Press, passim. Indexed.
> Describes Smollett's association of madness with city
> life and with dissenters and relates <u>Launcelot Greaves</u> to
> parliamentary reform of private madhouses.

8    COLE, RICHARD C. "Community Lending Libraries in Eighteenth-
Century Ireland," <u>Library Quarterly</u>, 44 (April), 111-23.
> Includes material on popularity of Smollett's work in
> Ireland.

9    COPELAND, EDWARD. "<u>Humphry Clinker</u>: A Comic Pastoral Poem in
Prose?" <u>Texas Studies in Literature and Language</u>, 16
(Fall), 493-501.
> Displaying an interest in the form, Smollett applied its
> generic characteristics in order to achieve cohesiveness in
> the novel.

10   DAICHES, DAVID. "Smollett Reconsidered," in <u>Miscellanea
Anglo-Americana</u>. Festschrift für Helmut Viebrock, ed. Kuno
Schumann et al. München: Karl Pressler, pp. 109-36.
> Insightful general essay uses <u>Launcelot Greaves</u> as basis
> for initiating the argument that Smollett is essentially
> a moralist and then seeks to locate and define the moral
> character of his novels.

11   DAY, ROBERT ADAMS. "Introduction," in Francis Coventry's <u>The
History of Pompey the Little</u>. Oxford English Novels.
London, New York, Toronto: Oxford University Press, pp.
ix, xi, xiv, xv, xxii, xxiv, 5.
> Compares reception, techniques of Coventry's and
> Smollett's works. Reprints comment on <u>Peregrine Pickle</u>
> from third edition in 1753.

12   DePORTE, MICHAEL V. "Don Quixote in England," in <u>Nightmares
and Hobbyhorses: Swift, Sterne, and Augustan Ideas of Mad-
ness</u>. San Marino, Calif.: The Huntington Library, pp. 112-
13.
> Use of <u>Don Quixote</u> in <u>Launcelot Greaves</u> and Smollett's
> failure to characterize accurately quality of madness in
> his hero.

13    EPSTEIN, WILLIAM H.   John Cleland: Images of a Life.   New
      York and London: Columbia University Press, passim.   In-
      dexed.
           Personal and literary relationships of Smollett and
      Cleland.

14    FABEL, ROBIN.   "The Patriotic Briton: Tobias Smollett and
      English Politics, 1756-1771," ECS, 8 (Fall), 100-14.
           Apolitical until 1756, Smollett neither a Whig nor Tory
      afterwards, but rather opposed to partisan government.
      Against radical changes, he believed it possible to make
      necessary institutional reforms.

15    FOLKENFLIK, ROBERT.   "Self and Society: Comic Union in Humphry
      Clinker," PQ, 53 (April), 195-204.
           Multiple point of view, examining ways individual char-
      acters reconcile their self-interests with social union,
      provides a unity of discordia concors in the novel.

16    GASSMAN, BYRON.   "Humphry Clinker and the Two Kingdoms of
      George III," Criticism, 16 (Spring), 95-108.
           Humphry Clinker presents a dualistic vision of England,
      which contrasts the real world through which group travels
      with an idealistic, mythic one that reflects the hopes that
      many Englishmen had had when George III became king.

17    GEDDES, J.   "Smollet [sic], Tobias George," in Great Scots.
      Devon: Arthur H. Stockwell, p. 117.
           Brief, unflattering account that does not mention the
      novels.

18    HAMILTON, OLIVE.   "In Search of Smollett at Livorno," in Para-
      dise of Exiles. Tuscany and the British.   London: André
      Deutsch, pp. 49-61.
           General, unscholarly, poorly informed account of
      Smollett and his work, with more specific comment on his
      Travels and details about his burial place and decline of
      interest in it.

*19   HANES, SARA LOUISE.   "Dialect in the Novels of Fielding and
      Smollett."   Diss., University of Georgia, 1974.
           Assesses accuracy and effectiveness of Smollett's uses
      of dialect material particularly in relationship to charac-
      terization.   Cited in Dissertation Abstracts, 35, 6694-A.

*20   HONHART, CAROL TAPLETT.   "Fielding, Smollett, Sterne, and the
      Development of the Eighteenth-Century Travel Book."   Diss.,
      Duke University, 1974.

1974

Contributions of Smollett's Travels and Humphry Clinker
to the development of travel literature in the eighteenth
century. Cited in Dissertation Abstracts, 35, 5348-A-
5349-A.

21 HOWES, ALAN B. Sterne: The Critical Heritage. The Critical
Heritage Series, ed. B. C. Southam. London and Boston:
Routledge & Kegan Paul, passim. Indexed.
Introduction, notes, and selections offer comment on
relationship and comparisons of Smollett's and Sterne's
works.

22 ISER, WOLFGANG. "The Generic Control of the Esthetic Response: An Examination of Smollett's Humphry Clinker," in
The Implied Reader: Patterns of Communication in Prose Fiction from Bunyan to Beckett. Baltimore and London: The
Johns Hopkins University Press, pp. 57-80.
Combining the epistolary novel, travel book, and picaresque, Humphry Clinker creates a new means of perceiving
reality, and its multiple perspective offers a variety im-
possible in any of the individual forms. Smollett's method
is related to eighteenth-century associational psychology
and Scottish empirical philosophy. Translation of 1972.21.

23 JACK, IAN. "Gray in His Letters," in Fearful Joy: Papers from
the Thomas Gray Bicentenary Conference at Carleton Univer-
sity, ed. James Downey and Ben Jones. Montreal and London:
McGill-Queen's University Press, p. 23.
Compares William Mason's ironic letter on travels to
Smollett's style in his Travels.

24 JARRETT, DEREK. England in the Age of Hogarth. New York:
Viking Press, pp. 47-48, 58.
Sees description of naval conditions in Roderick Random
as exaggerated and Smollett's attitude toward criminals as
harsh.

25 JOLIAT, EUGÉNE. Smollett et la France. Genève: Slatkine
Press, 279 pp.
Reprint of 1935.5.

26 KARL, FREDERICK R. "Smollett's Humphry Clinker: The Choleric
Temper," in The Adversary Literature: The English Novel in
the Eighteenth Century, A Study in Genre. New York:
Farrar, Straus and Giroux, pp. 183-204.
Even at his best, Smollett fails to offer more than the
realistic details of the clash in values between an older

and younger generation because he lacks the philosophical assessment necessary to give them meaning.

27  KELCH, RAY A.  <u>Newcastle. A Duke without Money: Thomas Pelham-Holles 1693-1768</u>.  Berkeley and Los Angeles: University of California Press, p. 12.
    Smollett's portrait of Newcastle in the <u>Atom</u> based on personal knowledge.

28  KNAPP, LEWIS M.  "Smollett 1721-1771," in <u>The English Novel: Select Bibliographical Guides</u>, ed. A. E. Dyson.  London: Oxford University Press, pp. 112-27.
    Bibliographical essay discusses and evaluates editions, critical studies and commentaries, biographies, and bibliographies.

29  KRONENBERGER, LOUIS.  <u>The Extraordinary Mr. Wilkes: His Life and Times</u>.  Garden City, N.Y.: Doubleday, pp. 28ff. and 217.
    Smollett and Wilkes's political controversy and their earlier personal relationship.

*30  LYNN, JOANNE LEWIS.  "Configurations of the Comic Grotesque in the Novels of Tobias Smollett."  Diss., University of California, Irvine, 1974.
    Strength of Smollett's novels in his comic grotesque vision which gives his work its stylistic energy and which he unites with psychological realism in his later writing.  Cited in <u>Dissertation Abstracts</u>, 35, 7259-A.

*31  MAYS, JACK THURSTON.  "The Use of Quixote Figures and Allusions to <u>Don Quixote</u> in the Novels of Tobias Smollett."  Diss., Ball State University, 1974.
    Smollett used his knowledge of <u>Don Quixote</u> to good effect in creating his characters and developing his structure in all five novels.  Cited in <u>Dissertation Abstracts</u>, 35, 1053-A-1054-A.

32  OLIVER, R. C. B.  "Diederick Wessel Linden, M.D.," <u>National Library of Wales Journal</u>, 18 (Summer), 241-67.
    Smollett's personal knowledge and parody of the work of the physician who was the original of Dr. L---m in <u>Humphry Clinker</u>.

33  PARK, WILLIAM.  "<u>Tristram Shandy</u> and the New 'Novel of Sensibility,'" <u>Studies in the Novel</u>, 6 (Fall), 268-69, 275-77.
    Changes in Smollett's later fiction from the conventions of the novel in the 1740s.

1974

34    PICKERING, SAM JR.  "'The most "harum-scarum" sort of novel we
      have ever encountered': Marryat's The King's Own and
      Shandyism," English Studies in Africa, 17 (September), 71-
      77.
          Argues against Marryat's indebtedness to Smollett and
      describes his dislike of Smollett's kind of realism.

35    PRESTON, THOMAS R.  "Disenchanting the Man of Feeling:
      Smollett's Ferdinand Count Fathom," in Quick Springs of
      Sense: Studies in the Eighteenth Century, ed. Larry S.
      Champion.  Athens, Ga.: University of Georgia Press, pp.
      223-39.
          Structure of the novel derives from tradition of man of
      feeling rather than that of rogue biography, and Renaldo
      learns from Fathom the ways in which villainy threatens
      unprotected virtue.

36    PRESTON, THOMAS R.  "The 'Stage Passions' and Smollett's
      Characterization," SP, 71 (January), 105-25.
          Argues the generally pervasive influence of drama on
      Smollett's techniques and examines particular relationship
      between eighteenth-century acting theories and Smollett's
      formulaic treatment of his characters.

37    PROBYN, CLIVE T.   "Gulliver and the Relativity of Things:
      A Commentary on Method and Mode, with a Note on Smollett,"
      Renaissance and Modern Studies, 18 (1974), 63-76.
          Contrasts manner and tone of Smollett's satire in
      Humphry Clinker with Swift's in Gulliver's Travels.

38    PROBYN, CLIVE T.  "Swift and the Physicians: Aspects of Satire
      and Status," Medical History, 18 (July), 250, 259.
          Comments on Smollett's medical knowledge and his de-
      scriptions in Roderick Random.

*39   PUTMAN, ALAN DAVID.  "George Meredith and the Eighteenth Cen-
      tury: A Study in Literary Parallels."  Diss., University of
      Toronto, 1974.
          Offers comparisons of motifs and allusions in the novels
      of Meredith and Smollett.  Cited in Dissertation Abstracts,
      36, 1533-A.

40    RAYMOND, MICHAEL W.  "The Romance Tradition in Eighteenth-
      Century Fiction: A Study of Smollett."  Diss., University
      of Florida, 1974.
          Argues that an understanding of the conventions and ob-
      jectives of the fictional romances provides the best means
      for studying Smollett's novels--particularly Peregrine

Pickle, Ferdinand Count Fathom, and Launcelot Greaves--
despite their satiric elements.

41    [RIDER, WILLIAM].  An Historical and Critical Account of the
      Lives and Writings of the Living Authors of Great-Britain
      (1762).  Augustan Reprint Society, No. 163.  Los Angeles:
      William Andrews Clark Memorial Library, pp. 11-12.
          Reprint of 1762.19.

42    ROGAL, SAMUEL J.  "Enlightened Enthusiasm: Anti-Methodism in
      the Literature of the Mid and Late Eighteenth Century,"
      Enlightenment Essays, 5 (Spring), 8-10.
          Considers reasons for change between Smollett's more
      tolerant treatment of Methodism in Humphry Clinker and
      earlier pronouncements in History of England.

43    ROGERS, PAT.  "Sterne and Smollett," in The Augustan Vision.
      New York: Barnes & Noble, pp. 293-98.
          Brief sketch of life and writing stresses Smollett's
      importance to development of the novel as a genre.

44    ROUSSEAU, GEORGE S.  Goldsmith: The Critical Heritage.  Criti-
      cal Heritage Series, ed. B. C. Southam.  London and Boston:
      Routledge & Kegan Paul, passim.  Indexed.
          Introduction and selections offer comment on comparisons
      of Smollett's and Goldsmith's works and on their personal
      and professional relationship.

45    RUSSELL, H. K.  "Unity in Eighteenth-Century Episodic Novels,"
      in 1974.35, pp. 183-96.
          Includes discussion of Smollett's various means for pro-
      viding unity in Humphry Clinker.

46    RYMER, MICHAEL.  "Another Source for Smollett's Lismahago,"
      N&Q, n.s. 21 (February), 57-59.
          Source for character in Humphry Clinker may have been
      Sir William Johnson, who appears as unnamed character in
      Charles Johnstone's Chrysal, or the Adventures of a Guinea.

47    SELLS, A. LYTTON.  Oliver Goldsmith. His Life and Works.  New
      York: Barnes & Noble/Harper and Row, passim.  Indexed.
          Smollett's character and literary relationships.

48    SIEBERT, DONALD T., JR.  "The Role of the Senses in Humphry
      Clinker," Studies in the Novel, 6 (Spring), 17-26.

74

        Smollett's use of the senses provides serious basis for commentary on the novel since his imagery derives from Lockean epistemological assumptions that suggest the senses provide the basis of knowledge.

*49   SMITH, LOUISE ZANDBERG. "The Transforming Eye: Response to Landscape as a Measure of Social Sensibility in Late Eighteenth-Century Fiction." Diss., University of Virginia, 1974.
        Influence of Ferdinand Count Fathom on treatment of relationship between landscape and character responses. Cited in Dissertation Abstracts, 35, 4558-A-4559-A.

50   SPACKS, PATRICIA MEYER. "Early Fiction and the Frightened Male," Novel, 8 (Fall), 5-15.
        Suggests relationship of the sexual fears of Smollett's heroes to the insecurities of a male-dominated society.

51   STAECK, WOLFGANG. "'Novelty' als Gestaltungsprinzip bei Smollett: Ein Beitrag zur Interpretation Seiner Sonderlingsfiguren," Germanisch-Romanische Monatsschrift, 24 (March), 71-87.
        Attempts to relate eighteenth-century theories of novelty to the manner in which Smollett develops his eccentric characters in each of his novels.

52   STEELE, JAMES. "Thomas Gray and the Season for Triumph," in 1974.23, pp. 209-12.
        Compares Smollett's and Gray's views of British military operations during the 1740s.

53   THOMSEN, CHRISTIAN W. "Tobias Smollett: Roderick Random; Peregrine Pickle; Ferdinand Count Fathom; Humphry Clinker. Pikareskes Erbe, Odd Characters und die Groteske der Verletzten Humanität," in Das Groteske im Englischen Roman Des 18. Jahrhunderts. Darmstadt: Wissenschaftliche Buchgesellschaft, pp. 142-223.
        Relates Smollett's use of the grotesque to the picaresque and examines it in relation to the Gothic, carefully assessing grotesque characteristics in Commodore Trunnion, Matt Bramble, Lismahago, and Tabitha.

54   TOBIN, TERENCE. "Scots Abroad, 1725-1750," in Plays by Scots, 1660-1800. Iowa City: University of Iowa Press, pp. 155-60 and passim.
        Objective account of Smollett's plays and some comparisons with those of other Scots.

55  TOLIVER, HAROLD.  "Fictional Documents and Letter Liaisons,"
    in Animate Illusions: Explorations of Narrative Structure.
    Lincoln: University of Nebraska Press, pp. 142, 145, 149,
    150.
        Function and technique of the epistolary method in
    Humphry Clinker.

56  WICKS, ULRICH.  "The Nature of Picaresque Narrative: A Modal
    Approach," PMLA, 89 (March), 240-49.
        Includes discussion of Smollett's theory and practice of
    the picaresque.

57  WILLIAMSON, AUDREY.  "The King and the North Briton," in
    Wilkes: "A Friend to Liberty".  New York: Reader's Digest
    Press/E. P. Dutton & Co., pp. 52-56.
        Smollett's motives and efforts as editor of the Briton.


                            1975

1   ALLEN, WALTER E.  "Smollett, Tobias," in The New Encyclopaedia
    Britannica.  "Macropaedia."  15th ed.  Chicago et al.: En-
    cyclopaedia Britannica, Inc.; William Benton; Helen
    Hemingway Benton, XVI, 908-9.
        Balanced account emphasizes vigorous comedy and use of
    the picaresque.

2   AUTY, SUSAN G.  "Smollett and Sterne and Animal Spirits," in
    The Comic Spirit of Eighteenth-Century Novels.  Port
    Washington, New York and London: National University Pub-
    lications, Kennikat Press, pp. 103-79.
        Amused rather than critical, Smollett accepts the world
    as it is, which removes satiric effect in his novels.
    Peregrine Pickle, in its comedy, conveys Smollett's own
    enjoyment of life, but with more mature manipulation and
    development of its comedy, Humphry Clinker more effectively
    expresses his balanced view of human experience.

3   BOUCÉ, PAUL-GABRIEL.  "The Duke of Newcastle's Levee in
    Smollett's Humphry Clinker," YES, 5 (1975), 136-41.
        Episode illustrates Smollett's complex use of reality
    and contradicts old-fashioned notion that he simply copied
    from life.

4   BOUCÉ, PAUL-GABRIEL.  "Smollett et le Roman du Dix-Huitième
    Siècle," EA, 28 (April-June), 183-89.
        Essay review argues the continued vitality of Smollett
    scholarship.

1975

5 BRACK, O. M. JR. "'Of making many books there is no end':
Editing Smollett," in Editing Eighteenth Century Novels.
Papers . . . at the Conference on Editorial Problems Uni-
versity of Toronto November 1973, ed. G. E. Bentley, Jr.
Toronto: A. M. Hakkert, pp. 91-115.
Detailed account of the vexing problems of producing an
edition of Smollett's novels.

6 BRACK, O. M. JR. "Toward a Critical Edition of Smollett's
Peregrine Pickle," Studies in the Novel, 7 (Fall), 361-74.
Complex problems of preparing a modern scholarly edition. Proposes first edition as copy text, correcting
errors overlooked by Smollett for revised second edition,
and including all authentic changes by Smollett.

7 BRACK, O. M. JR. "William Strahan: Scottish Printer and Publisher," Arizona Quarterly, 31 (Summer), 185, 190.
Smollett's importance to Strahan's publishing career.

8 BROOKS, DOUGLAS. "Smollett: Roderick Random, Peregrine
Pickle, Ferdinand Count Fathom" and "Smollett: Humphry
Clinker," in Number and Pattern in the Eighteenth-Century
Novel: Defoe, Fielding, Smollett and Sterne. London and
Boston: Routledge & Kegan Paul, pp. 123-43 and 144-59.
Smollett applied numerology in a variety of ways to the
patterning of these four novels and his schemes provided
structures distinct from those of his picaresque predecessors. Brooks sees Humphry Clinker as the final eighteenth-
century work carrying on a tradition derived from Renaissance humanism.

9 BROWN, P. S. "The Vendors of Medicines Advertised in Eighteenth-Century Bath Newspapers," Medical History, 19 (October), 360, 362, 365.
On the realism and satire of Humphry Clinker.

10 BUSH, DOUGLAS. Jane Austen. Masters of World Literature, ed.
Louis Kronenberger. New York: Macmillan, passim. Indexed.
Compares Smollett's and Austen's nautical characters.

11 BUTLER, MARILYN. Jane Austen and the War of Ideas. Oxford:
Clarendon Press, passim. Indexed.
Smollett's influence on Thomas Holcroft and Robert Bage
and a comparison of his and Henry Mackenzie's treatment of
social abuses.

12 CASH, ARTHUR H. Laurence Sterne: The Early & Middle Years.
London: Methuen & Co., passim. Indexed.

Sterne's knowledge of Smollett's work and Smollett's description of William Hewett in Humphry Clinker.

13   CHALKER, JOHN. Violence in Augustan Literature. An Inaugural Lecture Delivered at Westfield College (University of London), pp. 3-5.
Smollett's caricatured violence reflects a sense of the instability of life itself.

14   COLE, RICHARD C. "Smollett and the Eighteenth-Century Irish Book Trade," PBSA, 69 (July-September), 345-63.
Discusses in detail the many cheap Irish reprints of Smollett's work, their sales, their audience and its response. See 1977.36.

15   CUNNINGHAM, VALENTINE. Everywhere Spoken Against: Dissent in the Victorian Novel. Oxford: Clarendon Press, pp. 218, 221.
Smollett relatively mild in his treatment of non-conformity.

16   DAVIES, PAUL C. "Augustan Smells," Essays in Criticism, 25 (October), 404-6.
Smollett's use of the sensation of smell as a motif in his writings.

17   DEMPSEY, I. LINDSAY. "The Metamorphosis of Humphrey [sic] Clinker," New Laurel Review, 4 (Spring and Fall), 19-26.
Design of Humphry Clinker set in Matt's struggle with Tabitha, which represents his attempt to overcome the limitations and stultifying characteristics in his nature.

18   DONALDSON, IAN. "The Satirist's London," Essays in Criticism, 25 (January), 110-12.
Treatment of London crowds in Humphry Clinker emphasizes the subjective character of observations of the city.

19   FADER, DANIEL. The Periodical Context of English Literature, 1708-1907. Xerox Monograph Publishing Imprint Series. Ann Arbor: University of Michigan Press, pp. 17-19, 32.
Undocumented and uninformed comment regards Smollett as a hack writer as grotesque as his characters.

20   FELSENSTEIN, F. "An Early Abridgement of Smollett's Peregrine Pickle," N&Q, n.s. 22 (January), 13-14.
Bibliographical description of American edition; questions whether, as Knapp suggests (1954.3), it was for children.

1975

21    FIEBERLING, JOHN ERNEST. "The Real Substantial Chivalry:
        Character and Society in Smollett's Politics." Diss.,
        Johns Hopkins University, 1975.
            Examines the coherence of values in Smollett's novels,
        relates them to his histories and journalism, and argues
        the central importance of his self-conception as a Scottish
        gentleman. Sees him as a True Whig rather than a supporter
        of monarchy and aristocracy.

22    FLANDERS, W. AUSTIN. "The Significance of Smollett's Memoirs
        of a Lady of Quality," Genre, 8 (June), 146-64.
            Relates fictional characteristics of The Memoirs to
        Smollett's failure in early novels to present a cohesive
        work out of an individual's disparate experiences. Ina-
        bility to resolve social and moral problems leads to reli-
        ance on conventional endings.

*23   FLETCHER, CONSTANCE MARY. "The Eighteenth-Century Criminal in
        Law and Literature." Diss., Northwestern University, 1975.
            Treatment of criminals in Fathom severe, but more philo-
        sophical than discussions in Smollett's non-fiction. Cited
        in Dissertation Abstracts, 36, 4506-A.

24    FREEDMAN, RICHARD. "Birth of the Novel," in The Novel. New
        York: Newsweek Books, pp. 17-19.
            Conventional account of Smollett's novels.

*25   GIBSON, LOIS RAUCH. "Attitudes toward Childhood in Eighteenth
        -Century British Fiction." Diss., University of
        Pittsburgh, 1975.
            Chapter two describes Smollett's depiction of children
        as consistent with their mature picaresque characters.
        Cited in Dissertation Abstracts, 36, 4508-A-4509-A.

26    HUNTER, J. PAUL. Occasional Form: Henry Fielding and the
        Chains of Circumstance. Baltimore and London: The Johns
        Hopkins University Press, pp. 144, 147.
            Smollett's use of the journey motif.

27    JEFFREY, DAVID K. "Religious Metaphors in Humphry Clinker,"
        The New Rambler, Serial C, no. 16 (1975), pp. 26-28.
            Unconvincing discussion attempts to relate use of re-
        ligious metaphors to the biological in Humphry Clinker.

*28   KAWAI, MICHIO. "The Language of Satire in Smollett's Novels,"
        in Gengo to Buntai: Higashida Chiaki Kyoju Kanraki Kinen
        Ronbunshu [Language and style: collected essays commemorat-
        ing the 60th birthday of Prof. Chiaki Higashida], ed.

Chiaki Higashida.  Osaka: Osaka Kyoiku Tosho, pp. 81-92.
Cited in <u>MLA International Bibliography</u>, 1977.

29   KIEVITT, FRANK DAVID.  "Attitudes toward Roman Catholicism in
     the Later Eighteenth-Century English Novel."  Diss.,
     Columbia University, 1975.
         Direction of Smollett's satire determines the way in
     which he deals with Roman Catholicism.

30   KNAPP, LEWIS M. and LILLIAN DE LA TORRE.  "Smollett's Por-
     traits," <u>N&Q</u>, n.s. 22 (November), 493-95.
         Two letters, c. 1826, respond to Smollett's great grand-
     nephew's request for information about portraits of the
     novelist.

31   McINTOSH, CAREY.  "Quantities of Qualities: Nominal Style and
     the Novel," in <u>Studies in Eighteenth-Century Culture</u>, 4,
     ed. Harold E. Pagliaro.  Madison: The University of
     Wisconsin Press for ASECS, pp. 147-48.
         Relationship of diction, style, and meaning in <u>Roderick
     Random</u>.

32   McNUTT, DAN J.  <u>The Eighteenth-Century Gothic Novel: An Anno-
     tated Bibliography of Criticism and Selected Texts</u>.  New
     York and London: Garland Publishing, passim.  Indexed.
         References concerning Smollett's relationship to the
     Gothic.

33   MONTESER, FREDERICK.  "The Picaro in British Literature," in
     The <u>Picaresque Element in Western Literature</u>.  Studies in
     the Humanities, No. 5, Literature.  University, Alabama:
     University of Alabama Press, pp. 54-58.
         Unfavorable but unconvincing account of Smollett's
     varied dependence on the picaresque, Cervantes, and
     Fielding for all his novels except <u>Humphry Clinker</u>.

34   PRESTON, THOMAS R.  "Tobias Smollett--A Risible Misanthrope,"
     in <u>Not in Timon's Manner: Feeling, Misanthropy, and Satire
     in Eighteenth-Century England</u>.  Studies in the Humanities,
     No. 9, Literature.  University, Alabama: The University of
     Alabama Press, pp. 69-120.
         Smollett's work is a quest for combining social satire
     with a comic portrayal of the man of feeling, and he suc-
     cessfully achieves his purpose in <u>Humphry Clinker</u>.

35   PUNTER, DAVID.  "Smollett and the Logic of Domination," <u>Liter-
     ature & History</u>, no. 2 (October), pp. 60-81.

1975

       Marxist analysis examines Smollett's depiction of the
contradictions between professed ideals and practices of
British capitalism and attributes his ability and stance
as a social critic to his outsider's role and personal experience.

36    REGAN, MICHAEL ROBERT. "Satire and Comedy in the Novels of
      Tobias Smollett." Diss., Brown University, 1975.
       Relates development of Smollett's novels--four stages:
picaresque, satiric, didactic, and comic--to his expanding
view of the world and his continual concern for experimentation with fictional forms.

37    ROGAL, SAMUEL J. "Eighteenth-Century Bath: The Sink of Prof-
      ligacy," Studies in History and Society, 6 (Spring), 93-94.
       Portrait of Bath in Humphry Clinker attacks a wasteful
way of life.

38    ROSENBLUM, MICHAEL. "Smollett as Conservative Satirist," ELH,
      42 (Winter), 556-79.
       Despite variety, Smollett's novels consistently express
through satire his conservative concern for order, hier-
archy, and design in society, although Humphry Clinker
offers a less dogmatic attack on disorder and greater open-
ness to the energy of change.

39    ROTHSTEIN, ERIC. "Humphry Clinker," in Systems of Order and
      Inquiry in Later Eighteenth-Century Fiction. Berkeley,
      Los Angeles, London: University of California Press, pp.
      109-53.
       Relates novel's formal characteristics to Smollett's
skeptical epistemological views, which developed through a
search for order in his device of multiple perspective for
his characters.

40    ROUSSEAU, GEORGE S. and ROGER A. HAMBRIDGE. "David Herbert:
      Victorian Editor of Smollett," Library Review, 25 (Spring),
      17-20.
       Details Herbert's editing of Smollett's work and praises
his methods and annotation.

41    SENA, JOHN F. "Smollett's Matthew Bramble and the Tradition
      of the Physician-Satirist," PLL, 11 (Fall), 386-96.
       Bramble in tradition of the physician-satirist who re-
lates physical ailments to moral sickness. Discusses nar-
rator in the Travels and examines particularities and development of Bramble in Humphry Clinker.

1975

42  SHELDON, ESTHER K.  "What's an Impfiddle," American Speech, 50
    (Spring-Summer), 138-40.
        Use of folk-etymologies for Win's malapropisms in
    Humphry Clinker.

43  SPECTOR, ROBERT D.  "An Attack on the Critical Review in
    Political Controversy," N&Q, n.s. 22 (January), 14.
        Attacks Smollett's partisanship by showing inconsistency
    between his history and printed attacks on the North
    Briton.

44  STANLEY, MAXINE.  "A World in Transition: Structure and Moral
    Vision in the Novels of Tobias Smollett." Diss., Brown
    University, 1975.
        Sees Smollett's novels as a transition between eigh-
    teenth-century Rationalism and nineteenth-century Romanti-
    cism and argues that his concern for the difficulty of man
    in finding order in a disordered and fragmented universe
    marks him as a forward-looking novelist.

45  SUTHERLAND, JAMES.  "Tobias Smollett (1721-1771)," in The
    Oxford Book of Literary Anecdotes.  Oxford: Clarendon
    Press, pp. 95-96.
        Scott's accounts of Smollett's squabbles, particularly
    his trial for libelling Admiral Knowles.

*46 THOMAS, JOEL JORDAN.  "Smollett and Ethical Sensibility."
    Diss., University of Iowa, 1975.
        Smollett indebted to the philosophical theories of sym-
    pathy and ethical sensibility expressed in the writing of
    Hume and Adam Smith, and the structural weakness of his
    first four novels results from his inability to reconcile
    antithetical fictional intentions of satire and comedy.
    Cited in Dissertation Abstracts, 36, 2229-A-2230-A.

47  WAIN, JOHN.  Samuel Johnson.  New York: Viking Press, pp. 238,
    286.
        Johnson's unfavorable view of Smollett's Travels and
    Smollett's ambiguous opinion of Johnson.  Published in
    England in 1974.

48  ZIMMERMAN, EVERETT.  Defoe and the Novel.  Berkeley, Los
    Angeles, London: University of California Press, p. 50.
    Contrasts Defoe's and Smollett's attitudes toward their
    picaresque heroes.

1976

1    ABERNATHY, PETER L., CHRISTIAN J. W. KLOESEL, JERRY R.
     SMITTEN. "Tobias Smollett," in English Novel Explication.
     Hamden, Conn.: The Shoe String Press, pp. 204-7.
     Secondary works on the novels, including the Atom.

2    ADAMS, PERCY G. "The Anti-Hero in Eighteenth-Century Fic-
     tion," Studies in the Literary Imagination, 9 (Spring), 39,
     42-43.
     Character of the heroes and the genre of Roderick
     Random, Peregrine Pickle, and Ferdinand Count Fathom.

3    BAKER, VAN R. "A French Provincial City and Three English
     Writers: Montpelier as Seen in the 1760s by Sterne,
     Smollett, and Boswell," ECL, 2 (March), 54-58.
     Smollett's account in Travels is the most detailed eigh-
     teenth century English description.

4    BEASLEY, JERRY C. "Romance and the 'New' Novels of
     Richardson, Fielding, and Smollett," SEL, 16 (Summer), 437-
     50.
     Compares Smollett's opposition to the prose romances
     with Fielding's and Richardson's and finds him most criti-
     cal of and least affected by earlier representatives of the
     genre.

5    BELCHER, GERALD L. "Commonwealth Ideas in the Political
     Thought of the Defenders of the Eighteenth-Century English
     Constitution," ECL, 3 (December), 63-69.
     Smollett's views in History of England compatible with
     Whig assessment of the past.

6    BLACKALL, ERIC A. Goethe and the Novel. Ithaca and London:
     Cornell University Press, pp. 195-96, 202, 224.
     Smollett popular in Germany, but Goethe uninterested in
     his work despite some affinities.

7    BLONDEL, MADELEINE. Images de la Femme dans le Roman Anglais
     de 1740 a 1771. Paris: Librairie Honore Champion, 2 Vols.,
     passim. Indexed.
     Considers Smollett's treatment of women in all his nov-
     els, including the Atom, and relates them to the social
     milieu and customs of the period.

8    [BOSWELL, JAMES]. A View of the Edinburgh Theatre during the
     Summer Season, 1759. Augustan Reprint Series, No. 179.
     Los Angeles: William Andrews Clark Memorial Library, pp.
     49-50.
          Reprint of 1760.11.

9    BOUCÉ, PAUL-GABRIEL. The Novels of Tobias Smollett, trans.
     P. G. Boucé and Antonia White. London and New York:
     Longman, ix + 405 pp.
          Translation of 1971.7. Updates original notes and bib-
     liography, but omits chapters on Smollett's personality
     (pp. 69-93) and style (pp. 392-431).

10   BOWERS, FREDSON. "Recovering the Authors' Intentions," in
     Pages, The World of Books, Writers, and Writing. Detroit:
     Gale Research Co., p. 220.
          Confusion in modern editions of Smollett between
     London's Fleet prison and the maritime fleet.

11   BREWER, JOHN. Party Ideology and Popular Politics at the
     Accession of George III. Cambridge, New York et al.:
     Cambridge University Press, passim. Indexed.
          Smollett's political role in his periodicals, particu-
     larly the Briton.

12   BURKE, JOSEPH. English Art, 1714-1800. Oxford History of
     English Art, 9, ed. T. S. R. Boase. Oxford: Clarendon
     Press, p. 31.
          Accuracy of artistic description in Smollett's Humphry
     Clinker,

13   CURLEY, THOMAS M. Samuel Johnson and the Age of Travel.
     Athens, Ga.: University of Georgia Press, passim. Indexed.
          Smollett's Travels and novels in relation to travel
     literature of the period and to Johnson's work.

14   D., R. "Jonathan Corncob," Publishers Weekly, 210 (October
     25), 56.
          Because of eighteenth-century review comparing it to
     Smollett's work, American scholar rediscovered the novel.

15   DOUBLEDAY, NEAL FRANK. Variety of Attempt. British and Ameri-
     can Fiction in the Early Nineteenth Century. Lincoln and
     London: University of Nebraska Press, pp. 68, 212.
          Relation of Smollett's novels to Susan Ferrier's and
     Jane Austen's.

1976

*16   DOUGLASS, WAYNE JOSEPH. "Smollett and the Sordid Knaves:
        Political Satire in The Adventures of an Atom." Diss.,
        The University of Florida, 1976.
            Novel reflects the conservative, but not stereotypically
        Tory and Jacobite, politics characteristic of his History
        of England and Briton and his idea that a Patriot King is
        necessary for the general welfare. Cited in Dissertation
        Abstracts, 37, 6493-A.

17    DUNN, RICHARD J. "Humphry Clinker's Humane Humor," Texas
        Studies in Literature and Language, 18 (Summer), 229-39.
            Smollett finally finds the means of subjectively convey-
        ing a humane balance through the characterization, narra-
        tive technique, and diction in Humphry Clinker.

18    FABIAN, BERNHARD. "English Books and Their Eighteenth-Century
        German Readers," in The Widening Circle: Essays on the Cir-
        culation of Literature in Eighteenth-Century Europe, ed.
        Paul J. Korshin. The Haney Foundation Series. Philadel-
        phia: University of Pennsylvania Press, pp. 132, 142, 151-
        52, 159, 164.
            Availability of Smollett's work in Germany and influence
        of the Critical Review on German periodicals.

19    FURTWANGLER, ALBERT. "Mr. Spectator, Sir Roger, and Good
        Humour," UTQ, 46 (Fall), 47.
            Bramble and Jery in Humphry Clinker as type-pairing.

20    GOLDEN, MORRIS. "A Decade's Bent: Names in the Monthly Re-
        view and the Critical Review, 1760-1769," BNYPL, 79
        (Spring), 336-61.
            Use of names in the Critical suggests Smollett's edi-
        torial influence in its concern with medicine and its
        Scottish sensitivities and its lesser concern with re-
        ligion.

21    HATCH, RONALD B. Crabbe's Arabesque: Social Drama in the
        Poetry of George Crabbe. Montreal and London: McGill-
        Queen's University Press, pp. viii, 73, 255.
            Smollett's general influence on Crabbe's poetry.

22    HUNT, JOHN DIXON. "Postscript," in The Figure in the Land-
        scape: Poetry, Painting, and Gardening during the Eigh-
        teenth Century. Baltimore and London: The Johns Hopkins
        University Press, p. 246.
            Smollett's ideas on gardening in his Travels.

23    JEFFREY, DAVID K.  "Smollett's Irony in Peregrine Pickle,"
       JNT, 6 (Spring), 137-46.
            Style and language of "Memoirs of a Lady of Quality"
       indicate Smollett's authorship, and it is used in ironic
       contrast to the theme and narrative technique of the rest
       of the novel to provide a more positive view of Peregrine.

24    KELLY, GARY.  The English Jacobin Novel 1780-1805.  Oxford:
       Clarendon Press, passim.  Indexed.
            Smollett's influence on Robert Bage, Thomas Holcroft,
       and William Godwin.

25    KNAPP, LEWIS M. and LILLIAN DE LA TORRE.  "The Portraits of
       Tobias Smollett," N&Q, n.s. 23 (November), 500-504.
            Describes and analyzes evidence for purported portraits
       of Smollett.

*26   KOENIGS, KAREN JO ANN.  "Early Evaluation of the Novel: Peri-
       odical Reviews of Mid-Eighteenth-Century London."  Diss.,
       Loyola University of Chicago, 1976.
            Considers theory of the novel in the Critical Review.
       Cited in Dissertation Abstracts, 36, 7410-A-7411-A.

*27   McGRAW, PATRICIA MARIE.  "Ideas about Children in Eighteenth-
       Century British Fiction."  Diss., University of Connecti-
       cut, 1976.
            Smollett's treatment of children in his novels related
       to social attitudes and theories.  Cited in Dissertation
       Abstracts, 36, 7441-A.

28    MILES, PETER.  "Bibliography and Insanity: Smollett and the
       Mad-Business," Library, 5th ser., 31 (September), 205-22.
            No real evidence that Smollett's comments on illness of
       George III in fifth volume of Continuation of the Complete
       History led to suppression of the work.

29    NEALE, R. S.  "Bath: Ideology and Utopia, 1700-1760," in
       Studies in the Eighteenth Century, 3.  Papers Presented at
       the Third David Nichol Smith Memorial Seminar, 1973, ed.
       R. F. Brissenden and J. C. Eade.  Toronto and Buffalo:
       University of Toronto Press, p. 54.
            Moralistic attitude toward Bath in Humphry Clinker com-
       pared to contemporary viewpoints.

30    NEW, MELVYN.  "'The Grease of God': The Form of Eighteenth-
       Century English Fiction," PMLA, 91 (March), 235-44.

1976

> Argues reasonably that secular alteration of a provi-
> dential world view provides the context for the novels of
> Smollett and other major novelists.

31  NEW, PETER. "The Literary and Ethical Context of Crabbe's
    Poetry," in George Crabbe's Poetry. New York: St. Martin's
    Press, pp. 27, 37.
    > Detached quality of the inset of Miss Williams's story
    > in Roderick Random and its didactic function.

32  PAULSON, RONALD. "Life as Journey and as Theater: Two Eigh-
    teenth-Century Narrative Structures," NLH, 8 (Autumn), 54.
    > Significance of metaphors in Humphry Clinker.

33  PEARSON, GABRIEL. "Towards a Reading of Dombey and Son," in
    The Modern English Novel: the Reader, the Writer and the
    Work, ed. Gabriel Josipovici. New York: Barnes & Noble,
    Harper & Row, pp. 64-65.
    > Implications of the narrative technique of the opening
    > of Roderick Random.

34  PERRIN, NOEL. "Foreword," in Adventures of Jonathan Corncob.
    Loyal American Refugee. Boston: David R. Godine, p. xi.
    > Compares broad humor of the 1787 novel with Smollett's.

*35  PRATT, T. K. "A Study of the Language in Tobias Smollett's
    Roderick Random." Diss., University of London, 1976.
    > Cited in Index to Theses Accepted for Higher Degrees by
    > the Universities of Great Britain and Ireland.

36  PUZON, BRIDGET. "The Hidden Meaning in Humphry Clinker,"
    Harvard Library Bulletin, 24 (January), 40-54.
    > Humphry Clinker belongs to the genre of the Bildings-
    > roman of middle age--remarkable in its period but not un-
    > usual in earlier and later fiction.

37  RICE, SCOTT. "Smollett's Seventh Travel Letter and the De-
    sign of Formal Verse Satire," SEL, 16 (Summer), 491-503.
    > Smollett's Travels combines traditional writings on the
    > Grand Tour and classical formal verse satire and is not
    > merely a record of his own travel experiences.

38  ROGERS, DEBORAH C. "Further Shakespearean Echoes in Humphry
    Clinker," ANQ, 14 (March), 98-102.
    > Nine additional malapropisms of Win Jenkins in Humphry
    > Clinker derive from Shakespeare.

39    ROSENBLUM, MICHAEL. "Smollett and the Old Conventions," PQ,
       55 (Summer), 389-402.
            Smollett is a more self-conscious writer than he is gen-
       erally given credit for, and his narratives rework and
       modify traditional modes of the romances in order to
       achieve their satiric fiction.

40    ROUSSEAU, ANDRE MICHEL. "Tobias Smollett," in L'Angleterre
       et Voltaire. Studies in Voltaire and the Eighteenth Cen-
       tury, ed. Theodore Besterman. Oxford: The Voltaire Foun-
       dation, Vol. 147, pp. 768-73 and Vols. 144-47, passim.
            Unfavorable appraisal of Smollett's abilities as a his-
       torian and translator. Throughout there are comments on
       these and on his views of Voltaire.

41    ROUSSEAU, GEORGE S. "Nerves, Spirits, and Fibres: Towards
       Defining the Origins of Sensibility," in 1976.29, pp. 153,
       156.
            Sensibility in Smollett's work.

42    ROUSSEAU, GEORGE S. and ROGER HAMBRIDGE. "Smollett and Poli-
       tics: Originals for the Election Scene in Sir Launcelot
       Greaves," ELN, 14 (September), 32-37.
            Lord William Manners is probably the original of Sir
       Valentine Quickset and character of Isaac Vanderpelft may
       be a composite of Job Staunton Charlton and Sampson Gideon.

43    SILVERMAN, KENNETH. A Cultural History of the American Revo-
       lution. New York: Thomas Y. Crowell, p. 319.
            Publication of "Ode to Independence" in American maga
       zine as part of the revolutionary movement.

44    SPACKS, PATRICIA MEYER. Imagining a Self. Autobiography and
       Novel in Eighteenth-Century England. Cambridge, Mass.:
       Harvard University Press, passim. Indexed.
            Smollett's characters and their quest for identity.

45    SPECTOR, ROBERT D. "The End of the Briton and Auditor,"
       N&Q, n.s. 23 (August), 357-58.
            Surprise termination indicates Smollett was uninformed
       about Lord Bute's political intentions.

46    TOMLINSON, T. B. "Jane Austen's Originality: Emma," in The
       English Middle-Class Novel. London et al.: Macmillan, pp.
       22-23, 27.
            Contrasts Smollett's and Austen's work.

1976

47    WILES, ROY McKEEN. "The Relish for Reading in Provincial
       England Two Centuries Ago," in 1976.18, pp. 93-94, 97, 99.
          Availability and sales of Smollett's work in the
       provinces.

## 1977

1    ADAMS, GEORGIA. "The Technique of Interpolation in Selected
       Novels of the Seventeenth and Eighteenth Centuries."
       Diss., City University of New York, 1977.
          Relationship of interpolated stories in Humphry Clinker
       to its main theme.

2    ALCORN, JOHN. "Spirit of Place: The Travel Book," in The
       Nature Novel from Hardy to Lawrence. New York: Columbia
       University Press, pp. 43-44.
          On the journey-motif in Roderick Random.

*3    ARCHER, PATRICIA FAYE. "Rhetorical Elements of the Grotesque
       and the Absurd in Tobias Smollett's Humphry Clinker."
       Diss., Texas A&M University, 1977.
          Examines the rhetorical patterns through which Smollett
       creates "comic grotesque and absurd effects" and argues
       its stylistic importance in his earlier novels as well.
       Cited in Dissertation Abstracts, 38, 2134-A.

4    AUBURN, MARK S. "The Rivals," in Sheridan's Comedies. Their
       Contexts and Achievements. Lincoln and London: University
       of Nebraska Press, pp. 40-41.
          Win Jenkins's malapropisms in Humphry Clinker compared
       to those used by Sheridan's character.

5    BJORNSON, RICHARD. "The Picaresque Hero as Young Nobleman:
       Victimization and Vindication in Smollett's Roderick
       Random," in The Picaresque Hero in European Fiction.
       Madison: The University of Wisconsin Press, pp. 228-45 and
       passim.
          Changes in plan, tone, and characterization in Roderick
       Random provide a meaning diametrically opposed to that of
       the traditional Spanish picaresque. Briefly discusses
       picaresque elements in Ferdinand Count Fathom.

6    BJORNSON, RICHARD. "The Picaresque Novel in France, England,
       and Germany," Comparative Literature, 29 (Spring), 147.
          Smollett's changes from the traditional picaresque.

7   BOUCÉ, PAUL-GABRIEL. "References in Roderick Random," TLS,
        November 25, p. 1380.
            Asks about two references in the novel and makes sugges-
        tions about both.

*8  BRYANT, MARCIA LANGLEY. "Magnificence and Foppery: France
        According to Eighteenth-Century English Travel Writers."
        Diss., The University of Iowa, 1977.
            Finds a developing "social conscience" reflected in
        Smollett's ironic and satiric Travels. Cited in Disserta-
        tion Abstracts, 38, 2135-A-2136-A.

9   CARNOCHAN, W. B. Confinement and Flight. An Essay on English
        Literature of the Eighteenth Century. Berkeley, Los
        Angeles, London: University of California Press, pp. 61,
        63-65, 67, 95.
            Sees prison episode in Roderick Random as a "rite of
        passage" for the hero.

10  EAGLE, DOROTHY and HILARY CARNELL. Oxford Literary Guide to
        the British Isles. Oxford: Clarendon Press, passim. In-
        dexed.
            Places related to Smollett and his work.

11  GOLD, JOEL J. "John Wilkes and the Writings of 'Pensioner
        Johnson,'" SBHT, 18 (Spring), 86-90.
            Smollett's Briton and political controversy.

12  GOLDEN, MORRIS. "Travel Writing in the Monthly Review and
        Critical Review, 1756-1775," PLL, 13 (Spring), 213-23.
            Aesthetic principles of reviews of travel literature in
        the Critical and responses to Smollett's Travels.

13  GRANT, DAMIAN. Tobias Smollett. A Study in Style. Manches-
        ter: Manchester University Press; Totowa, N.J.: Rowman and
        Littlefield, xii + 232 pp.
            Argues from a linguistic and stylistic approach to
        Smollett's work against traditional critical treatments.
        Contrasts Smollett's attitude toward, and use of, language
        and style with those of his contemporaries and specifically
        analyzes these in his work. Examines comic procedures by
        which Smollett achieves his moral statements by combining
        distancing and detachment from his subject with intensify-
        ing techniques.

14  GREENE, DONALD J. Samuel Johnson: Political Writings. Yale
        Edition of the Works of Samuel Johnson, 10. New Haven and
        London: Yale University Press, passim. Indexed.

1977

Notes include comment on Smollett's relationship with Johnson, Roderick Random, and the History of England.

*15    HAMBRIDGE, ROGER A.  "An Annotated Edition of Tobias Smollett's Life and Adventures of Sir Launcelot Greaves (1760-1761)."  Diss., University of California, Los Angeles, 1977.
        Introduction provides background of composition and notes and appendices give specific rather than interpretive detail.  Collation of the text in the British Magazine with that in the 1762 edition supplements work of Richard Lettis, 1957.11.  Cited in Dissertation Abstracts, 38, 2806-A.

16    ISERNHAGEN, HARTWIG.  "Vermittlungsmodell und Thematische Struktur: zu Robinson Crusoe und Humphry Clinker," Deutsche Vierteljahrsschrift für Literaturwissenschaft und Geistes-geschichte, 51 (June), 181-207.
        Seeks a "theoretical foundation for the integration of reader-oriented, structuralistic, and hermeneutical approaches" to Humphry Clinker in order to account for the tensions arising in the novel from the relationship between its theme and its epistolary method of communication.

17    JEFFREY, DAVID K.  "The Epistolary Format of Pamela and Humphry Clinker," in A Provision of Human Nature: Essays on Fielding and Others in Honor of Miriam Austin Locke, ed. Donald Kay.  University, Alabama: The University of Alabama Press, pp. 145-54.
        Despite some incisive comments about Lydia and her situation in Humphry Clinker, an otherwise unfounded comparison of relationship of the epistolary technique to the development of the young women in Richardson's and Smollett's novels.

*18    JONES, MARCIA BELL.  "Self-Images: A Study of Female Auto-biography Written in England from 1660 to 1800."  Diss., University of North Carolina at Chapel Hill, 1977.
        Considers the popularity of Lady Vane's "Memoirs" in Peregrine Pickle.  Cited in Dissertation Abstracts, 39, 297-A.

19    LINDSAY, JACK.  Hogarth. His Art and His World.  London: Hart-Davis, MacGibbon, passim.  Indexed.
        Smollett's political, social, and aesthetic values.

20    LINDSAY, MAURICE.  "The Eighteenth Century," in History of Scottish Literature.  London: Robert Hale, pp. 264-71 and passim.

General, sympathetic, but dated account of Smollett's
life and work.

21  MILES, PETER. "Radical Reform and Tobias Smollett," N&Q, n.
    s. 24 (June), 265-69.
       Relationship of Smollett's social commentary in his
    History and Humphry Clinker to arguments of nineteenth-
    century advocates of social reform indicates that
    Smollett's reputation as a Tory historian is an oversimpli-
    fication.

22  [PERCY, THOMAS and WILLIAM SHENSTONE]. The Percy Letters.
    The Correspondence of Thomas Percy and William Shenstone,
    7, ed. Cleanth Brooks. New Haven and London: Yale Univer-
    sity Press, pp. 23, 27, 42, 50-51.
       Attacks on Smollett in four letters of 1759 and 1760.

23  PICKERING, SAMUEL F. JR. "The Evolution of a Genre: Fictional
    Biographies for Children in the Eighteenth Century," JNT,
    7 (Winter), 5.
       Relationship between the Atom (misdated) and the devel-
    opment of fictional biographies for children.

24  ROSS, IAN CAMPBELL. "Smollett and the Jew Bill of 1753,"
    ANQ, 16 (December), 54-56.
       Rejects idea that Jewish character in Fathom originated
    in his support of the Jewish Nationalization Act and sug-
    gests influence of a German novel and thematic function of
    character.

25  ROUSSEAU, GEORGE S. "Beef and Bouillon: A Voice for Tobias
    Smollett, with Comments on His Life, Works, and Modern
    Critics," British Studies Monitor, 7 (Winter), 4-56.
       Abrasive analysis of Smollett and his critics argues
    that the experimental and varied characteristics of his
    novels deny any possibility of labeling them or easily
    defining their uneven achievement. Suggests that the most
    profitable critical approach should focus on the person-
    ality and psychology of the man and the content of his
    novels.

26  RUNTE, ROSEANN. "Gil Blas and Roderick Random: Food for
    Thought," French Review, 50 (April), 698-705.
       Food and meals play a major role in delineating the
    actions, chronology, theme, and characterization in the
    two novels.

1977

27 SEKORA, JOHN. <u>Luxury: The Concept in Western Thought, Eden to Smollett</u>. Baltimore and London: The Johns Hopkins University Press, xv + 340 pp.
Uses Smollett as a key figure in discussing attitudes toward luxury in the eighteenth century. Finds him, particularly in his historical, political, and journalistic publications and in <u>Humphry Clinker</u>, to be the most powerful defender of the classical attitude which regarded luxury as the basic human vice and sees that as the major theme in his final novel.

28 SEKORA, JOHN. "Some Political Figures in <u>Humphry Clinker</u>," <u>N&Q</u>, n.s. 24 (June), 270-73.
Using <u>Briton</u> as a source, identifies pseudonymous characters and explains attitudes toward particular political figures.

29 SENA, JOHN F. "Smollett's Portrait of Narcissa's Aunt: the Genesis of an 'Original,'" <u>ELN</u>, 14 (June), 270-75.
Character in <u>Roderick Random</u> based on medical studies of hysteria, but heightened for comic purposes.

30 SIEBER, HARRY. <u>The Picaresque</u>. Critical Idiom Series. New York: Barnes & Noble, passim. Indexed.
Picaresque characteristics in Smollett's work.

*31 SIWILA, JAMES EDWARD. "Narrative and Social Order: the Novels of Tobias Smollett." Diss., University of Kentucky, 1977.
Novels are an attempted resolution of Smollett's conflict between realistic social views and "more optimistic liberal ideology." Relates Smollett's own conflict in values to the structure of his novels and argues that his sympathies are with an older aristocratic order. Cited in <u>Dissertation Abstracts</u>, 39, 1602-A.

32 SKILTON, DAVID. "Tobias Smollett," in <u>The English Novel. Defoe to the Victorians</u>. Comparative Literature Series. London: David & Charles; New York: Barnes & Noble/Harper & Row, pp. 40-44 and passim.
Regards Smollett as inferior to Fielding, but praises his experimentation as a contribution to the genre.

33 SMITH, ALBERT. "<u>Sir Launcelot Greaves</u>: A Bibliographical Survey of Eighteenth-Century Editions," <u>The Library</u>, 5th ser., 32 (September), 214-37.
Publication details from appearance in the <u>British Magazine</u> through various British, Irish, and unauthorized editions.

34    SMITH, RAYMOND J.  Charles Churchill.  Twayne's English Au-
         thors Series, 197, ed. Sylvia E. Bowman.  Boston: Twayne
         Publishers, G.K. Hall, pp. 17, 19, 30-32, 53.
            Churchill's various literary quarrels with Smollett.

35    STONE, LAWRENCE.  "Parent-Child Relations," in The Family,
         Sex and Marriage in England 1500-1800.  New York et al.:
         Harper & Row, p. 441.
            On the audience appeal of a scene in Roderick Random.

36    SUTHERLAND, GUILLAND.  "Smollett and the Irish Book Trade: A
         Reply," PBSA, 71 (October-December), 494-97.
            Qualifies, corrects, and adds to points about Smollett's
         works in Ireland made by Robert C. Cole.  See 1975.14.

37    TAYLOR, S. ORTIZ.  "Episodic Structure and the Picaresque
         Novel," JNT, 7 (Fall), 218-25.
            Sees a circular shape to seemingly random structure in
         such picaresque narratives as Roderick Random.

38    TRIPATHI, P. D.  The Doctrinal English Novel (Later Eighteenth
         Century).  Calcutta: K. P. Bagchi, passim.  Indexed.
            Smollett's social and political attitudes and relation
         to later novelists.

39    WILSON, EDMUND.  Letters in Literature and Politics 1912-1972,
         ed. Elena Wilson.  New York: Farrar, Straus and Giroux,
         p. 717.
            1970 letter describes inability to read Peregrine
         Pickle.

## 1978

1     ANDRES, SOPHIA.  "Tobias Smollett's Satiric Spokesman in
         Humphry Clinker," in Studies in Scottish Literature, 13,
         ed. G. Ross Roy.  Columbia, S.C.: University of South
         Carolina Press, pp. 100-110.
            Matt Bramble serves as satiric spokesman in Humphry
         Clinker, which attempts to preserve classical satiric tra-
         dition.  Smollett attacks individual evils as basis of
         social evils and argues for social harmony and stability.

2     ANON.  "Smollett, Tobias," in Lives of the Georgian Age. 1714-
         1837, compiled by Laurence Urdeng Associates, ed. William
         Gould.  New York: Barnes & Noble, Harper & Row, pp. 392-95.
            Generally unsympathetic account of life and work.

1978

3   BATTEN, CHARLES L. JR.   Pleasurable Instruction. Form and
    Convention in Eighteenth-Century Travel Literature.
    Berkeley, Los Angeles, London: University of California
    Press, passim.   Indexed.
        Considers Humphry Clinker and Travels in the context of
    eighteenth-century travel literature and discusses
    Smollett's editing of A Compendium of Authentic and Enter-
    taining Voyages.

4   BERTELSEN, LANCE.   "The Smollettian View of Life," Novel, 11
    (Winter), 115-27.
        Examines characteristics of scenes in Smollett's novels
    and finds a common concern for displaying the "dynamics of
    human 'communication,'" which provides a unifying force,
    but which is never adequately achieved until Humphry
    Clinker.

5   BJORNSON, RICHARD.   "Victimization and Vindication in
    Smollett's Roderick Random," in 1978.1, pp. 196-210.
        Reprint of 1977.5.

6   BRIDEN, EARL F.   "Smollett and the Bankruptcy Laws, N&Q, n.
    s. 25 (February), 45-47.
        Ties Smollett's concern in Launcelot Greaves and his
    Continuation of the Complete History about the inequity of
    the laws to his prison experience and parliamentary actions
    of 1758-59.

7   BYRD, MAX.   London Transformed.   Images of the City in the
    Eighteenth Century.   New Haven and London: Yale University
    Press, pp. 29, 63, 89-90.
        Treatment of London life in Peregrine Pickle, Roderick
    Random, and Humphry Clinker.

*8  CHANDA, ASOKE KUMAR.   "From the Picaro to the Young Man from
    the Provinces: the Theme of Social Climbing in European
    and American Fiction."   Diss., University of Illinois at
    Urbana-Champaign, 1978.
        Roderick Random an example of a bourgeois picaro.   Cited
    in Dissertation Abstracts, 39, 270-A.

9   CORDASCO, FRANCESCO.   Tobias George Smollett. A Bibliograph-
    ical Guide.   New York: AMS Press, xiv + 157 pp.
        Includes 875 items arranged according to General Bibli-
    ography and Reference Guides, Bibliographies, Texts,
    Letters, Biography and General Criticism, Translations and
    the Travels, Historical Works and Periodicals, and
    Miscellanea.   Scant annotation, but lists reviews of major

secondary works. Unreliable in its listings and annotations and misleading about the forged letters published by
Cordasco in articles and in his edition of Smollett's letters.

10   HAMBRIDGE, ROGER A. "Smollett's Legalese: Giles Jacob's New
     Law-Dictionary and Sir Launcelot Greaves," Revue des
     Langues Vivantes. Tijdschrift voor Levende Talen, 44, No.
     1 (1978), 37-44.
         Smollett's legal jargon in the novel derives from
     Jacob's work.

11   HART, FRANCIS RUSSELL. "Scottish Variations of the Gothic
     Novel," in The Scottish Novel from Smollett to Spark.
     Cambridge, Mass.: Harvard University Press, pp. 13-19 and
     passim.
         Reprint and slight expansion of 1973.21.

12   HILSON, J. C. "Another Smollett Portrait?" N&Q, n.s. 25
     (February), 47.
         Suggests Smollett sat for a miniature by Charles Dixon.

13   JEFFREY, DAVID K. "'Ductility and Dissimulation': The Unity
     of Ferdinand Count Fathom," Tennessee Studies in Litera-
     ture, 23 (1978), 47-60.
         Use of image clusters provides the structural and
     thematic unity in the novel, and the dual plots are paral-
     lel and intertwining.

14   JOHNSON, CLIFFORD R. Plots and Characters in the Fiction of
     Eighteenth-Century English Authors. Hamden, Conn.: Archon
     Books; Kent: Wm. Dawson & Sons, II, passim.
         Detailed plot summaries of Smollett's five novels, The
     History and Adventures of an Atom, and Habbakkuk Hilding.
     These appear alphabetically under "Plots." A section on
     "Characters" identifies major and minor figures under
     alphabetical listing.

15   ROPER, DEREK. Reviewing before the "Edinburgh" 1788-1802.
     Newark: University of Delaware Press, passim. Indexed.
         Smollett's role on the Critical Review and his reviews
     for the Monthly Review.

16   ROSS, IAN CAMPBELL. "Language, Structure and Vision in
     Smollett's Roderick Random," EA, 31 (January-March), 52-63.
         Smollett's vision of a disordered world provides the
     novel's thematic unity and its diction underlines a concern
     for the moral disorder it deals with.

1978

17    SCHWARTZ, RICHARD B.  "The Life-Writer's Task," in <u>Boswell's</u>
      <u>Johnson. A Preface to the "Life"</u>.  Madison: The University
      of Wisconsin Press, pp. 16-17.
           Smollett's satire of Pallet's artistic opinions in
      <u>Peregrine Pickle</u>.

18    SCHWEITZER, KARL W.  "The Origins of the 'Press War' of 1762:
      A Reappraisal," <u>N&Q</u>, n.s. 25 (February), 47-50.
           Includes discussion of Smollett's <u>Briton</u>.

19    SPACKS, PATRICIA MEYER.  "The Dangerous Age," <u>ECS</u>, 11 (Sum-
      mer), 417-38.
           As a novel of maturation, <u>Roderick Random</u> suggests that
      a hero's passage to adulthood requires not only that he
      learn to control his passions, but that he receive guidance
      and financial support from members of the adult society.
      <u>See</u> pp. 434-38.

20    SUTHERLAND, GUILLAND.  "John Moore's Biography of Smollett: A
      Letter," <u>EA</u>, 31 (January-March), 64-66.
           Sensible brief discussion of Moore's intentions and
      problems in writing his prefatory life of Smollett.

21    SZLADITS, LOLA L.  <u>Patrons & Publishers. The Economics of</u>
      <u>English Literature</u>.  New York: New York Public Library, p.
      10.
           Smollett's commercial success for his publisher.

22    WEINSHEIMER, JOEL.  "Defects and Difficulties in Smollett's
      <u>Peregrine Pickle</u>," <u>Ariel, A Review of International English</u>
      <u>Literature</u>, 9 (July), 49-62.
           Inadequate treatment of hero and inability to blend
      literary types of satire and comic-picaresque <u>Bildungsroman</u>
      result in the novel's failure.

23    WEINSHEIMER, JOEL.  "Impedance as Value: <u>Roderick Random</u> and
      <u>Pride and Prejudice</u>," <u>PTL: A Journal for Descriptive</u>
      <u>Poetics and Theory of Literature</u>, 3 (1978), 139-66.
           Failing to engage the reader and leaving him with
      nothing to do, <u>Roderick Random</u> is a weak novel.

24    WICKS, ULRICH.  "The Romance of the Picaresque," <u>Genre</u>, 11
      (Spring), 31, 42, 43.
           Romance and picaresque in Smollett's novels.

25    WRIGHT, TERENCE.  "The Imperfect Ideal of the Novel," <u>MLR</u>, 73
      (January), 2.
           The anti-heroic character of Smollett's work.

# Index

Note: All numbers refer to entry numbers rather than to pages.

Dempsey, I. Lindsay, 1975.17
Denizot, Paul, 1971.15; 1972.11
Denne, Clarence John Jr., 1971.16
Dennie, Joseph, 1936.10
De Porte, Michael V., 1974.12
De Quincey, Thomas, 1848.1;
    1881.4
Dermody, Thomas, 1807.2
Derrick, Samuel, 1779.1
Deutsch, Otto Erich, 1948.15
Devine, M. E., 1971.69
Devonshire, M. G., 1929.3
Dewhurst, Kenneth, 1972.12
Dialogues of the Living, 1762.11
Dibdin, Charles, 1795.5; 1891.4
Dibelius, Wilhelm, 1910.7
Dibon, Roger, 1950.6; 1971.62
Dickens, Charles, 1836.1; 1837.1,
    3; 1838.2, 3; 1840.2; 1842.4;
    1845.5; 1846.4; 1849.1;
    1851.1; 1869.3; 1872.6;
    1873.2; 1875.3; 1877.1;
    1879.1; 1882.6; 1888.6;
    1892.6, 14, 15; 1909.1, 2;
    1922.3; 1923.4, 10; 1925.10;
    1928.14; 1931.6; 1936.9;
    1952.9; 1954.7; 1957.4;
    1958.16; 1959.4; 1963.9, 13;
    1964.12; 1965.14, 24, 31;
    1968.30, 32; 1969.4; 1970.1,
    15, 21, 29, 42; 1971.13, 40,
    42; 1973.30; 1976.33
Dictionary of National Biography,
    1898.7; 1924.4
Digeon, Aurélien, 1940.4
Dillingham, William B., 1970.13
D'Israeli, Isaac, 1795.6; 1812.3
Dixon, Charles, 1978.12
Dobson, Austin, 1880.3; 1892.7;
    1894.2; 1902.5
Dobson, Jesse, 1957.5
Donaldson, Ian, 1975.18
Donovan, Robert Alan, 1966.12
Dooley, D. J., 1958.9
Dooley, Roger B., 1956.5
Doran, John, 1876.1
Doubleday, Neal Frank, 1976.15
Doublet, George, 1934.4
Doughty, Katharine F., 1918.3
Doughty, Oswald, 1926.7
Douglas, John, 1757.9

Douglass, Wayne Joseph, 1976.16
Downs, Brian W., 1928.3
Doyle, Arthur Conan, 1908.4
Dr. Wilson's Remarks upon Some
    Passages of the Critical
    Review..., 1761.13
Drake, Nathan, 1798.9; 1810.5
Drinker, Cecil K., 1925.7
Drinkwater, John, 1923.5
Driskell, Leon V., 1967.10
Duane, William, 1874.2
Dudden, F. Homes, 1952.6
Duffield, Pitts, 1897.3
Duke, Loraine Joanna, 1970.14
Du Laurens, 1971.41
Dunbar, Howard Hunter, 1946.2
Duncan, Alexander, 1896.1
Duncan, Jeffrey L., 1968.14
Dunlop, John C., 1814.5; 1888.2
Dunn, Richard J., 1976.17
Dyson, Anne Jane, 1973.31
Dyson, H. V. D., 1940.5

E., H., 1802.5
Eagle, Dorothy, 1977.10
Eastwood, W., 1949.5
Eaves, Thomas Cary Duncan,
    1944.3; 1971.17
Eclectic Review, 1821.3
Edgar, Pelham, 1934.9
Edgeworth, Maria, 1812.2; 1895.2;
    1931.3; 1964.27
Edinburgh Magazine, 1786.4
Edinburgh Review, 1809.1; 1815.1;
    1839.1; 1861.1; 1865.1
Egan, Pierce, 1821.7; 1825.4;
    1931.6; 1971.52
Eickelberg, Frederick Charles,
    1969.6
Eliot, George. See Evans, Mary
    Ann.
Elistratova, A. A., 1953.5;
    1955.1; 1966.13
Ellison, Lee Monroe, 1929.4
Elmer, Robert Watson, 1965.12
Elton, Oliver, 1928.4
Elwin, Malcolm, 1934.6
Elwin, Whitwell, 1902.6
Emerson, Ralph Waldo, 1910.8;
    1960.7; 1965.13
Emery, John Pike, 1946.3

Golden, Morris, 1959.7; 1966.16;
    1972.16; 1976.20; 1977.12
Goldknopf, Irma, 1968.17
Goldsmith, Oliver, 1757.10;
    1759.9, 10; 1760.13; 1762.15;
    1767.5; 1848.1, 2; 1849.2;
    1885.5; 1924.8; 1926.19;
    1927.8; 1928.13; 1933.8;
    1946.4; 1952.1; 1957.22;
    1959.7; 1961.14; 1966.17;
    1967.23, 39; 1969.12; 1971.3;
    1974.44, 47
Göller, Karl Heinz, 1972.17
Goodall, W., 1752.3
Goodhugh, William, 1827.2
Gordon, Ian A., 1966.18
Gordon, Peter, 1784.3
Gordon, Robert C., 1969.8
Gosse, Edmund, 1888.6; 1906.3;
    1919.2
Gosse, Philip, 1952.7
"Gothic," 1790.1; 1883.5; 1899.1;
    1902.9; 1921.2; 1927.6;
    1932.28; 1934.14; 1947.3;
    1953.1; 1957.21; 1963.28;
    1972.33; 1973.21; 1974.53;
    1975.32
Gove, Philip Babcock, 1941.2
Graband, Gerhard, 1972.18
Graham, Henry Grey, 1899.2;
    1908.5
Graham, R. B. Cunninghame, 1925.8
Graham, Robert, 1925.8
Graham, W. H., 1949.9
Graham, Walter, 1930.5
Grainger, James, 1759.2, 11;
    1848.3
Granger, Rev. James, 1805.4
Grant, A. J., 1935.3
Grant, Anne, 1806.7
Grant, Damian, 1966.19; 1967.18;
    1968.15; 1971.24; 1977.13
Grant, Douglas, 1951.9
Grant, James, 1882.2
Grant, M. H., 1937.4
Granville, A. B., 1874.4
Graves, Richard, 1934.7. See
    also The Spiritual Quixote
Graves, William Thomas, 1970.19
Gray, Charles Harold, 1931.5
Gray, Ernest Weston, 1931.6

Gray, John, 1804.1
Gray, Thomas, 1757.12; 1900.3;
    1948.24; 1974.23, 52
Green, David Bonnell, 1949.10
Green, F. C., 1935.4
Green, Robert M., 1914.3
Greene, Donald, 1970.20; 1971.25;
    1977.14
Gregory, George, 1808.3
Greiner, Walter F., 1969.9
The Grenville Papers, 1852.1
Grierson, H. J. C., 1932.8
Griffinhoofe, Harry G., 1886.3;
    1893.3
Griffith, Philip Mahone, 1961.7
Griffiths, Ralph, 1751.16;
    1753.4; 1755.1; 1762.16;
    1764.3; 1773.4; 1934.16
Grimm, Friedrich Melchior, 1877.2
Groome, Francis H., 1884.2
Grossvogel, David I., 1968.18
Grunder, Henry, 1968.19
Guillén, Claudio, 1962.7; 1971.26
Guirand, Alexandre, 1824.5
Guliev, G., 1971.27

H., G., 1784.3
H., M., 1797.7
Habbakkuk Hilding. See Smollett,
    Tobias, works attributed to,
    Habbakkuk Hilding
Habel, Ursula, 1930.6
Habib, Mohammed, 1973.20
Hahn, Barbara M., 1923.2; 1929.2
Hallenback, Chester T., 1932.9
Halsband, Robert, 1956.6
Halsey, William D., 1956.2
Hambridge, Roger A., 1975.40;
    1976.42; 1977.15; 1978.10
Hamilton, Lady Anne, 1807.4
Hamilton, Anthony, 1951.8
Hamilton, Archibald, 1956.7
Hamilton, Olive, 1974.18
Hamilton, William, 1955.21
Hammond, Reginald J. W., 1964.15
Handel, George Frederick, 1776.6;
    1901.7; 1946.17; 1948.15;
    1966.28
Handover, P. M., 1965.16
Hanes, Sara Louise, 1974.19